To Stefan

NICOLAS PARTY

STÉPHANE AQUIN
STEFAN BANZ
ALI SUBOTNICK
MELISSA HYDE

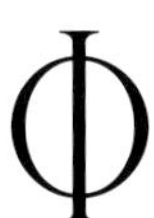

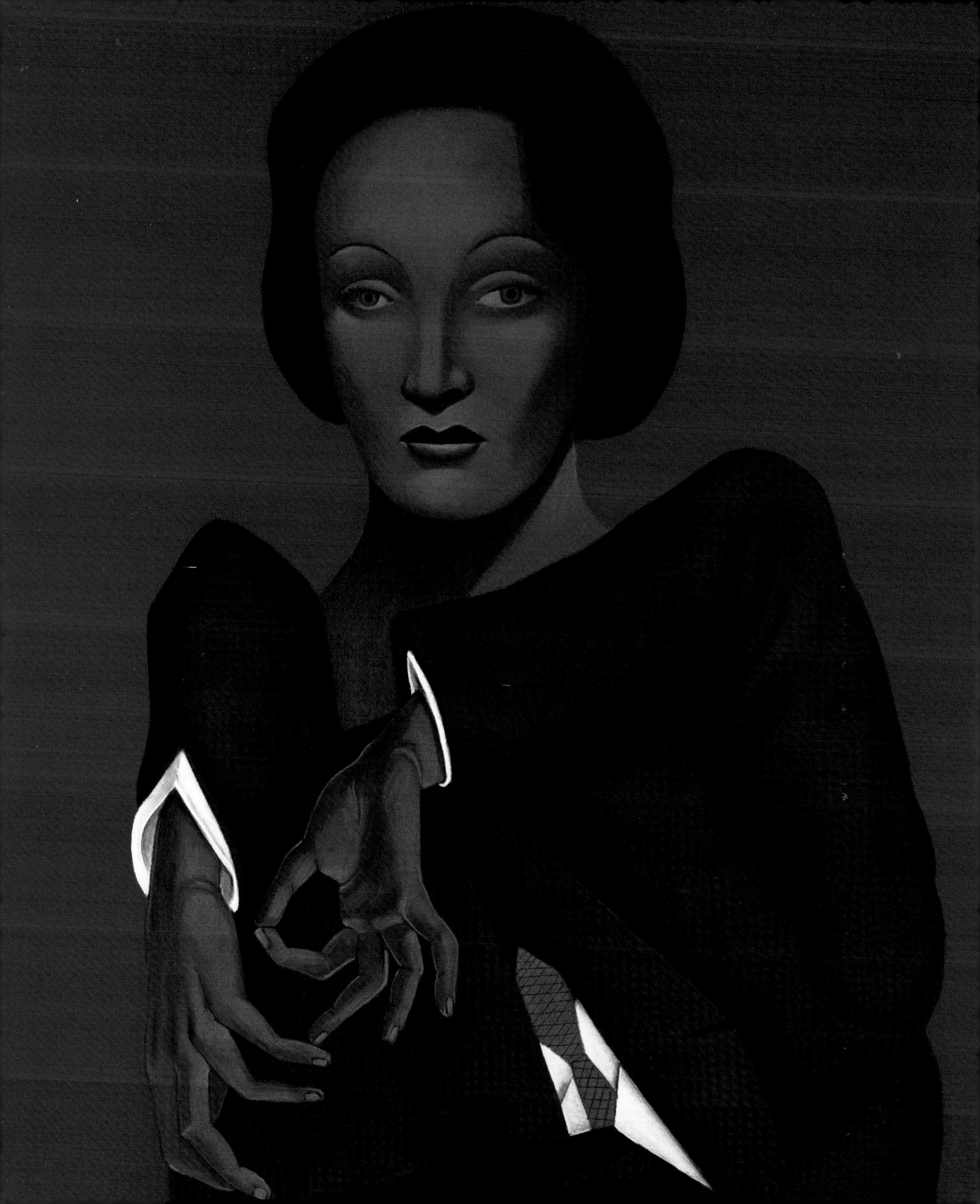

PORTRAIT WITH A LAWYER,
2021
SOFT PASTEL ON LINEN
150 X 127 CM

CONTENTS

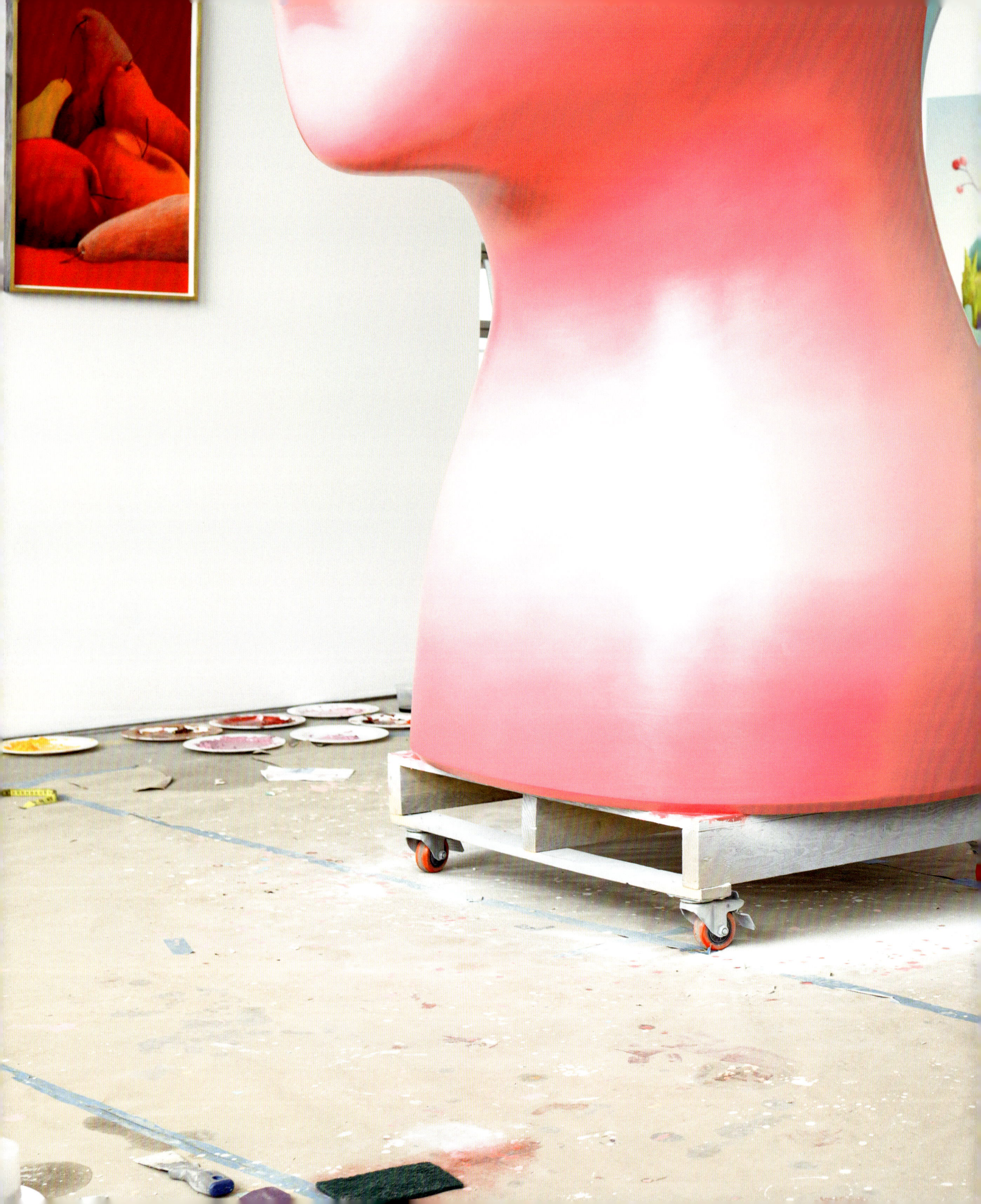

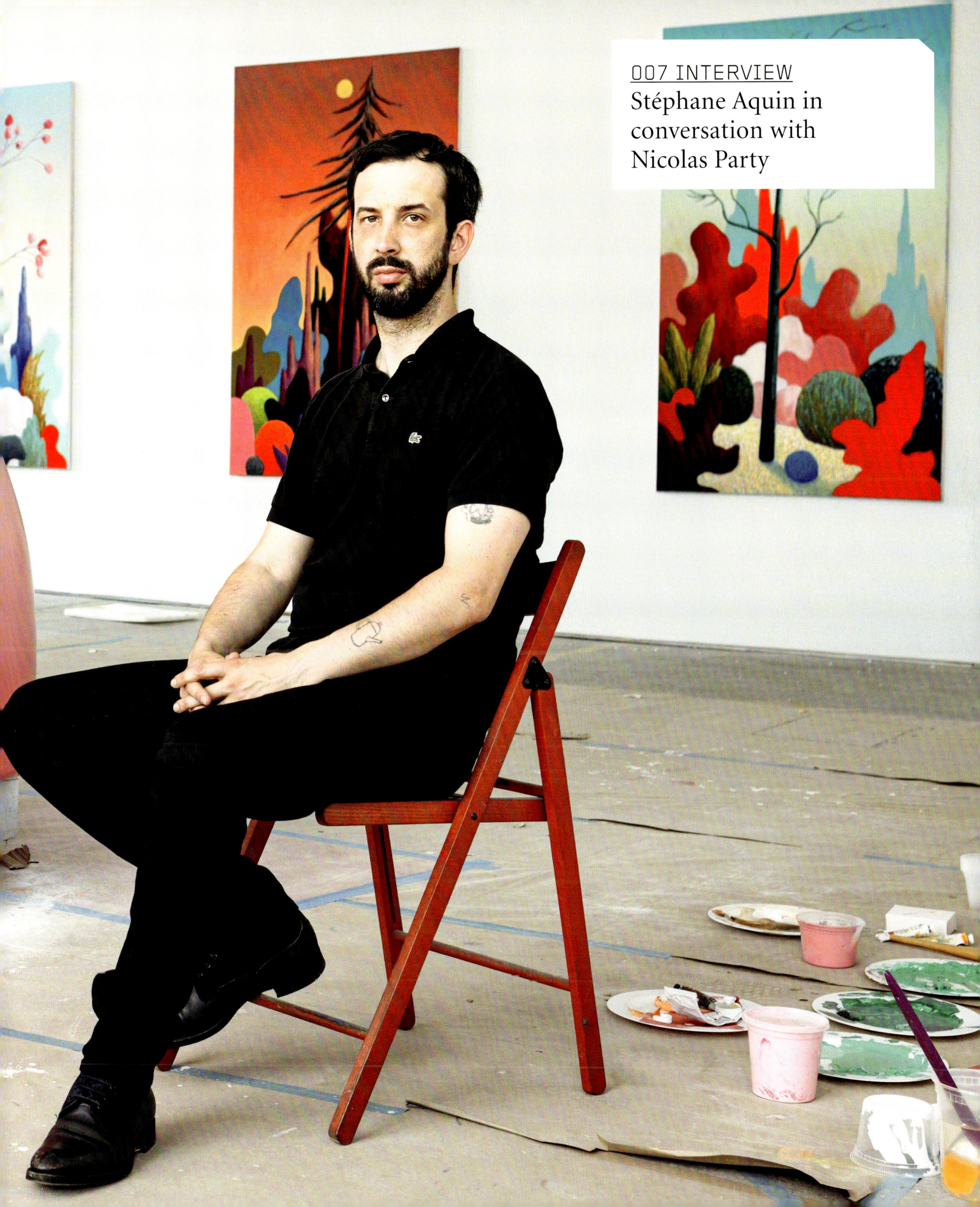

007 INTERVIEW

Stéphane Aquin in conversation with Nicolas Party

STÉPHANE AQUIN: *How did you get into art growing up?*

NICOLAS PARTY: I grew up in a small village called Villette, near Lausanne, on the border of the Lac Léman. It's a very picturesque place, surrounded by vineyards, and one of the first exposures I had to art was watching the local painters do watercolours for the wine labels. Friends of my parents worked as janitors at a museum that opened in Lausanne when I was four years old. They lived in the custodians' house beside the museum, in this beautiful park, and quite often we'd visit them on the weekend. That's how I started going to museums. I have great memories of those visits and I remember seeing some fantastic exhibitions there. I saw a Magritte show, and that looked so magical to me at age seven. When I was ten, they organized an exhibition of François Bocion, an artist born in Lausanne in 1828, who made many paintings of the lake and the surrounding landscape. I remember being fascinated by the translation into painting of my own surrounding landscape. My parents bought me a set of oils and I started copying Bocion's paintings from the catalogue that my dad had brought home. It was the first time I felt a great sense of joy in painting.

AQUIN: *Were you still in Villette when you started doing graffiti?*

PARTY: I did my first graffiti when I was twelve with my neighbour, who was three years older. He told me that two friends from his school had showed him how to get inside a motorway bridge. He drove us on his 'vélomoteur', a sort of scooter with pedals for teenagers – and very old people – to a massive highway bridge close by. We broke the lock of an entrance at one extremity of the bridge and got in. He'd brought some spray paint to do some drawings on the wall. That first experience was so thrilling that I instantly became addicted to the adrenalin. It was the perfect way to mix my passion for drawing and that very teenage sense of adventure that comes with breaking the rules.

AQUIN: *It became very serious, and you went on doing graffiti for more or less a decade. Did you develop any kind of style or imagery? Was it tags?*

PARTY: In 2001, I did my last painting on the side of a train, ten years after my first graffiti inside that bridge. During those ten years a lot happened in connection with this activity, and more or less my whole life was dictated by it: most of my time out of school was devoted to either being outside painting or inside making sketches with friends. We drove all over Switzerland, but also France, Italy and Germany to paint, and to meet other graffiti artists. I became very skilled at using spray paint to create designs that got more and more elaborate, but graffiti was never really about the visuals – it was mostly about the act. What mattered was to do it in the most visible and difficult location. For example, painting the TGV (Train Grande Vitesse), the fast train from Paris that stayed overnight in Lausanne, was greatly valued by your graffiti colleagues. It was very difficult to paint on it because of security. You only had twenty minutes to paint between security-guard rounds. But the reward was big – your painting would be in Paris the next morning.

AQUIN: *Graffiti also got you into trouble: there are stories that circulate about nights spent in Swiss jails.*

PARTY: I got caught for the first time when I was fifteen, then later in Italy when I was eighteen. We got locked in for police 'interviews' many times – it was part of the excitement of it all. You had all the ingredients of a cops and bad guys movie, but without the gravity of the crime – we were just painting. I got caught one last time two years after I'd actually stopped, because someone talked. There was a trial a year later, in 2014, and I was fined around $50,000. I was a student at art school at that point and that amount was pretty scary. It took me ten years to pay it back. But I'll always look back at that decade as an extremely exciting time, when we were painting as a group, always looking for extraordinary thrilling adventures.

AQUIN: *Can you tell me more about the social aspect of graffiti and tagging? How significant was this for you?*

opposite,
SUNRISE, 2018
SOFT PASTEL ON LINEN
160 X 180 CM

previous pages,
NICOLAS PARTY, NEW YORK, 2020

next pages,
TWO POTS, 2016
SOFT PASTEL ON LINEN
100 X 80 CM

STILL LIFE, 2016
SOFT PASTEL ON LINEN
170 X 140 CM

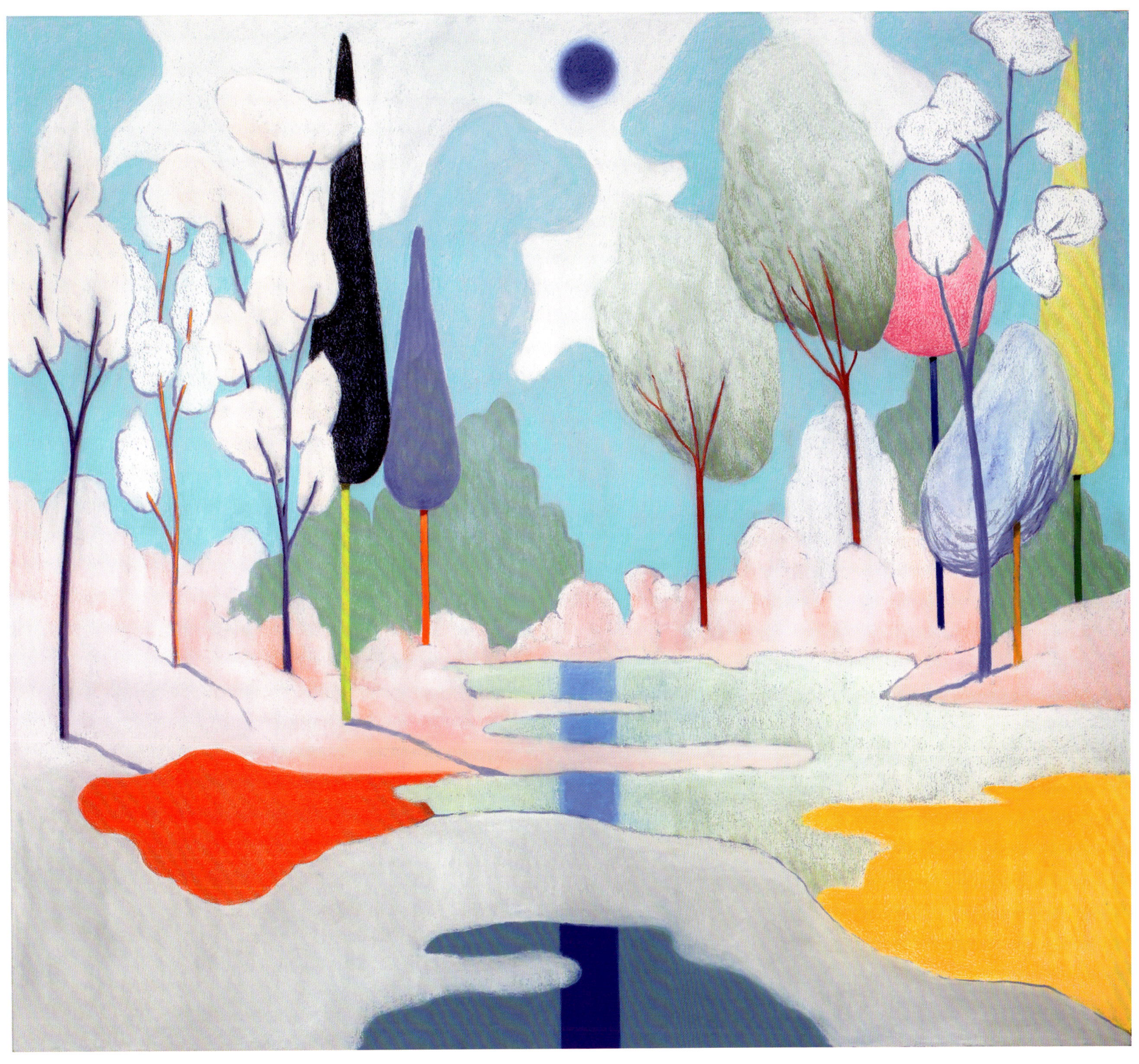

PARTY: There was definitely a sense of coming-of-age rebellious energy. We felt that we were reclaiming the street for our own purposes, as a band, in a very similar way to how skateboarding does. It's a way of taking ownership of the world that surrounds you by visually disturbing the order of the streets. There was also a shared conviction of being 'anti-system', behaviour that's typical for a teenager, and I still feel it's important for society to tolerate that sort of expression.

AQUIN: *How would you chart the influence of graffiti on your work today?*

PARTY: Quite a lot of my practice can be linked to that decade. I still paint on walls. But more than mural-making, which has a long tradition in the history of art, the way that I approach it is directly connected to graffiti. In graffiti the action of painting is

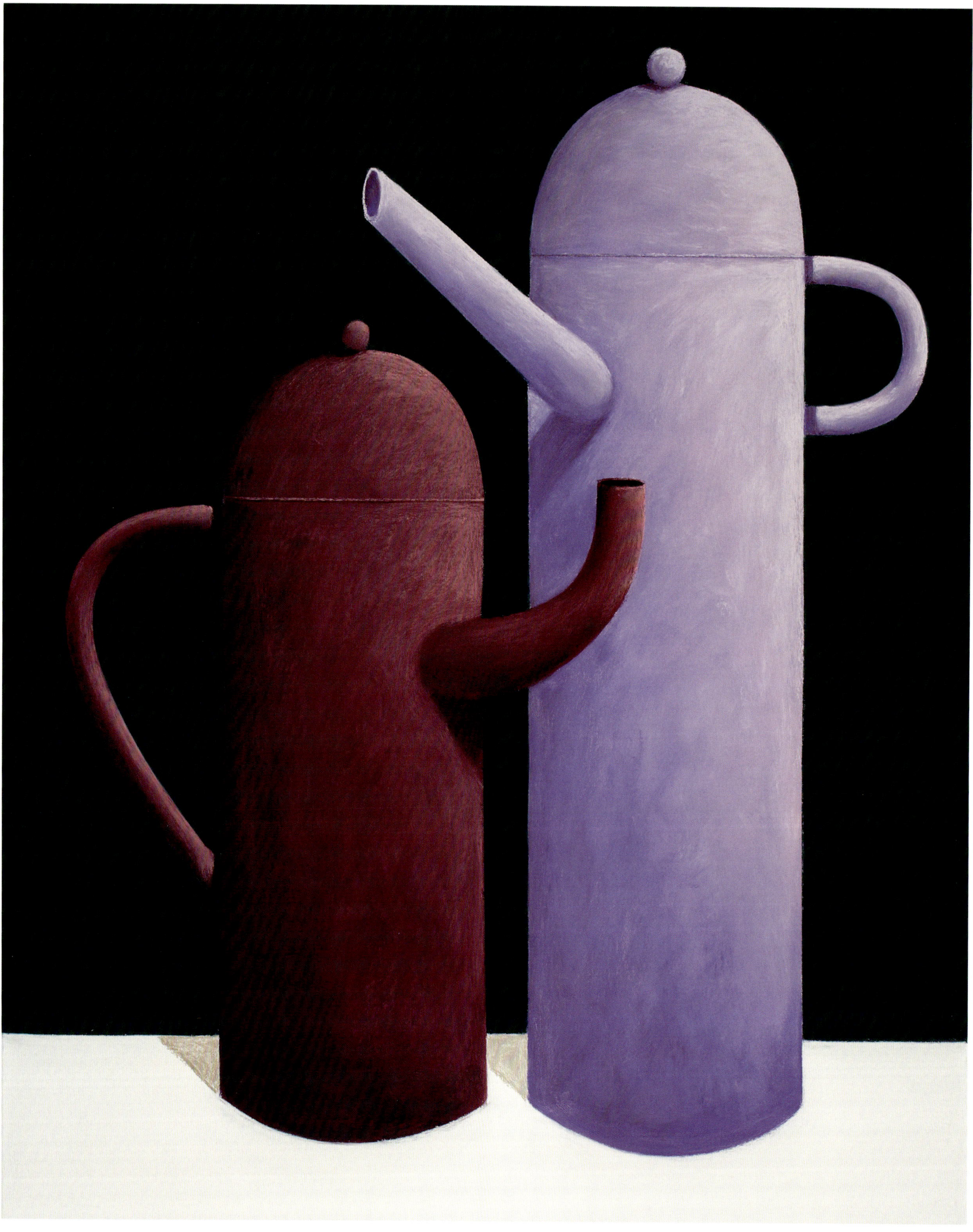

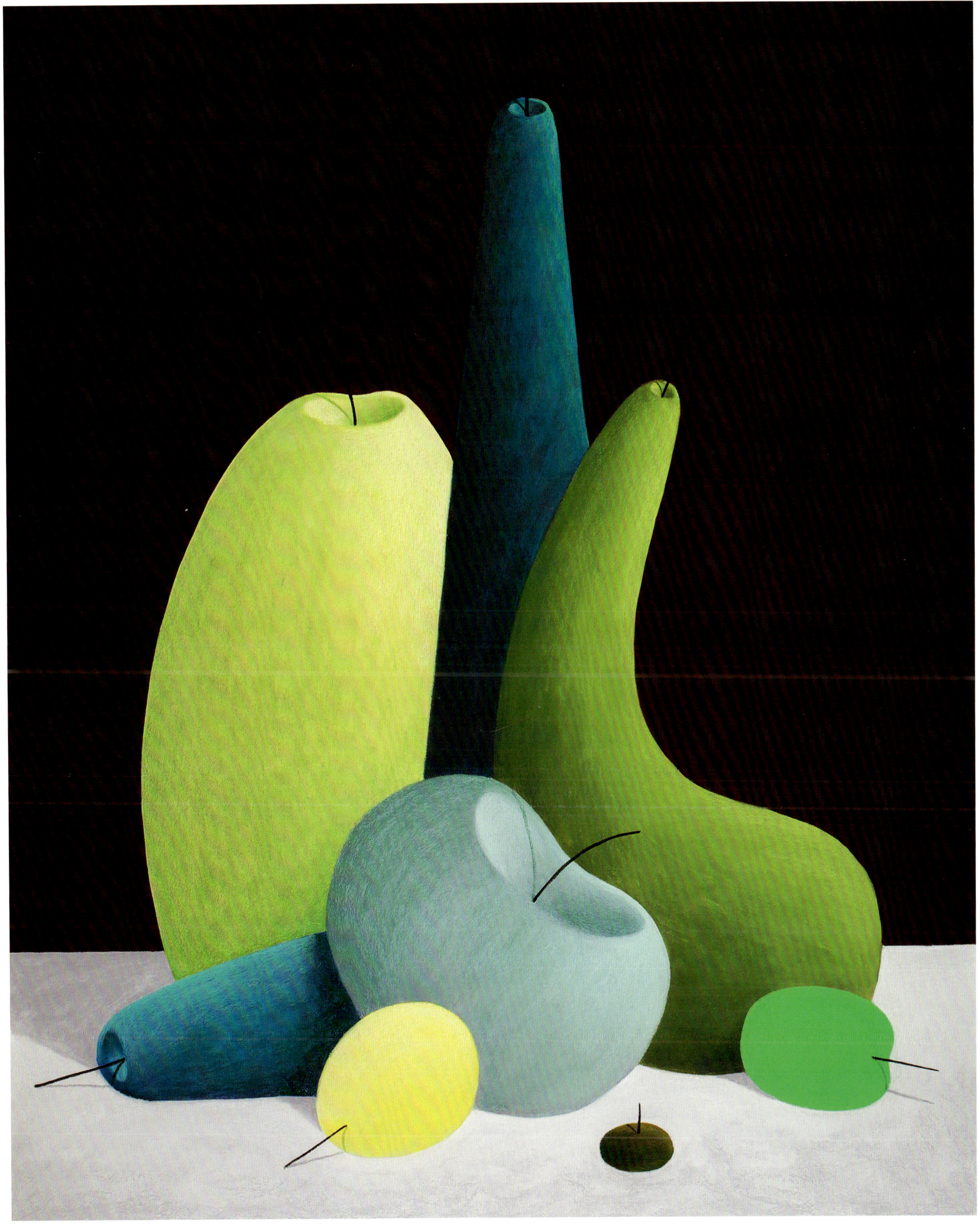

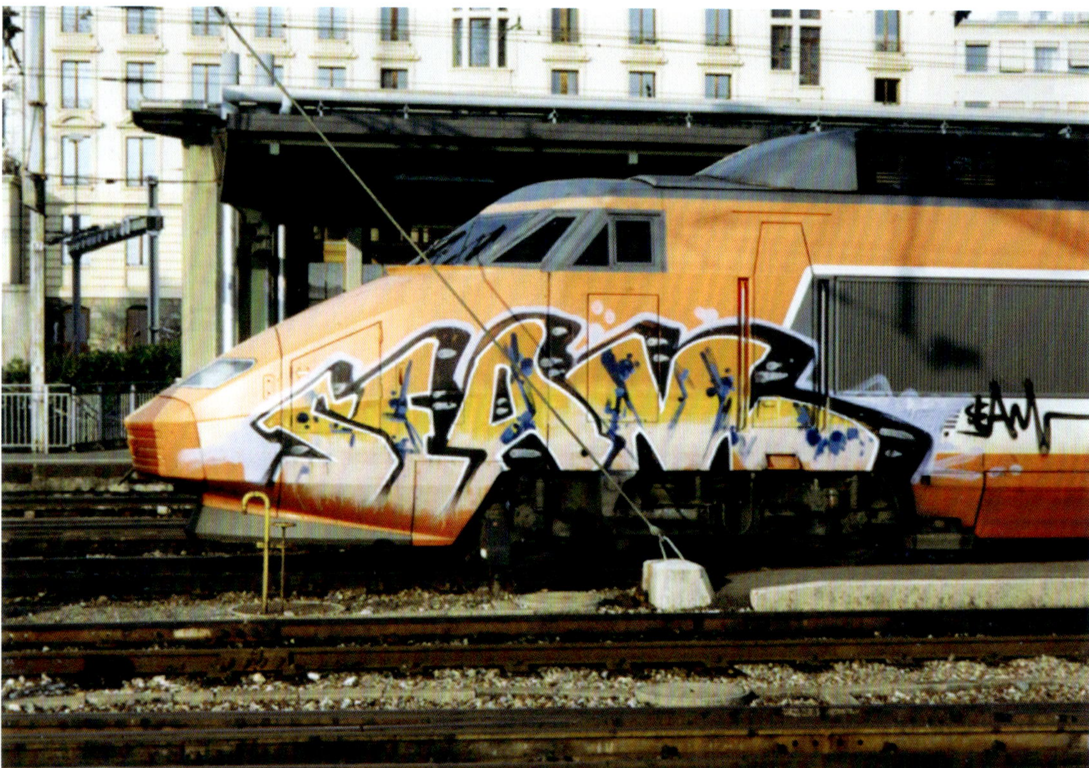

A TGV TRAIN WITH GRAFFITI BY THE ARTIST, LAUSANNE, 1998

probably more important than the visual result. It doesn't really matter if the painting that I did on a train would be washed out or scrubbed off the next day: what's important is that you were there doing it. In some way, you can connect it to live art, where the performance is the work and not the result. In a lot of my murals of the last ten years, I've tried to find that same energy. One way that I found is to leave a large space open for improvisation during the execution – if you start out knowing only half of what you're going to do, you put yourself in a place where the stress of resolving the work during the very finite period of the installation creates a rush of adrenalin that's very enjoyable, and generative.

Another important influence of graffiti on my current work is its aesthetic. When you paint on the train or by the side of the highway you need to choose very bold colours and graphic depictions. The image that you try to make visible is often in a place where either the viewer or the work itself are in movement. Those visual strategies still operate in my work today: bold and contrasting colours, graphically defined compositions.

AQUIN: *You stopped graffiti, and entered the ECAL, the École Cantonale d'Art de Lausanne, notorious for its conceptual bent; a very different social context and worldview of art from that of graffiti.*

PARTY: The art school provided a social environment that was as exciting as graffiti. But the ethos was completely different. All the teachers hated graffiti, and anything that looked even remotely like it was regularly pointed at as exactly what not to do. At that point, I was very curious about the immense world of novelty that art school provided, and it didn't take me very long to forget about graffiti and absorb as much I could from all that the teachers had to offer. The only thing that I missed from my graffiti years was the adrenalin, and it's something that I've tried many times, and sometimes successfully, to reproduce.

AQUIN: *What did you study and discover during those three years at ECAL?*

PARTY: I actually started in the cinema department, and after six months I moved into graphic design with a focus on interactive design, which centred on learning how to create design directly for the screen. I mainly did 3D animation and the work for

foreground,
STILL LIFE A STRIPED POT,
2010
OIL ON CANVAS
153 X 102 CM

background,
DECORATIVE PATTERN
NUMBER 1, 2010
SPRAY PAINT ON WALL
DIMENSIONS VARIABLE

INSTALLATION VIEW AT
THE GLUE FACTORY,
GLASGOW INTERNATIONAL
FESTIVAL, 2010

my degree was a thirty-minute abstract 3D animation. I still quite like this work, and a lot of the aesthetic of the pots that I did for a few years were directly influenced by how a 3D programme simulates volume on basic geometrical elements.

AQUIN: *So to sum it up, you started with the graffiti in relation to street life and architecture, and after that a conceptual framing comes into place. And then you had an art group for three years.*

PARTY: Yes, during the last year of art school a few friends started to meet every week to play music. But none of us actually knew how to play any instruments, so it was more like us mimicking all the experimental music that we were discovering at the time, artists like John Cage, Terry Riley, Tony Conrad, Moondog, La Monte Young and many others. We had a great teacher, Pierre Baudevin, who was extremely knowledgeable about music, and every week he'd make us listen to sounds that we'd never heard before. So, every time we had a session, we'd record it and make a little CD with a cover and a title. We made around thirty of those – not that they're really listenable to, I have to say. At some point the music activity faded away and with two other friends, Charlotte Herzig and Stéphane Devidal, we started to make art projects together.

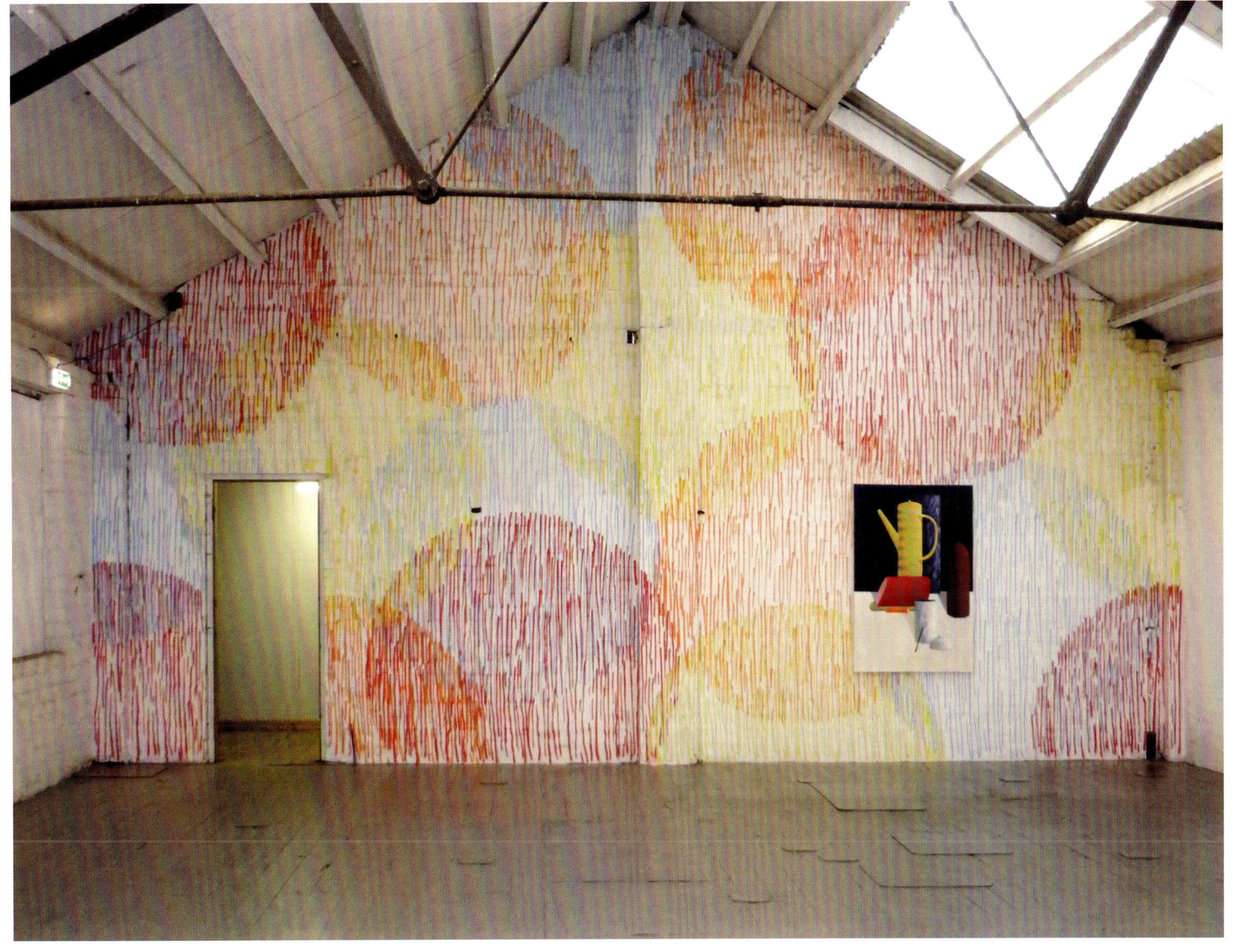

AQUIN: *And did your group have a name?*

PARTY: Blakam. It comes from an onomatopoeic word from the manga Akira. It's the sound of very big explosions.

AQUIN: *Can you tell me about the projects you did together?*

PARTY: It was a wide variety of activities. We also painted together – but what was most exciting was starting to work on site-specific installations. We organized a series of concerts, inviting musicians to perform in an environment that we created. We'd paint and design all sort of items in order to create a setting that would visually interfere with the experience of the music. We also used similar set-design strategies to display our painting works in different installations. We made a few mural paintings as a backdrop for our paintings, but we also made homemade frames and different objects that interacted with the paintings. It was during those projects that we created the stones that I continued to do after this period with Blakam, called *Blakam's Stones*. During a project where we invited different artists to design a crazy golf course, we first painted stones to look like fruits, cheese and various other food items. We then placed those painted stones as obstacles on a board painted like a Jackson Pollock action painting. It was during that time that my interest in creating environments really took shape, and I think a lot of my ideas about how to install a show can be traced to that period.

AQUIN: *And you also curated projects by other artists as part of Blakam.*

PARTY: Yes, we also opened a project space in the warehouse where we all had our studios. We named the gallery Bellevaux, which was the name of the neighbourhood. We invited artists to do projects and we also used that space to do several of our Blakam music projects. We created a logo and a website, and for each show we'd design a poster and organize an opening and hold parties. I have great memories of that period. I even lived in the warehouse for a few months. Under this arrangement, it was easy to be creative and productive, and it was a lot of fun.

AQUIN: *You leave ECAL, you leave Lausanne altogether, and you move to Glasgow and enter the Glasgow School of Art. Once there, you start your 'Sweet Geranium' projects, in which you bring together a number of interests that you'd been developing in Switzerland – more specifically, making a work of art out of installing the work of others.*

PARTY: I went to Glasgow to focus on my practice as an individual, after four years of working within a group – but I missed my time with Blakam and the shared energy surrounding it. I started this project in my studio during the second year of my MFA. I called it 'Sweet Geranium'. It was a prolongation, or extension, of the ideals of Blakam. Every other month I invited one artist to lend me a few works, and I created a display for their work. My display could be very invasive, and I was experimenting with how far the display could affect the work shown in a space. I worked on all sorts of visually invasive frames, murals, plinths and floor paintings. I also made screen-print posters for each show.

AQUIN: *Can you tell me about your association with the Poster Club in Glasgow?*

PARTY: With the 'Sweet Geranium' projects, I learned how to screen print and I wanted to keep practising it after I graduated. I became a member of the Glasgow Print Studio, which had great facilities, to make more screen prints. There I met Ciara Philips, a Canadian artist who primarily uses screen printing in her practice. Collaboration is an essential part of her work, and with other artists from Glasgow she started a project called Poster Club. Every Wednesday from 6 to 9pm, we'd meet at the print workshop to make a poster. I think we called that weekly print a 'poster' instead of an artwork to take some pressure off, even if the poster never actually 'posted' anything but itself. We also had a few shows where we displayed the prints, including one in Shanghai at the Himalayas Museum, where we all went to install the show, which was a fantastic experience.

MINI GOLF, 2006
(WITH BLAKAM)
ACRYLIC ON STONE
AND OIL ON WOOD

INSTALLATION VIEW AT CIRCUIT, LAUSANNE, 2006

opposite,
BLAKAM MADAME 2
(WITH BLAKAM), 2006
MURALS: ACRYLIC ON WALL
STONES: ACRYLIC ON STONE
FABRIC, INSTRUMENTS

INSTALLATION VIEW AT FORDE, GENEVA, 2006

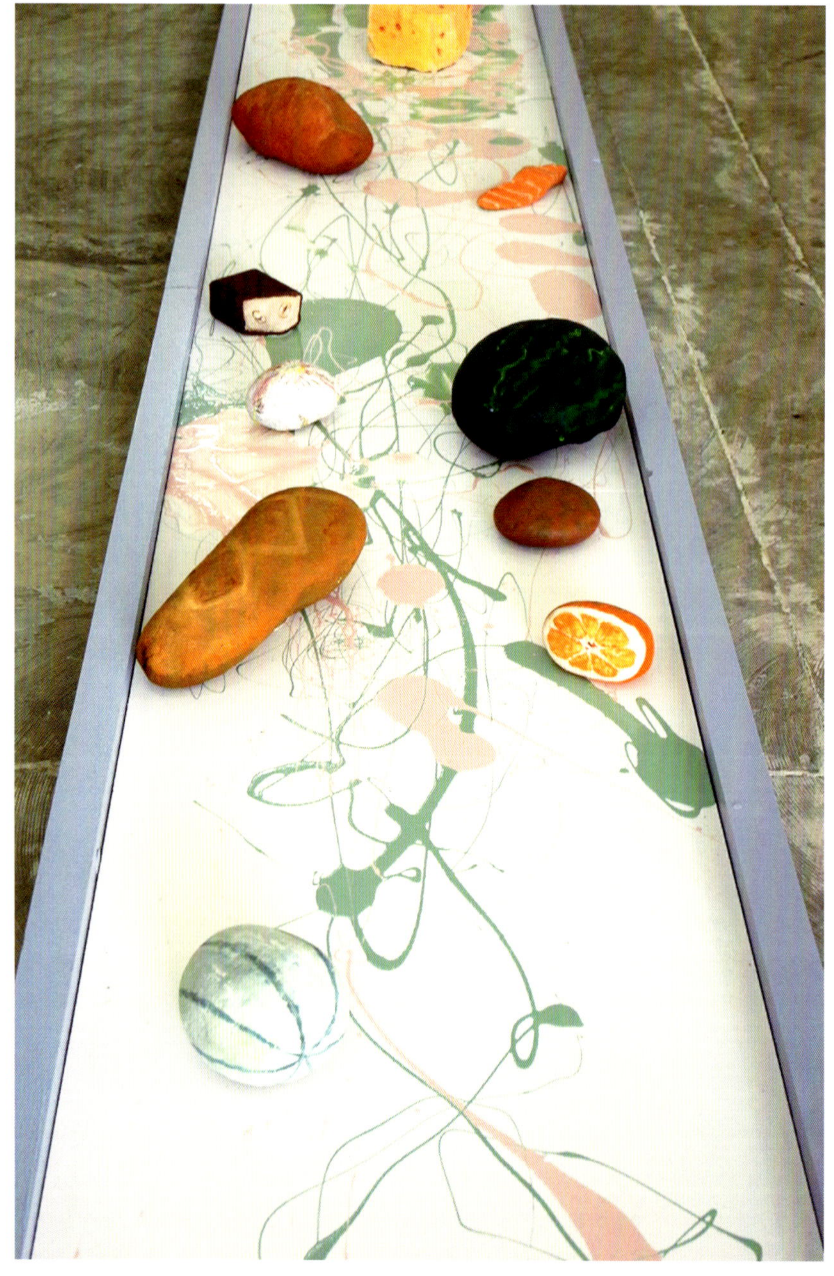

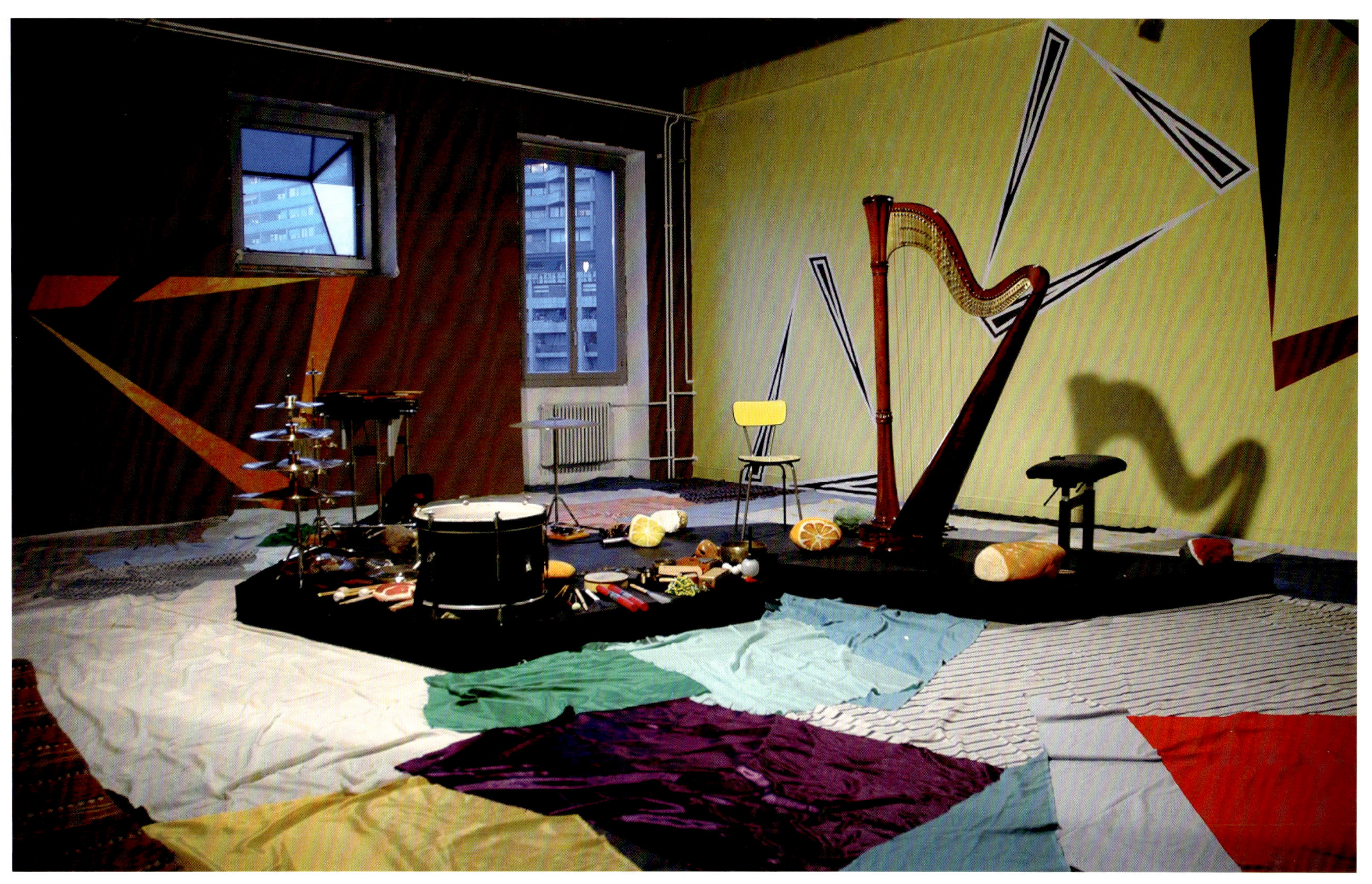

AQUIN: *All these are exciting projects, but you said you didn't go to Glasgow just to pursue collaborative projects. You went there to develop as an artist in your own right. Can you expand on this?*

PARTY: The big change in Glasgow wasn't really 'Sweet Geranium'. I went to Glasgow to focus on my painting practice. I was still struggling a lot to understand what my interests in that field were. Subject matter, style, technique, everything that defines an artistic practice was very blurry. It's one thing to know that you love art and that you want to spend all your time painting; it's another thing to understand what specifically defines your art, and how it relates to your personality. It's an introspective process that's unending. Sometimes there's some breakthrough that can feel very liberating, and I had a few moments like that in Glasgow. One discovery was to determine the question of the subject matter. Around 2017–18, I decided that I would only paint landscapes or still lifes and that I would only work within those historical genres defined by Western art. It was liberating because suddenly the pressure of having to find new subjects to paint was lifted off my mind – the stress that comes with the idea that art is about novelty and originality. Nothing was really new about painting a still life or a landscape, but there's still a lot to explore conceptually within those fields. A few years later I added portraits to my repertoire of subject matter.

AQUIN: *Your first major project in Glasgow, after leaving the art school is the* Dinner *for 24 Elephants, held at the Modern Institute in Glasgow. But there are no paintings in this show. Can you tell us more about this project?*

PARTY: Well, this needs a bit of explanation. I'd embarked on my journey as a painter, but I was struggling with another element of my art practice, which was the technique.

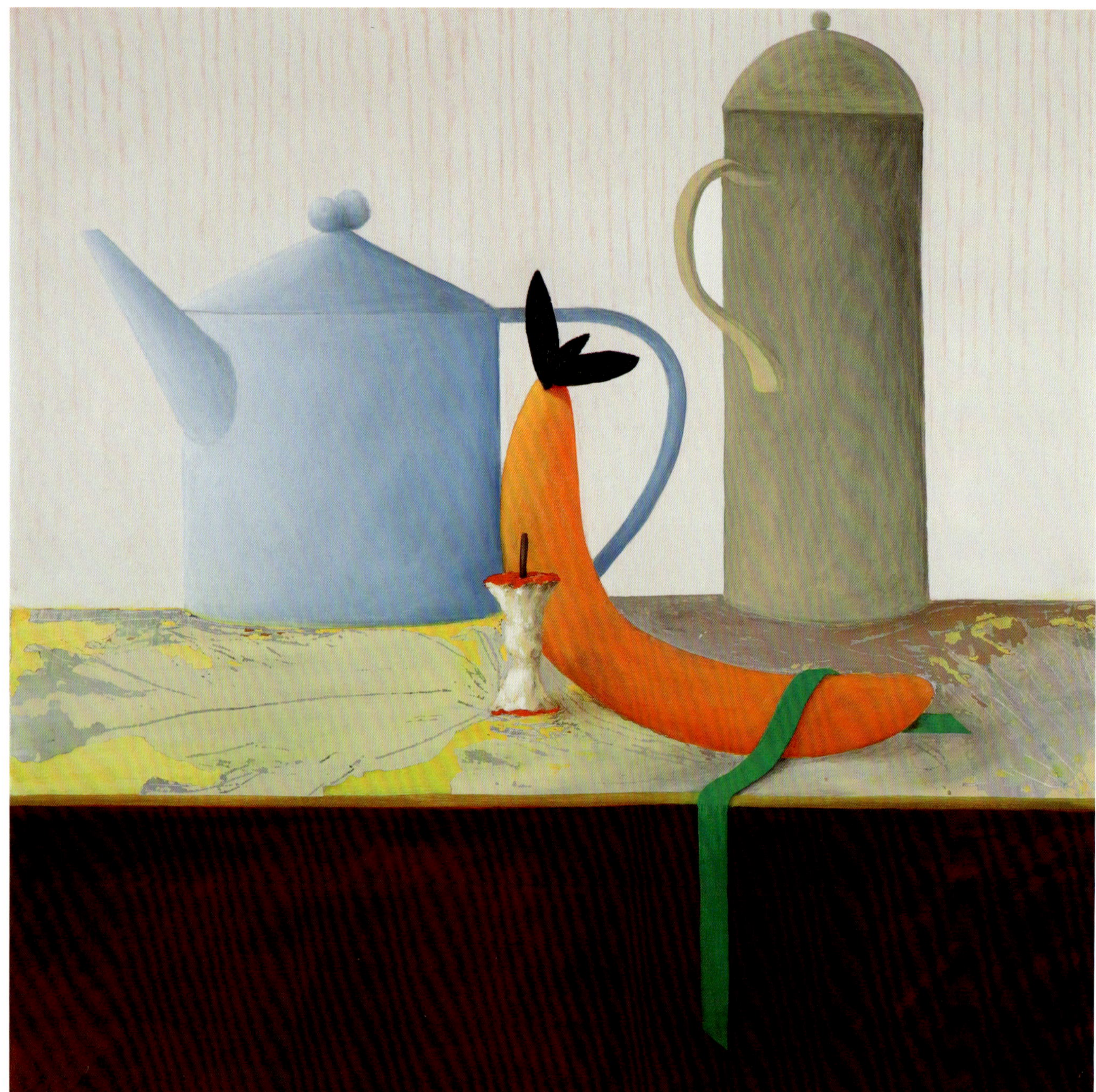

STILL LIFE WITH AN APPLE,
2009
OIL ON CANVAS
100 X 100 CM

Finding a medium and a way to use it that feels natural to you is challenging – I only really achieved that when I moved from Glasgow to Brussels and picked up pastel. But at that time, I was mainly using oil and my process was very slow. I could take up to sixteen months to finish a painting. That meant that I never really had enough paintings to do a show – I actually only did one show with oil paintings, in 2013. After that, anytime I had an exhibition, because I didn't have enough paintings to show, I began using the number of days provided by the galleries to produce a series of works onsite, mainly drawing and painting directly onto the walls. This way of doing a show was directly related to my graffiti years, where the location and the duration was completely linked to the art created. I often used spray paint to do those projects because of my experience with that medium and its ability to cover walls very fast.

AQUIN: *So this explains the dinner, at least partly. That* Dinner for 24 Elephants *was your first big coup. But others were to follow and they're an important part of your practice now. I'd like to hear more about these dinners.*

PARTY: The *Dinner for 24 Elephants* was the first time that I was invited to do a project in a commercial gallery. Toby Webster, the director of the Modern Institute, actually

DINNER FOR 24 ELEPHANTS, 2011
4 TABLES ACRYLIC ON WOOD
EACH 78 X 237 X 119 CM

DINNER FOR 24 ELEPHANTS STOOL, 2011
24 STOOLS ACRYLIC ON WOOD
EACH 45 X 45 X 45 CM

INSTALLATION VIEW AT THE MODERN INSTITUTE, GLASGOW, 2011

invited me to do a project in their viewing room. I explained that I could organise a dinner in the main space, but I would only use the main space for one day, then we could pile up all the tables, stools and plates in the viewing room. It was an exciting way of using the two very different spaces within the same project.

The idea for the *Dinner for 24 Elephants* was to create a set design for an 'artist's dinner', where all the participants would perform their own role. The characters of the play were the people who attend a classic 'artist's dinner': the gallerist, the collector, the curator and the artist. Everybody would be playing their usual role in this ritual, except for the two directors of the gallery and myself, who became the waiters for the dinner.

AQUIN: *You were basically staging the art world, with its sociology and its economy, but in a very theatrical way. Why did you call this* Dinner for 24 Elephants?

PARTY: I wanted to create a humorous feeling right from the title. When you're invited to a dinner for twenty-four elephants, you feel a sense of irony. When the guests arrived in the room, they saw four large tables surrounded by twenty-four cubic stools painted to look like elephants. It appeared that twenty-four elephant guests had already got there before they arrived. Then people sat on them, and it looked as if each guest was riding an elephant. The image of a human on top of an elephant brought to mind a few different thoughts, and one of my intentions was to evoke the power dynamic suggested by this

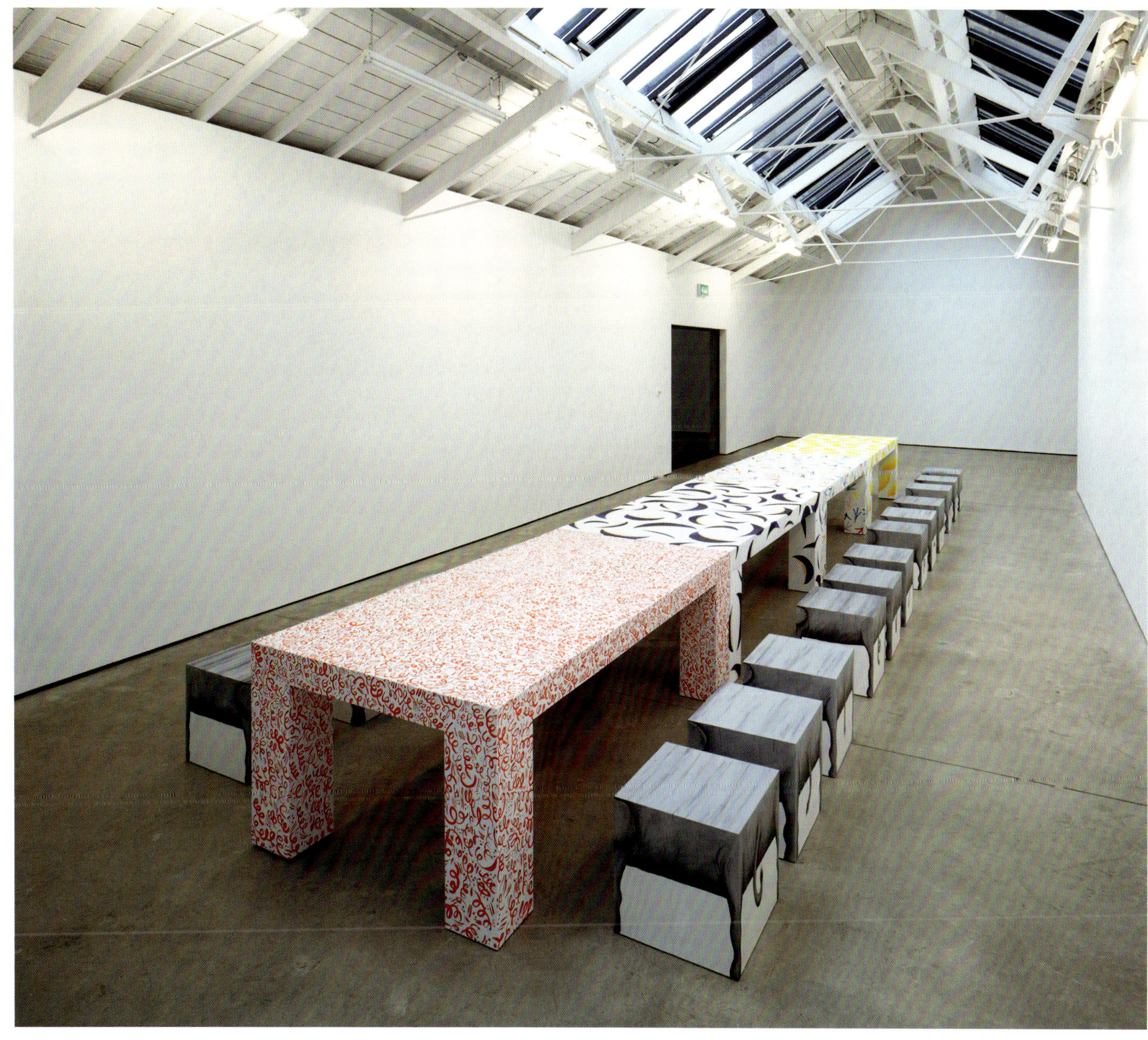

image. Humans take pride in riding the biggest animals that walk on earth; it gave us a sense of power and superiority over nature. But because of the proportions of the elephant, the elephant being a stool, the animal looked tiny with a giant human sitting on it.

AQUIN: *And the food was also artistically thought out, right?*

PARTY: I wanted to play with idea of proportions, again, in dining culture. You can practically make class distinctions just by looking at how big portions are in a restaurant. The more expensive the restaurant, the smaller the portions are. Another aspect of fine dining is the number of courses that will be served during one meal. The guests of the dinner were served ten courses – very small portions of food placed in the middle of a big plate. Some elements of the menu evoked fine dining, such as the course of just one oyster. Others suggested fast-food dining – for example, the lonely sausage placed on a big plate.

AQUIN: *Can you tell me more about the plates, since everything in this performance was designed?*

PARTY: I wanted to control the visual atmosphere with the design of the plates and tables as well as the lighting. I painted different colourful patterns on the tables and plates, to create an overtly decorative aspect to the project. It was important to design

DINNER FOR 24 ELEPHANTS, 2011
HAND PAINTED CERAMIC PLATES, FOOD, 7 PIECES
EACH Ø 33 X 3 CM

INSTALLATION VIEW AT THE MODERN INSTITUTE, GLASGOW, 2011

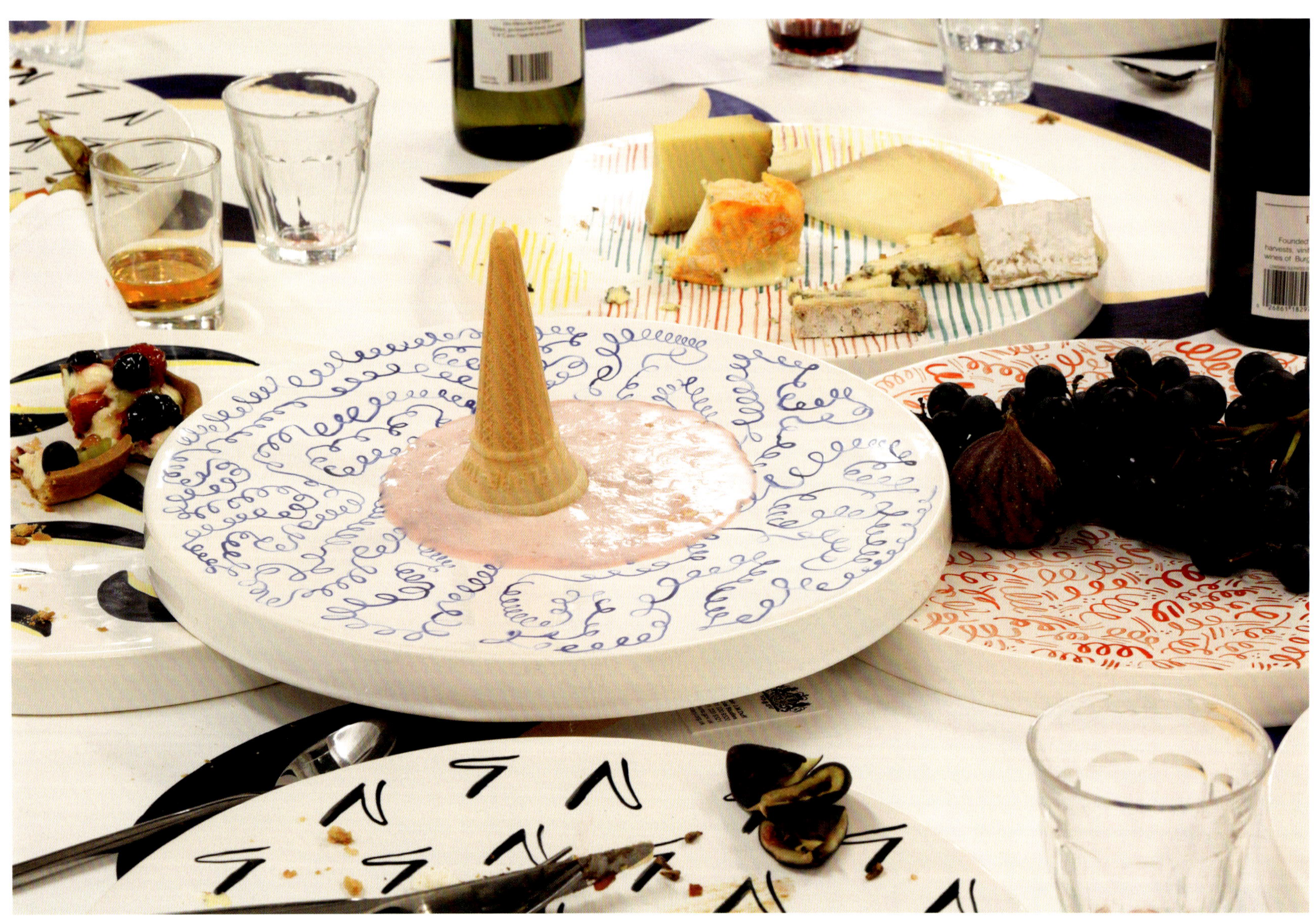

the shapes of the tables and plates, in order to be in charge of the full experience. The shapes are influenced by Brutalism and the pattern and colours by Memphis design. I wanted to create a visual environment that was the opposite of a refined dining restaurant. It looked more like a bulky overly patterned cafeteria. As for the lighting, the room was lit like a gallery usually is, quite in opposition to the ambient fine restaurant lighting culture. The food, the colourful patterns, and the guests were under spotlight.

AQUIN: *I can't help but think of your fellow Swiss compatriot, Daniel Spoerri, who also staged dinners from the 1960s onwards. Did you have him in mind in any way? Or other examples in the history of art of works involving dinners and meals?*

PARTY: There are a lot of remarkable art projects involving a dinner that served as references for *Dinner for 24 Elephants*. One of the common aspects of all those projects is the importance of the social event of a dinner: a dinner party is a social ceremony, from Leonardo's *Last Supper* (1495–1498), where the presence of the guests reveals the future of the host, to Judy Chicago's *The Dinner Party* (1974–79), where the absence of the guests at the table reveals their power to us. Every year, at the G20 forum, the twenty most powerful leaders of the world sit down to share the same food and wine, with the knowledge that sharing food is a known symbol of unity between parties that are in known conflict with each other.

AQUIN: *The dinners were to become a recurrent staple of your work. But the first exhibition where we instantly recognize Nicolas Party's installation/pictorial work is the one in Athens where you paint the walls of an apartment with charcoal, and on this backdrop you hang your paintings.*

PARTY: Those two shows happened in exactly the same week! We did the dinner, and the next day I flew to Athens, painted five rooms, then I flew back to Glasgow to open the project room show, and then I flew back to Athens for the opening. That was my introduction to the professional art world!

AQUIN: *Well, we'll take it as a sign of how coherent these two aspects of your work are. Can you tell me more about this particular project?*

PARTY: The premise of the project was quite particular. Several galleries were invited to take over different spaces in a neighbourhood in Athens that was run down by the 2008 economic crisis. There were a lot of empty buildings in Athens then. The gallery was given this beautiful apartment in a town house in which they asked me to do a project. Two other galleries occupied the other apartment in the building. The building was in a street affected by the devastating consequences of drug addiction on a neighbourhood. I painted all the walls of the deteriorating apartment to evoke the appearance of an elegantly decorated home. No objects were brought to the space and it was still completely empty when the show opened – only the appearance of the wall was transformed. The surfaces had changed, but the haunting feeling of emptiness of the place remained. I used spray paint to do a pattern on all the walls, decorating the room as if it was wallpapered. In the three main rooms, I drew three still lifes using charcoals. I used gold leaf to create a frame around the drawings. Using three characteristic techniques (spray paint, charcoals and gold leaf) was an important part of the project. Visually, each technique acted very differently on the surface of the walls and each media had a distinctive connotation. Spray paint is a very recent medium that was invented for DIY purposes, and later was taken up by street artists to paint outside on walls and trains. It's now strongly associated with street art and urban culture in general, so the use of that technique brought the street into the rooms. It's a paint that covers the walls extremely well. Charcoal might be the oldest mark-marking tool and is still used today. It's a very fragile medium that's quite hard to use on the wall. It reveals the marks of the walls and can be removed very easily from the surface. Gold leaf is also a very ancient technique, probably first used by the ancient Egyptians, and one associated with power and luxury. The use of the technique in the project brought a precious material into the rooms.

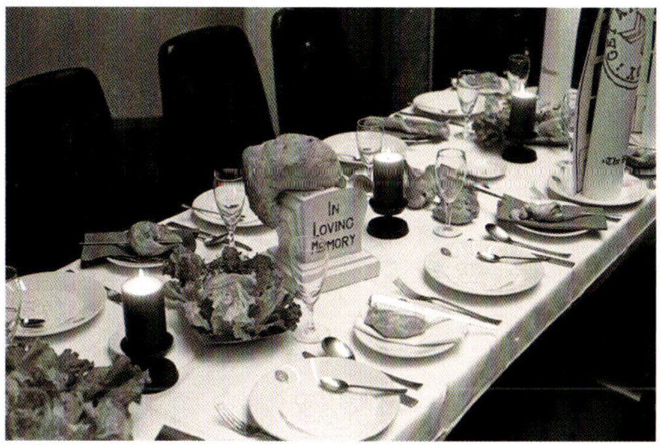

DANIEL SPOERRI
THE BANANA TRAP DINNER, 1970
EDINBURGH COLLEGE OF ART

DINNER FOR 24 ELEPHANTS
(DETAIL), 2011
HAND PAINTED CERAMIC
PLATES, SAUSAGE
7 PIECES
EACH Ø 33 X 3 CM

INSTALLATION VIEW AT THE
MODERN INSTITUTE, GLASGOW,
2011

DINNER FOR 24 ELEPHANTS
(DETAIL), 2011
4 TABLES ACRYLIC ON WOOD
EACH 78 X 237 X 119 CM

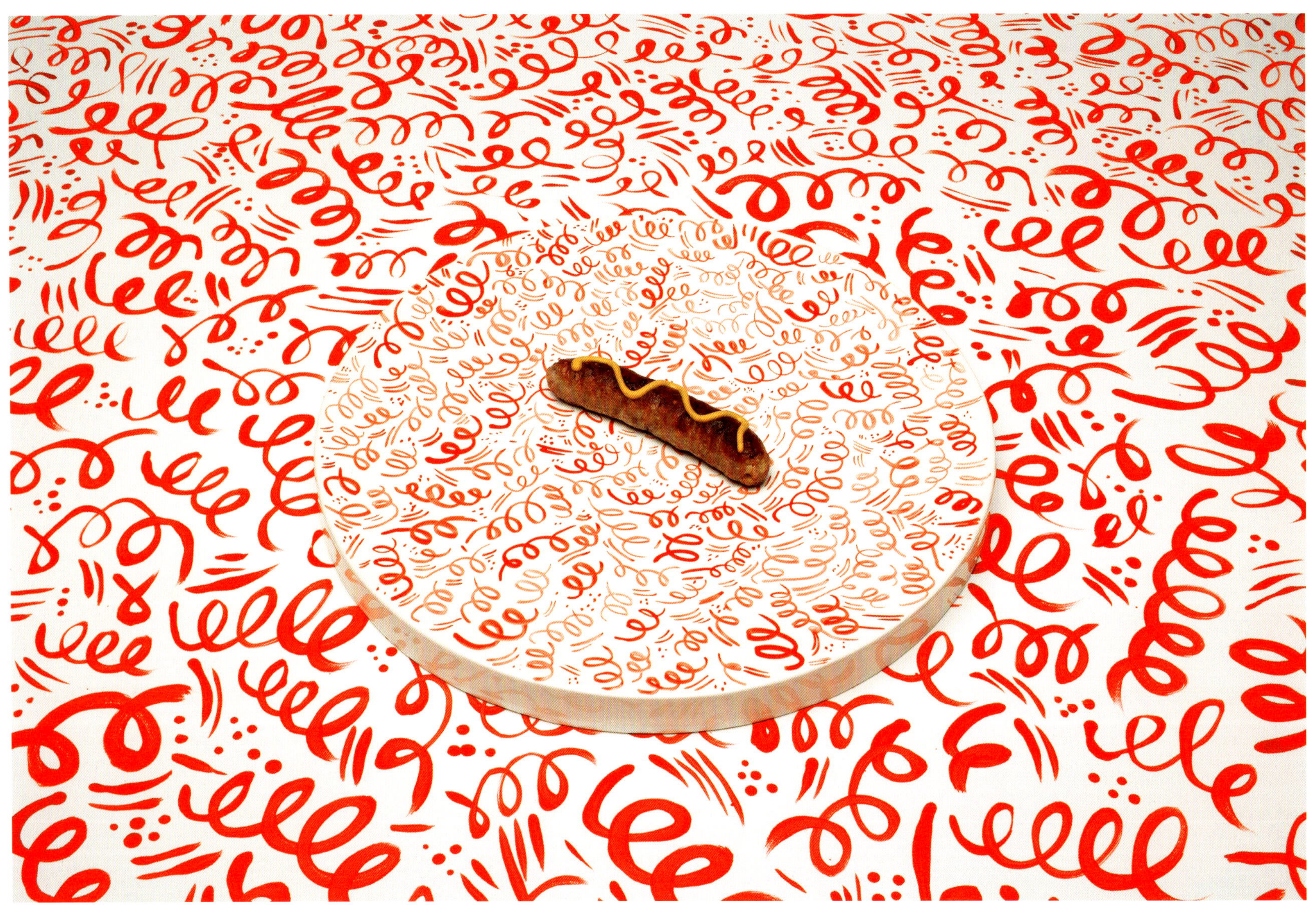

DINNER FOR 24 DOGS
(DETAIL), 2012
HAND PAINTED CERAMIC
PLATE, COMPTE,
8 PIECES
EACH 36 X 3 CM

INSTALLATION VIEW AT SALON
94 FREEMANS, NEW YORK, 2011

DINNER FOR 24 DOGS
(DETAIL), 2012
TABLE: ACRYLIC ON FURNITURE
GRADE BIRCH PLYWOOD
CHAIRS: GRAPHITE ON
PLYWOOD, 24 PARTS
TABLE: 75 X 267 X 230 X 222 CM
CHAIRS: EACH 45 X 45 X 45 CM

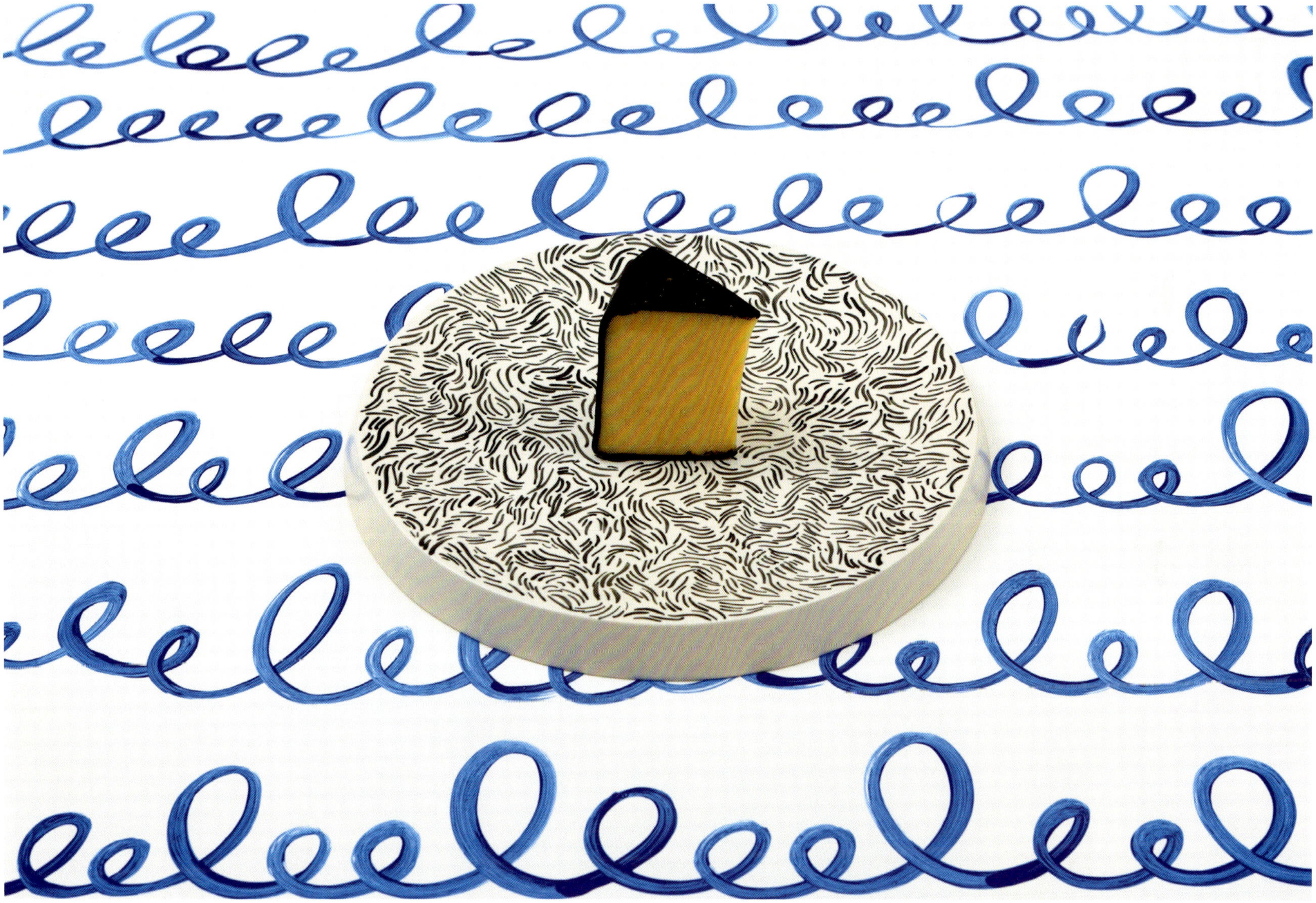

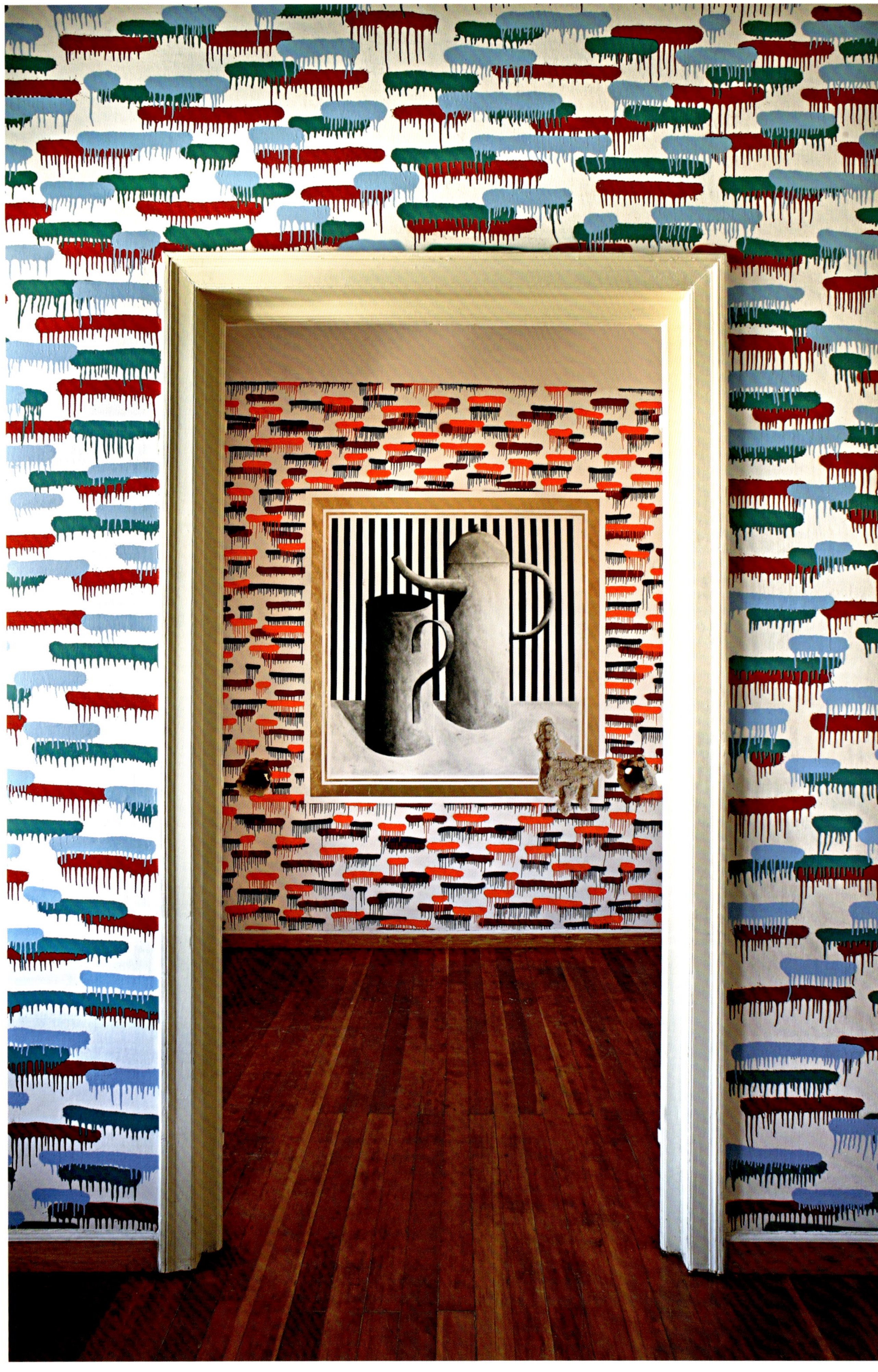

STILL LIFE, GOLD AND PEELING PAINT 1, 2011
SPRAY PAINT AND CHARCOAL ON WALL, GOLD LEAF

INSTALLATION VIEW AT REMAP 3, ATHENS, 2011

from left,
STILL LIFE WITH A CANDLE, 2012–13
OIL ON CANVAS
133 X 94 CM

STILL LIFE WITH PETALS, 2012
OIL ON CANVAS
160 X 160 CM

STILL LIFE WITH AN ORANGE TABLE, 2012–13
OIL ON CANVAS
104 X 104 CM

STILL LIFE WITH A RIBBON, 2012–13
OIL ON CANVAS
104 X 154 CM

STILL LIFE WITH A BOTTLE, 2012–13
OIL ON CANVAS
167.2 X 166 CM

MURAL: SPRAY PAINT ON WALL

INSTALLATION VIEW AT THE MODERN INSTITUTE, GLASGOW, 2013

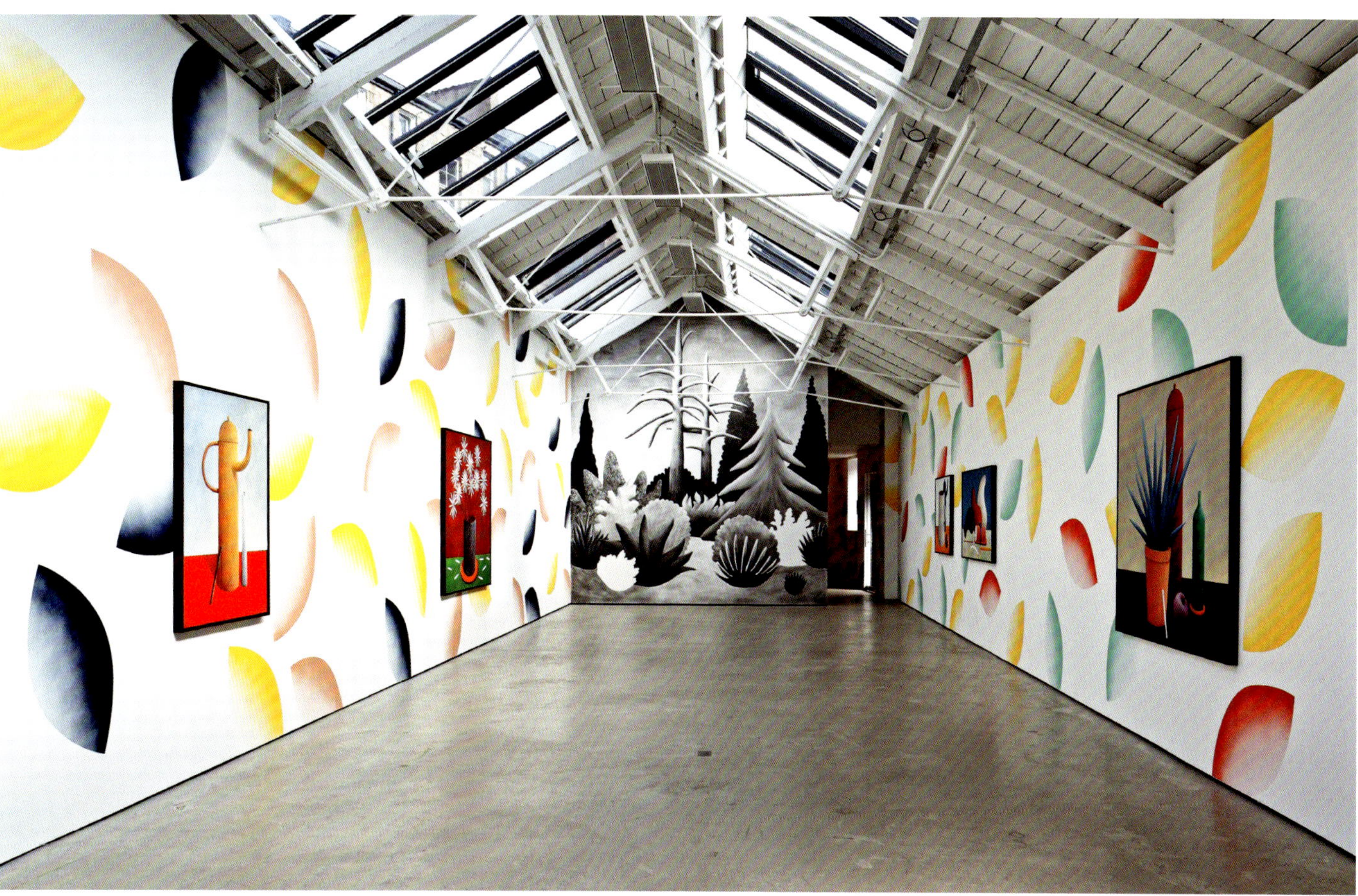

AQUIN: *When I look at the course of your career, there seems to be a gradual coming together of many interests that had been shaped in your younger years: the stage setting with Blakam; graffiti and urban subcultures; the conceptual thinking learned at school, and painting, of course. And it comes together in these two projects. But also there's a gradual expansion of motifs and scale, and genres too – one being the portraiture that comes in at some point.*

PARTY: Two years after the dinner project, for my second show at the Modern Institute, I did my first painting show where I displayed a series of still-life paintings, two charcoal landscape murals and a series of watercolour landscapes. All the walls had a pattern painted with spray paint. The show really established the way I did many other shows after that.

AQUIN: *You may show works from different genres in the same exhibition, but you never mix them up in the actual works. Each genre is treated separately, as if you were gaining control, piece by piece, of the traditional classifications of the history of painting.*

PARTY: It was around 2013 that I decided to distinguish those classic genres in my practice. I still hadn't done any portraits yet, only still lifes and landscapes, and I knew that I wanted to maintain those clear classifications. I named the Modern Institute show 'Still Life Oil Paintings and Landscape Watercolours' for that reason – I wanted to make clear that those different painting were indeed a still life or a landscape. I began trying to explore the depth of those classifications by reducing them to their essence – what is a still life, a landscape or a portrait? – and maybe by extension questioning why we created those categorizations between object, nature, human, animals, elements.

AQUIN: *For each of these different genres, you seem to be in search of the defining, essential element. The pot stands for still lifes, the tree for all landscapes.*

PARTY: I like how each of those classifications addresses distinct questions. For example, simplified that way, a landscape naturally addresses questions about our relation to nature, a portrait interrogates our relation to ourselves, a still life confronts us with an objectified world. I try to reduce the elements represented in each category, following the great example of an artist like Giorgio Morandi, an Italian artist who spent his career representing different pots and bottles. His ability to reduce his still life to the essence of the subject makes the viewer perceive the existentiality of such a task. It then allows the viewer to share Morandi's experience while he was observing his pots for long hours, making us understand that if you look hard enough, you can see God in a pot.

AQUIN: *Tell me more about your fruit still lifes.*

PARTY: Fruits are the simplest form of food: they exist and can be consumed without any effort – just pick the apple from the tree. They don't require any transformation prior to their consumption. You eat what's directly given by nature. Eating berries doesn't require any skills and we can imagine that the way we eat them must be similar to the way that a caveman enjoyed them. That makes the visual aspect of fruits timeless and consequently a great subject for painters, not unlike our bodies, which also haven't changed much through the ages – without clothes and accessories, Adam and Eve's bodies looked like ours. Lately, I like to imagine my fruit still lifes as a group of bodies, tired and slowly melting on each other. I think about the painting by Ingres,

LANDSCAPE, 2013
WATERCOLOUR ON PAPER
56 X 76 CM

opposite,
LANDSCAPE, 2013
WATERCOLOUR ON PAPER
76 X 56 CM

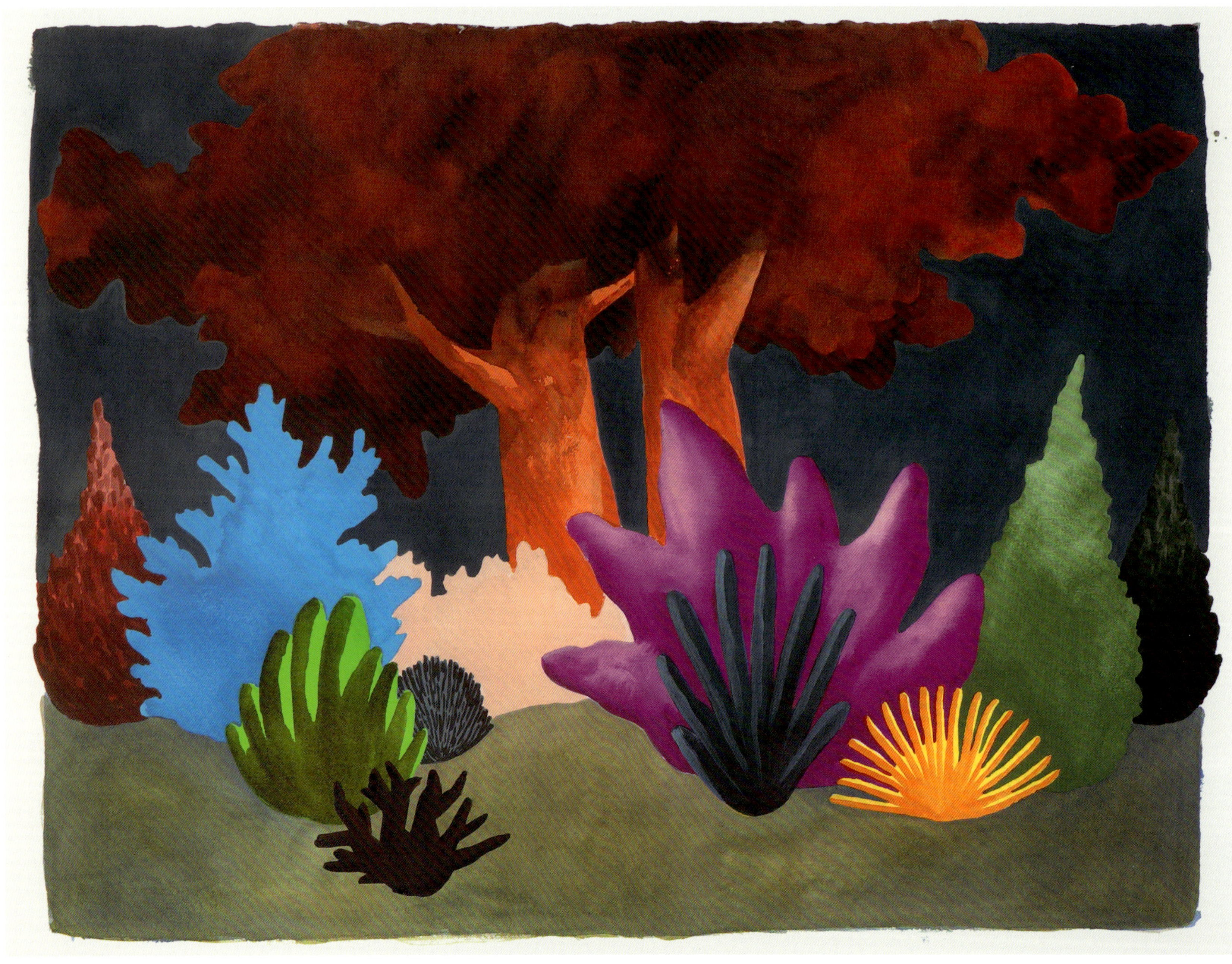

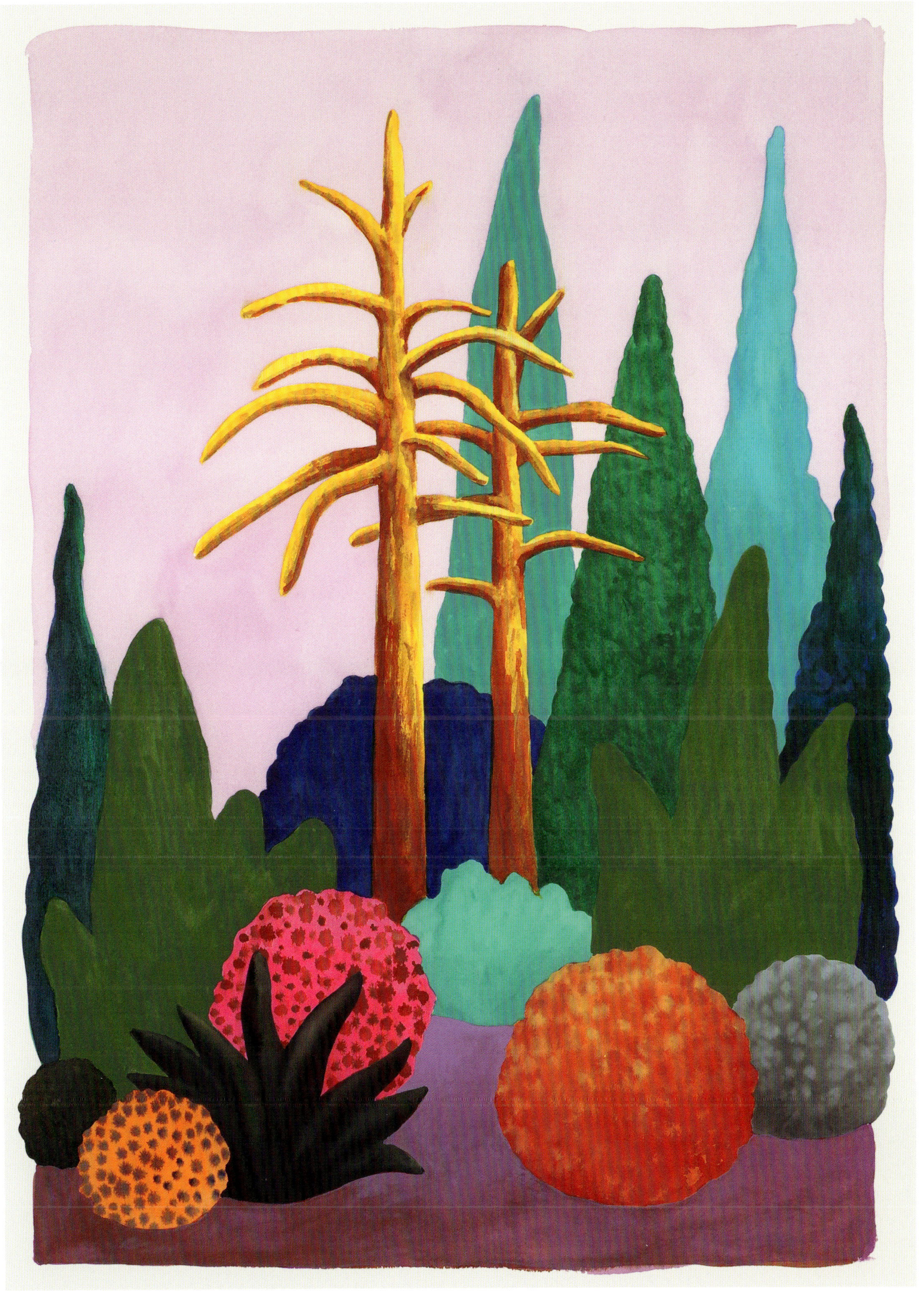

Le Bain Turque (1852–59) where a multitude of bodies lean against each other with great sensuality. This association between fruits and the human body is a longstanding tradition in western art, where fruits have been used to evoke human flesh. Especially in still life, the sexual connotations in the representation of food give the painter a playful set of elements to have fun with. Fruits, oysters, flowers and other features give the painter erotic subjects without having to name them directly. Today, we don't have any emojis that illustrate our sexual features, so we use peaches, aubergines and strawberries to communicate our sexual desires, in similar ways to Flemish still lifes, which used this coded language.

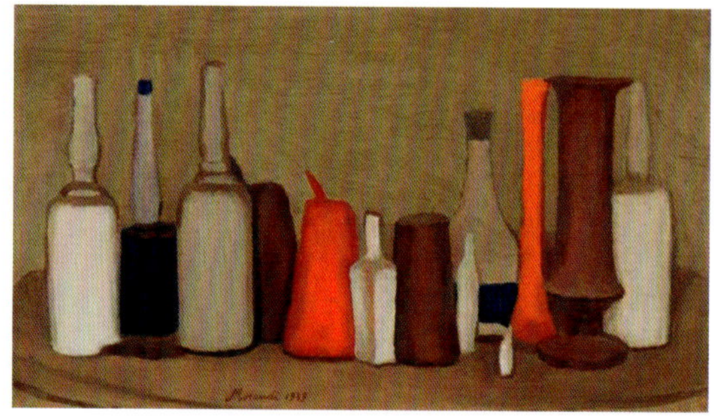

GIORGIO MORANDI
NATURA MORTA, 1939
OIL ON CANVAS
32 X 57 CM

AQUIN: *Of all the genres, landscape is the one that has come to characterize your work the most acutely. Is it because the symbolism of the tree reaches deeper than, for instance, that of the pot? You can see God in a tree.*

PARTY: Landscape in western art has always interrogated the idea of nature and our relation to it. In the first representations of the garden of Eden, where nature is depicted as a lost ideal, the question of humans in conflict with nature seems already to be central. Is humanity part of nature or is it an external force that dominates and destroys our environment? The history of landscape painting retraces humanity's continually shifting relationship to our natural environment. For a long time, the natural world was dangerous for humans, and conquering it was an imperative step in the course of the dominance of our species, but each step of that conquest brought a sense of loss. Landscapes often depict either a glorification of our conquest of our environment or the nostalgia of a lost paradise that existed before we destroyed it. We could say that the greatest landscape paintings both contain ideas and question the viewer about it.

AQUIN: *In your case – but tell me if I'm wrong – your landscapes include no trace of human activity. These are all 'natural' scenes, untouched, unaltered by the presence of man.*

PARTY: Very quickly, I decided to paint landscape with no traces of humanity, no houses, fences, roads, canals, farmland, etc. I paint an environment that belongs either to a time before or long after humanity, a time when human culture doesn't affect the landscape. An element that became crucial to my landscapes is the tree. Trees might be the object most frequently painted to represent the natural world, an essential symbol in cultures around the world. Today, the tree is still the fundamental symbol of the anxiety that we have about the future of our planet, our landscape.

AQUIN: *Have you developed a knowledge of botany, as many painters who painted trees and plants did – Claude Monet, to name the most famous?*

PARTY: None of the trees that I paint are inspired by a tree that exists in our natural environment. I like the idea of walking through a forest made up of every single tree ever painted by humans, with all their different shapes and meanings. It's in that forest that I walk to find inspiration. I paint subjects with a long history in image-making culture. I find it comforting to paint something that has been represented so many times in the past. It makes the subject rich. In other landscape paintings, I choose to depict rocks, which also have an abundant symbolic history. Lately, I've started to paint caves, which again have a rich history of representation. When you depict a cave, it echoes back to the first known images. The subjects that I use are in continuous use in human culture, and their roots and branches are endlessly growing.

AQUIN: *You did a few murals entirely of trees – at the Dallas Museum of Art, for instance, and at the Marciano Art Foundation. These aren't single trees, but forests, so to speak.*

PARTY: I've painted quite a few murals that depict tree landscapes. What made this subject work well with my mural practice is the relation between trees and architecture. Trees naturally have straight vertical lines created by the growth of the trunk. Those perfect straight lines are rare in nature, which is, in our perception, more organic. Trees do also have roots, branches and leaves, all very organic shapes. A radically simplified tree is a circle on top of a straight line. Architecture is structured by horizontal and

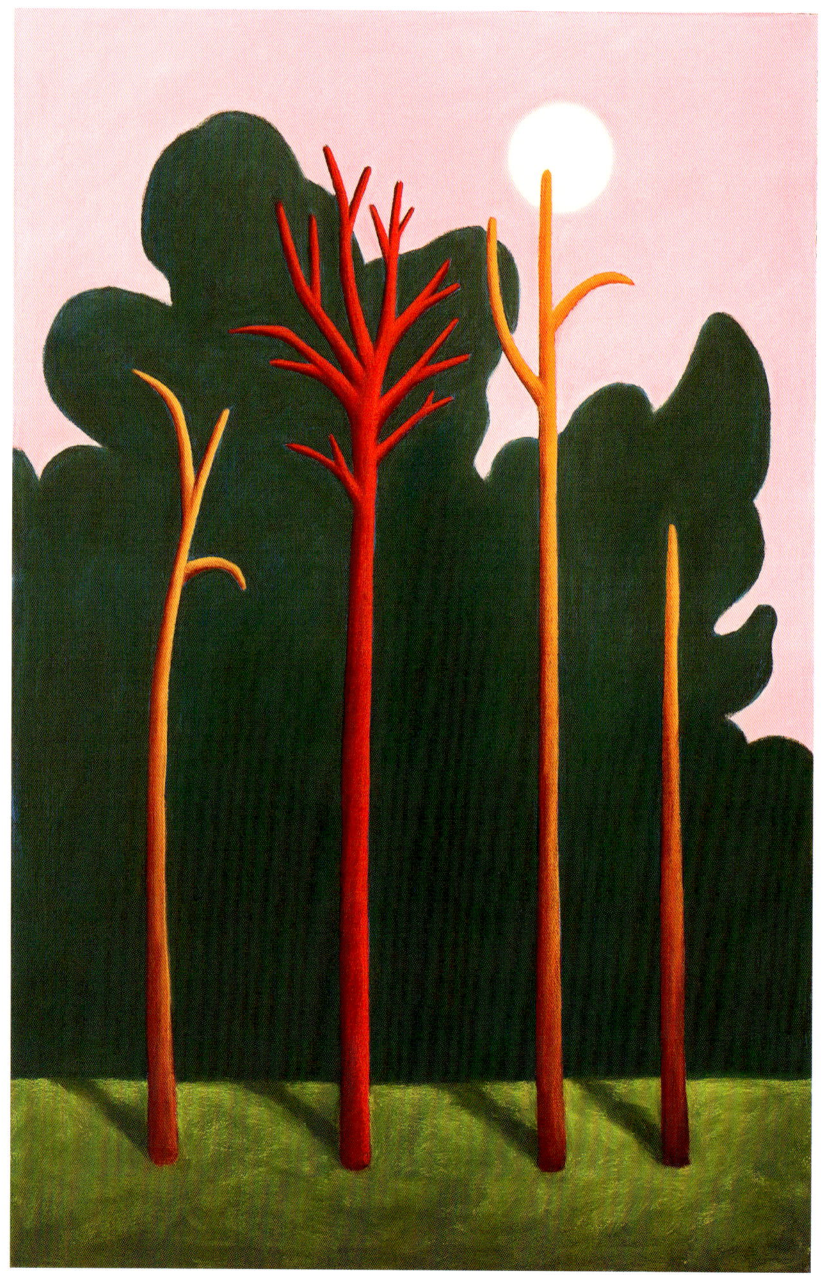

opposite,
LANDSCAPE, 2014
SOFT PASTEL ON LINEN
150 X 100 CM

below,
STILL LIFE, 2014
SOFT PASTEL ON LINEN
110 X 140 CM

vertical lines, and this graphic geometry is an artist's visual canvas when we start to paint on the walls. You're constantly playing with it, either by making use of its geometry or by breaking it. A tree is perfectly shaped to simultaneously create organic and geometric forms, making it possible to make shapes either contrasting with or matching the architecture. In 2019 at the Marciano Art Foundation in Los Angeles, I was asked to do a mural in their four-storey service staircase. The constant interruptions in the architecture – rails, steps, pipes, angles, doors etc. – made the project quite challenging, the opposite of the perfectly regular rectangular wall. To try to encompass all those aspects in the design, I painted trees that grew from the bottom floor to the top, the straight shapes of the tree trunk often repeating the different existing vertical lines of the space.

AQUIN: *Can you tell me about your rocky landscapes?*

PARTY: Mineral matters, as opposed to organic ones, are lifeless. A rocky landscape looks similar on Mars and on Earth. What Mars seems to be missing is not the rocks, but the trees and streams. A desert landscape is a place of emptiness and if a person is wandering in it, he probably won't encounter anyone, making it a place for stories and myths related to solitary revelation and introspective discovery. In my rock landscapes, no evidence of vegetation or even water is visible. Life is absent. I also use the rock landscapes as a counterpoint to the tree landscapes, where life is abundant and flourishing. My caves series followed the rock paintings. The cave pastels also depict a space without life.

AQUIN: *You said that it's the echo of prehistoric art that interests you in the cave paintings.*

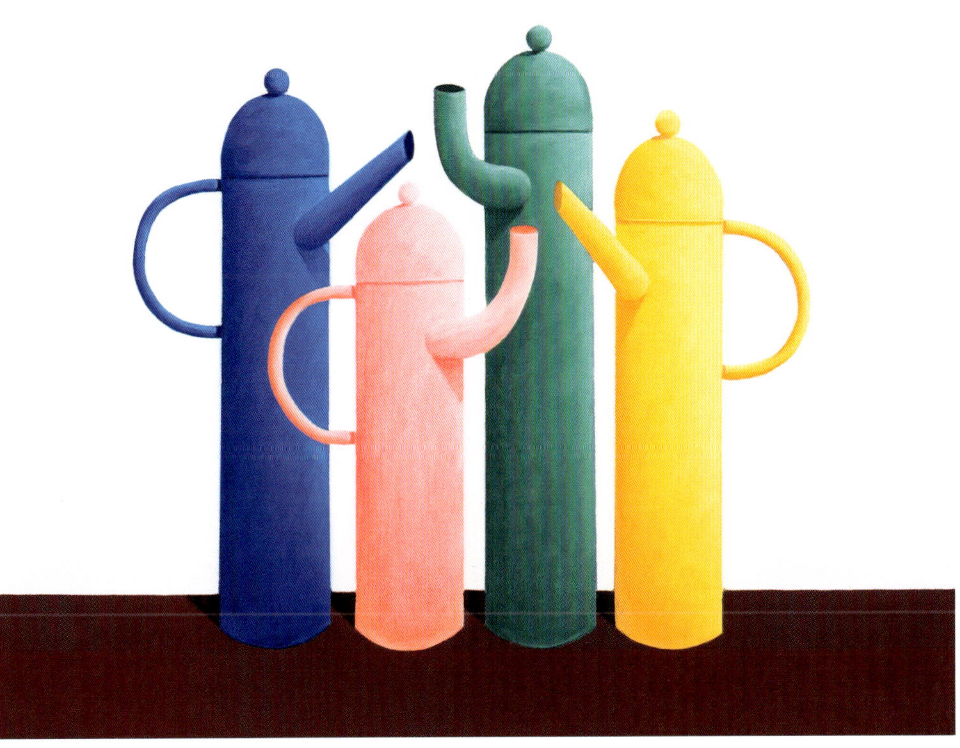

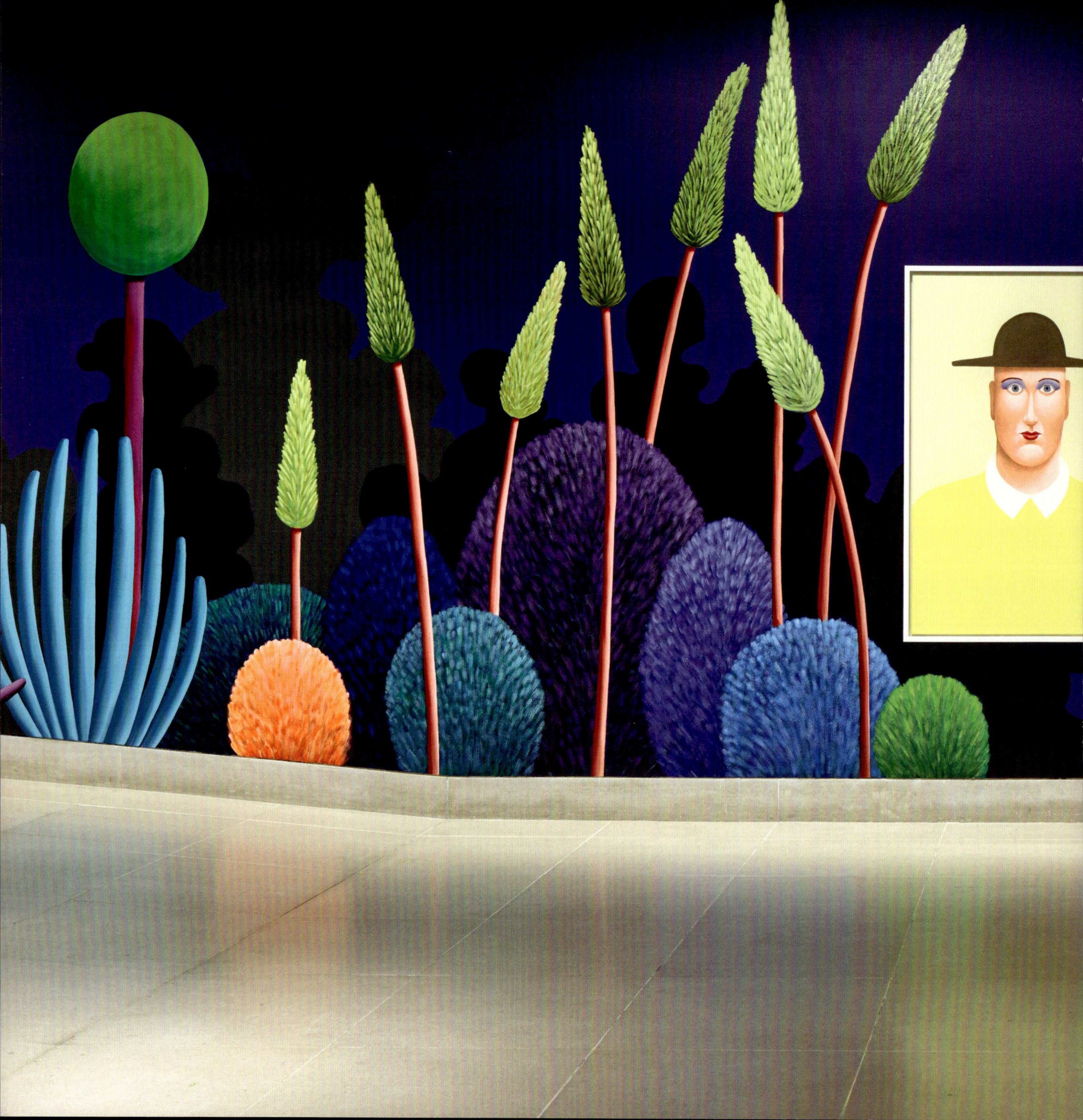

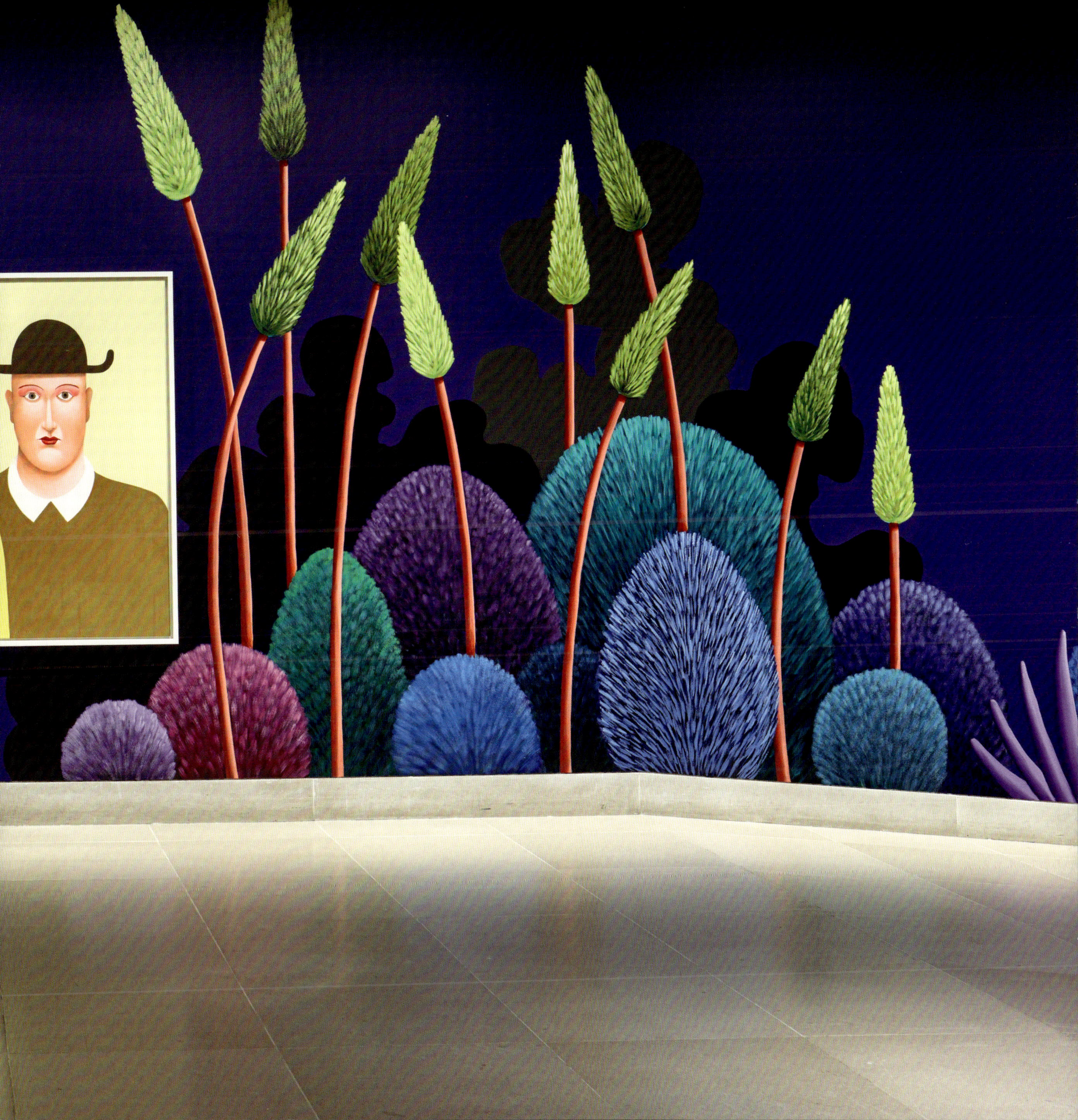

STILL LIFE, 2015
SOFT PASTEL ON LINEN
150 X 90 CM

MURAL: CHARCOAL ON WALL

INSTALLATION VIEW AT
INVERLEITH HOUSE,
EDINBURGH, 2015

previous pages,
TWO MEN WITH HATS, 2016
SOFT PASTEL ON LINEN
150 X 170 CM

MURAL: ACRYLIC ON WALL

INSTALLATION VIEW AT THE
DALLAS MUSEUM OF ART, 2016

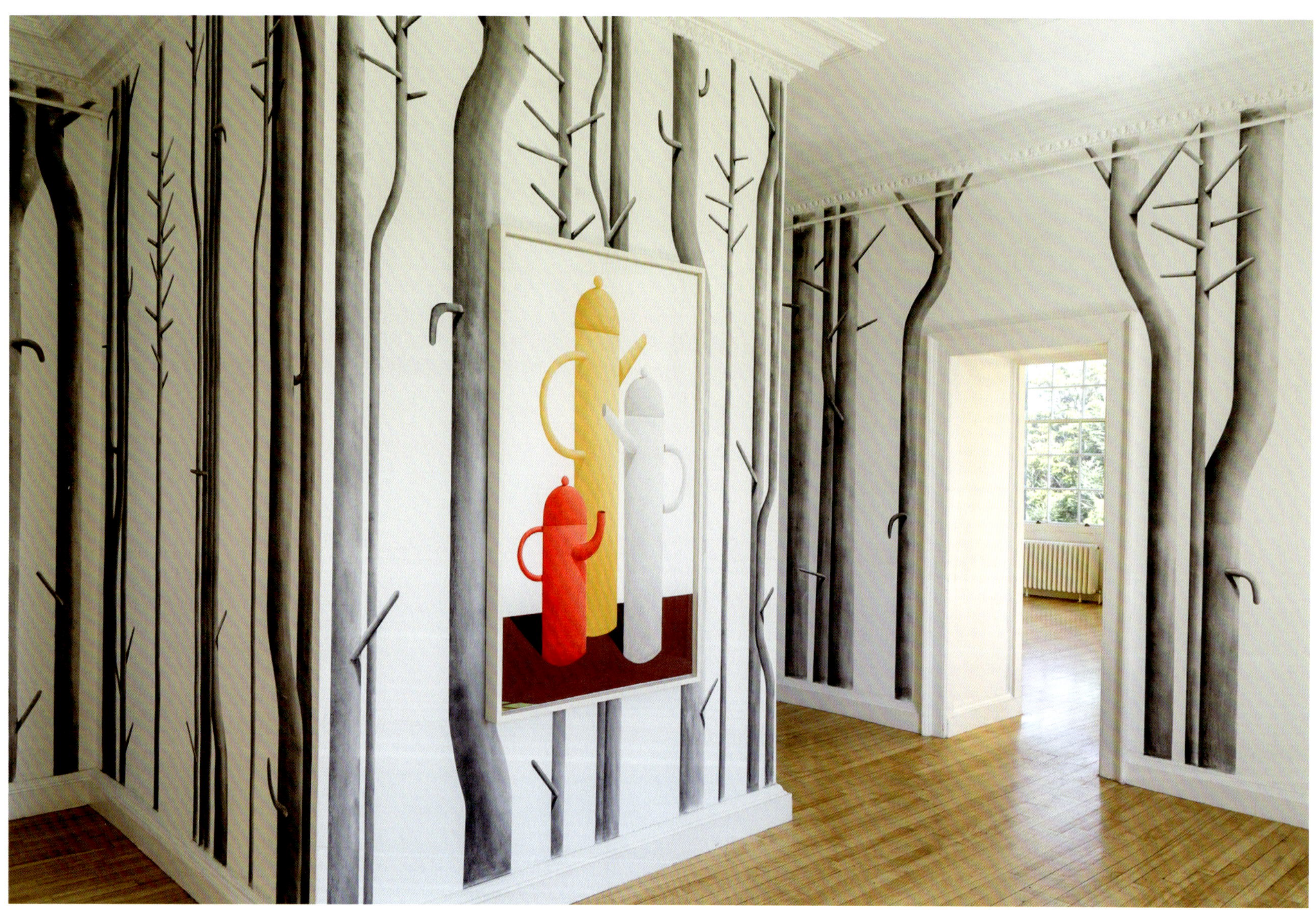

TREE TRUNK, 2015
SOFT PASTEL ON LINEN
150 X 80 CM

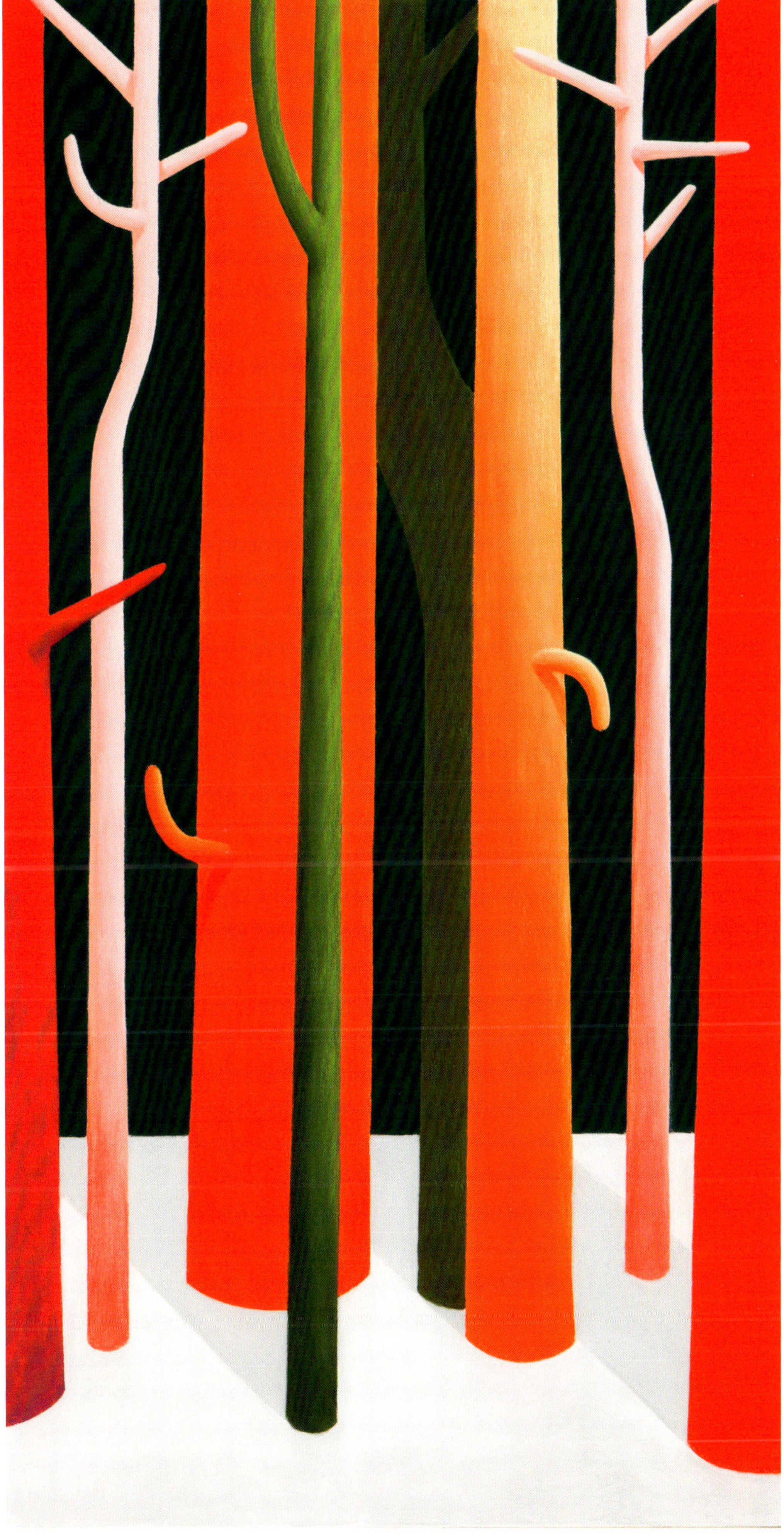

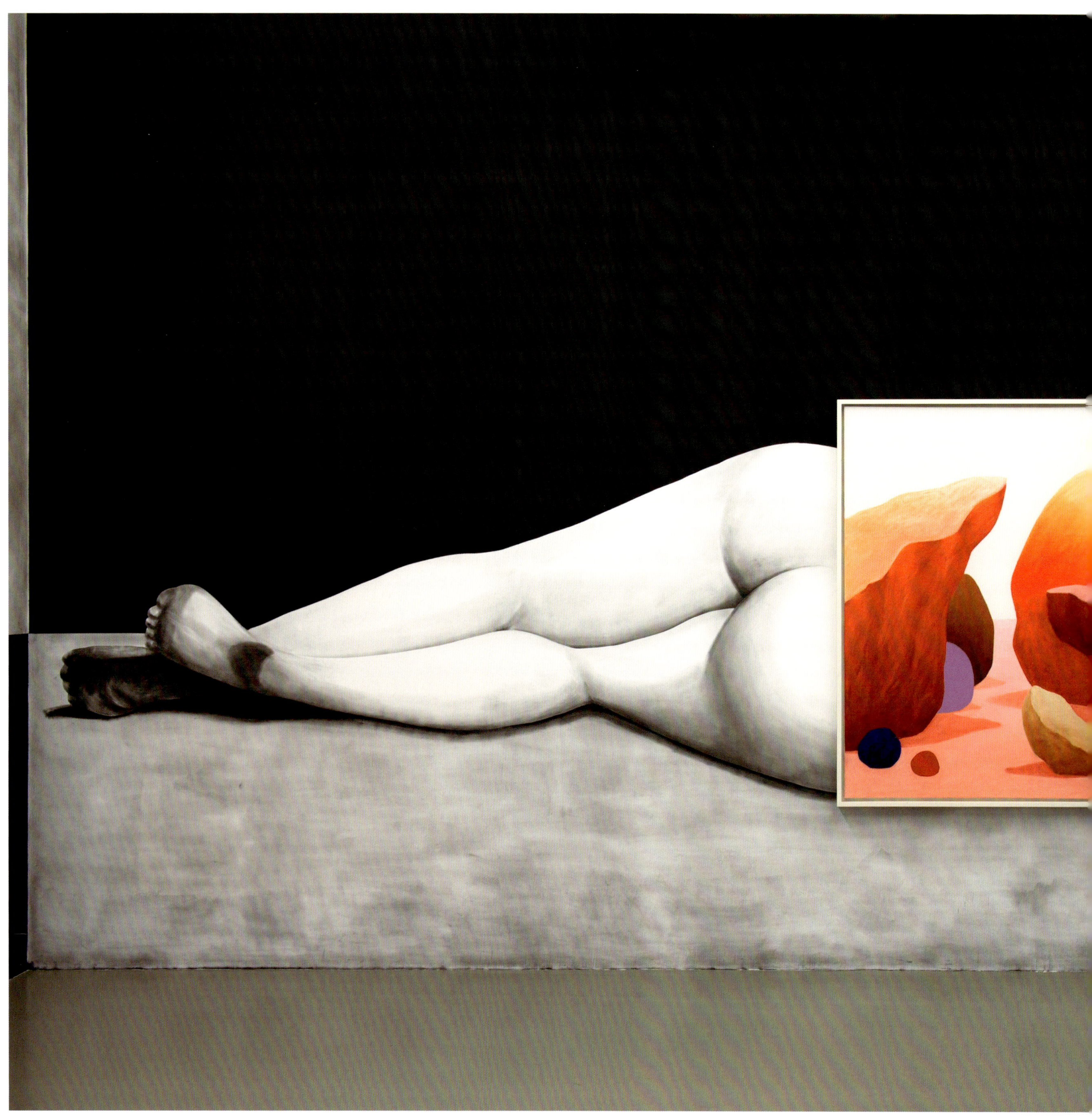

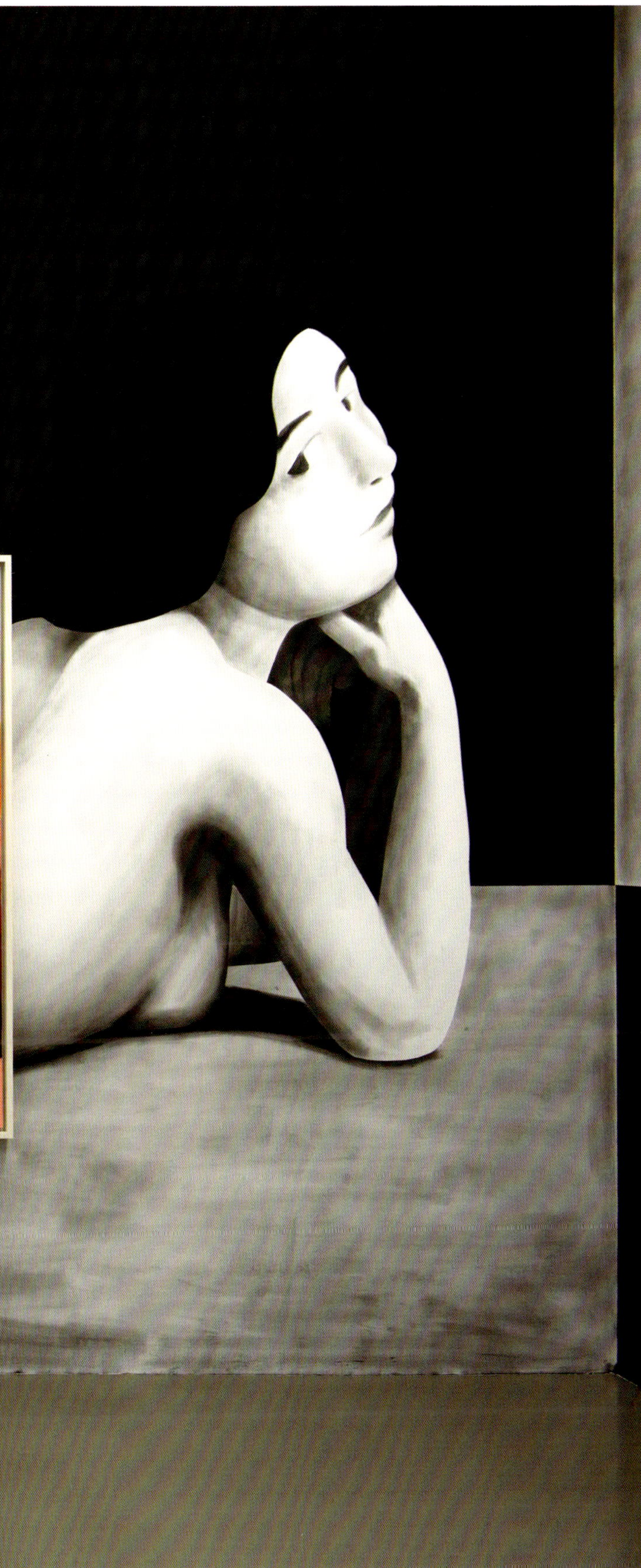

ROCKS, 2014
SOFT PASTEL ON LINEN
155 X 126 CM

INSTALLATION VIEW AT CENTRE CULTUREL SUISSE, PARIS, 2015

next pages,
SUNRISE, SUNSET, 2017
OIL ON WALL

INSTALLATION VIEW AT THE HIRSHHORN MUSEUM AND SCULPTURE GARDEN, WASHINGTON, DC, 2017

PARTY: There are many stories throughout history where a cave plays a central role. The oldest traces of art are found inside caves, reminding us that these underground places have formidable power in our imagination. The absence of light makes a cave an uninhabitable place, but also reminds us of how we spend our first nine months in the dark, making it a place for birth as well as death. Humans used caves as a burial site as well as a place for resurrection. It's a territory where things are upside down, where forms are growing from the floor and the ceiling. Stalagmites and stalactites create the architecture of rooms that are unimaginable from the surface. Like other subjects in my practice, the caves that I paint are inspired by paintings from the past. *The Grotto of Manacor* (1901) by William Degouve de Nuncques is an image that greatly inspired me, as well as the *Grotto in the Gulf of Salerno* (1774) by Joseph Wright of Derby. Those two paintings are great examples of the evocative power of this mysterious environment.

AQUIN: *There's something we haven't talked about yet, but that's a key part of your work, and that's your use of the work of others. You've used paintings by Picasso and Vallotton as murals upon which to install your own works, as you did at the Independent Art Fair in 2015, or at the Centre Culturel Suisse in Paris the same year; or you've sometimes directly quoted or 'sampled' the work of another artist in one of your works.*

PARTY: This may come from the graffiti years, when it was very common to reproduce a character from a comic book, for example. In Glasgow, I did a painting that depicted a sweet potato resting in a glass of water that I saw in my friend's studio. When I painted it, I added a plate I took from a William Nicholson painting. It was pretty discreet, but I liked how this plate travelled from one painting to another. The plate became a time-travelling tool, the way the hero of the Chris Marker film *La Jetée* (1962) uses extremely accurate visual memory of one image from the past to travel in time.

AQUIN: *The project that you did at the Hirshhorn Museum and Sculpture Garden in 2017, 'Sunrise Sunset', was almost all sampling, from artists ranging from Caspar David Friedrich to Georgia O'Keefe and Félix Vallotton.*

PARTY: For the Hirshhorn show, I made a series of twenty-seven wall paintings depicting sunrises and sunsets, displayed on eight distinctive wall sections. Most of the painting sampled landscapes by other artists in various ways. Some were cropped reproductions, and some took only a detail of a painting. On one wall I painted two icebergs, each taken from two works by Lawren Harris. I copied the icebergs and placed them in my own environment, so it looked as if they'd drifted from his painting into mine. Another wall looked like a Henri Rousseau painting. I didn't directly copy any distinctive plants from his work, but rather used his very recognizable style in my landscape. I also painted a red sun floating in a pale green sky, which was directly taken from a Rousseau jungle work.

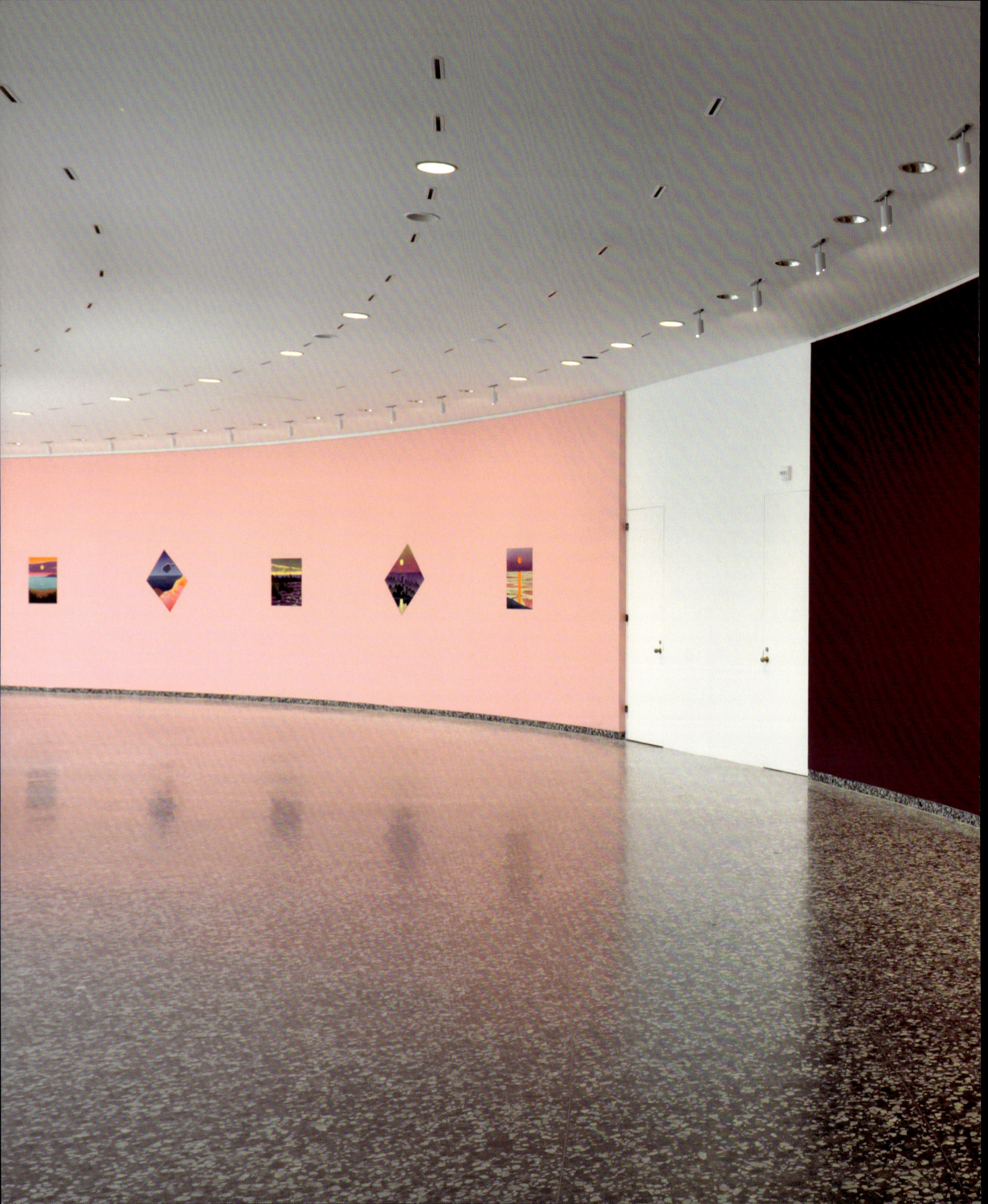

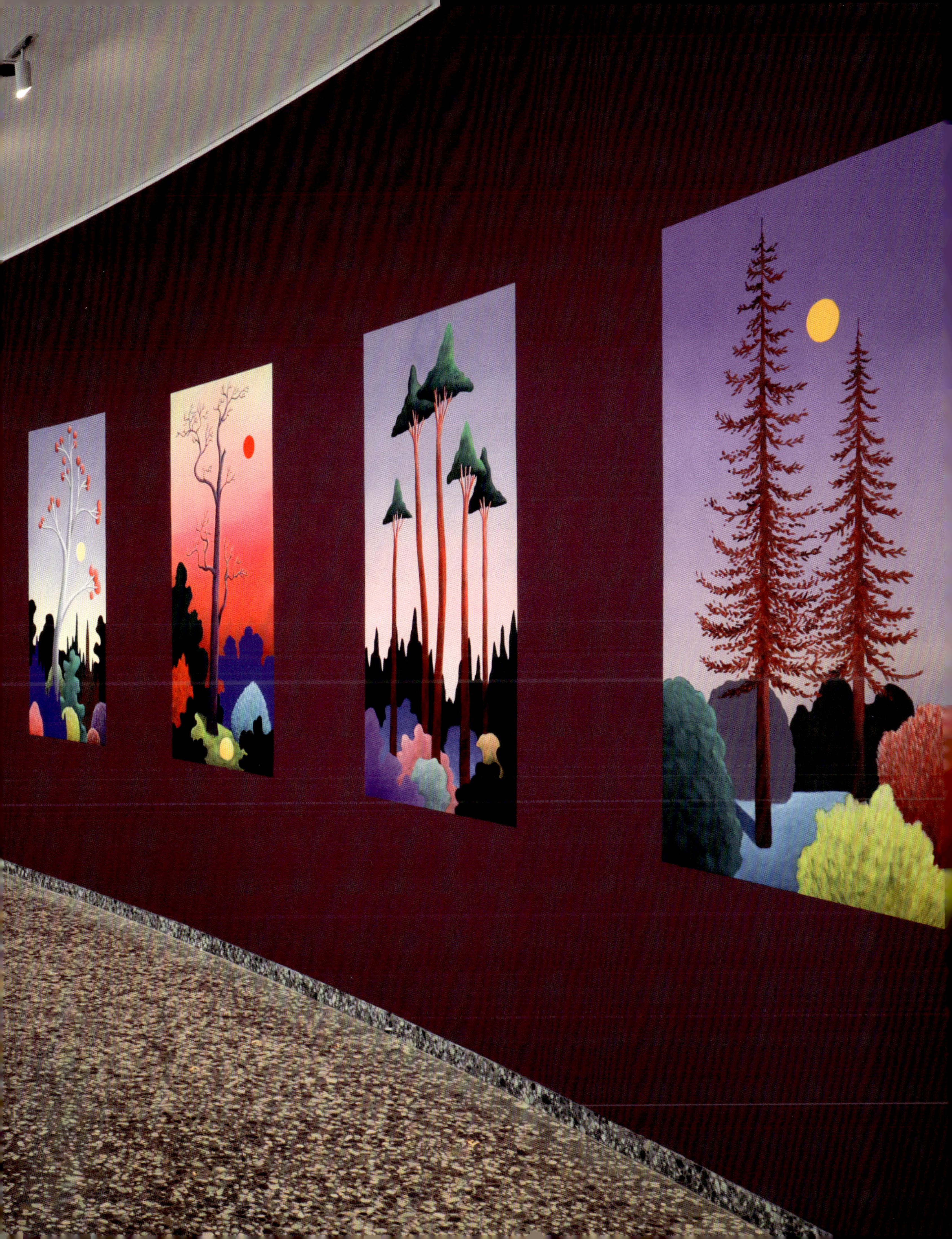

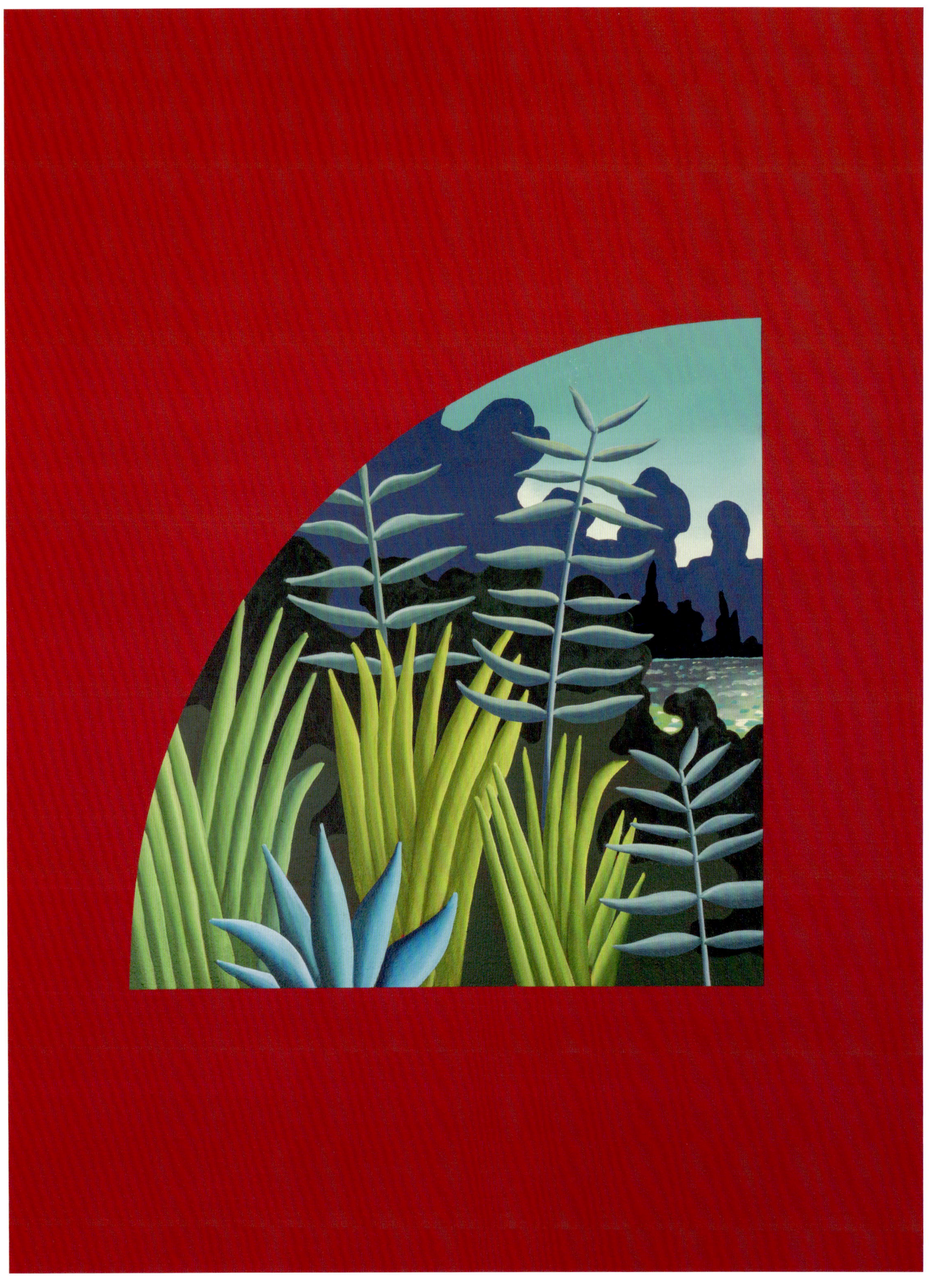

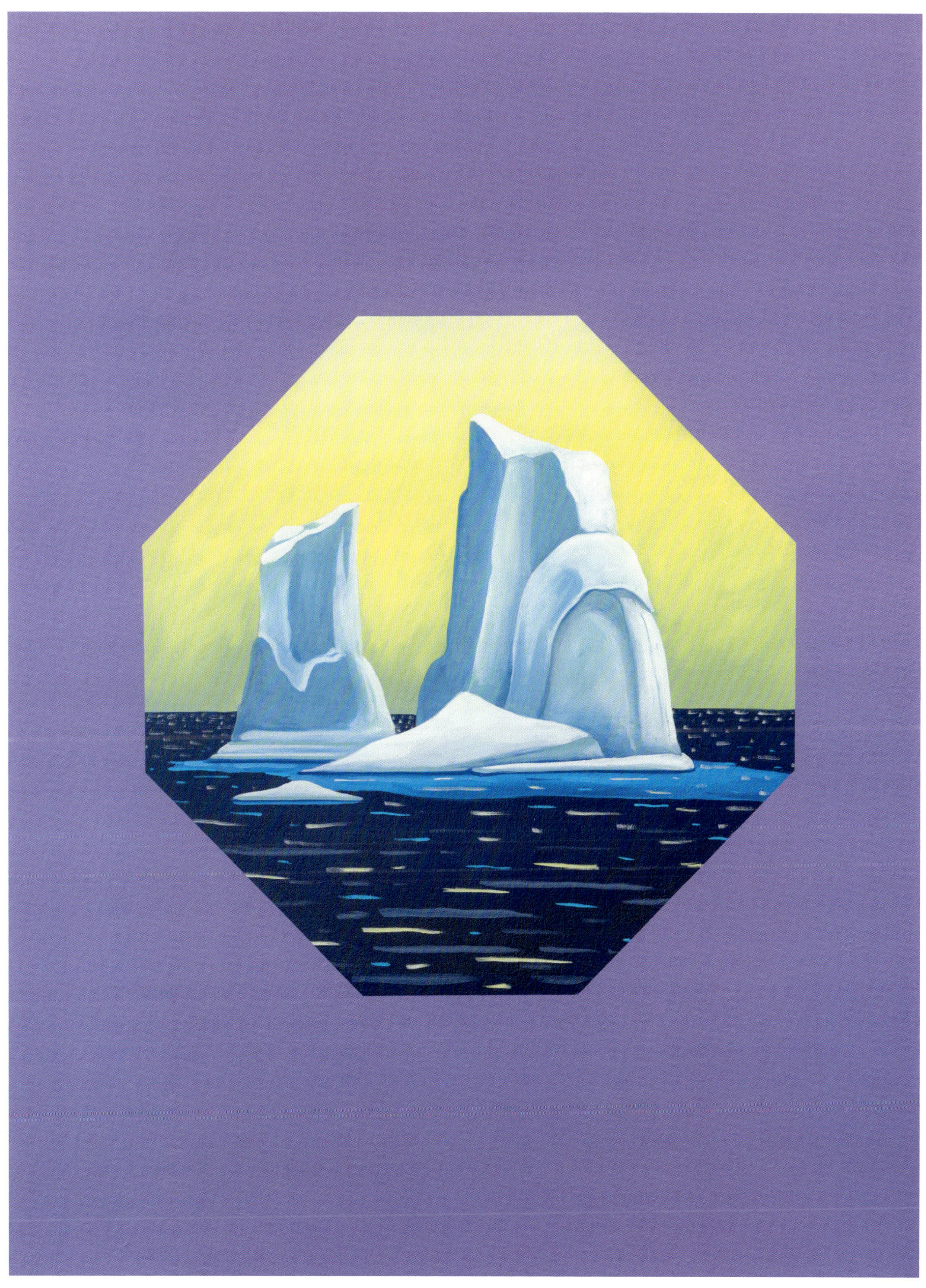

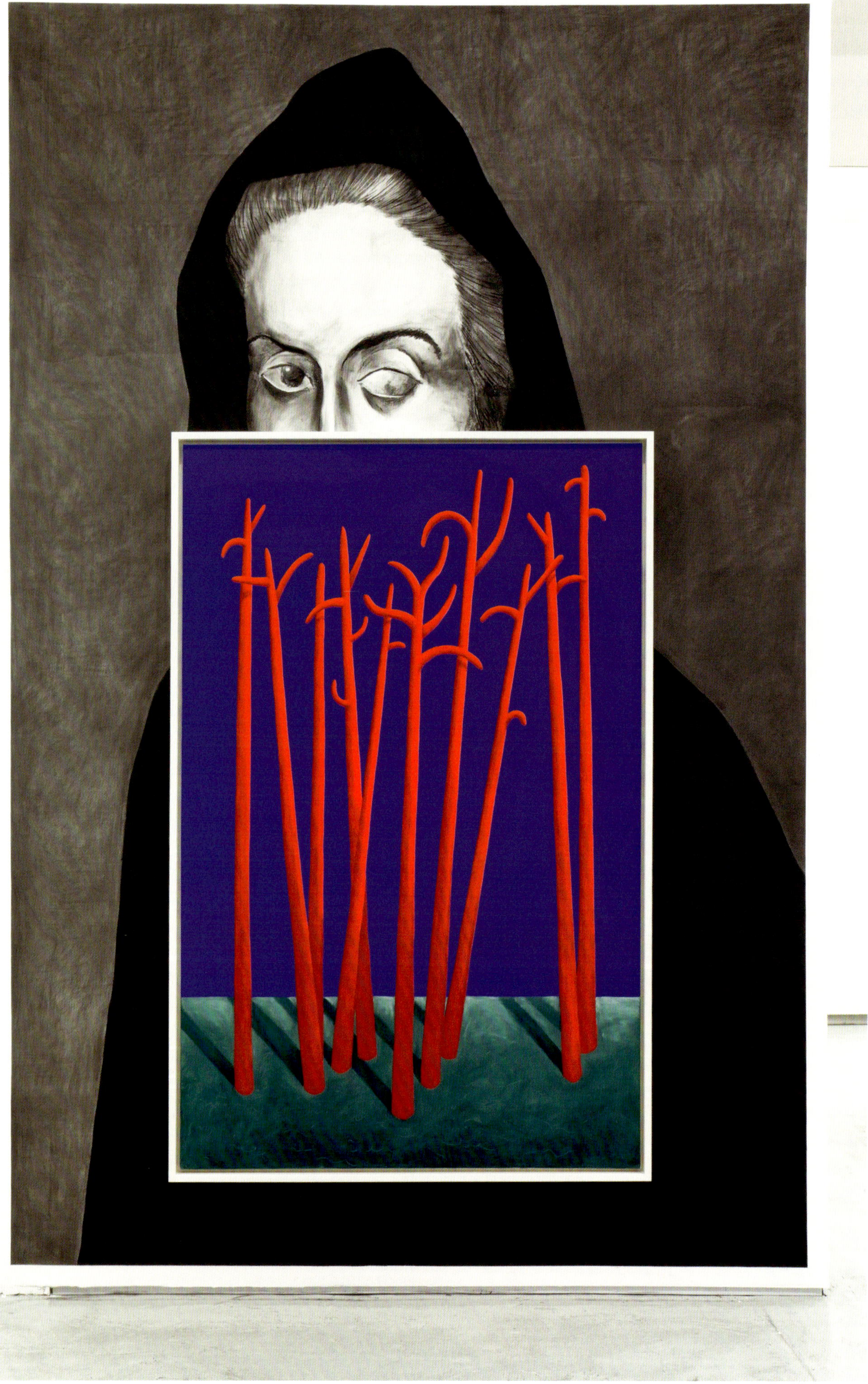

TREES, 2014
SOFT PASTEL ON LINEN
200 X 130 CM

background,
LA CÉLESTINE, 2015
CHARCOAL WALL DRAWING

INSTALLATION VIEW AT
INDEPENDENT, NEW YORK, 2015

opposite,
PORTRAIT, 2017
SOFT PASTEL ON LINEN
140 X 110 CM

MURAL: SOFT PASTEL ON WALL

INSTALLATION VIEW AT
FONDATION DE L'HERMITAGE,
LAUSANNE, 2018

previous pages,
SUNRISE, SUNSET (DETAIL),
2017
OIL ON WALL

INSTALLATION VIEW AT
THE HIRSHHORN MUSEUM
AND SCULPTURE GARDEN,
WASHINGTON, DC, 2017

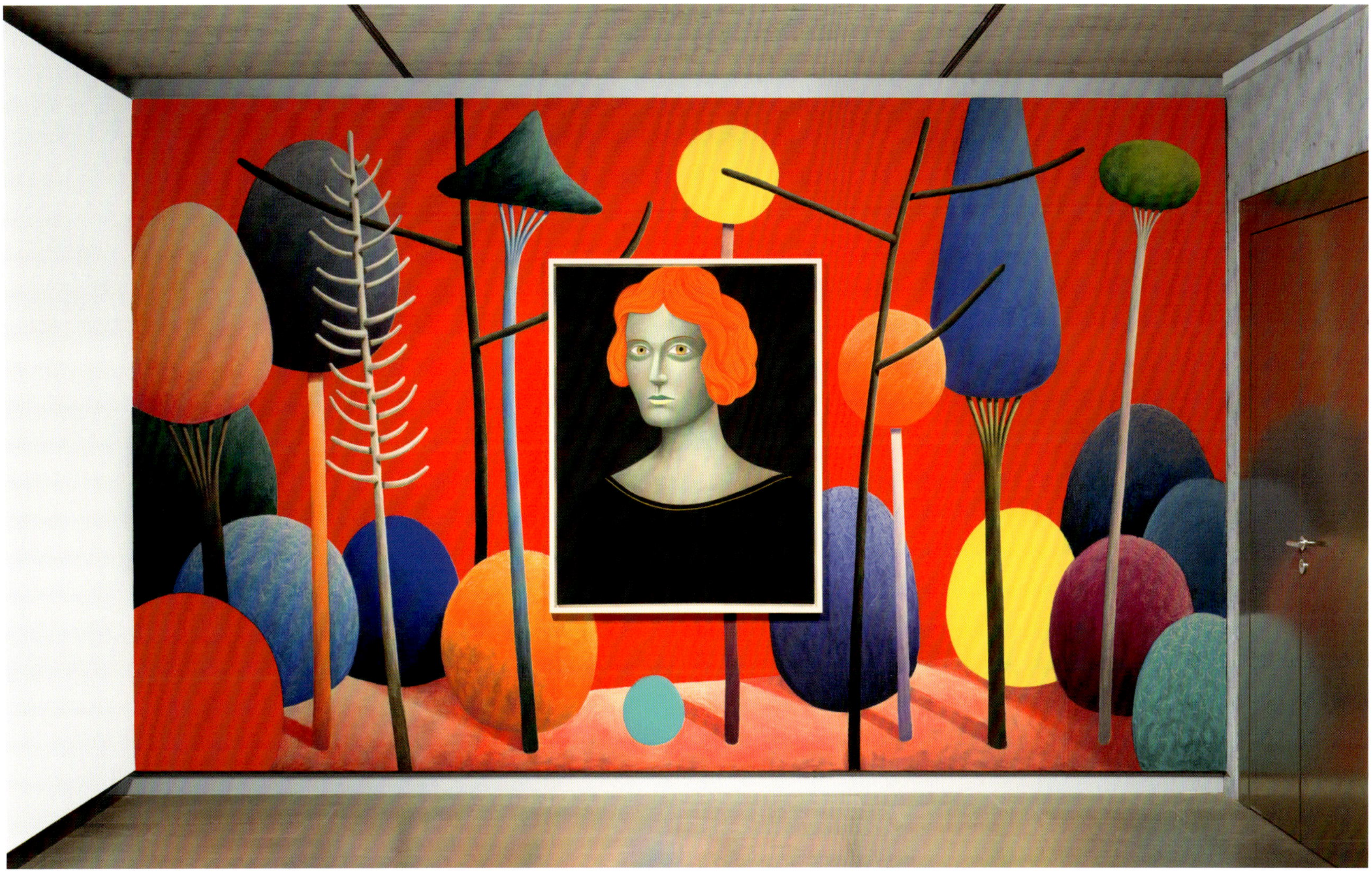

AQUIN: *This wasn't the first time you'd developed an entire project around the work of another artist. You'd done that in Norway at the Kunsthall Stavanger in 2014.*

PARTY: The Kunsthall Stavanger exhibition was based around the figure of the Norwegian painter Lars Hertervig (1830–1902). That was the first project where the idea of creating murals by sampling and reproducing another artist was fully explored. The premise was that a large group of Hertevig's paintings had been on display in the museum in the past, before being given to another museum in Stavanger. In four different rooms, I created a series of sixteen charcoal wall drawings based on several works by Hertevig. Each wall drawing was encircled by a spray-painted pattern that covered all the walls of the rooms. Most of the drawings were not loyal copies of the original works, but cropped or edited versions. In one room, for example, I drew four different cloud compositions based on landscape details. The scale of the reproduction was an important aspect of the process. In another room, I drew three large tree compositions, taking up the entire height of the room. Those works were all based on very small sketches by Hertevig. Using charcoals, a very delicate medium, to draw directly on the wall, emphasized the transitory nature of the project. All the drawings were ghostly presences of Hertevig's paintings on those walls.

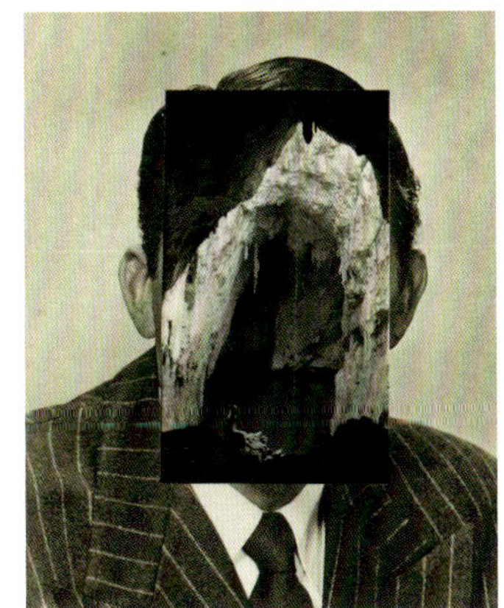

JOHN STEZAKER
MASK IV, 2005
COLLAGE
21 X 17 CM

AQUIN: *We've used the word 'sampling', but actually your quotational practice encompasses a wide variety of strategies: full and direct quotation of a work of another artist, cropping, use of a single recognizable motif, stylistic imitation, full-blown reproduction …*

PARTY: Two years after the show in Norway, at the Independent art fair in New York, I did another wall painting that reproduced another artwork. I used charcoals to draw on a wall an imitation of the Blue Period painting by Picasso, *La Celestine* (1968), then hung a landscape on top of it. The painting covered most of the Picasso image, only revealing the top half of her face, showing her glass eye. The effect was very close to the imagery of collages, where distinct images interact with each other. I was inspired by the work of an artist who uses collage in his work, John Stezaker. He often juxtaposes only two images to create his collages. Following that first attempt, I did a few similar 'collages' in a show at the Centre Culturel Suisse in Paris, by drawing nude paintings by the artist Félix Vallotton on the wall, on top of which I hung rock landscapes. More recently, in the show 'Pastel' at The FLAG Art Foundation in New York, I used a similar strategy, this time using pastel to create the mural and hanging works by various artists on top.

AQUIN: *We've covered so much already – you've shed light on large areas of your work – but we haven't yet spoken about what you've have come to be known for, which is your use of pastel. You're one of the very few artists currently using pastel almost exclusively as your primary medium. You were even invited to show at the Fondation de l'Hermitage in Lausanne in 2017, in a large survey of the history of pastel. It must have been doubly important for you to be included in that great art-historical narrative and at the same time recognized in your home town. Can you tell me about your very unique dedication to this medium?*

PARTY: In the summer of 2013, I saw a Picasso show in Basel where I was struck by a pastel portrait titled *Tête de femme* (Head of a Woman, 1921). My first reaction was that I wanted to do the same portrait, so I bought the postcard and the next day I went to the art store and bought a pastel set and some paper. I started to draw portraits using pastel for the first time, regularly looking at the Picasso portrait for inspiration. From the first drawing I made that summer I felt that this new technique was something that I loved. It was fast and versatile; the colours were vibrant and pure. Using your finger to draw made the process sensual and immediate. I fell in love with pastel that summer of 2013. Almost immediately, pastel became my primary medium and I started to spend most of my time trying to learn and explore the technique. The first series of pastels that I made that summer were almost exclusively portraits. It felt very natural to depict those faces with make-up, making them look androgynous, I didn't know it at the time, but pastels have a distinctive relationship to make-up.

AQUIN: *More recently, at The FLAG Art Foundation, you brought your love and your knowledge of pastel to a whole other level in your show entitled 'Pastel'. You showed – in a very stage-designed and immersive way – your own work alongside a number of works by other artists that read as a retrospective of the history of pastel, from Jean-Basptite Perronneau to Mary Cassatt to Billy Sullivan. You even had a Rosalba Carriera that was installed on your mural backdrop reproducing tree tops cropped from a work by François Boucher. There was a deep Rococo streak running through the whole show.*

PARTY: As a medium, pastel was really born in the eighteenth century. The technique was extremely popular during that period. That popularity completely vanished after the French Revolution. Rosalba Carriera, a celebrated Venetian artist who worked in Paris for a few years, really embodied that moment and she's arguably responsible for the rise of interest in the medium. She used pastels to create, almost always, portraits, creating the face of the Rococo aesthetic. One of the aspects of that eighteenth-century look is the use of make-up by both men and women, displaying a playfulness regarding gender identification. Men and women covered their faces with white powder and then added rouge to their cheeks. Those powders could be bought in the same shop as pastels, and were often made out of the same pigment. The model was already a painting when posing for the artist.

AQUIN: *The Rococo moment certainly did have some gender-bending aspects to it, at least in the way certain court amusements and leisure activities were represented, and pastel was taken on by some notable male artists such as Perronneau, or Quentin de la Tour, but the pastel definitely remained associated with women.*

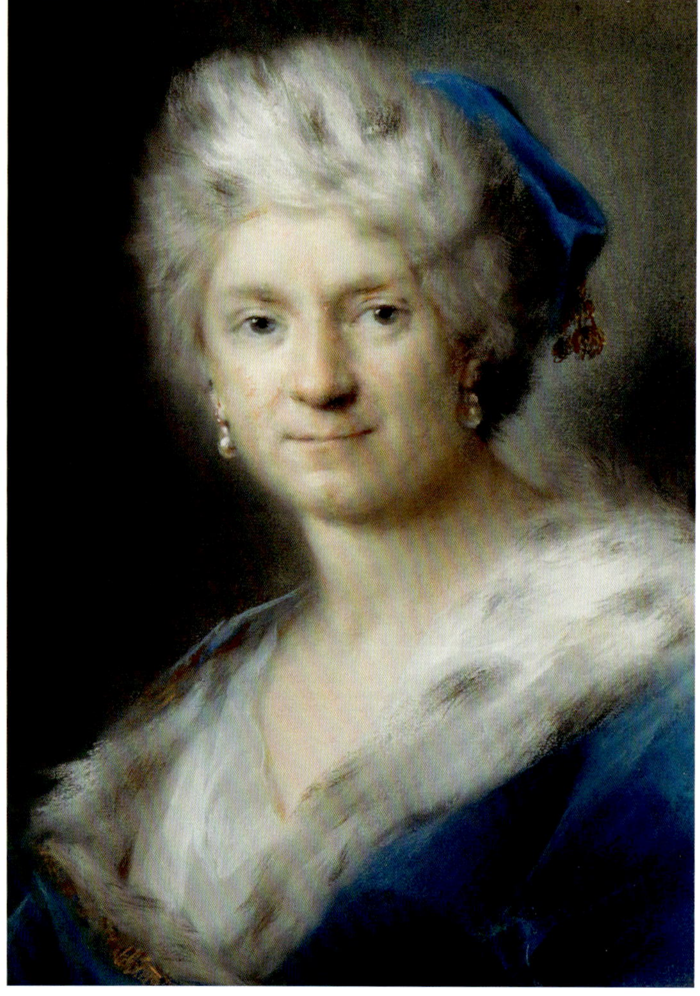

ROSALBA CARRIERA
SELF-PORTRAIT AS WINTER, 1731
PASTEL ON PAPER
465 X 340 CM

TREE, 2020
WATERCOLOUR ON PAPER
31 X 23 CM

PARTY: For various reasons, pastel was extremely popular among women. Pastel sticks could be used at home. In the eighteenth century, being an artist required the technical knowledge to fabricate paint, since paint in tubes only came later. The ease of access and practicality of pastel made it possible for many women to become well-known professional artists. So the medium became strongly associated with women and was attacked for that reason by the conservative art academy, who argued that it was a technique for women as a hobby at home and not for serious artists, who should use oil to create their work. This damaging campaign against the medium, and its effect on the rise of women artists in the eighteenth century, can still be felt today. In my opinion, it's why this medium is underused in the art world today.

AQUIN: *Given the links between pastels and painting one's face, it makes sense that your discovery of pastel led to the addition of portraiture to your work.*

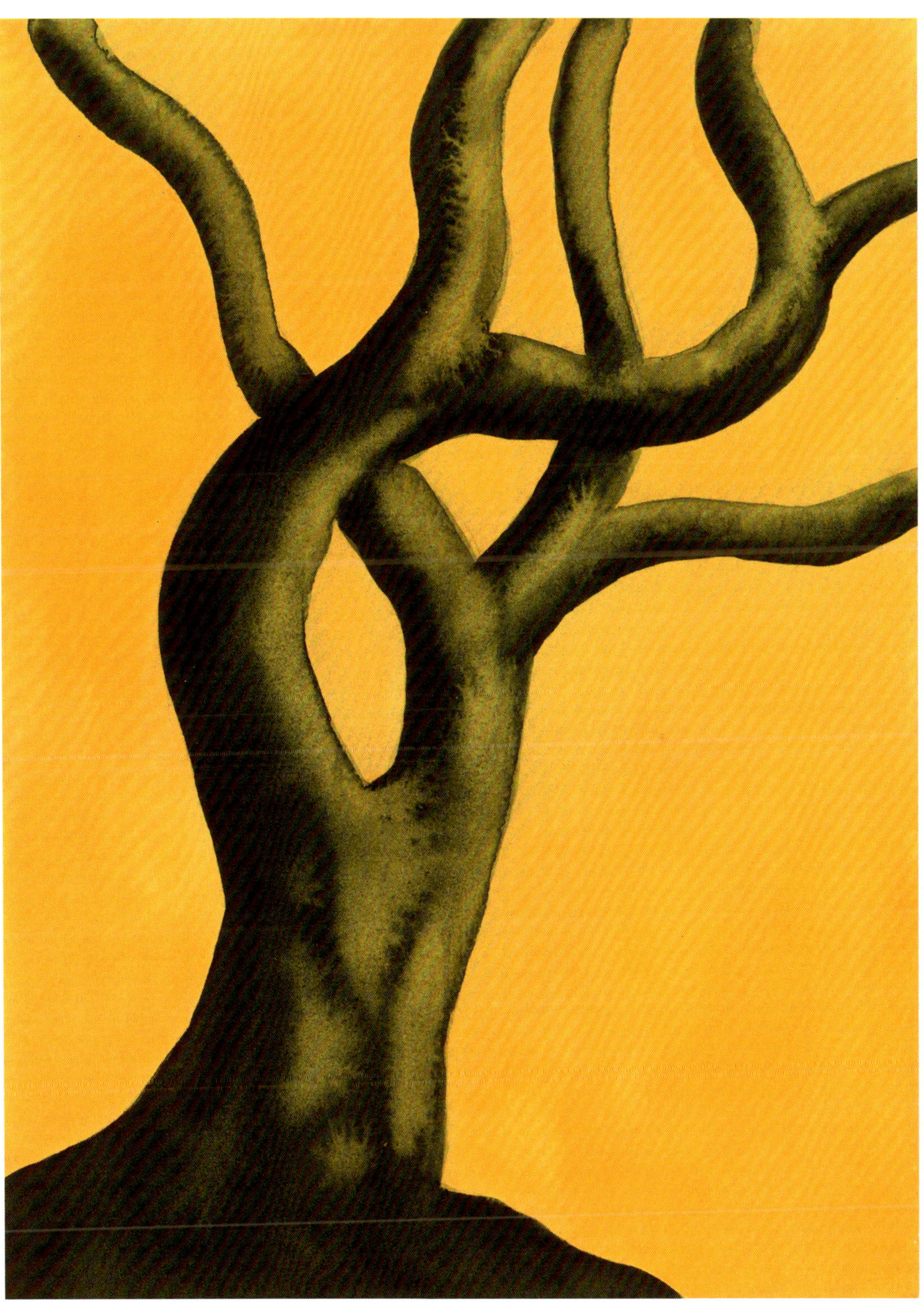

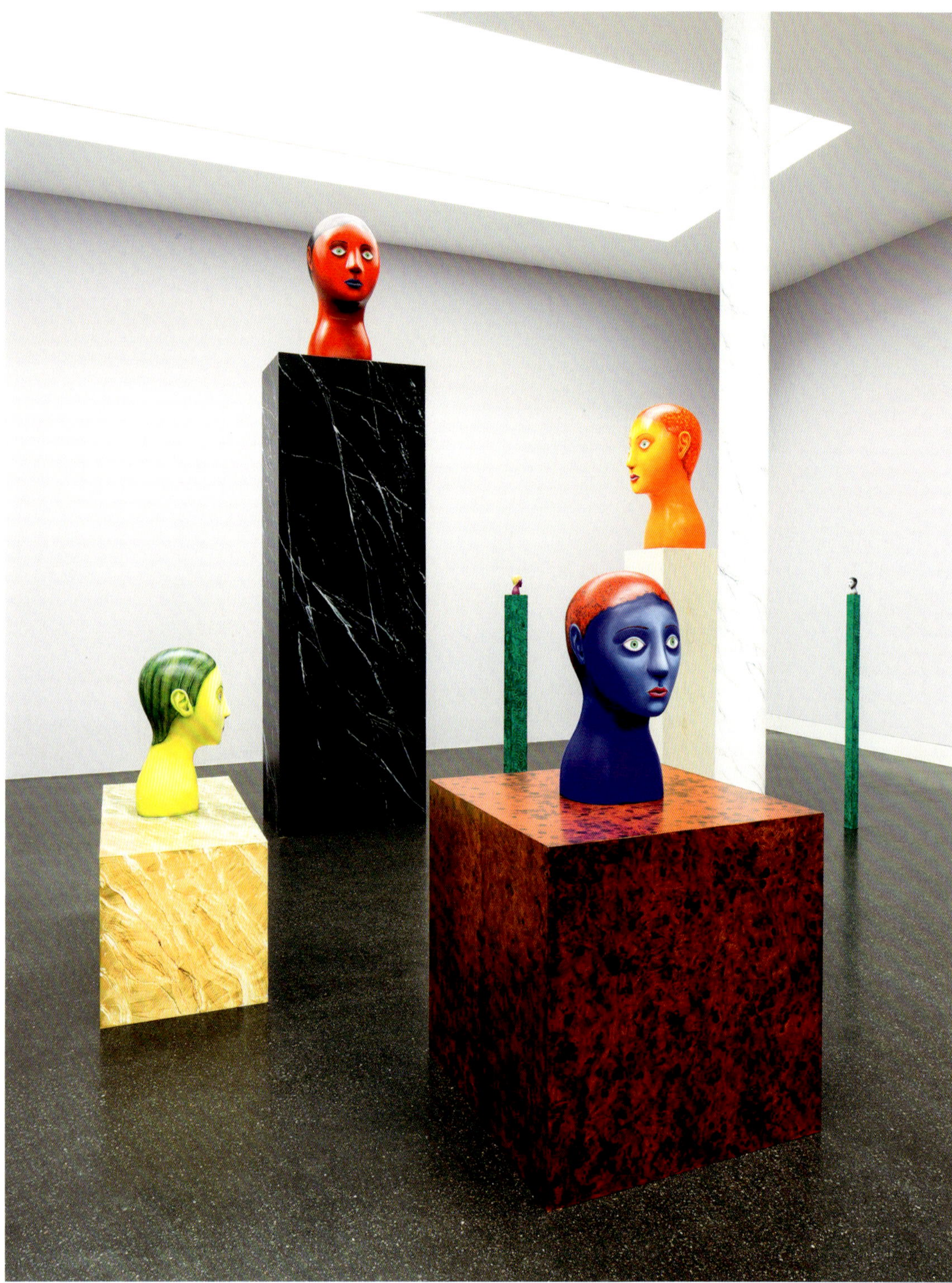

from left,
HEAD, 2018
OIL ON WOOD
70 X 38 X 30 CM

HEAD, 2018
OIL ON COATED POLYSTERENE
100 X 64 X 50 CM

HEAD, 2018
OIL ON WOOD
10 X 7 X 5 CM

HEAD, 2018
OIL ON WOOD
70 X 38 X 30 CM

HEAD, 2018
OIL ON COATED POLYSTERENE
100 X 64 X 50 CM

HEAD, 2018
OIL ON WOOD
10 X 7 X 5 CM

PAINTED OIL PLINTHS
DIMENSIONS VARIABLE

INSTALLATION VIEW AT
GALERIE GREGOR STAIGER,
ZURICH, 2018

PARTY: Yes. As I mentioned earlier, I started to use this medium after seeing the pastel portrait by Picasso and for the first year I only experimented with pastel in that genre. Historically, this technique is strongly associated with the portrait. That can be explained by different factors, such as the rapidity of execution in comparison to oil painting, making the length of posing for the model much shorter and consequently more practical. Almost all the famous pastel artists of the eighteenth century primarily painted portraits. Carriera, Maurice Quentin de La Tour or Jean-Baptiste Perronneau are paragons of the golden age of the pastel portrait in Europe. When I started using pastel, the medium naturally guided me into doing portraits and more specifically exploring the idea of transforming the human face using make-up to paint the skin.

AQUIN: *Pastel has survived as a medium – the material is still being produced and sold by a handful of specialized firms – in large part due to the amateur artist market. The same is true of watercolour, another medium with which you've shown a deep affinity.*

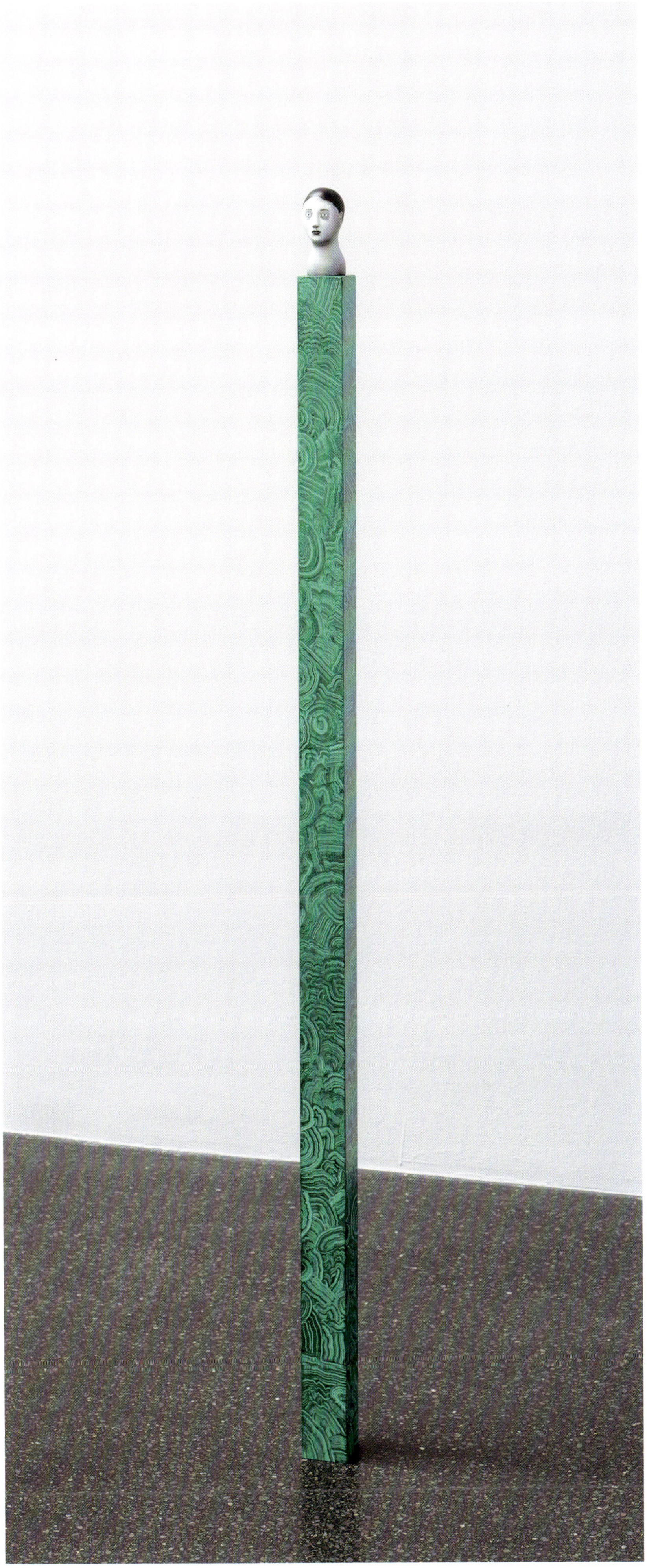

left,
HEAD, 2018
OIL ON WOOD
10 X 7 X 5 CM

PAINTED OIL PLINTH
150 X 6 X 6 CM

INSTALLATION VIEW AT
GALERIE GREGOR STAIGER,
ZURICH, 2018

below,
SPEAKER, 2017
WOOD, METAL MESH FRAME,
GYPSUM PLASTER, ACRYLIC
AND OIL PAINT
140 X 140 X 200 CM

INSTALLATION VIEW AT
MODERN ART OXFORD, 2018

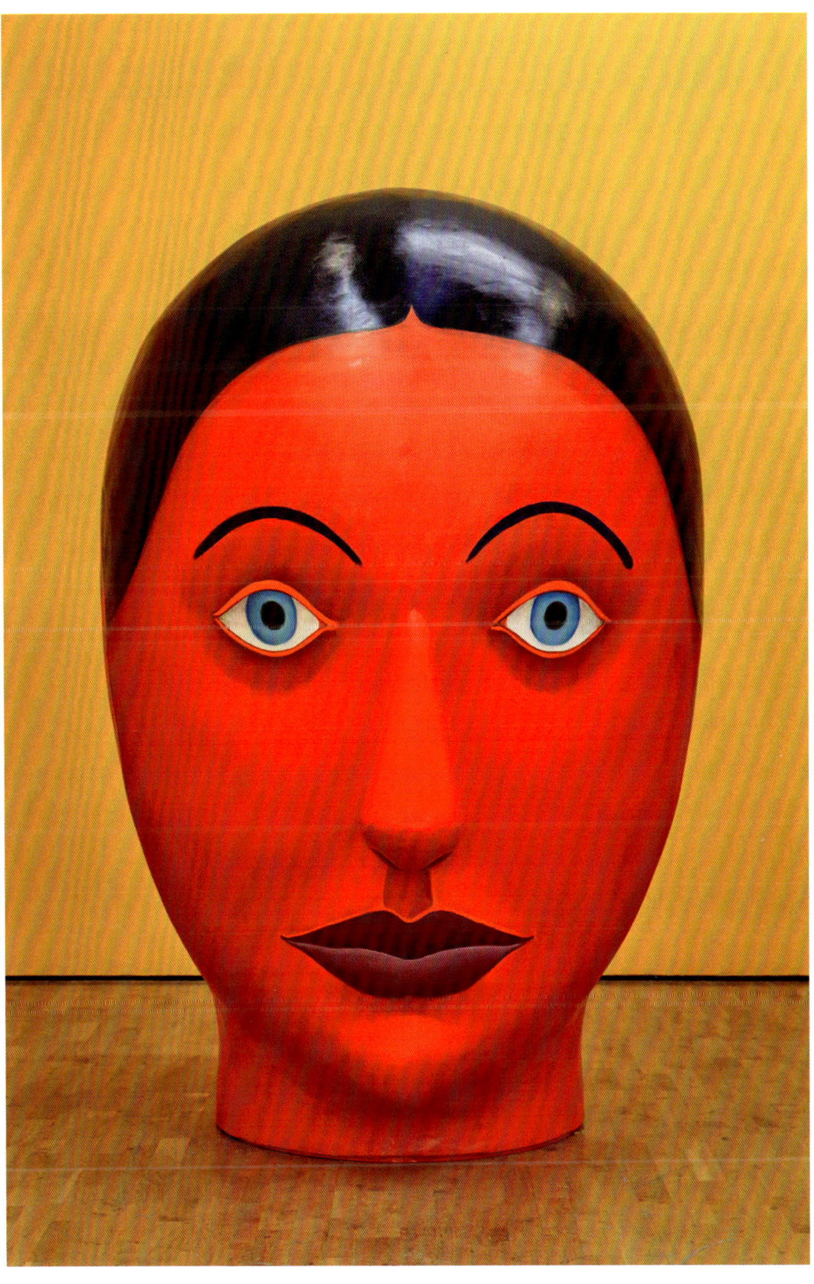

PARTY: I love using watercolours. It's of course a very practical medium: it doesn't require complicated materials that demand a studio. But the thing that attracts me the most is how water is actually the medium itself. You use water in all sorts of painting, like gouache and acrylic, but in watercolours water isn't just a tool that you can force to your own intentions; it has its own agenda and in order to paint you have to work with it. It almost feels like a collaboration with this element. You can't control what the paint will do when it interacts with the water on the paper. It moves by itself and decides to stay in place whenever the water evaporates.

AQUIN: *We've talked extensively about your work in two dimensions, murals, painting, pastel, etc, your staged performances, your sampling of the work of others, and your forays into immersive installations such as with The FLAG Art Foundation show, but in the last few years, you've also come to be known for your sculptural work. Can you tell me where this comes from?*

PARTY: My first show displaying only sculptures was at Modern Art Oxford in 2017. The exhibition consisted of a series of five large painted heads resting directly on the floor. All the heads had the same shape and measured two metres, but were each painted in a different colour tone.

For my second show presenting only sculptures at Galerie Gregor Staiger in Zurich in 2018, nine painted heads of different sizes were displayed on various plinths painted to imitate marble and wood surfaces. The shapes were modified from the previous show in Oxford but were based on the same idea: to create a simplified head based on a doll's shape, a hat displaying form or mannequin design. Each head was painted in a different colours but they all shared the same features. They didn't have any individual expressions and felt inhuman, staring at nothing in particular, having a sort of digital presence.

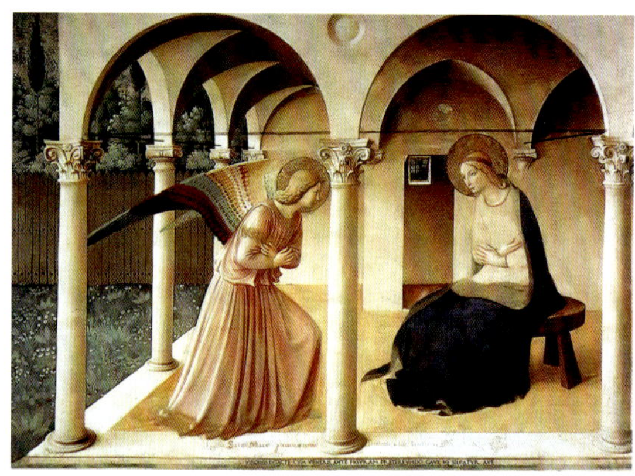

FRA ANGELICO
THE ANNUNCIATION, C. 1440–45
FRESCO
230 X 321 CM

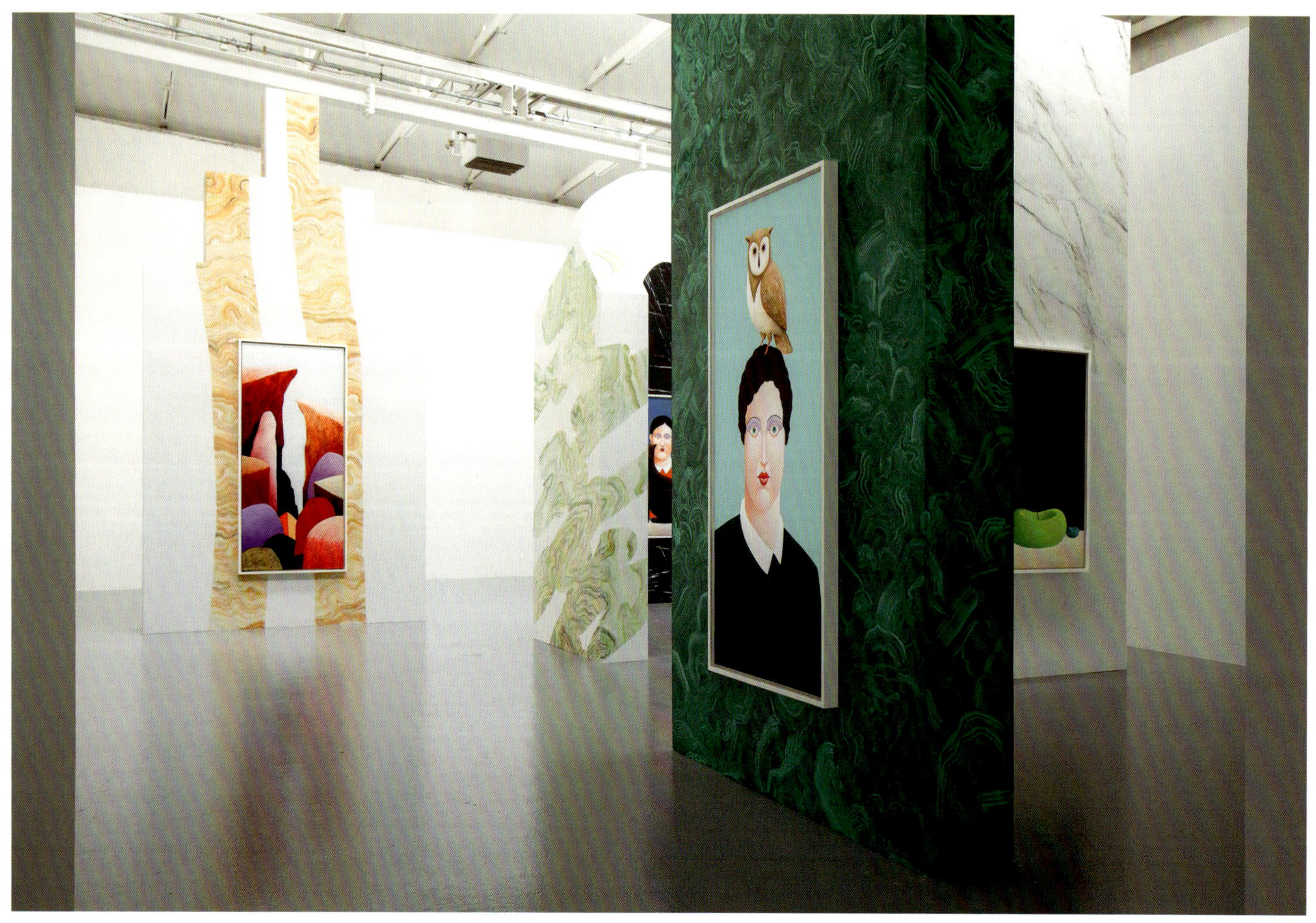

PORTRAIT WITH A CAT, 2016
SOFT PASTEL ON LINEN
156 X 106 CM

opposite, from left,
ROCKS, 2016
SOFT PASTEL ON LINEN
200 X 90 CM

PORTRAIT WITH A CAT, 2016
SOFT PASTEL ON LINEN
156 X 106 CM

PORTRAIT WITH AN OWL, 2016
SOFT PASTEL ON LINEN
200 X 90 CM

MURALS: OIL ON WALL

INSTALLATION VIEW AT
CENTRE D'ART NEUCHÂTEL,
SWITZERLAND, 2016

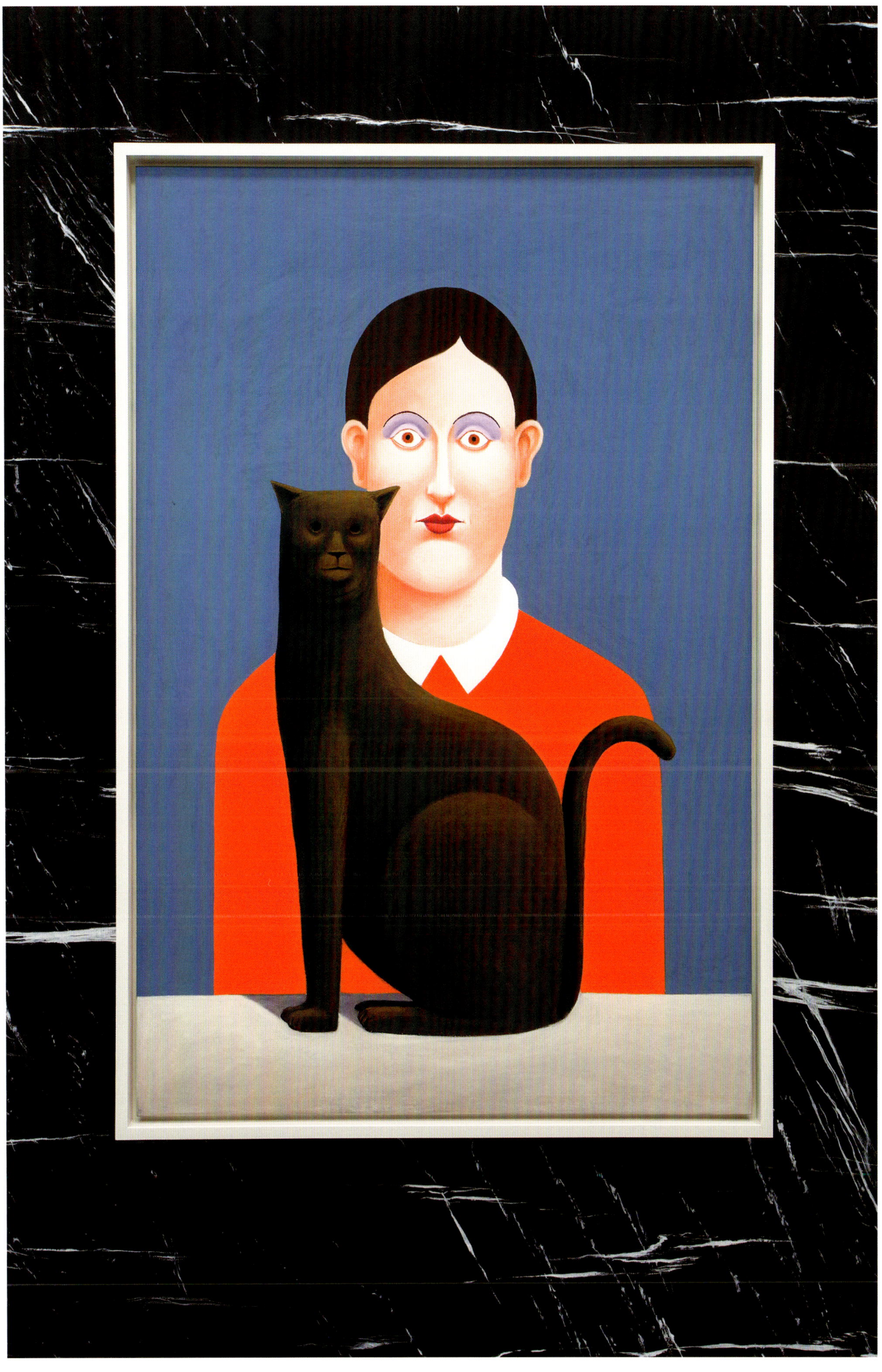

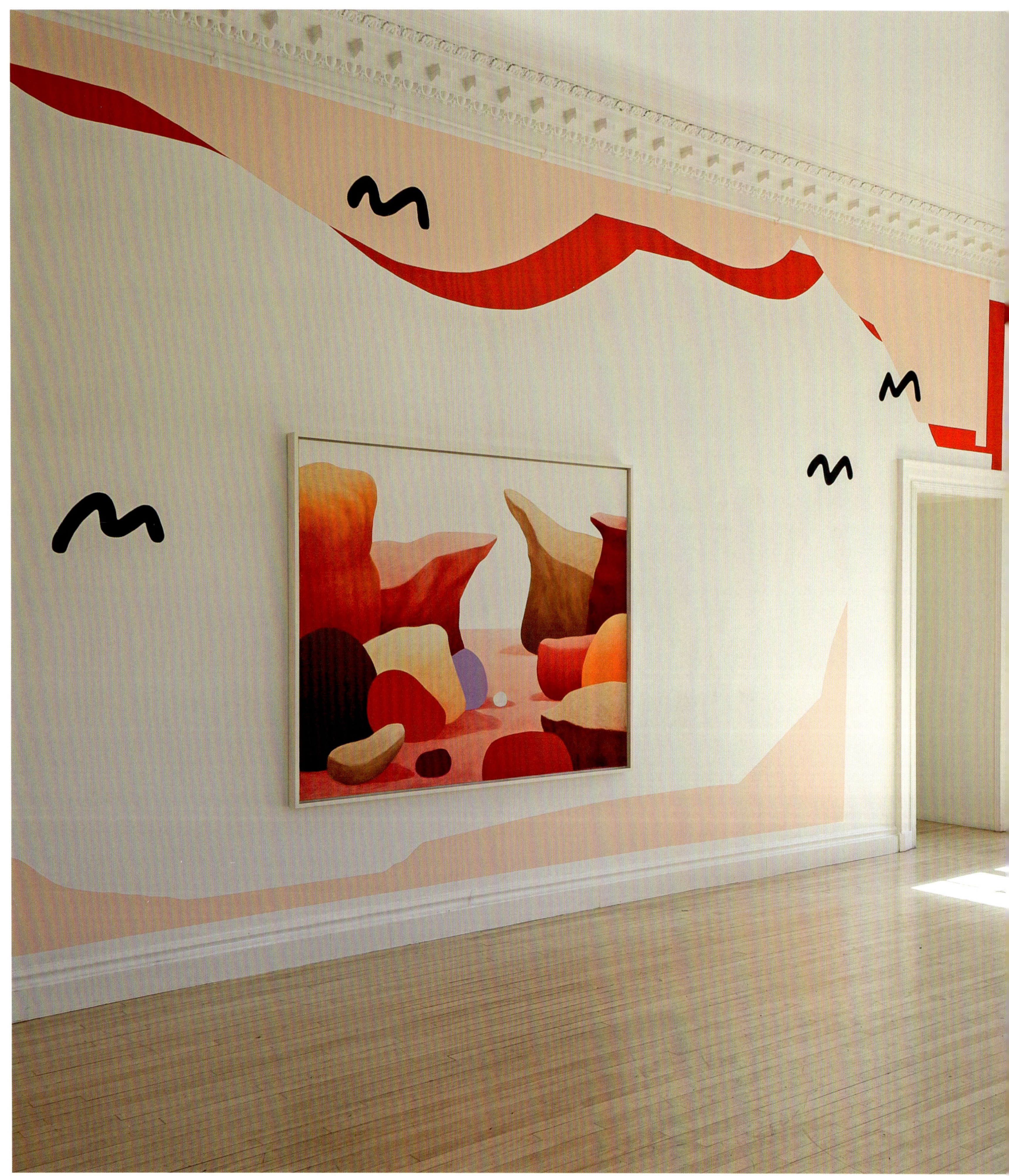

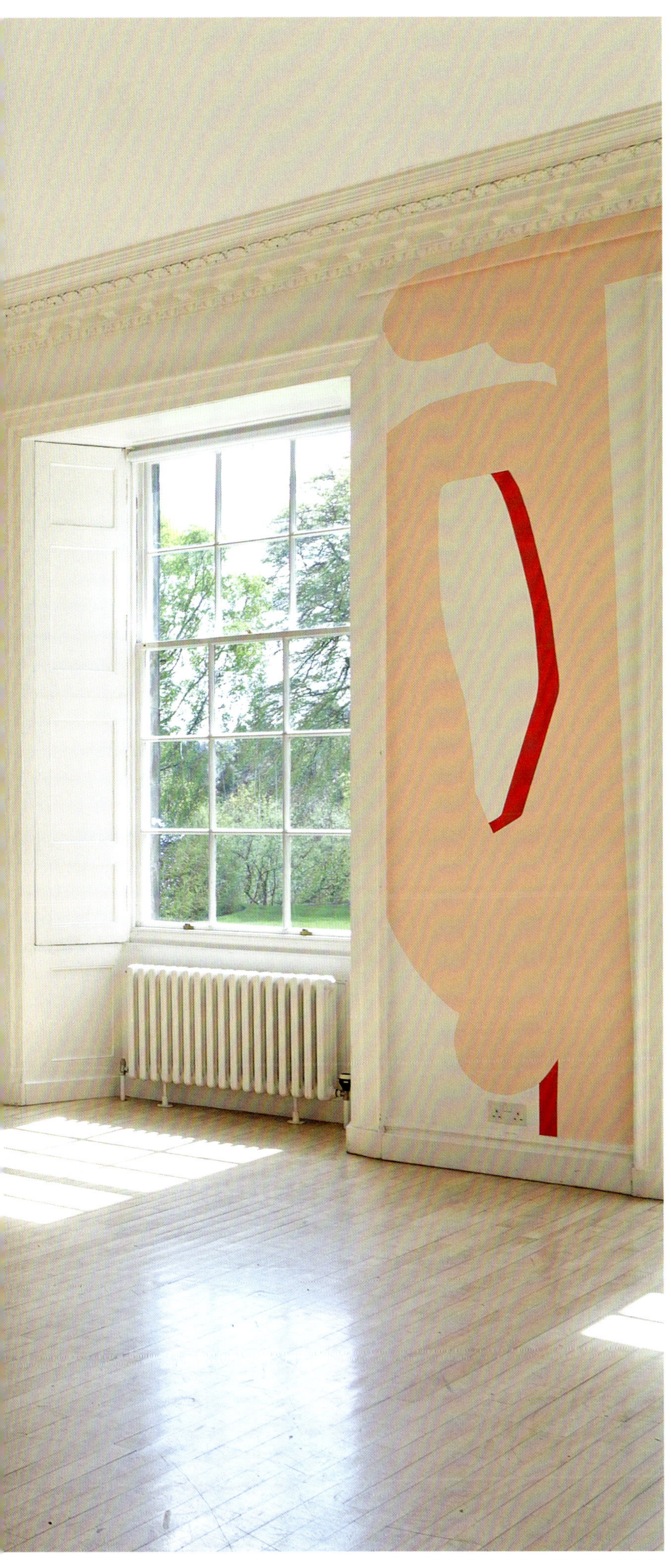

The notion of painted sculptures echoes the history of the reinterpretation of Greek sculpture during the Renaissance. When the Italians started to base their aesthetics on the works of antiquity, all the objects they were looking at were white. It was believed that the Greek and Roman sculptures looked like this when they were created. It was only much later, in the nineteenth century, that people discovered that all the classic sculptures were painted with bright colours. This misunderstanding accounts for a major aesthetic parameter in western sculpture history: the overwhelming authority of white marble sculptures. The growing western taste for pristine white bodies can't be detached from the parallel cultural history of races defined by skin colour, with all the attendant consequences, of which we're familiar.

AQUIN: *Another chapter of the history of art that you've engaged with, and that isn't that foreign to the one of polychrome sculpture, is that of the trompe-l'oeil tradition, by which the painter imitates various surfaces such as marble or wood. But this type of work refers to the world of architecture, which has come to hold a preeminent place in your work in recent years. Can you tell me about this?*

PARTY: I first used painted trompe l'oeil for the show at the Centre d'Art Neuchâtel (CAN) Switzerland in 2016. The title was 'Cimaise,' which is the French word for the fabricated wall used to hang art in a museum. The museum, CAN, was situated in an old factory and the architect built different cimaises to partially cover the original brick walls. The effect was similar to a movie set, where the artificial part of the set is perceptible when you step back and see the whole view. That encouraged me not to hang any paintings on the existing walls and instead to build a series of free-standing walls in the space. The nine cimaises each had different shapes and proportions that were inspired by the various architectural shapes of the original design of the factory. Each of these new walls was painted to create an illusion that they were made out of marble or wood using the traditional technique of trompe l'oeil painting. These painted effects have a long history, as early as the Roman frescoes of Pompeii, and were used frequently in the Renaissance in various frescos. The effects perfectly illustrate the affiliation of painting with the notion of illusion.

AQUIN: *There's a story of you having some sort of aesthetic epiphany or satori while visiting the Basilica di San Marco and its convent in Florence.*

PARTY: True. During a visit there, I felt a physical emotion when walking through the architecture looking at the different frescoes of Fra Angelico. The entrances of each monastic cell situated in the dormitory hallway are arches. There's an overwhelming presence of this form in the building: in the contours of the ceiling of the monastic cells, the windows, and most of the frescoes are painted inside an arch shape. That has an incredible effect on the viewer's experience. In an architectural arch, the centre holds all the energy of both sides that construct the shape, creating a profound sense of weight for what' passes beneath it. That load on you makes you feel smaller and causes your body and mind to bend, creating a feeling of humility. The effect of the architecture on the overall experience of the frescoes is remarkable and is a reminder of how architecture and painting were interlaced for centuries.

AQUIN: *I distinctly remember The FLAG Art Foundation arches, and the sense of ceremony that overtook you as you moved from one room to the other.*

PARTY: Actually, I did my first arches for the show at KARMA in 2017. I divided the gallery into four rooms, building new walls, and all the entries from one room to another were arches. When the construction was finished, I was astonished to see how different that simple intervention made the experience, and I've been building arches in almost all my shows since then.

AQUIN: *You and I have often talked about the fictional and irritatingly dogmatic idea of 'neutrality' that the white cube supposedly confers on the experience of art, when in fact it's a cultural construct.*

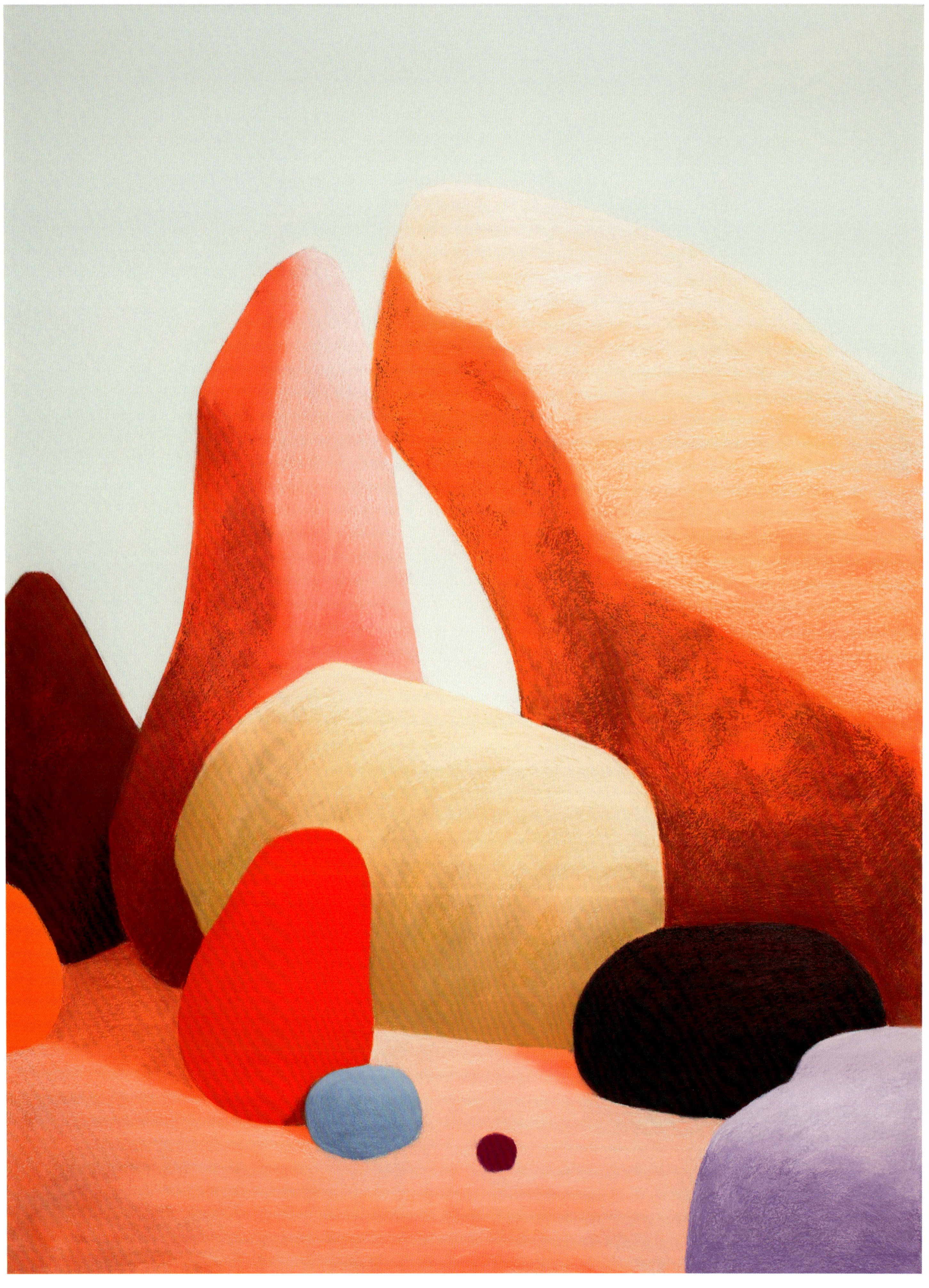

LANDSCAPE, 2015
SOFT PASTEL ON LINEN
150 X 100 CM

opposite,
ROCKS, 2016
SOFT PASTEL ON LINEN
105 X 80 CM

previous pages,
ROCKS, 2014
SOFT PASTEL ON LINEN
150 X 180 CM

MURAL: ACRYLIC ON WALL

INSTALLATION VIEW AT
INVERLEITH HOUSE,
EDINBURGH, 2015

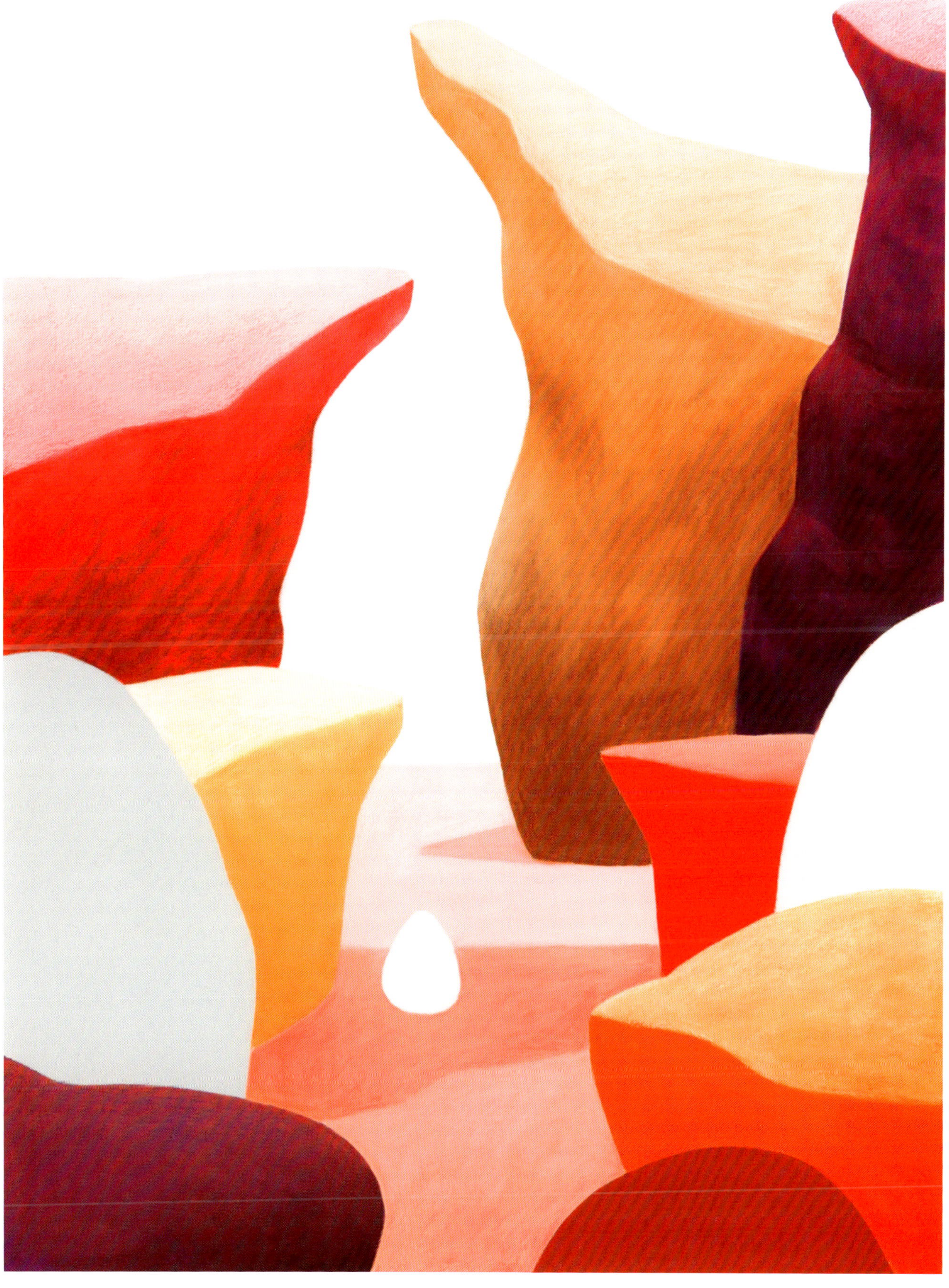

PARTY: Today, the vast majority of contemporary paintings are shown in spaces that have attempted to be neutral and invisible, making the experience only about the works on display and rarely about the interaction between the two. The notion of neutrality associated with the colour white for the walls of a gallery is a good example of this misunderstanding. If you ask most artists which colour they painted the walls for an exhibition they'll say, 'I didn't paint it, I kept it white', implying that white isn't a colour. In fact, white is a colour like any other, with its attendant history and cultural meanings. Its association with neutrality is a construct resonating with the notion of white skin being the only skin that is ostensibly non-coloured.

AQUIN: *Not to mention white's damaging effects on the perception of any coloured object you place on it.*

PARTY: When you hang a painting on a wall, its colour is very important and changes the perception of the work. It's surprising to me that most artists and curators find that only one colour, white, seems a good solution. Very often white is the wrong choice and is detrimental to the work. White reflects light more than most other colours. Surrounding a painting with brightness has the same effect as taking a photo facing the sun.

AQUIN: *You're a great lover and a great practitioner of the history of art. Your studio is filled with books and catalogues raisonnés about the work of other artists. You're also a collector in your own right, and your holdings show the scope of your embrace of the history of art, with works by artists ranging from Rosalba Carriera and Jean-Baptiste Perronneau, to pieces by Léon Spilliaert, one of your favourites, Georg Grosz, Albert Bierstadt, Félix Vallotton …*

PARTY: As we've discussed, the work of other artists is sometimes directly present in my work, and my main inspiration is the art of other artists. I discover new artists almost daily, but some I always go back to. Félix Vallotton's paintings are an unending inspiration for me. His ability to transform common subjects into a complex psychological material is masterful. His use of colours is also a perfect example of how some chromatic arrangements can give life to complex emotions in an ordinary subject. I'm thinking about his *Nude Seated in a Red Armchair* (1897) – the chair and the rug are painted a vivid red and the walls green. This combination of colours brings a whole psychological dimension to the image, making the viewer physically feel the tension of the scene. These chromatic strategies are also used by Edward Hopper, where common scenes are infused with emotional tension largely by his expert use of colour.

AQUIN: *Paradoxically, you conceive of many of your works as ephemeral. Pastels, to start with, are one of the most fragile and least durable media. But many of your murals, such as the one at the Hirshhorn, are made with the full awareness, and acceptance, that they'll be painted over. It's actually an intrinsic part of their idea, to be ephemeral.*

PARTY: Almost every mural that I do has a brief and impermanent existence; only a few are permanent public or private commissions. Most of the wall paintings only exist for the duration of the show. It can be as brief as a few days, in the instance of a wall painting made for an art fair, for example. Going back to the graffiti years, that ephemeral aspect was part of the process – we painted on surfaces that would sometimes be cleaned the day after we painted it. It's a distinctive approach, to create a work that will only exist for a predefined period and is specific to a location, again, similar to how live art is approached, where what exists after the performance is documentation and not the work itself. The transitory nature of the wall paintings also interrogated the need in our culture to preserve objects from the past. We devote tremendous energy to altering the effect of time on selected artefacts created in the past, with entire museums constructed to protect our collective memories. But the effect of time is inevitable and, as the title of the movie by Chris Marker and Alain Resnais declares, 'Statues Also Die'.

ARCHES, 2018
INSTALLATION VIEW AT
M WOODS, BEIJING, 2018

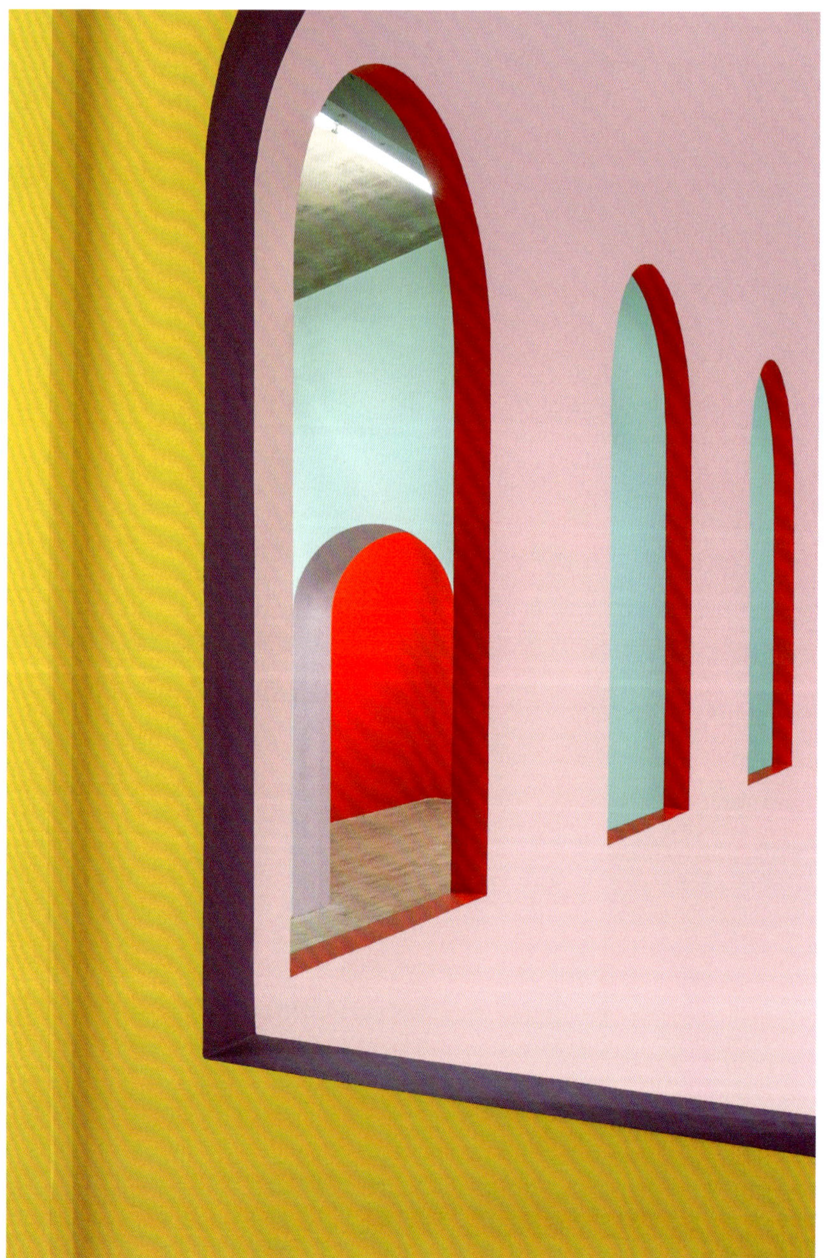

ARCHES, 2018
INSTALLATION VIEW AT
M WOODS, BEIJING, 2018

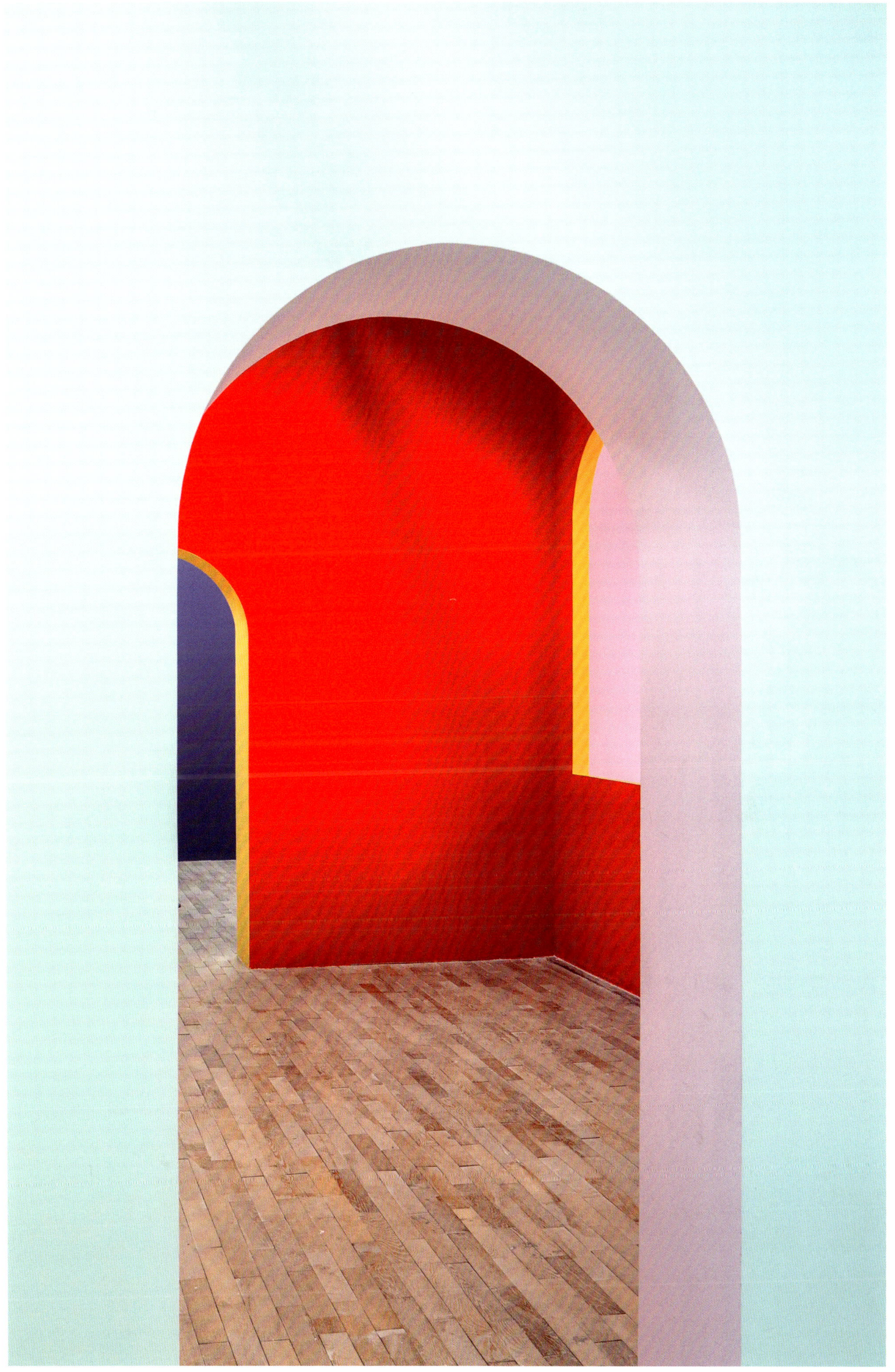

from left,
PORTRAIT WITH MUSHROOMS,
2019
SOFT PASTEL ON LINEN
150 X 127 CM

OTTO MARSEUS VAN SCHRIECK
FOREST FLOOR STILL LIFE
WITH THREE SNAKES, LIZARD
AND TOAD, 1663
OIL ON CANVAS
61 X 51 CM

MURAL OIL ON WALL

INSTALLATION VIEW AT HAUSER
& WIRTH, LOS ANGELES, 2019

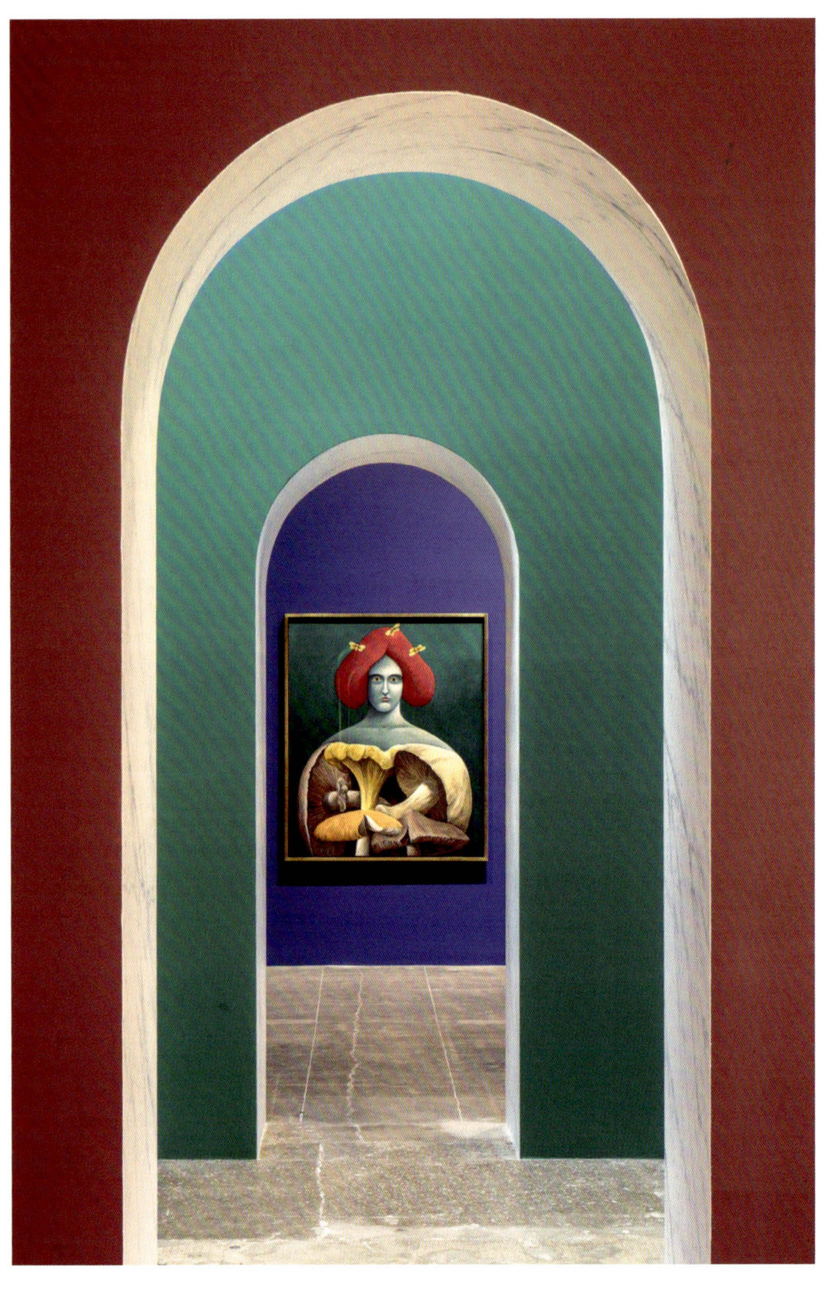

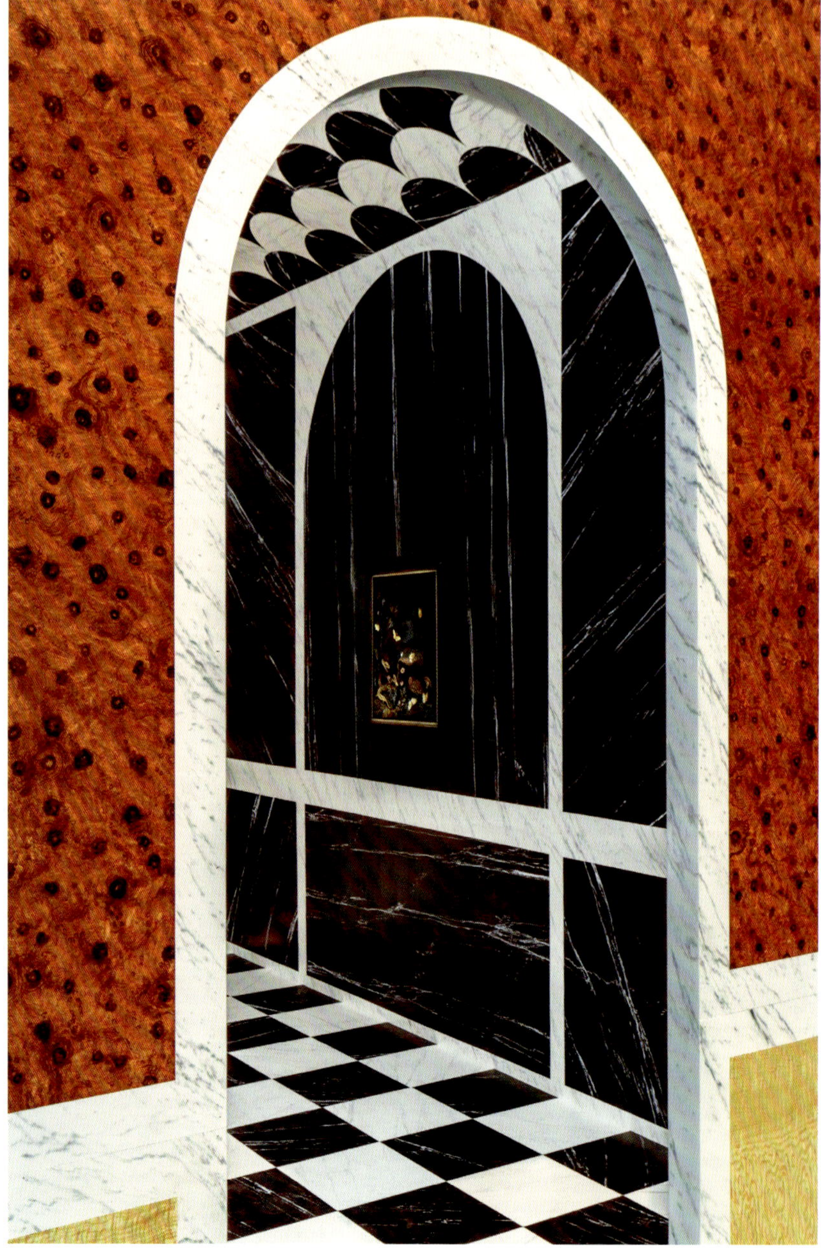

from left,
LANDSCAPE, 2019
SOFT PASTEL ON LINEN
191 X 165 CM

LANDSCAPE, 2019
SOFT PASTEL ON LINEN
191 X 165 CM

MURAL, OIL ON WALL

INSTALLATION VIEW AT HAUSER & WIRTH, LOS ANGELES, 2019

next pages, from left,
LANDSCAPE, 2019
SOFT PASTEL ON LINEN
191 X 165 CM

LANDSCAPE, 2019
SOFT PASTEL ON LINEN
191 X 165 CM

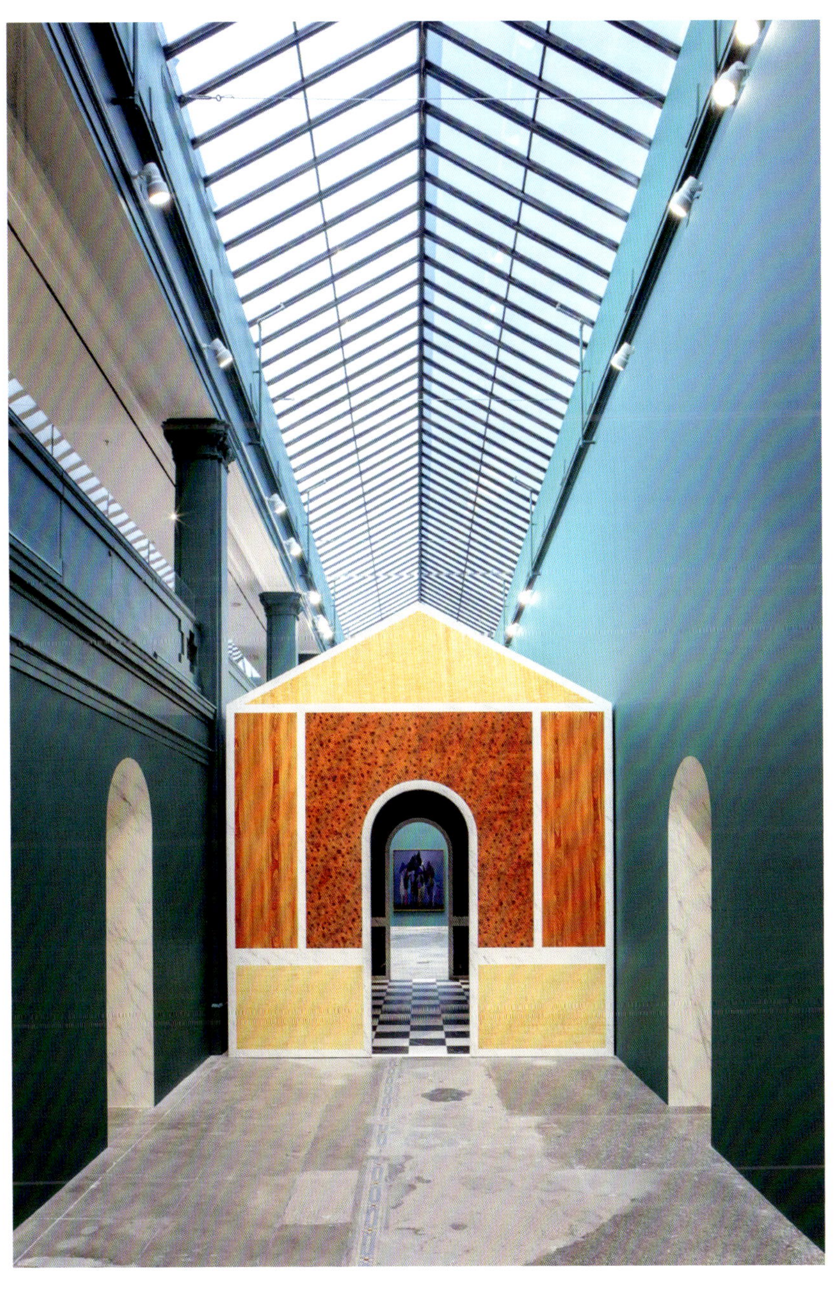

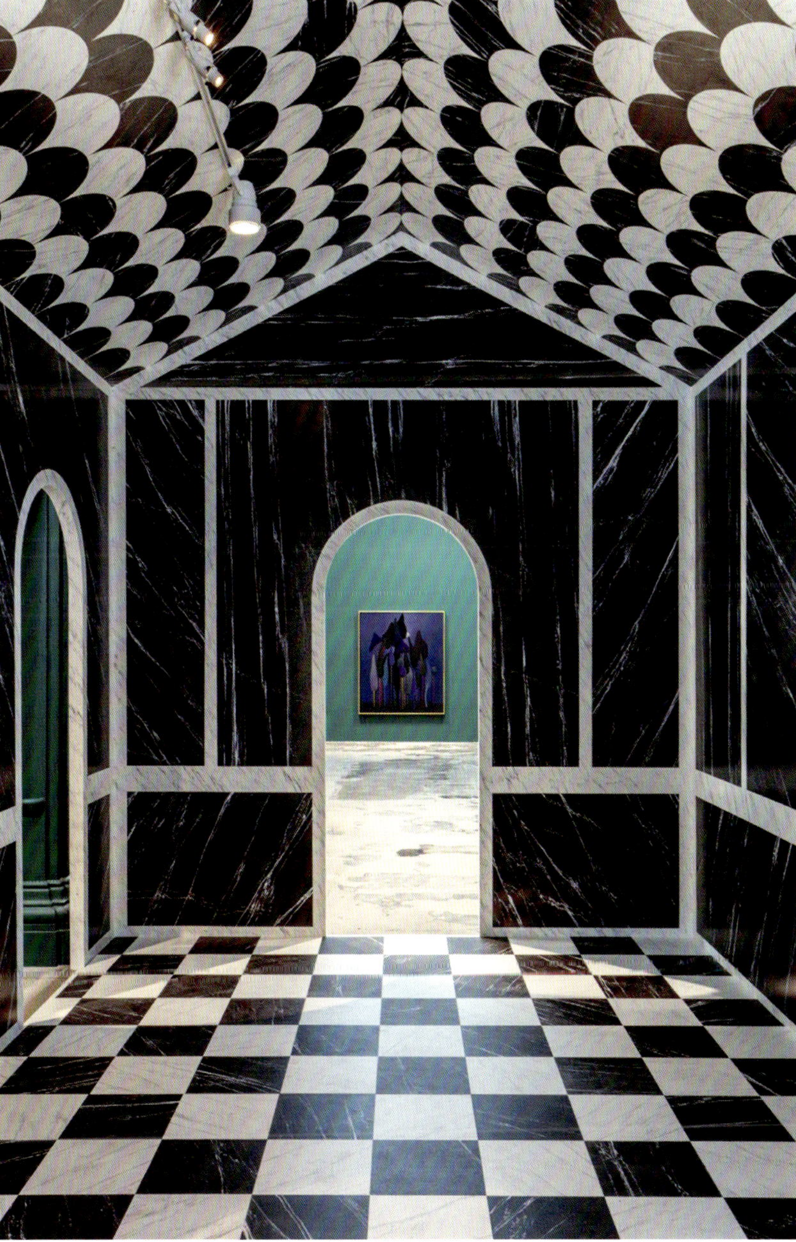

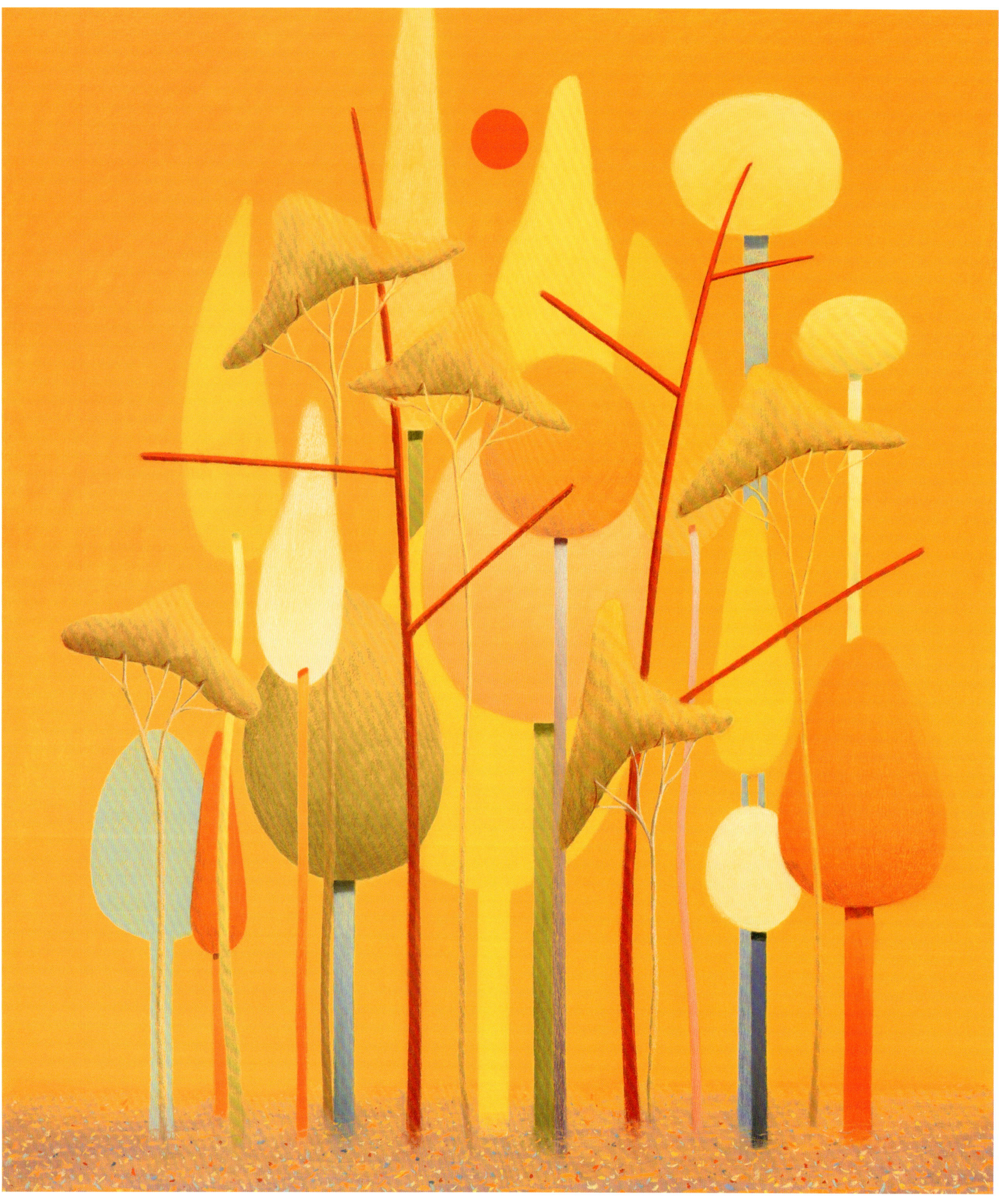

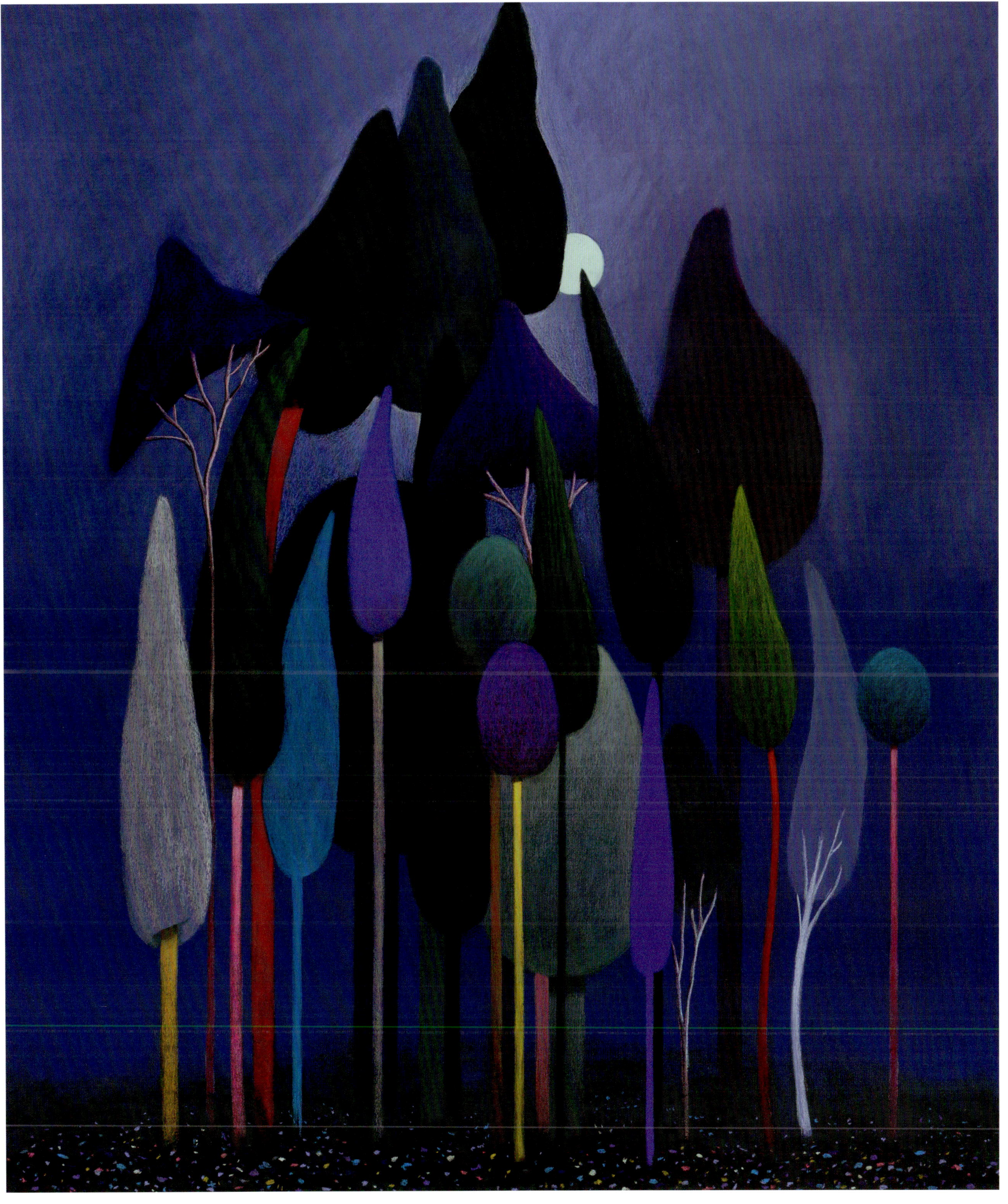

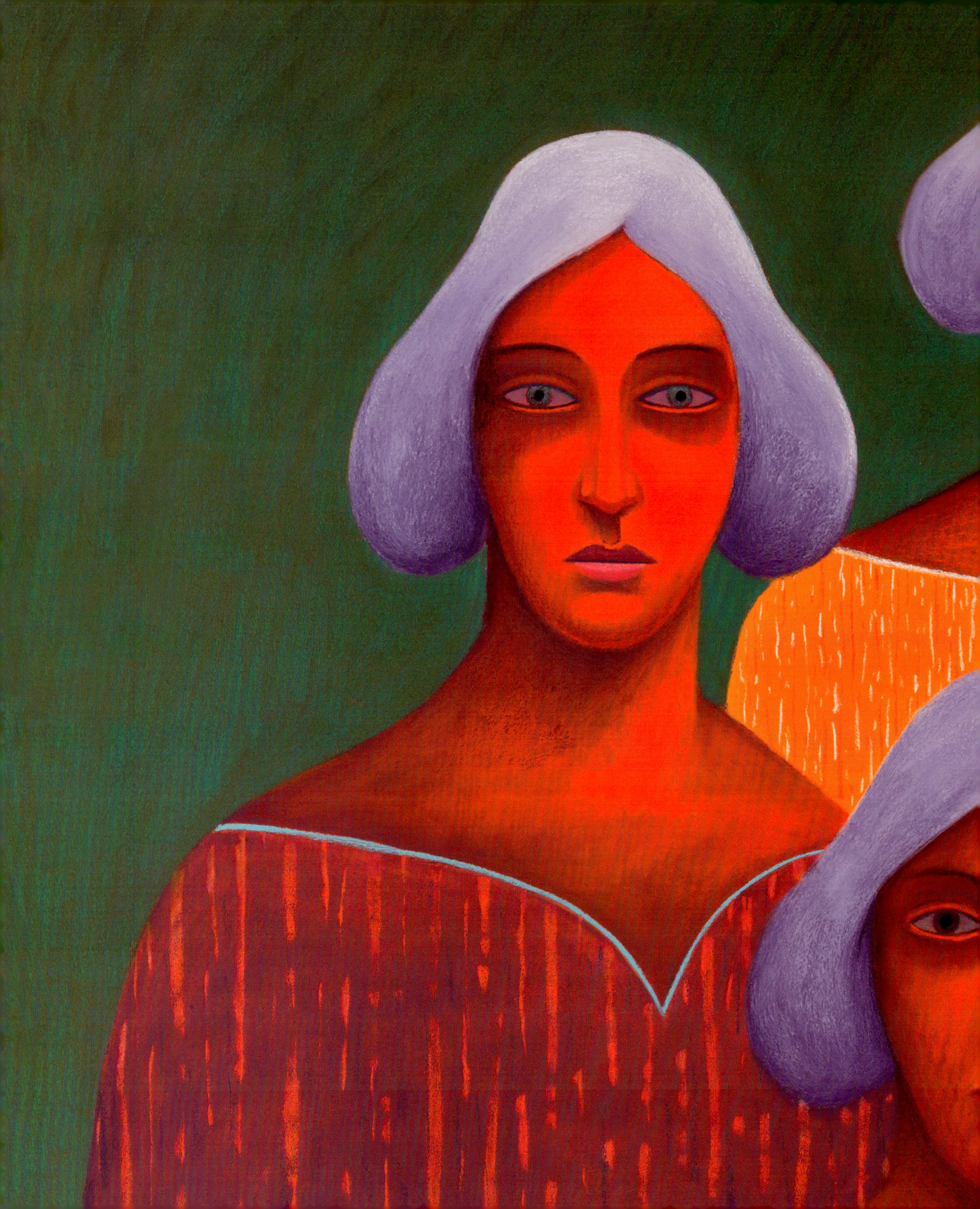

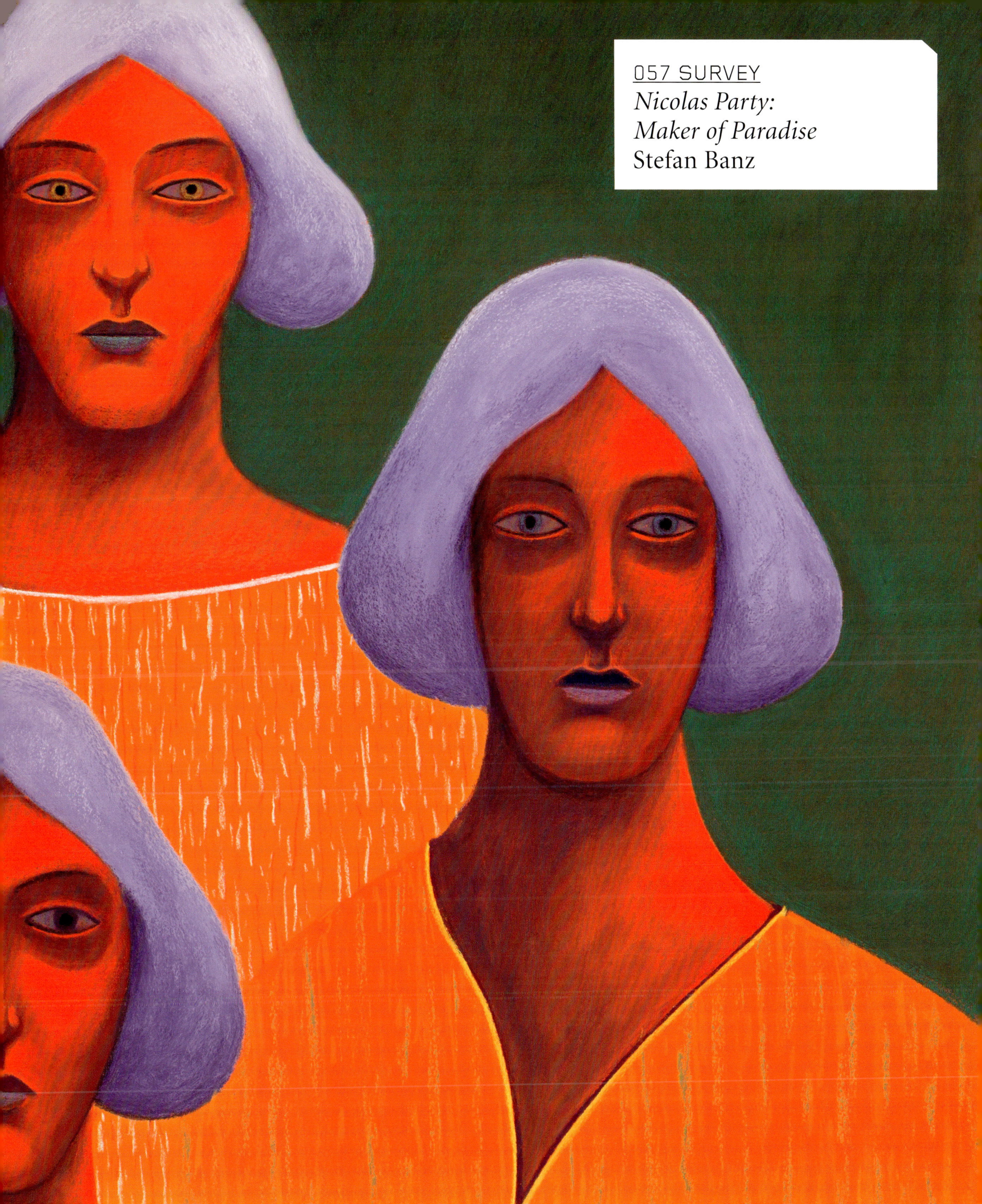

057 SURVEY

Nicolas Party: Maker of Paradise

Stefan Banz

Elephant

Nicolas Party's work touches a nerve that is located in a region of our consciousness, beyond suggestion, influence and everyday conflicts, a region where emotion, imagination, empathy and longing are not yet guided by preconceived interpretational constraints. For Party does not force us to read his pastels and sculptures in a preordained way. Instead, they induce a sense of being-with-ourselves that encourages us to see everything with totally fresh eyes, just as children do when they first encounter things, events and phenomena, artlessly and without filters and preconceptions.

I would like to begin this survey of Party's work along these lines, with the depiction of a rather touching elephant that the artist showed in his solo exhibition 'Three Cats' at the Modern Institute in Glasgow from 10 September to 29 October 2016. Elephants are a recurring subject in his work, appearing on different levels of reality and meaning, depending on the exhibition design.

Who among us would not like to live in such an ingenuous and trusting state? We long for paradisiacal conditions to lift our spirits, knowing full well that they do not exist in reality. It is only the longing, the

ELEPHANT, 2016
SOFT PASTEL ON LINEN
145 X 165 CM

MURAL: OIL ON WALL

INSTALLATION VIEW AT
THE MODERN INSTITUTE,
GLASGOW, 2016

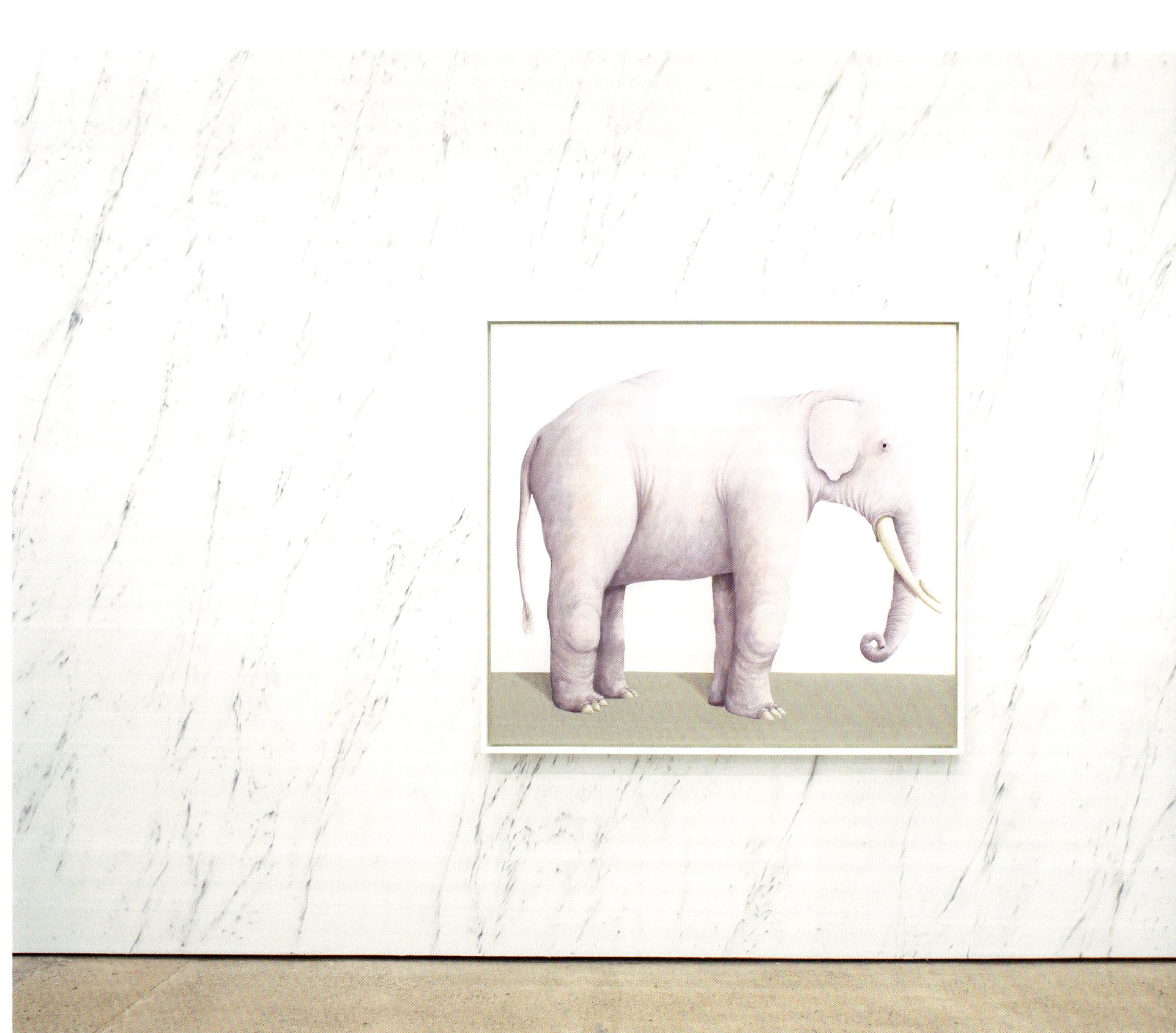

previous pages,
FOUR PORTRAITS, 2018
SOFT PASTEL ON LINEN
150 X 180 CM

imagination or the fantasy that counts. Paradise itself is meant to be merely a projection and not a reality. But we can neither overcome this fundamental paradox of our existence nor expunge it from our consciousness. This becomes particularly obvious when we go to the cinema, for example, where nobody wants to see paradise for two hours. In truth, we go to the cinema to experience a journey to reach paradise. But as soon as the plot touches it, up come the credits.

With his art, Party not only succeeds in awakening this longing for paradise, but also in playfully and pleasurably giving it a face. And in his exhibitions he gives us the feeling that paradise is never far off. They encourage us to take matters into our own hands and picture our own paradise. This is one aspect of what makes his art so appealing and successful.

In 'Three Cats', his second exhibition at the Modern Institute, the artist showed a painting of a white elephant in profile against an equally white background, standing on a beige floor. The painting is large, though smaller than life-size, framed with thin, white squared timber, and hangs on a trompe-l'oeil painted wall imitating white Carrara marble. In this simple mise-en-scène, almost all the ingredients of Party's art are represented. The miniature elephant, painted in profile, which resembles a shy, trusting child, seems to look straight at us as. We are instantly touched by its innocent look. And so we immediately establish an emotional relationship with this poignant portrayal. Is the elephant frightened? Does it feel ill at ease in its unfamiliar surroundings? Can we viewers do anything about it? Why is the elephant standing in this artificial environment that could itself be an exhibition room? Is it the untouched Modern Institute gallery that we see depicted here, just before the artist reinterpreted the room for his exhibition, in the very place where the picture of the elephant now hangs on a wall that in turn has been transformed into marble through the medium of painting?

We quickly realise that this elephant is not only a touching animal depiction that seeks direct contact with the viewer, but also a virtuosic element of an overall enactment that raises questions of perception, shifting reality and confusion. In addition, the artist almost casually addresses the tradition of portrait painting: the depiction of a human as an animal, or the pictorial humanisation of an animal as a parable. In doing so, he presents the elephant in profile, a mode of depiction familiar to us since the Renaissance and that artists like Joseph Stella (1877–1946) rediscovered in the classical modernism of the twentieth century in order to give it new meaning and new artistic expression.

The elephant is a creature long rich in associations across cultures. Its majestic appearance, column-like legs, ponderous movements, and thick, wrinkled skin evoke a sense not only of history and tradition, but of human congruence as well. Party's elephant seems to be a male Asian specimen: Asian elephants have smaller ears than their African counterparts, as well as a slightly smoother and lighter skin. Only the males have tusks. In Asia, the elephant is the royal mount of Indra and Shiva. It is also a symbol of power, wisdom, peace and happiness. Four elephants are even believed capable of carrying the entire universe, which is why they often appear in Indian and Tibetan architecture as caryatids. In Greek and Roman literature, the elephant is additionally associated with chastity, scholarship, gentleness and helpfulness. In Western antiquity it is an attribute of the god Mercury, owing to its intelligence. Because of its longevity, it also symbolises the overcoming of death.

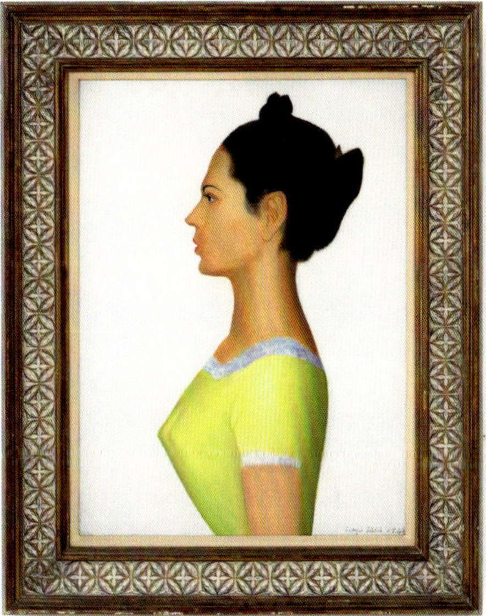

JOSEPH STELLA
WOMAN IN PROFILE, 1942
OIL ON CANVAS
61 X 46 CM

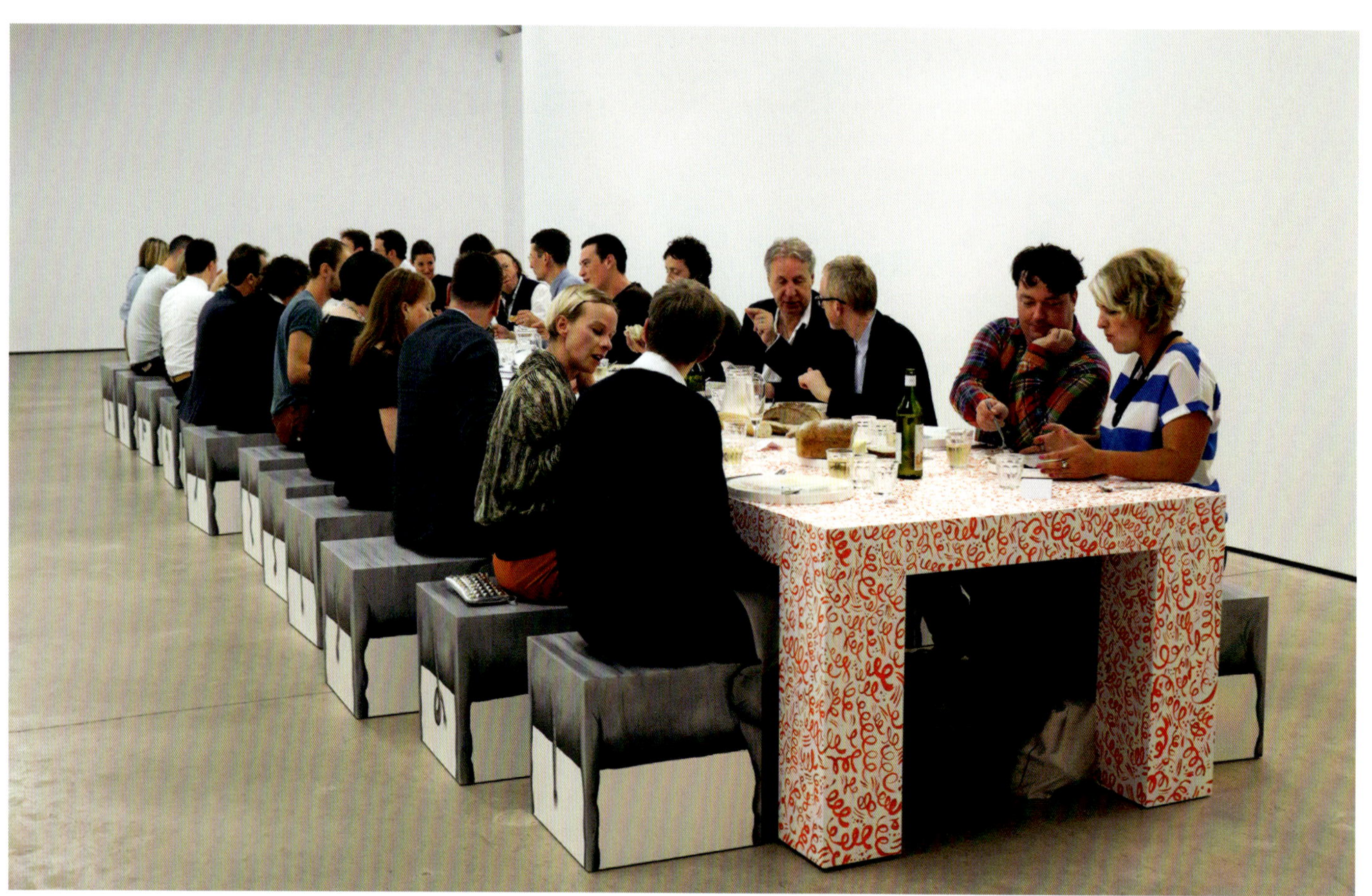

DINNER FOR 24 ELEPHANTS TABLE, 2011
4 TABLES ACRYLIC ON WOOD
EACH 78 X 237 X 119 CM

DINNER FOR 24 ELEPHANTS STOOL, 2011
24 STOOLS ACRYLIC ON WOOD
EACH 45 X 45 X 45 CM

DINNER FOR 24 ELEPHANTS, 2011
HAND PAINTED CERAMIC PLATES, FOOD
7 PIECES
EACH Ø 33 X 3 CM

INSTALLATION VIEW AT THE MODERN INSTITUTE, GLASGOW, 2011

And according to legend, after the Buddha crawled back into the womb of his mother Maya, he was reborn as a white elephant.

The German idiom 'wie ein Elefant im Porzellan-Laden', equivalent to the English-language 'bull in a china shop', describes the inappropriate use of force or clumsy, rude or tactless behaviour. The German phrase 'auf einem Elefanten reiten', on the other hand, describes a state of elation. Today, we often use the elephant to symbolise the importance of leading figures in politics and business, so that an 'elefantenrunde' ('elephant round'), for example, refers to a summit meeting bringing together top-level leaders. The term 'elefantenhochzeit' ('elephant wedding') is used in German to describe the merger of two large corporations. The elephant also represents groundedness, stability, endurance, reliability and – viewed as an éminence grise – the embodiment of strength and wisdom. Since it is thick-skinned, we believe that it can rarely be wounded. In addition 'Riding on an elephant' signifies having a sense of security, feeling wonderfully supported by its solid body. Finally, in certain contexts, trunks and tusks can be phallic symbols.[1]

In Party's installations, the elephant appears in different semantic contexts. Particularly playful and ambiguous is, for example, his *Dinner for 24 Elephants*, his first presentation at the Modern Institute in Glasgow, which is formally reminiscent of Katharina Fritsch's famous 1988 installation *Tischgesellschaft* (Dinner Party) at the Museum für Moderne Kunst in Frankfurt. On Friday 2 September 2011, a week before the official opening of the exhibition, the artist organised a dinner that resembled a performance and was a kind of 'elephant round'. Just twenty-four selected guests from the Glasgow art scene were invited to the event.

In the collection of the Museum of Modern Art in Frankfurt, Fritsch's *Tischgesellschaft* serves as the inspiration for a similar ritual, which has been repeated for several years on the first Monday in February: sixteen hosts invite sixteen guests and gather at a long table in dark clothing. The museum director presides over the evening, which includes a festive meal and an artistic contribution by a celebrated guest of honour. The following year, each guest becomes a host himself and in turn nominates a person to join the dinner party. In this way, a select circle is formed, dedicated to the promotion of the museum in a special way. For implicit in becoming a member of the *Tischgesellschaft* is the willingness to make a financial commitment to the museum.

On that Friday evening, Party's guests at the Modern Institute ate a seven-course menu devised by the artist including a single oyster, a fish, a sausage and a poached pear, each served on a plate specially painted by Party. The invited guests gathered around a large dining table painted by the artist sitting on cube seats resembling a pedestal and with perspective views of an elephant on all sides. In other words, Party's dinner was not

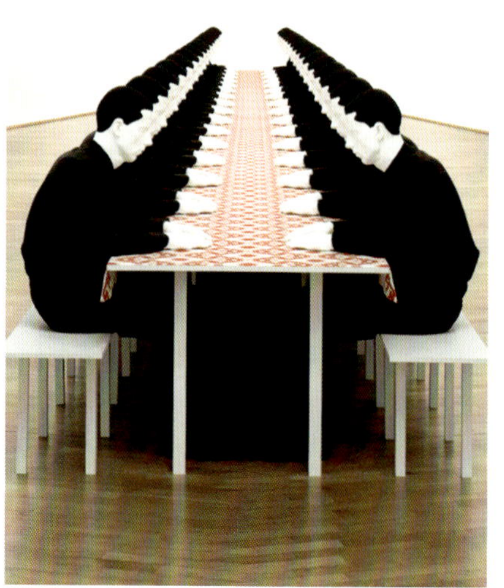

KATHARINA FRITSCH
TISCHGESELLSCHAFT, 1988
POLYESTER, WOOD, COTTON, PAINT
140 X 1600 X 175 CM

from left,
PORTRAITS, 2014
SOFT PASTEL ON LINEN
150 X 190 CM

ELEPHANTS (DETAIL), 2014
CHARCOAL ON WOOD
9 PARTS
EACH 410 X 75 X 75 CM

TREES, 2014
SOFT PASTEL ON LINEN
200 X 110 CM

INSTALLATION VIEW AT
THE WESTFALISCHER
KUNSTVEREIN, MÜNSTER, 2014

just an 'elephant round', but each guest seated on these pedestals depicting elephants also became part of this Gesamtkunstwerk, a living sculpture eating their 'amuse-bouches'. The event, audience and performance thus merged into a single entity, raising the concept of the artwork to a new level of reality.

The elephants painted on the cube seats were highly stylised and thus acquired a somewhat decorative touch. The artist developed this feature further in his next solo exhibition at the Westfälischer Kunstverein in Münster entitled 'Trunks and Faces' (8 November 2014 to 18 January 2015), for which he painted the same elephants on elements that were again block-like, but this time reminiscent of pilasters or caryatids. Thus, in this new presentation, the cubes no longer served as seats or pedestals for visitors, but instead became architectural elements placed against the wall and exploiting most of the available headroom in the museum. As a result, the elephants' legs, wrapped around corners, suddenly resembling curious-looking ornaments, with the painted tails hanging down recalling ropes one might pull to ring a bell or otherwise activate a mechanism that, for example, induces our artistic thinking and perception to resonate.

Elephants have been a subject, too, in recent Western art history; we need only think of Katharina Fritsch's life-size African elephant from 1987 or Carsten Höller's reclining baby elephants from 1999. An elephant perfectly embodies the eternal paradox of gracefulness and exploitation. We feel a strong liking for this unusual animal; we are impressed by its manner and its majesty, and yet we have exploited it for its ivory in the course of history to the extent that it is now in serious danger of extinction.

At the beginning of this survey study, I noted that Party's artistic works did not deal explicitly with the sweeping socio-political issues of our time. But the example of the elephant as a recurring theme in his works and installations demonstrates that he does touch poignantly on these burning issues. He addresses them not in moralising fashion, but playfully, in a roundabout way, as a grand visual experience or perceptual phenomenon.

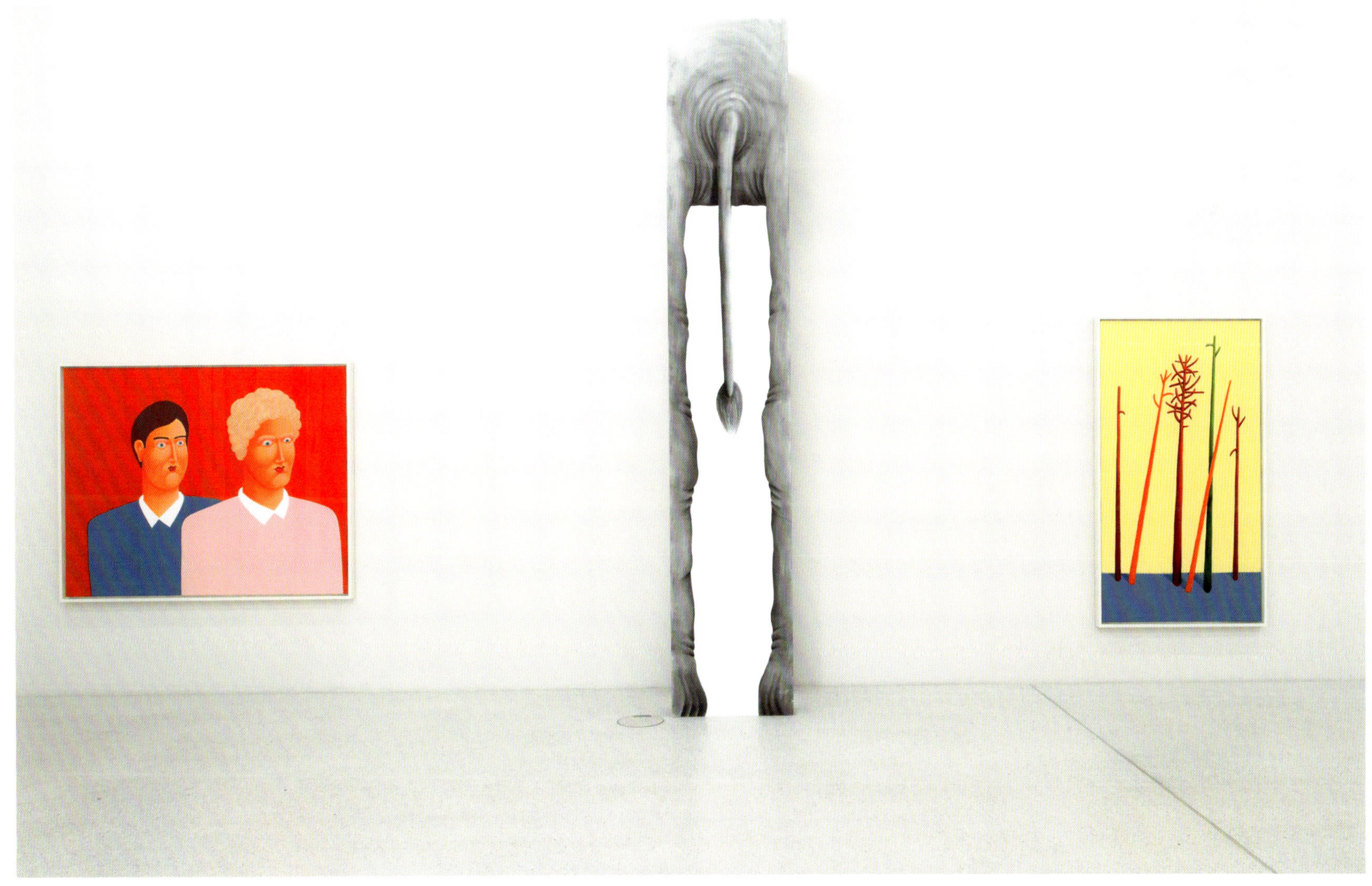

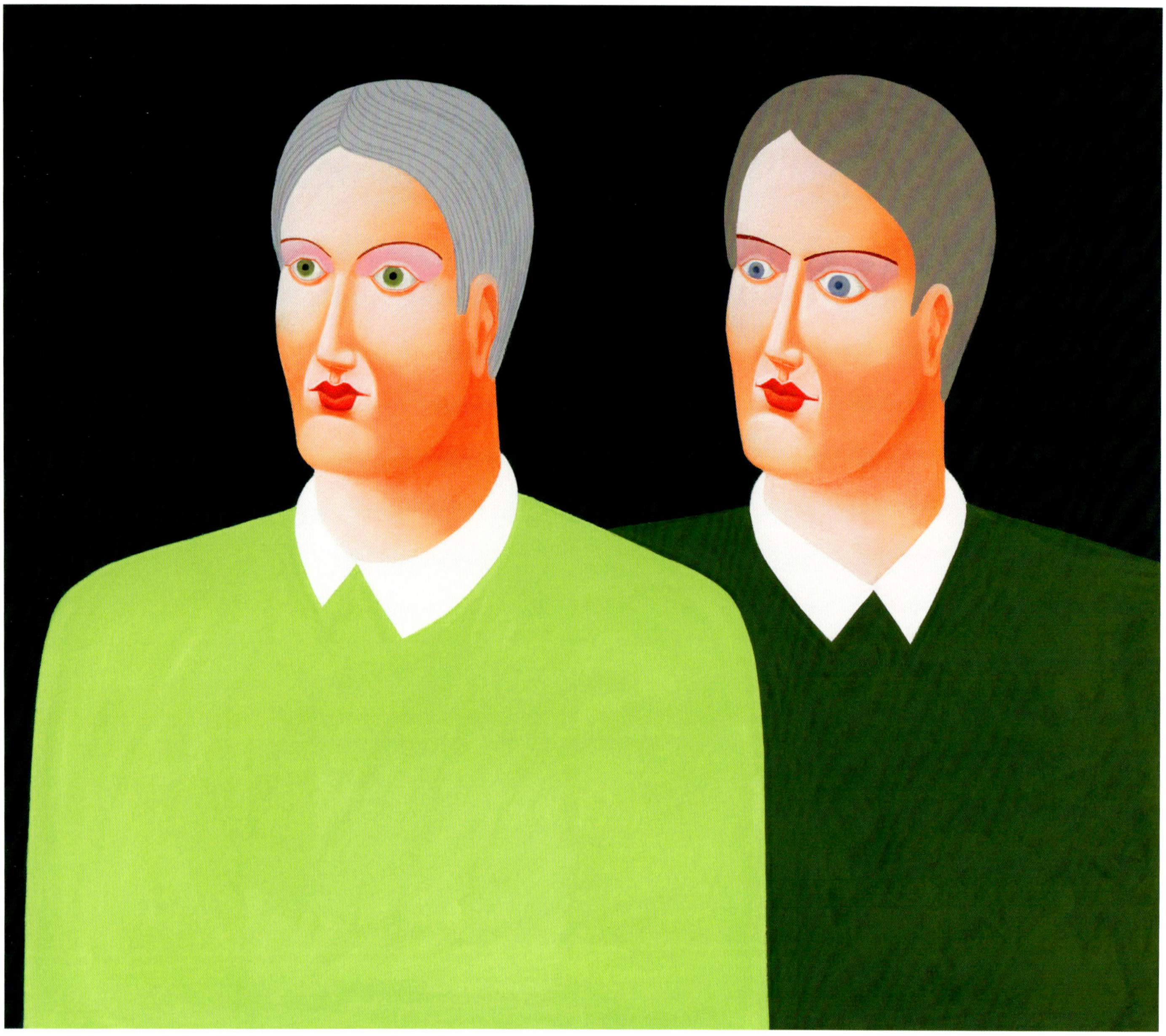

PORTRAITS, 2015
SOFT PASTEL ON LINEN
150 X 170 CM

Têtes Humaines 1

Hung amongst the various painted architectural elements at the Westfälischer Kunstverein, Party also exhibited highly stylized double portraits and pictures of leafless tree trunks. These are two more themes that repeatedly appear in his work in different contexts and constellations. We find single, double and group portraits in profile, semi-profile and frontal views, mostly painted in pastel on linen panels or primed linen. More recently, these have been increasingly joined by such attributes as insects, birds and reptiles. In addition, he has started to produce portrait sculptures in various sizes and to exhibit them in different contexts. A key inspiration for all these works, Party has stated, is Picasso's pastel *Tête de Femme* from 1921, which is now in the Fondation Beyeler in Riehen near Basel.

If we compare this famous painting of a woman's head with, for example, Party's *Portrait* from 2016 (p. 64), first shown at the Cimaise exhibition at Centre d'Art Neuchâtel (CAN), there is indeed a strong resemblance. However, since Party reveals this kinship from the very beginning, perhaps it is the differences – which give the work a different artistic presence – that are more striking. Party was fascinated by the portrait's enigmatic form of individualization, unique and unmistakable in its stark execution. In his own portrait pictures, Party adopts this individualization as a new theme and to pursue it further. With his knowledge of current image processing programmes he has neutralized and standardized the heads in his paintings so systematically that his depictions – in contrast to Picasso's – seem almost genderless (as for example in *Red Portrait*, 2016, p. 66). Although perhaps hinted at through the bright colours of the face and background and the additional attributes in the pictures, one could say that gender, origin and age vanish to a large extent in his portrayals. Moreover, we ask ourselves whether the depicted figures are not in fact portraits of portraits or sculptures.

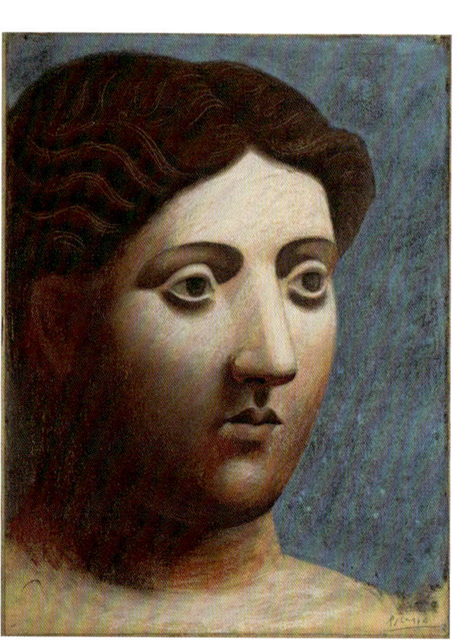

PABLO PICASSO
TÊTE DE FEMME, 1921
PASTEL ON PAPER
63.5 × 48 CM

PORTRAIT, 2015
SOFT PASTEL ON LINEN
170 X 150 CM

It is fascinating to see how these paradoxical impressions overlap in Party's work, and how these portraits conjure up different personalities and moods. We feel impelled to ask what sorts of lives they have led and what roles they play in society. And yet they remain strangely anonymous. The earlier portraits, especially, are almost always executed with uniform hairstyles and only slight variations in physiognomy. Even the clothes they wear have something neutral, timeless and indeterminate about them. This explains their highly enigmatic air. And yet they have a capacity to arouse strong feelings in the viewer.

Blue Portrait – exhibited by Party in a room painted Prussian blue in the 'Pastel' exhibition (pp. 64–5) at Karma in New York from 26 September to 5 November 2017 – is one of the most compelling examples in this regard. It is rare to witness a setting in which a portrait placed against the colouration of the exhibition space generates such an intense emotional presence. This room, steeped in Prussian blue, with its portraits of figures in different shades of blue, grey and black, arrests us before we can even think a single thought. The incredibly bizarre and at the same time beguilingly beautiful atmosphere in this room has an immediate, profoundly visceral effect. And if the wall were painted only half a tone lighter, darker, greener or yellower, and if the painting were also painted in only a slightly different tone, the entire effect of the scene, which spreads throughout the body via the retina and acquires a physical quality, would be lost. Everything seems so light and natural, as if this setting has come about of its own accord.

The Prussian blue of the wall forms the perfect frame for the frontal portrait of this genderless portrait. A viewer might identify the depicted person as female only through her hairstyle and because the lips seem to be reddened by lipstick. The figure's bust is slender rather than muscular, but there are no signs of breasts in the grey-painted clothing. There is nevertheless a strange form of eroticism in the mise-en-scène, elicited exclusively by the colours. It is a cool eroticism. However, before we become aware of any of this, we are immediately captured by the gaze of the large, round eyes staring straight at us. It feels as if we only look at the picture because it is looking at us.

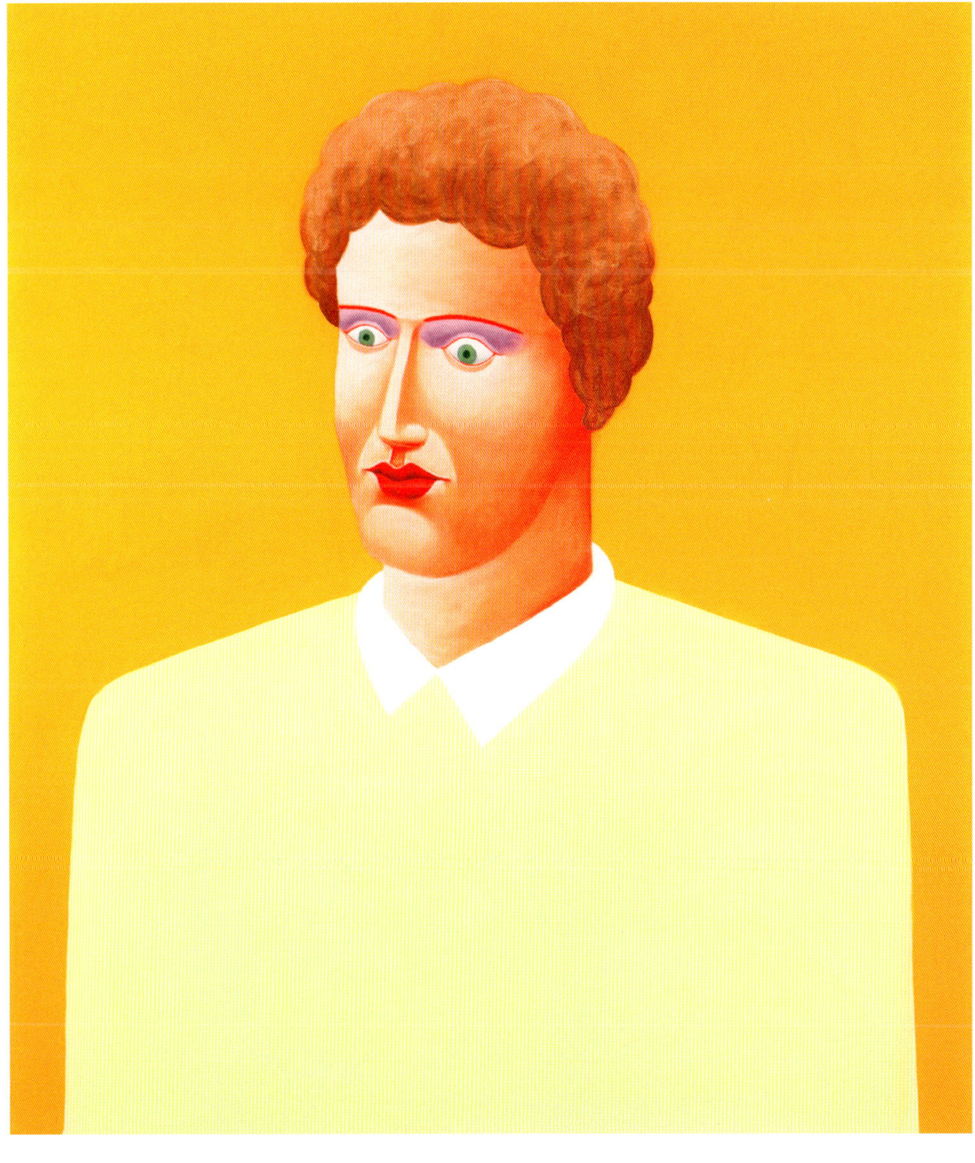

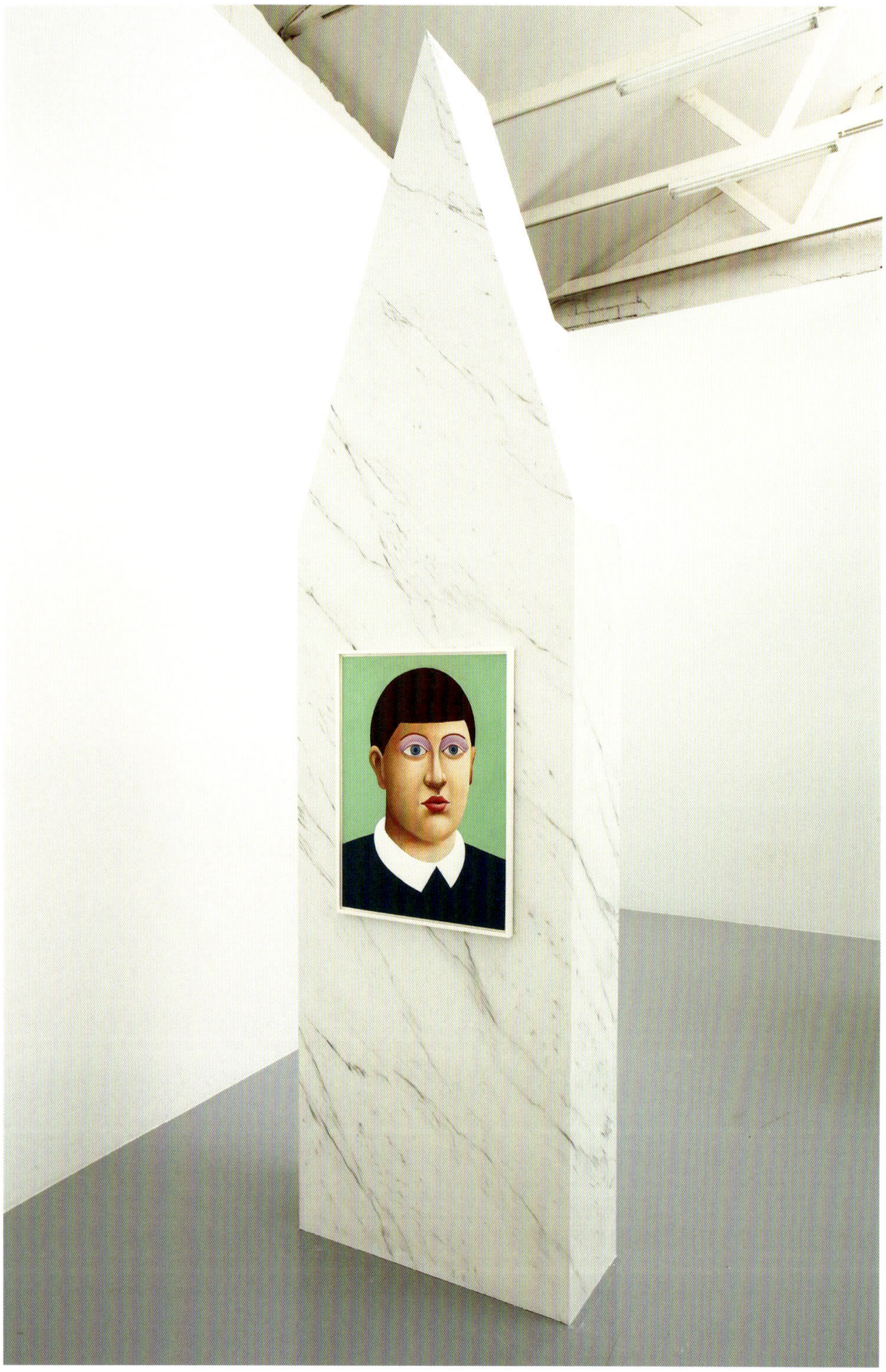

PORTRAIT, 2016
SOFT PASTEL ON PASTEL CARD
80 X 60 CM

MURAL: OIL ON WOOD

INSTALLATION VIEW AT CENTRE
D'ART NEUCHÂTEL, 2016

RED PORTRAIT, 2017
SOFT PASTEL ON PASTEL CARD
80 X 57 CM

INSTALLATION VIEW AT KARMA,
NEW YORK, 2017

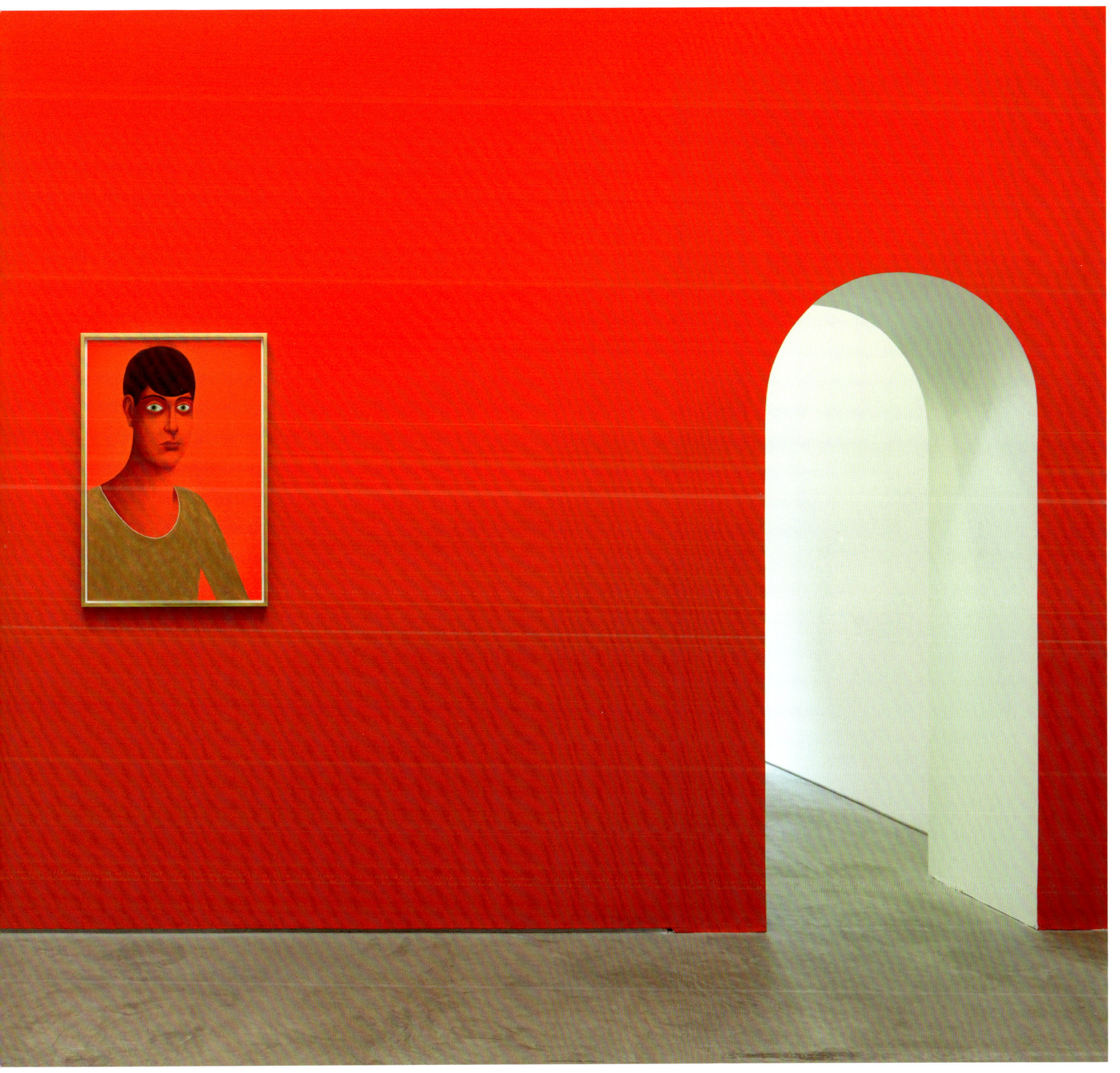

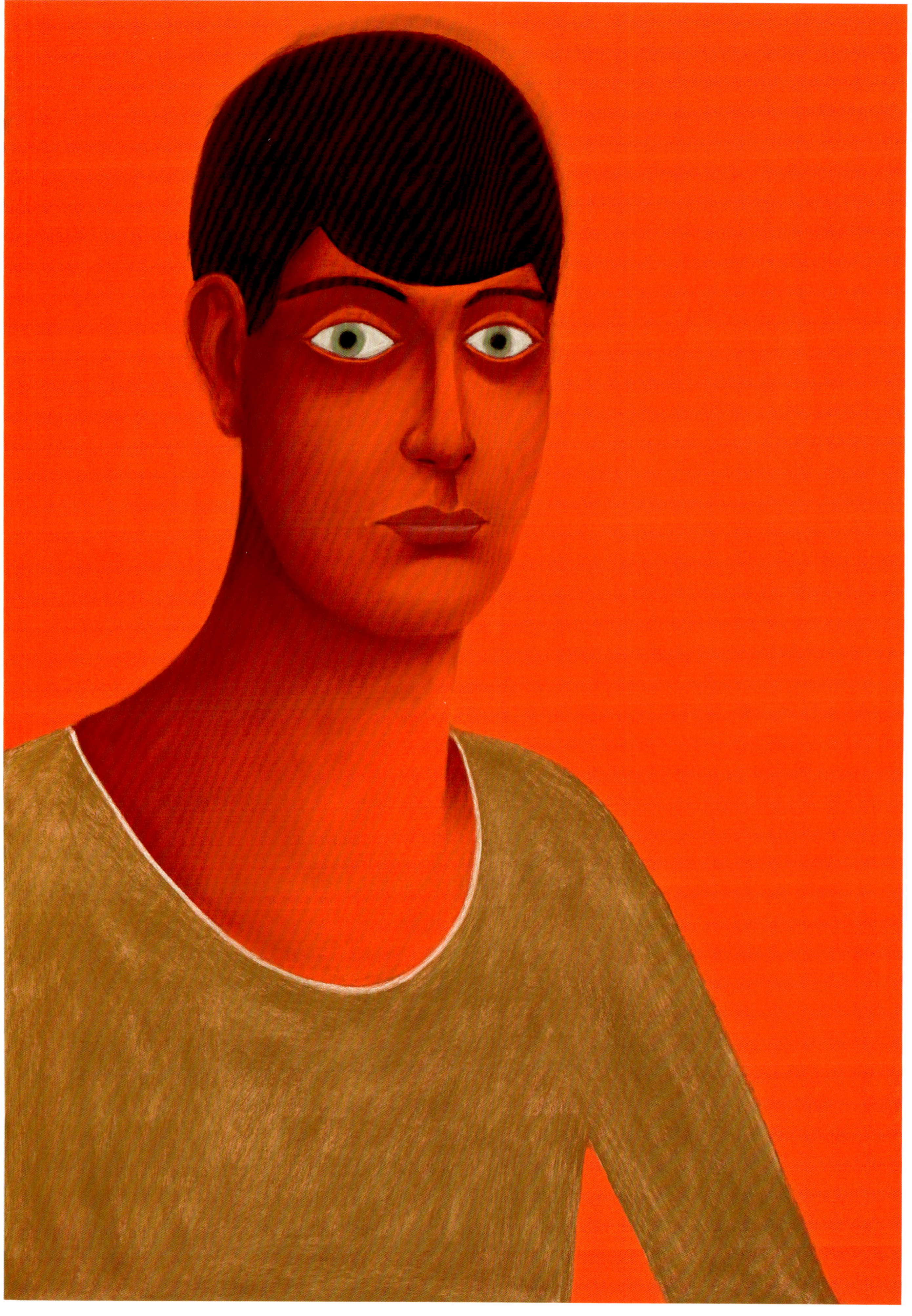

RED PORTRAIT, 2017
SOFT PASTEL ON PASTEL CARD
80 X 57 CM

BLUE PORTRAIT, 2017
SOFT PASTEL ON PASTEL CARD
82 X 62 CM

The artist creates these effects, all without any narrative. In the same exhibition, the picture *Tree Trunks* hung just to the right hints at a possible story, one that only manifests if we invent it ourselves. Thus, this blue room appears on the one hand strangely mysterious, while also being pervasively calm, neutrally charged, and steeped in tradition but lacking in history. The colouring is melancholic and gloomy, but the staging is utterly effortless. This gives rise to the indefinable tension, and the tradition-steeped lack of history finds expression in the paintings' direct historical references to artists such as Georgia O'Keeffe (*Dark Tree Trunks,* 1946) and Picasso (especially his 1901 blue portrait *Self-Portrait*). These are ingredients that occur in almost all of Nicolas Party's exhibitions and ultimately form the essence of his work.

Recently, Party has also enriched his portraits with various attributes taken from art history, such as Balthus' famous cat (see *Portrait with a Cat*, 2016, p. 45), depictions of flowers by Rachel Ruysch (*Portrait with Flowers*, 2018, p. 68) and butterflies from paintings by Otto Marseus van Schrieck (*Portrait with Langoustine*, 2019, p. 69). These quotations help to give the depictions greater individuality, while at the same time seeming more surreal and removed from reality. In the most

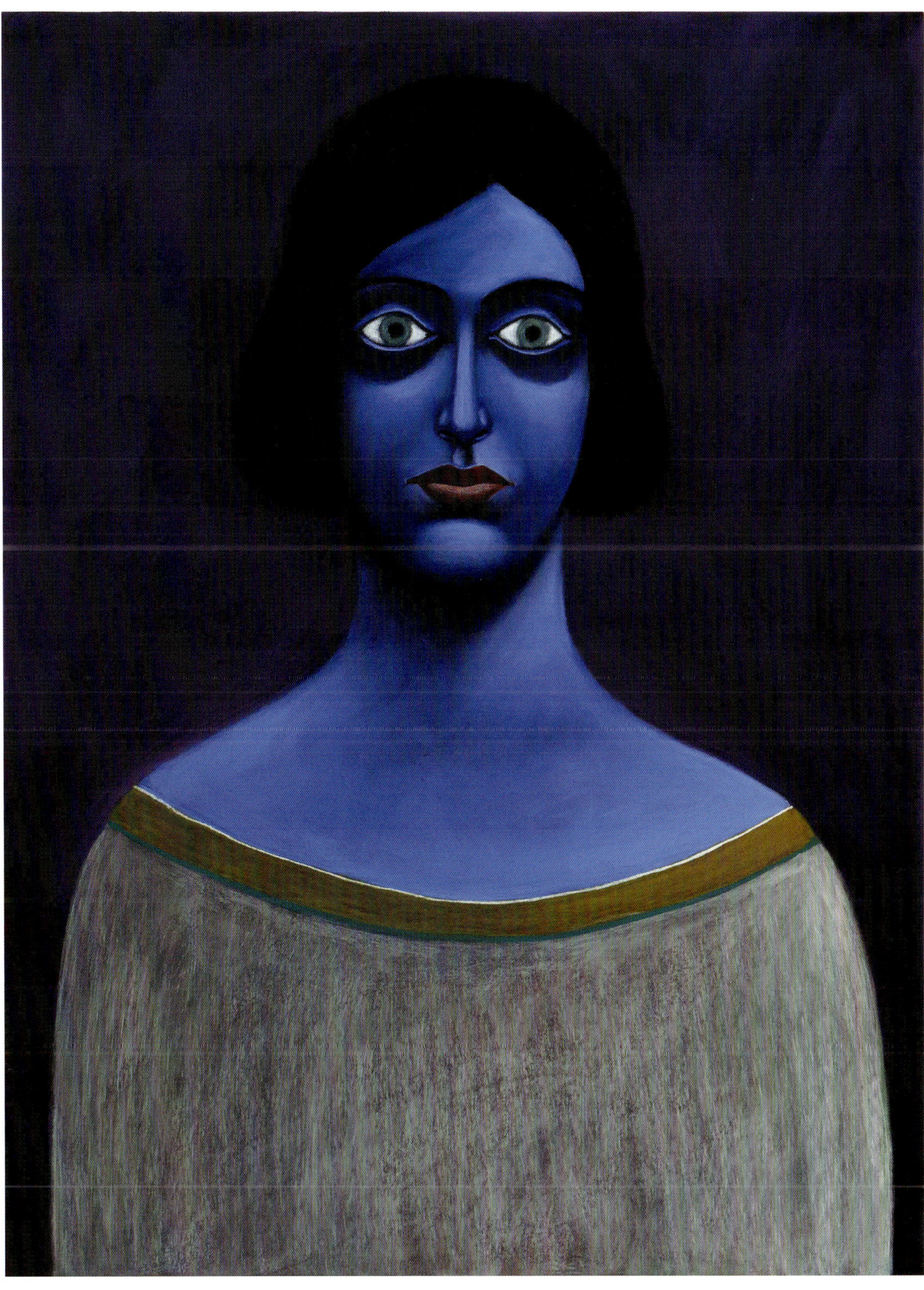

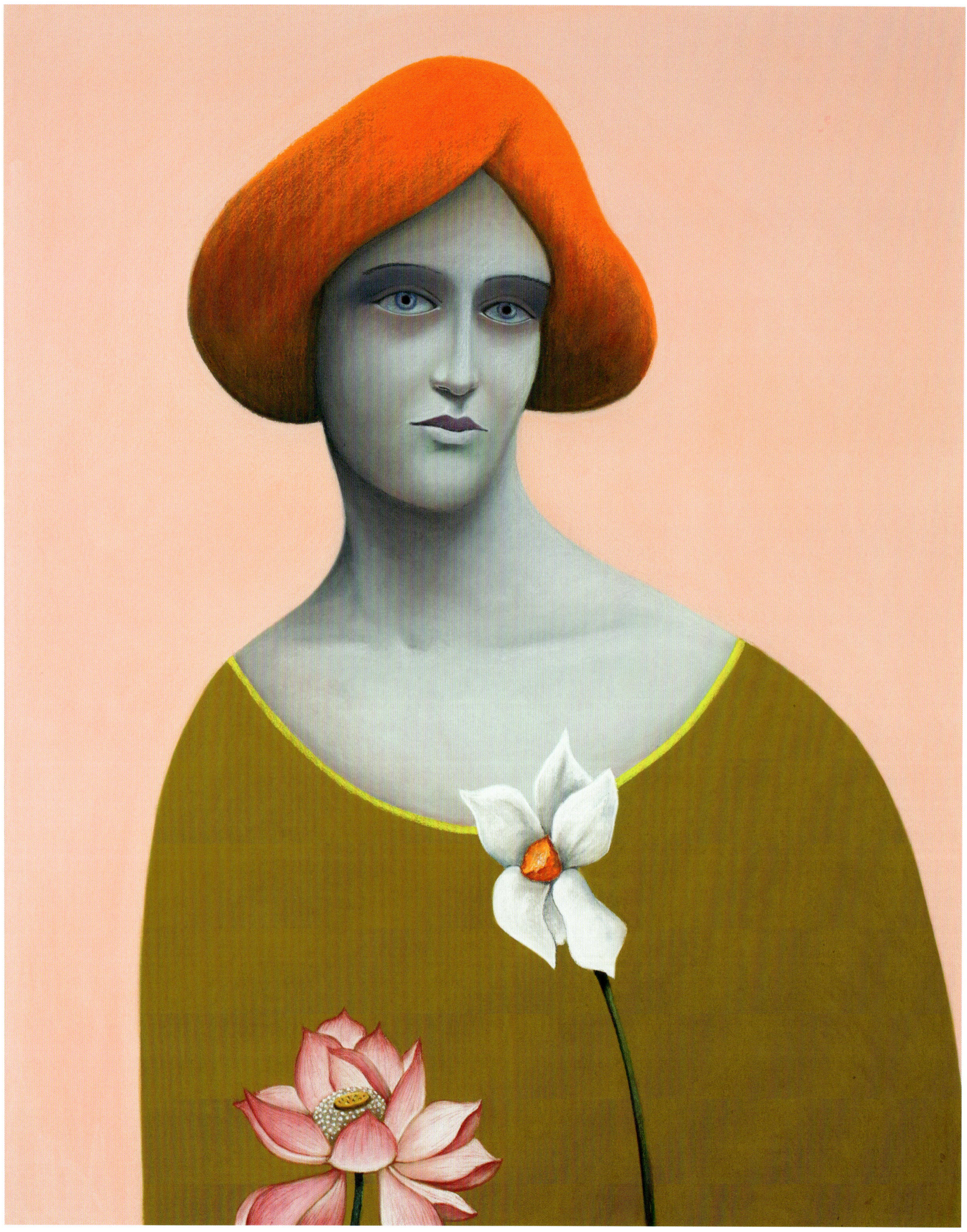

opposite,
PORTRAIT WITH FLOWERS,
2018
SOFT PASTEL ON LINEN,
156 X 125 CM

below,
PORTRAIT WITH LANGOUSTINE,
2019
SOFT PASTEL ON LINEN
170 X 90 CM

next pages, from left,
SUNSET, 2020
SOFT PASTEL ON LINEN
114 X 97 CM

PORTRAIT WITH SNAKES, 2019
SOFT PASTEL ON LINEN
150 X 127 CM

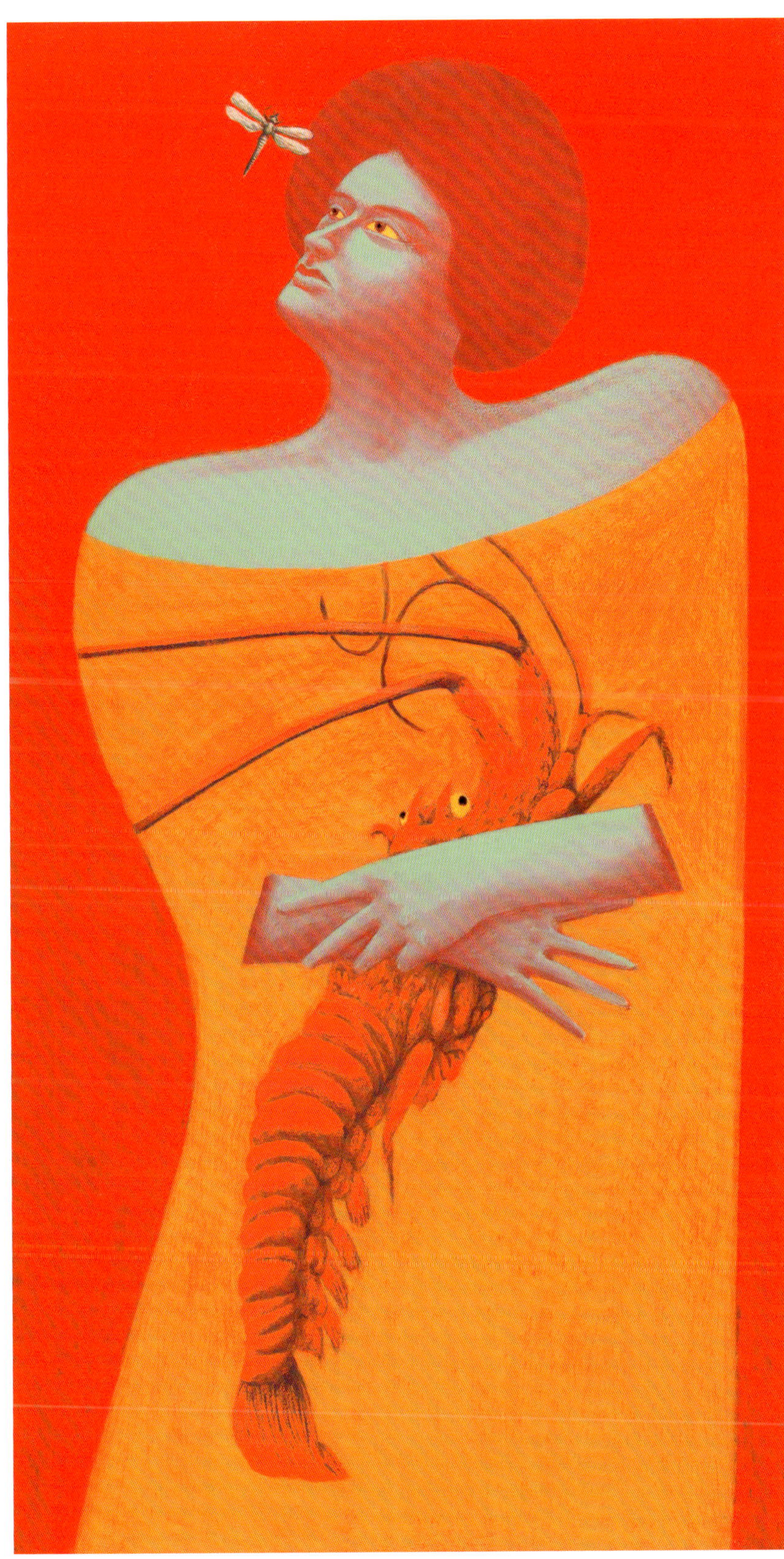

recent portraits, in particular, where, for example, items of clothing are no longer made of fabric but of reptiles (*Portrait with Snakes*, 2019, p. 71), the reference to immediate actuality seems at first glance to be even less distinct than in earlier paintings. But only at first glance. For if we think a little more about what is represented, we are suddenly thrown back into reality, into the here and now. A portrait wearing a frog dress, a snake dress or a reptile dress may indeed seem surreal. And it does indeed seem highly absurd to imagine a human being enjoying a stroll in public with two toads around her neck. In other words, Party's colourful, playful and joyful portraits evoke a curious form of reflection in us as well.

Sampling

Party's method in his portraits has a great affinity with the technique of sampling, a creative process, elemental in music since the 1940s, of extracting an excerpt from an already finished or published recording and integrating it into a new musical context. It is intriguing to see how Party uses this technique to bring together disparate subjects from differing periods of art history and contexts and turn them into harmonious art compositions of his own. This text will draw attention to quotations from art history, even though the artist uses sampling to pursue a strategy in which the classic forensic search for the original sources of his themes becomes superfluous. For he uses anything from art history that is useful to him. In recent years, he has adopted pictorial elements, extracts and subjects from famous, less famous or largely forgotten artists, including Félix Vallotton, Ferdinand Hodler, Hans Emmenegger, Henri Matisse, Picasso, Balthus, Joseph Stella, Milton Clark Avery, Georgia O'Keeffe, Lars Hertervig, Léon Spilliaert, Rosalba Carriera, Gustave Courbet, François Boucher, Jean-Honoré Fragonard and Otto Marseus van Schrieck.

Party is not quite an appropriation artist. He does not – like Elaine Sturtevant or Mike Bidlo, for example – take up specific works from art history in order to celebrate complete appropriation as an authentic artistic act. Instead, he juggles with quotations from different epochs of art history. They are as fundamental to his colourful and spatially expansive pictorial epics as modern life in Paris was for Manet or Mont Sainte-Victoire was for Cézanne. For Party, this creative working method is about as obvious and natural as the fitting and furnishing of our homes with items from different eras and contexts.

Têtes Humaines 2

This working method – and this unusually atmospheric concentration within his works and installations – he shares with, among others, Ugo Rondinone, another well-known Swiss artist. For example, when looking at

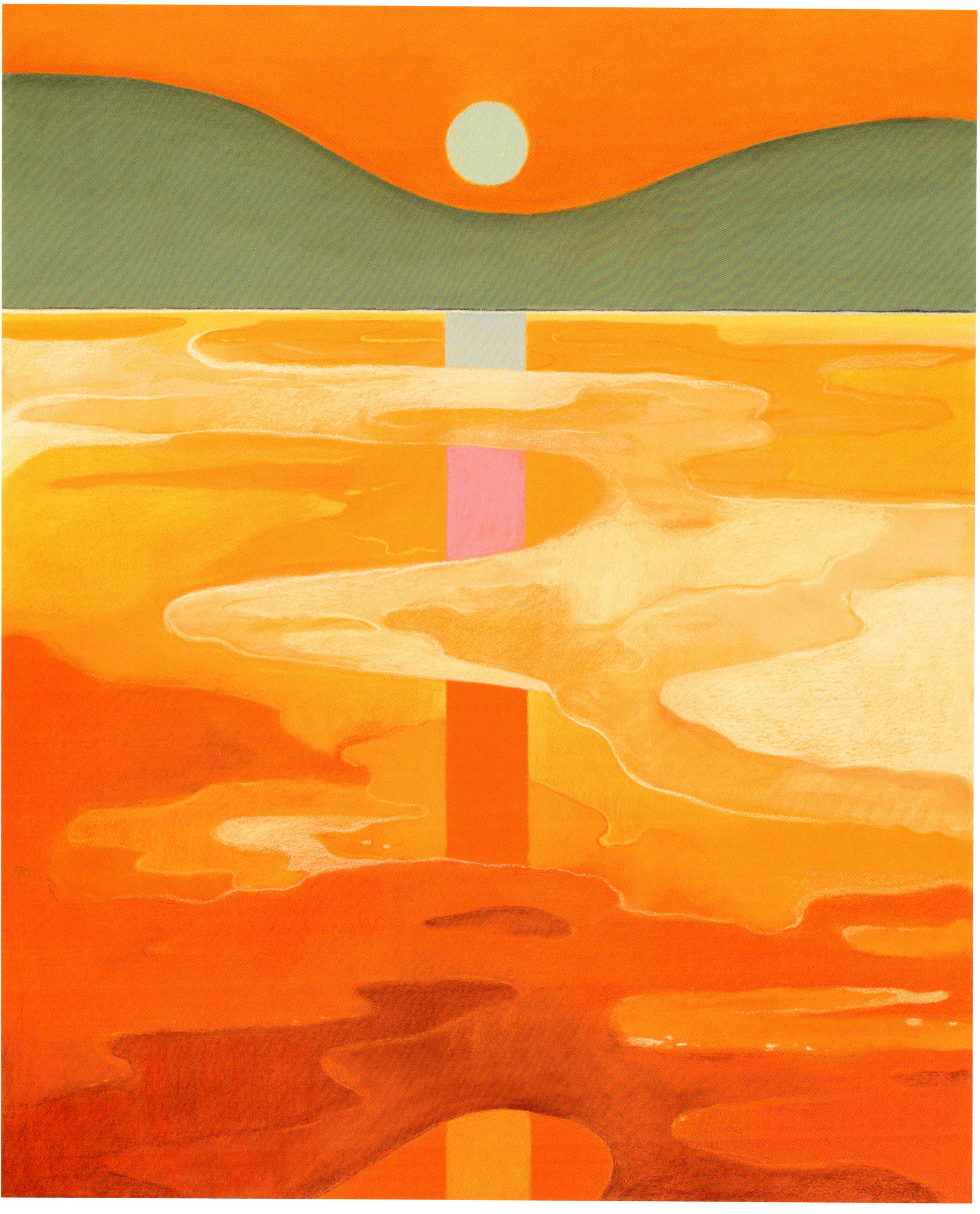

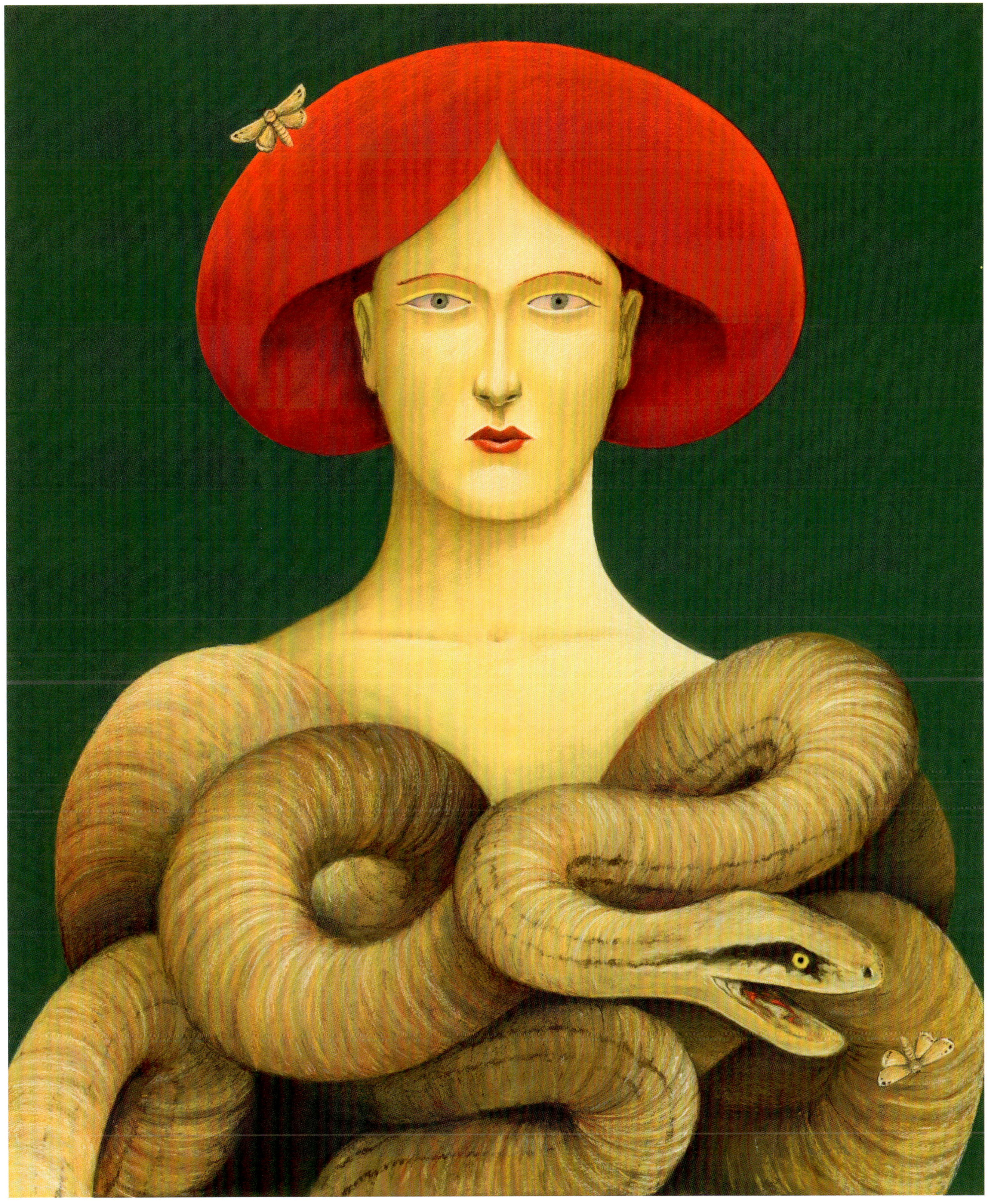

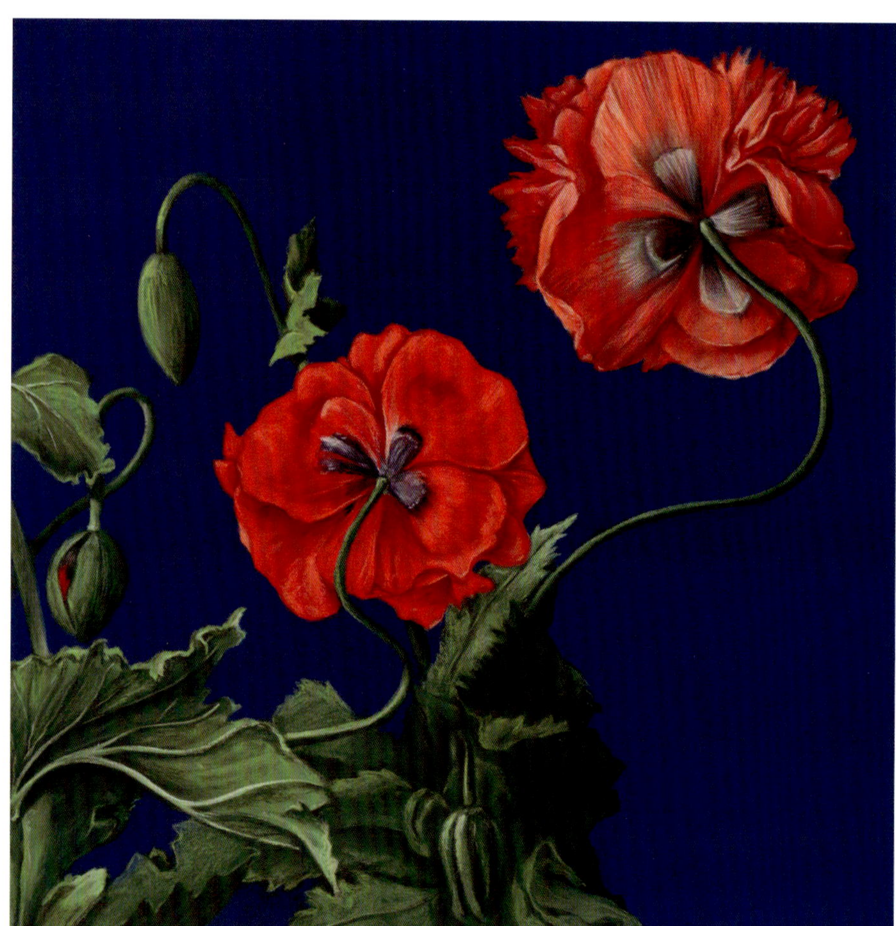

TWO POPPIES, 2019
SOFT PASTEL ON PASTEL CARD
60 X 60 CM

opposite,
HEAD, 2019
ACRYLIC AND OIL ON FIBERGLASS AND STYROFOAM
290 X 135 X 170 CM

INSTALLATION VIEW AT THE MARBLE HOUSE, NEWPORT, RHODE ISLAND, 2019

Party's oversized head sculptures (*Speakers*, 2017, pp. 74–5), we immediately sense an aesthetic and spiritual affinity with Rondinone's large-format sculptures *Sunrise Masks, Moonrise Masks* (2005) and *Nuns + Monks* (2020). In these typically Rondinonean work titles, however, there is also a remarkable difference from Party's artistic approach. While Rondinone's titles help to intensify the melancholy, nostalgia or romanticism of his works, Party always remains prosaic, with such titles as *Speakers* or *Heads*, so as not to burden his works and installations with advance interpretations. Although the artist claims the *Speakers* refer to female pioneers of the City of Oxford (where they were shown), the title does not indicate this. Further, it seems to contradict the sculptures' expression, because all the heads, rather than actually speaking, simply sit silently, with a solemn mien.

Party also plays with the dimensions of these heads, thus additionally distancing them from reality and allowing them to be perceived even more distinctly as autonomous sculptural entities. At Galerie Gregor Staiger in Zurich in 2018, for example, he exhibited eight heads, only five of which were similar in size to a human head, while another was much smaller and two others relatively tiny (see the installation views on pp. 42 and 77). What makes this staging especially distinctive, however, is that he did not just place the individual heads on pedestals, which were painted with different mock marble and wood patterns, but that each of these pedestals was out of proportion – both in height and width – to the sculpted head, although together they formed a unit.

In the same year, the artist exhibited a comparable installation at the M WOODS museum in Beijing, but this time only with a single head in human life-size, all the others being larger than life. Finally, in 2018 he placed one of these hand-painted, CNC-cut sculptures in the gardens of the Modern Institute in Glasgow (Aird's Lane Green Space) and another in the palatial Marble House in Newport, Rhode Island, whose entire furnishings are museum pieces that Party could not be alter, displace or remove. And so he placed one of his *Speakers* in the salon behind an imposing, grand piano (pp. 72 and 73). This is a particularly remarkable decision in that it once again beautifully highlights the playful and mischievous nature of Party's art: the head peeps out coyly from behind the instrument, just as a child would do when playing hide and seek, believing that it is well hidden but in fact visible to everyone.

Because of their typology Party's head sculptures have been compared to mannequins from the worlds of fashion or cosmetology. These figures are usually depicted as stereotypically as possible, in order to better highlight the individuality or diversity of the garments or products presented upon them. Party's heads, however, are extrapolated from his portrait paintings, a fact underscored by their rich and varied colouration. Dealing with current visual phenomena is the artist's

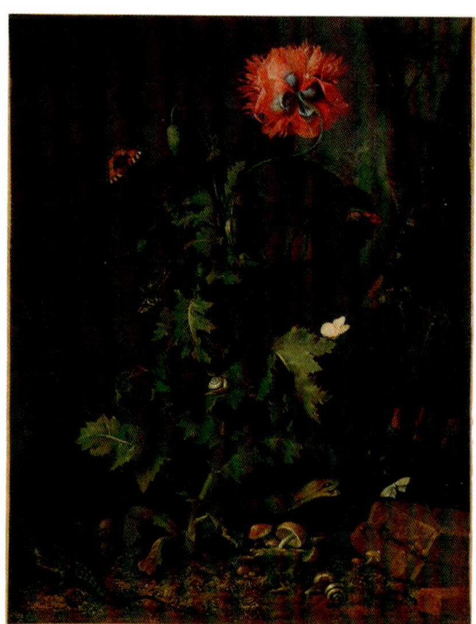

OTTO MARSEUS VAN SCHRIECK
STILL LIFE WITH POPPY, INSECTS, AND REPTILES, C. 1670
OIL ON CANVAS
68 X 52 CM

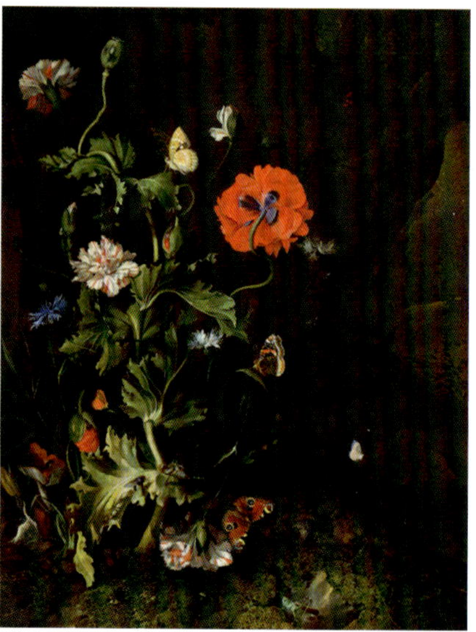

RACHEL RUYSCH
STILL LIFE OF A THISTLE BETWEEN CARNATIONS AND CORNFLOWERS ON A MOSSY FOREST FLOOR, WITH BUTTERFLIES AND A CRICKET, 1683
OIL ON CANVAS
65 X 51 CM

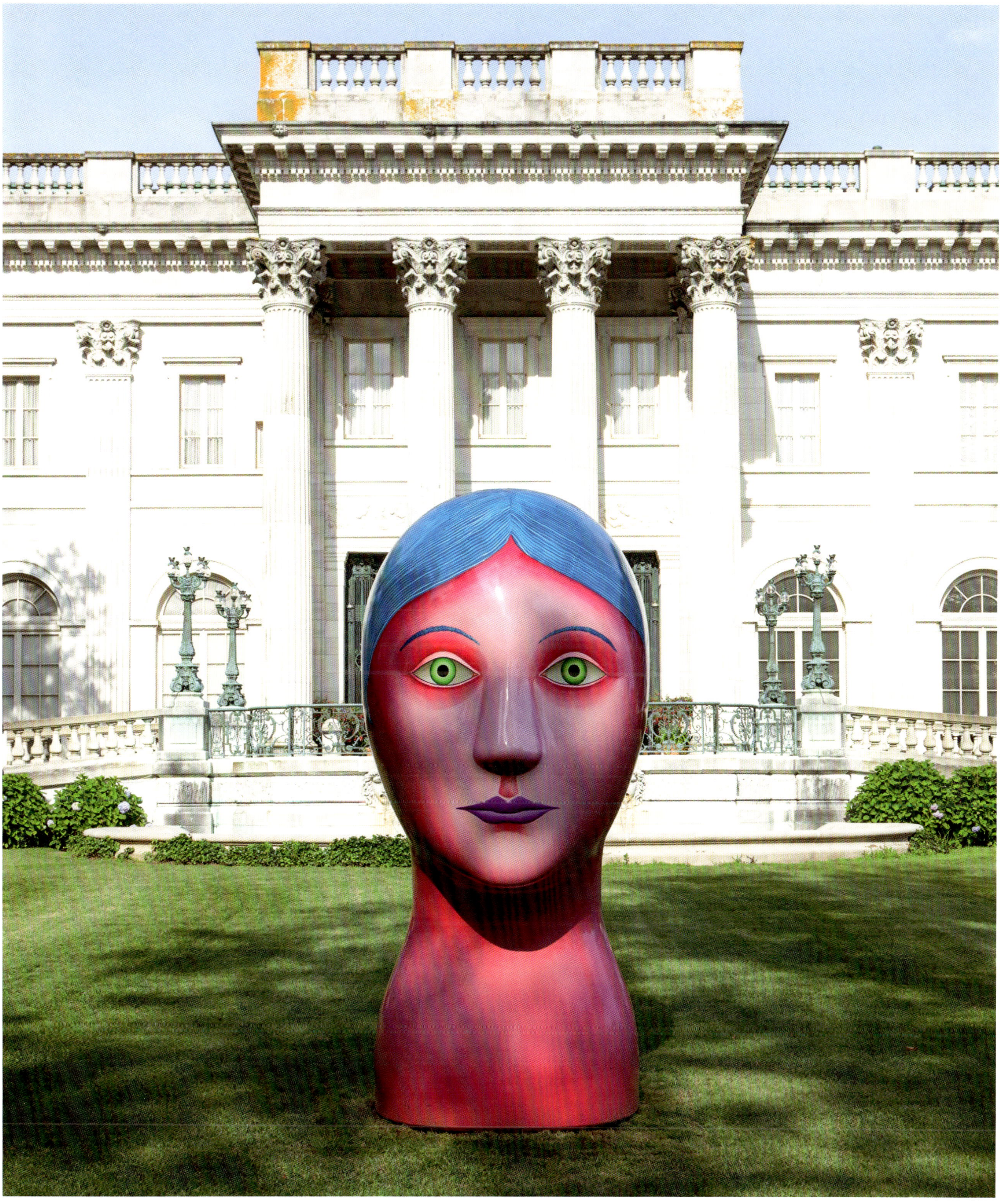

from left,
SPEAKER, 2017
WOOD, METAL MESH FRAME, GYPSUM, PLASTER, ACRYLIC AND OIL PAINT
140 X 140 X 200 CM

SPEAKER, 2017
WOOD, METAL MESH FRAME, GYPSUM, PLASTER, ACRYLIC AND OIL PAINT
140 X 140 X 200 CM

SPEAKER, 2017
WOOD, METAL MESH FRAME, GYPSUM PLASTER, ACRYLIC AND OIL PAINT
140 X 140 X 200 CM

SPEAKER, 2017
WOOD, METAL MESH FRAME, GYPSUM PLASTER, ACRYLIC AND OIL PAINT
140 X 140 X 200 CM

INSTALLATION VIEW AT MODERN ART OXFORD, 2018

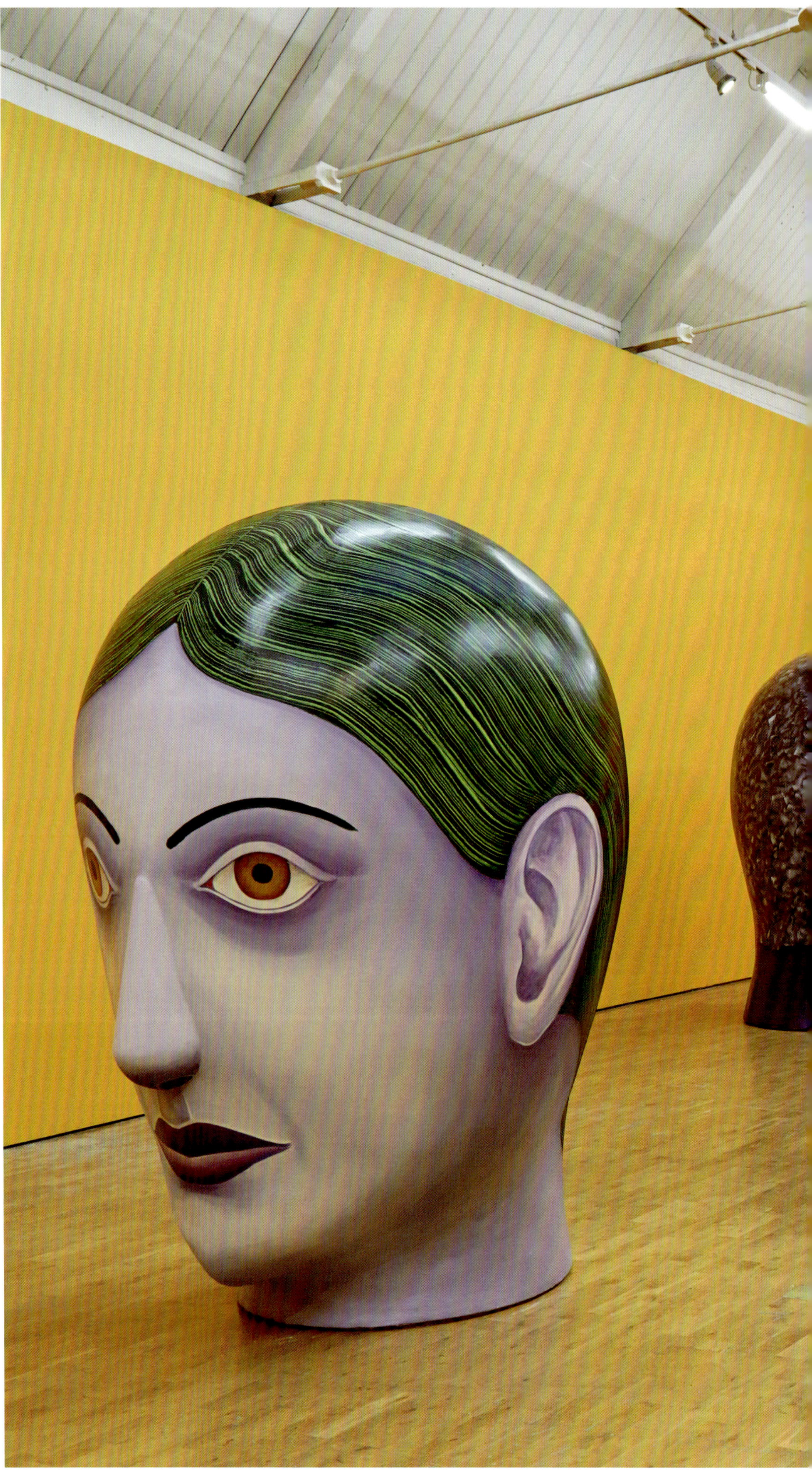

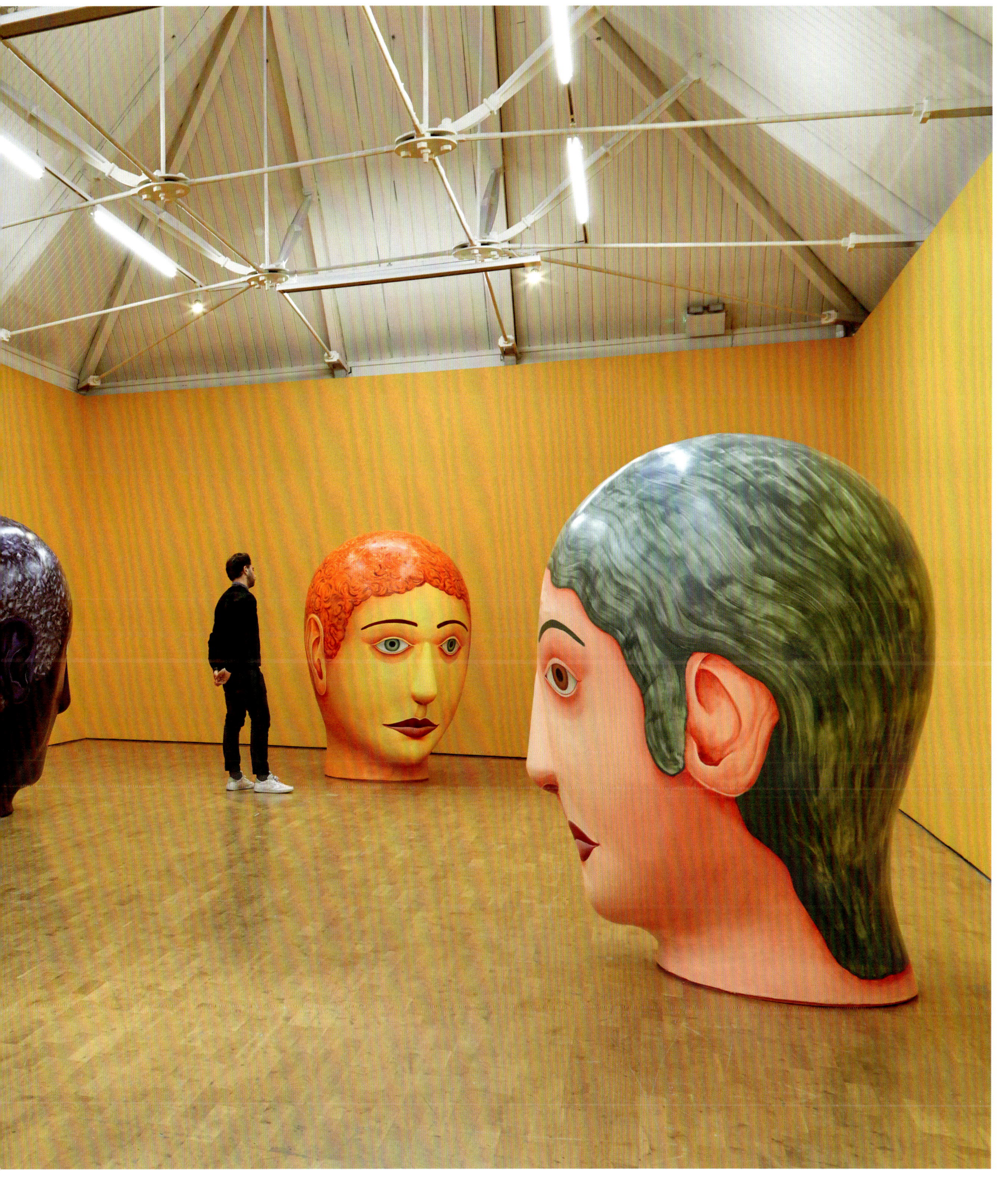

primary concern, and could there be anything more relevant today than the serene co-existence of heads of different shades? So here, too, our reflections have brought us to the big issues of our time.

Beginnings

Communality, the collaborative, has been essential to Party's practice since his beginnings as an artist. Even as a student he worked with other artists. In 2006, during his studies at the École Cantonale d'Art de Lausanne (ECAL), he co-founded the artist group Blakam with two fellow Swiss artists, Charlotte Herzig and Stéphane Devidal. As well as pursuing their own artistic work, Blakam was a curatorial group whose work mainly involved the programming, organisation, communication and design of the events at Kunstraum Bellevaux. When the group, for example, designed stage sets for concerts (see p. 78), the aesthetic approach was always devised in collaboration with the invited musicians, because the event was intended to be a performance, exhibition and concert in one. Finally, the artistic work of each individual dwelt ultimately and especially on the question of how, when and in what way painting could manifest itself as a picture as well as an object in space.

One could say that what made Blakam unique was that it was able to light-heartedly and nonchalantly launch work that defied categorization. It did not matter if the work created was called art, decoration, illustration or installation. And it was precisely from this attitude that the group ultimately developed its artistic credo: everything is painting, from eye-catching floor coverings to ceilings, holiday baubles, lamps and furniture. Their art was the colourful all-over, and resisred being stuffed into a crude drainpipe of definition.[2] And in this sense, the three artists made use of anything that seemed of interest to them for the realisation of their pictorial ideas – from references to the Renaissance to classical modernism, or from the emotionally charged sunsets of a Félix Vallotton to the ironic performances of the Lausanne Dada poet Arthur Cravan (1887–1918), nephew of Oscar Wilde.[3]

When Party graduated from the ECAL in 2008, he left Lausanne for Glasgow to complete the MFA programme at the Glasgow School of Art, BLAKAM's diverse activities became a thing of the past. In Glasgow, however, he soon embarked on a new project, which he called 'Sweet Geranium'. And this too existed for as long as his studies lasted. 'Sweet Geranium' was a series of exhibitions curated by the artist in his studio. Here, he transcended the defined framework of a classical curator by creating his own environments for the exhibitions and at the same time designing his own pedestal or frame for each exhibited work by the artists he invited (p. 81). Under 'Sweet Geranium', Party organised a total of six exhibitions from 2008 to 2010. At the Woodmill Studios in London, he staged a seventh, entitled 'Elephants' at the Woodmill from 12 to 27 February

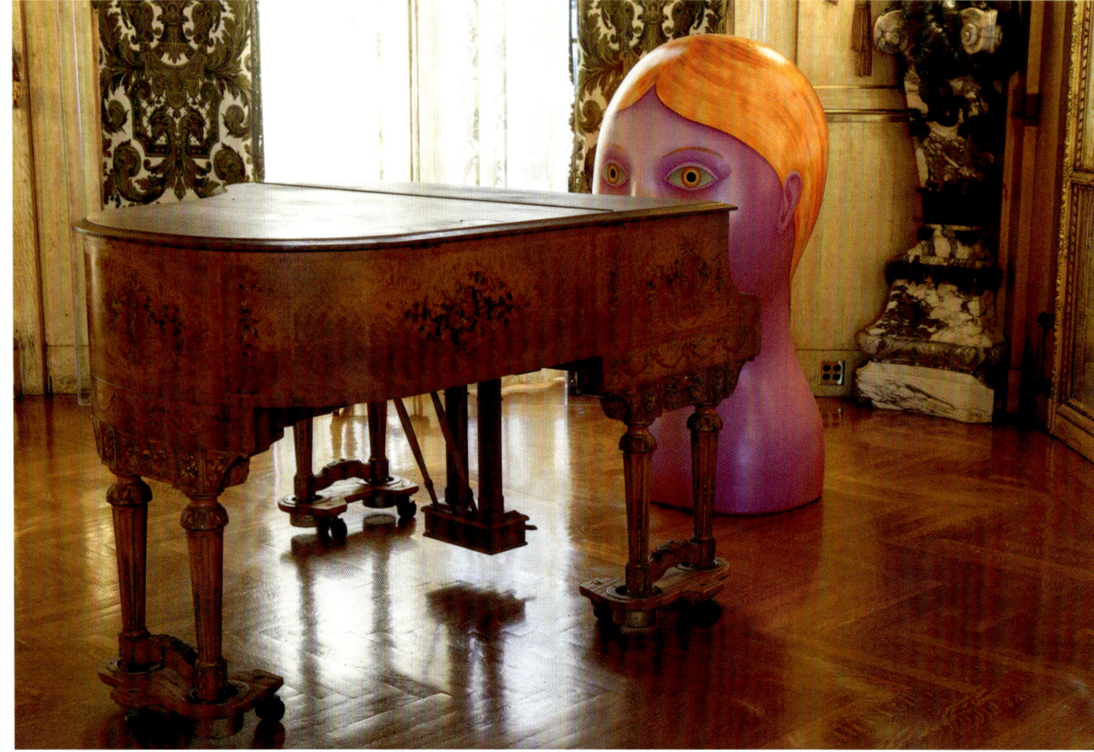

HEAD, 2019
ACRYLIC AND OIL ON FIBERGLASS AND STYROFOAM
150 X 60 X 80 CM

INSTALLATION VIEW AT MARBLE HOUSE, NEWPORT, 2019

HEAD, 2018
OIL ON COATED POLYSTERENE
100 X 64 X 50 CM

PAINTED OIL PLINTH
180 X 50 X 50 CM

INSTALLATION VIEW AT
M WOODS, BEIJING, 2018

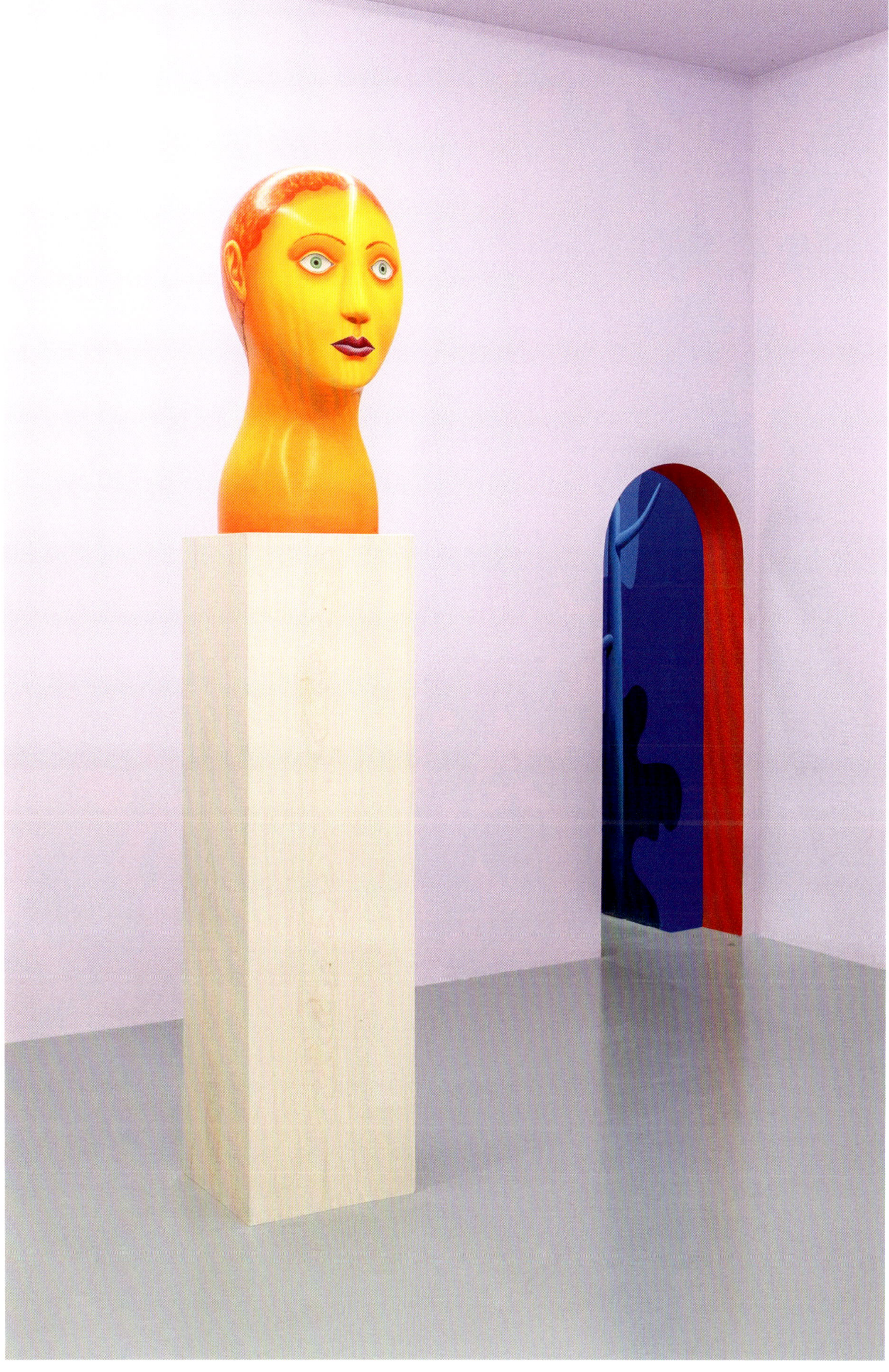

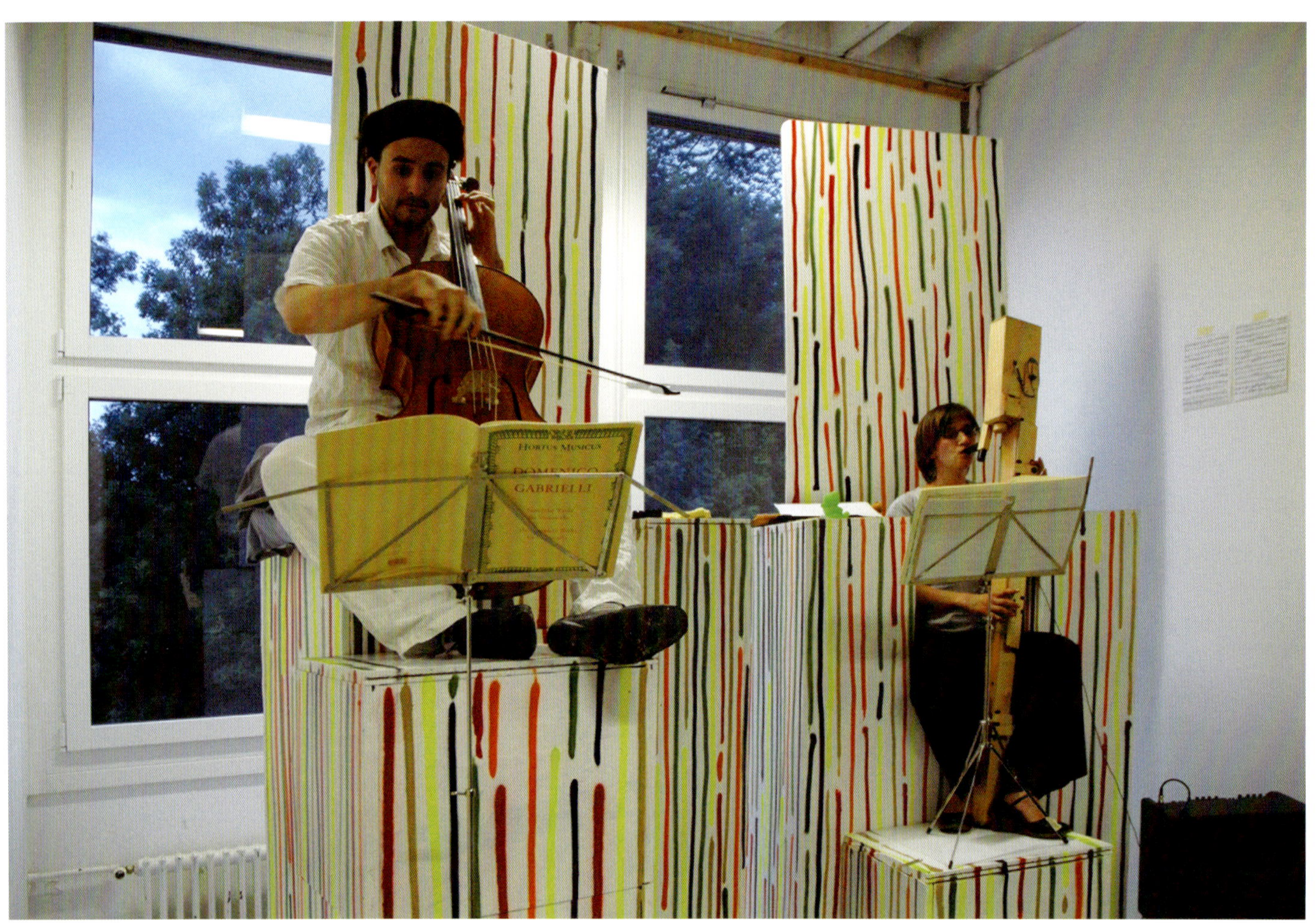

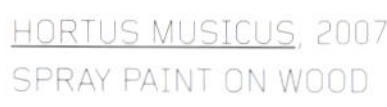

HORTUS MUSICUS, 2007
SPRAY PAINT ON WOOD

INSTALLATION VIEW AT ESPACE BELLEVAUX, LAUSANNE, LAUSANNE, 2007

2011, where painted cubes with elephants appeared for the first time. The cubes did not serve as stools for invited guests, but rather as pedestals showcasing the works of participating artists at the Woodmill Studios.

As part of his 'Sweet Geranium' project, Party produced an artist's book. *Staub: A Journal of Entropy* was produced in 2010 in collaboration with the artists Joanne Tatham and Tom O'Sullivan. John Calcutt, the then Acting Head of Programme at the MFA, Glasgow School of Art, writes:

The result is as awkward and gauche as the objects in his paintings, too unwieldy to hang on a wall, sit in a bookcase, or nestle comfortably in the hands. In each instance of the publication project, Party invites artists who work with text to submit a piece of writing that he will then respond to by manually transcribing and ornamenting it with imagery and assorted graphic marks (abstract and decorative) that serve to highlight the pictorial aspects of writing and the linguistic aspects of imagery.[4]

Interaction with Art History

With the natural culmination of 'Sweet Geranium', Party began to modify his concept of 'collaboration' again. The following period inaugurated an imaginary dialogue between him and art history. In other words, for a time he paused inviting artists to provide him with a work of art to which he responded artistically in kind, by conceiving of his own environment for it. Instead, he selected works from art history for his solo exhibitions and room installations or else found them directly in the collections of those institutions that invited him to stage solo exhibitions.

He realised one of the first projects of this kind in 2014 with Landscape at Kunsthall Stavanger (formerly Stavanger Kunstforening) in Norway (pp. 79 and 80). For this exhibition, occupying a total of five exhibition rooms in the museum Party created a distinctive environment by painting vertical lines of different colours onto the walls themselves, which are reminiscent, in its essentialism of minimalism and gesture, of Daniel Buren's stripes. Interspersed with these coloured 'ornaments,' Party painted selected pictorial elements in black and white from works by the Romantic artist Lars Hertervig (1830–1902), himself from Stavanger and well known in Norway despite having spent most of his life in seclusion. The largest collection of Hertevig paintings had once been hosted by the Kunstalle and then, during a restructuring, was given over to the larger Stavanger Art Museum. Landscape, in this sense, pays homage both to the painter Hertervig and to the history of the collection of the Kunsthall Stavanger by creating a phantom

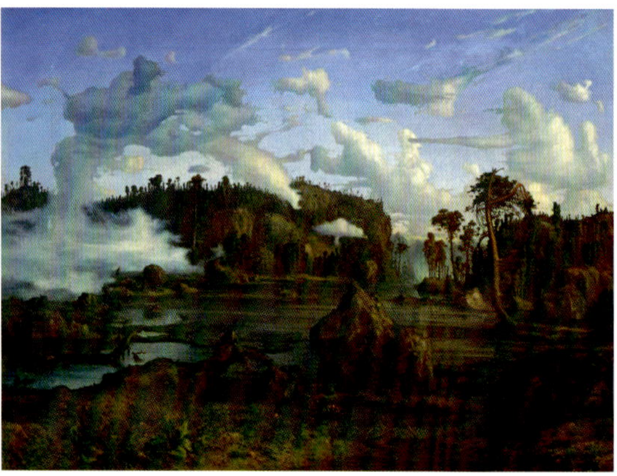

LARS HERTERVIG
THE TARN, 1865
OIL ON CANVAS
47 X 63 CM

from left,
LANDSCAPE, 2014
SPRAY PAINT AND CHARCOAL ON WALL

INSTALLATION VIEW AT KUNSTHALL STAVANGER, NORWAY, 2014

presence of the paintings which had once been located in the same space of Party's exhibition.

In this exhibition, Party combined two disparate elements from different periods of art history and unified them by replicating everything by hand. The manner of painting draws upon graffiti art, which is where he has his origins. Before beginning formal studies at the ECAL in Lausanne, Party lived the life of a nimble graffiti artist who left his sprayed images scattered around the city of Lausanne, on trains, bridges, and tunnels. Because of the risk of being caught in the act at any time, he learned to produce his graffiti pictures on the spot as quickly as possible. Given the constraints of time for the installation, 'Landscape' also seems to have been executed at speed and in a carefree manner. The exhibition has something impromptu and spontaneous about it, which is underlined by the media he used to produce the wall paintings. Applying charcoal straight to the walls, he succeeded in creating a memorable, multi-room mural painting in a short space of time.

But this spatial painting, this environment, was not only intended to stand for itself, but also to be a place for social interaction and participation. The artist organised a dinner – similar to *Dinner for 24 Elephants* in Glasgow – which he served on plates that he himself had painted and whose menu he devised in collaboration with a local chef. Various events also took place during the exhibition: a concert, a scenic performance and several workshops for children.

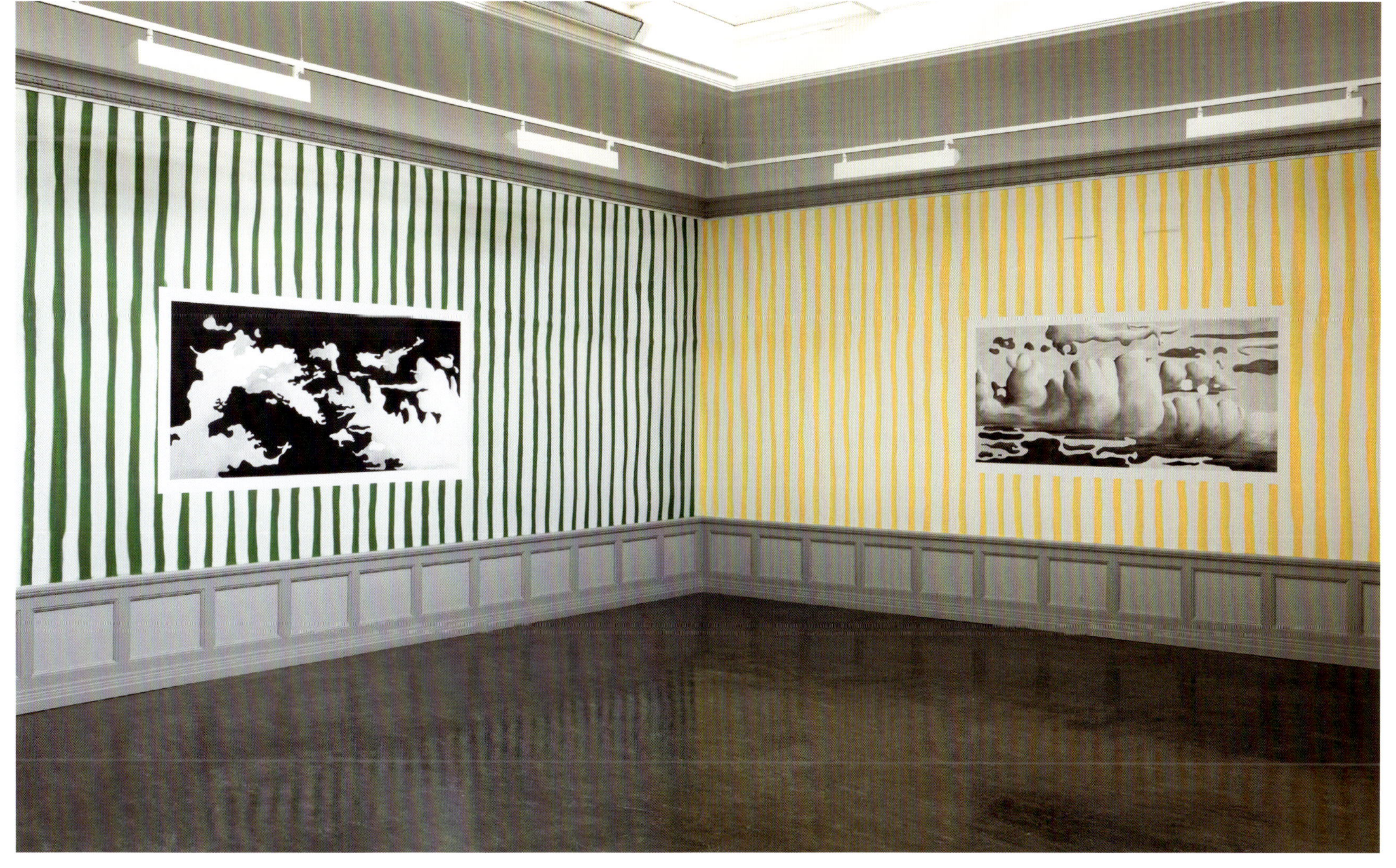

In 'Landscape', one also had the feeling that he was following two unusual artistic creeds that we associate with a largely forgotten painter, Louis Michel Eilshemius (1864–1941), who was Duchamp's favourite artist and whom Party has cited as an influence.[5] In roughly 1909, Eilshemius developed:

his own, highly unusual stylistic strategy that essentially embodied two prime elements: firstly, he tried to paint as many pictures as possible in a given period of time without subsequently correcting them. He refused to revise any of his works. He wanted his pictures to be as unpremeditated and authentic as possible. At the same time, he started to display his pictures in richly ornamented, painted frames in order to strengthen the focus on the depicted and elevate it to a different level of reality.[6]

Eilshemius's framings are astonishing pictorial inventions 'and have an exceptionally mysterious painterly quality'.[7] His painting is 'light, poetic, inspired, subtle, romantic, spontaneous, timeless and respectful towards the depicted subjects. It is, as it were, enraptured, wondrous and topical, and it is produced amid an ascendant avant-garde that ignores it. Eilshemius' pictures render visible the longing for authentic feeling, for the transfiguration of the commonplace, and for the charm of integrity'.[8] Party's work shares these very same qualities, especially in his wall paintings of the 'Landscape' exhibition, where he combines this spontaneous and rapid execution, without correcting anything, with the idea of the painted framing.

Magritte Parti

While in 'Landscape' the focus was still on the efficient execution of wall paintings, which gave the exhibition a somewhat provisional and fragmented air, the artist pursued a reverse strategy in his exhibitions thereafter. In the exhibition 'Magritte Parti', which was held at the Musée Magritte Museum in Brussels from 23 May to 18 November 2018, Party visualised a completely different treatment of art history. The project was only possible because several of Magritte's works had been sent to the USA to be shown in the exhibition 'René Magritte: The

LANDSCAPE, 2014
SPRAY PAINT AND CHARCOAL ON WALL

INSTALLATION VIEW AT KUNSTHALL STAVANGER, NORWAY, 2014

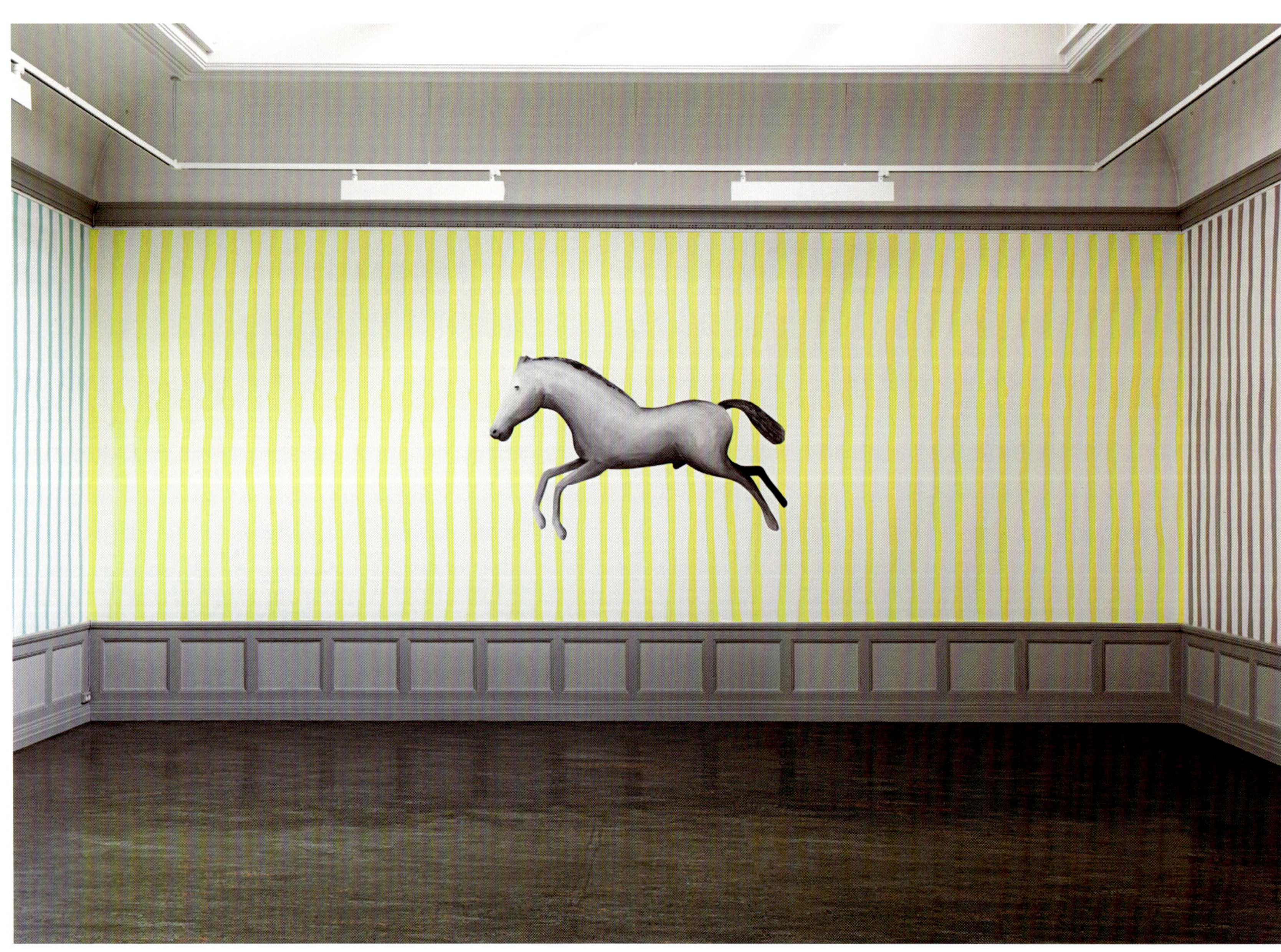

CLAIRE GREENSHAW
UNTITLED, 2008
PAINTED PAPIER-MÂCHÉ AND
OIL PAINTINGS

MURAL PAINTING (ACRYLIC
ON WALL) AND FRAMES
BY NICOLAS PARTY

INSTALLATION VIEW AT
SWEET GERANIUM STUDIO,
GLASGOW, 2008

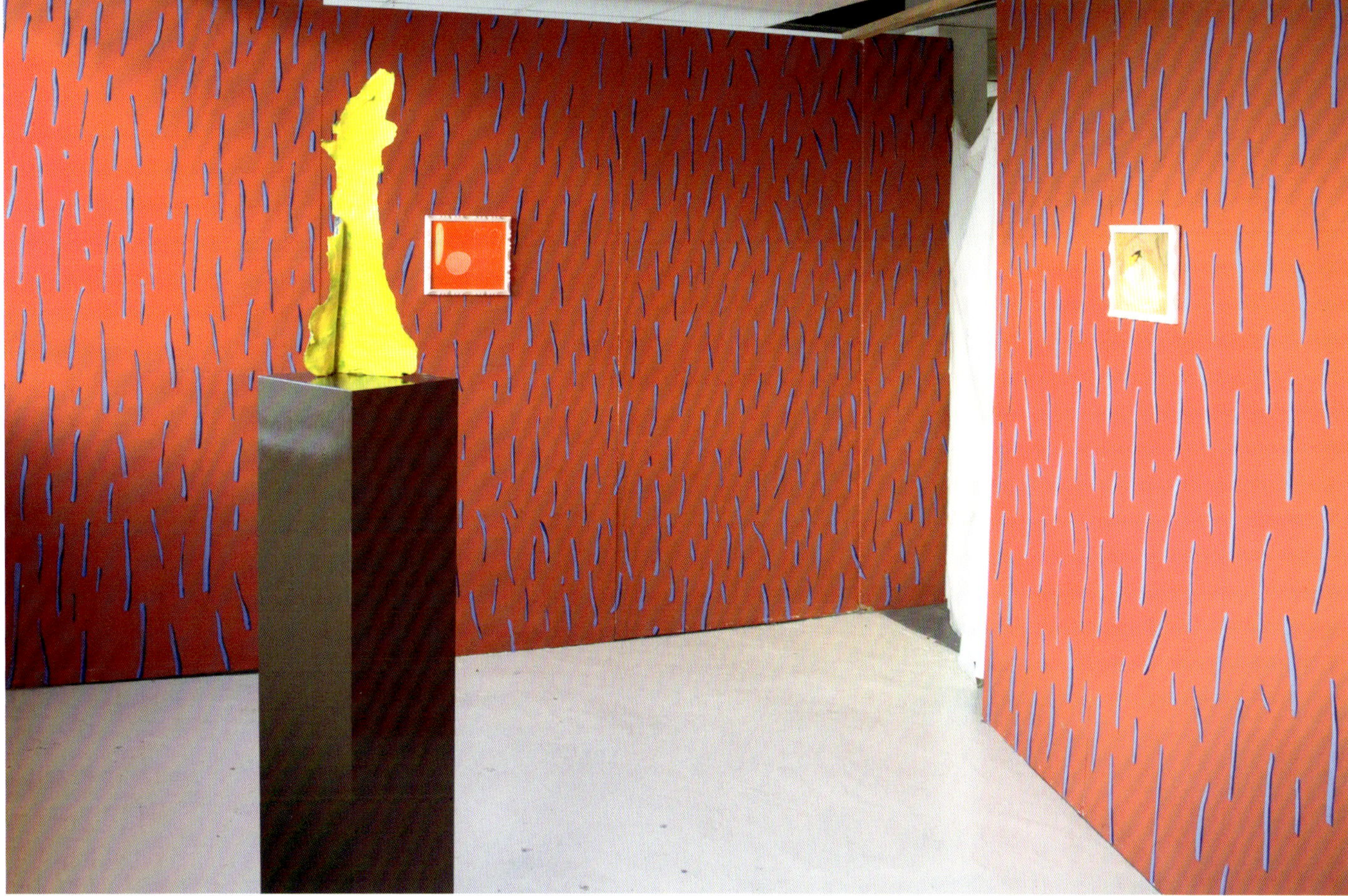

Fifth Season' at the prestigious San Francisco Museum of Modern Art (SFMoMA).[9] During this period, Party was invited to stage an exhibition in dialogue with the other works of the great Surrealist. This was a brilliant move on the part of those responsible, since Party's carefree, colourful pastels and wall paintings bear a direct affinity with the sophistic mischief of Magritte's paintings. Both feed off a meta-world that is at once sensitive, electrifying and ironic. Also fundamental to both artists is a remarkable feeling for the mysterious, their revival of the miraculous, and their efforts to enchant a utilitarian world. The very title of the exhibition ambiguously suggests Party's new approach. On the one hand, it literally says that Magritte has 'left' (*parti* in French), while also implying the artistic dialogue 'Magritte – Party' as a possibility of creative incongruity.

The exhibition kicked off with a large mural (p. 82) in which the artist visualised the Surrealist world of Magritte without quoting him directly. Instead, he applied the latter's visual language and approach to the depiction of materiality to his own composition, presenting trees, bushes and branches in imitation marble, making them look like petrified sculptures. The dark background was more reminiscent of a scratched, black wall than of a night sky, and the yellow, grainy moon could just as well have been a dull sun. A pastel picture of a man against a bright red background with an owl perched on his head was superimposed, adding an unsettling effect. This portrait possesses a certain ambivalence in the context of the exhibition. It could connote both Party himself, but also – when we consider the extremely smart clothing – Magritte. To cut a long story short: the wall painting is an electrifying interweaving of Magritte's and Party's ingenious visual worlds. The artist thus presented viewers with an abundant scope for interpretation, in terms not only of the metaphorical content of the individual pictorial elements, but also of the superimposition of subjects and the divergence of materiality from reality, a phenomenon familiar from many of Magritte's paintings.

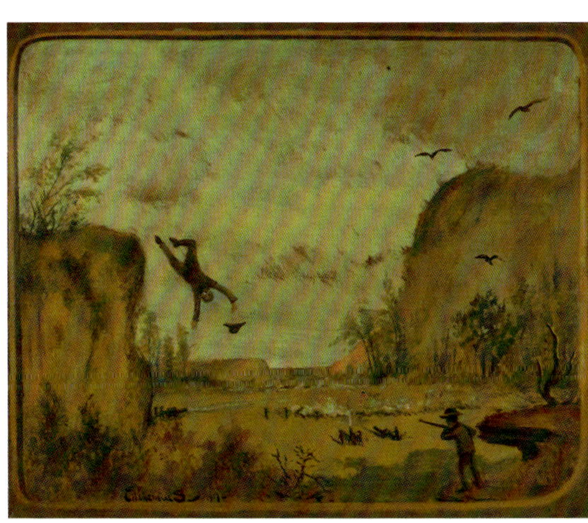

LOUIS MICHEL EILSHEMIUS
WAR, 1917
OIL ON BOARD
79 X 100 CM

The exhibition itself consisted of numerous juxtapositions in dialogue. In a first comparison (p. 83), Party responded to Magritte's painting *La Réponse imprévu* (1933). He juxtaposed the amorphous opening in the door with a dark void, also reminiscent of a human silhouette, with a similarly shaped painted fruit still-life sculpture, whose grey pears, apples and bananas look as if they have seen better days. The painting is set within a mount that imitates white Carrara marble. The subject and its framing are thus in balance, and the formal congruence with *La Réponse imprévu* culminates, in terms of content, in pure paradox. In another dialogue we see Magritte's painting *Découverte* (1927) juxtaposed with a mysterious portrait depiction. Party's picture shows a figure dressed in dark clothes with three black cats that resemble Dobermans in their size and bearing. Magritte's lady in *Découverte* is naked and covered with blotchy tattoos extending from face to thigh. They recall

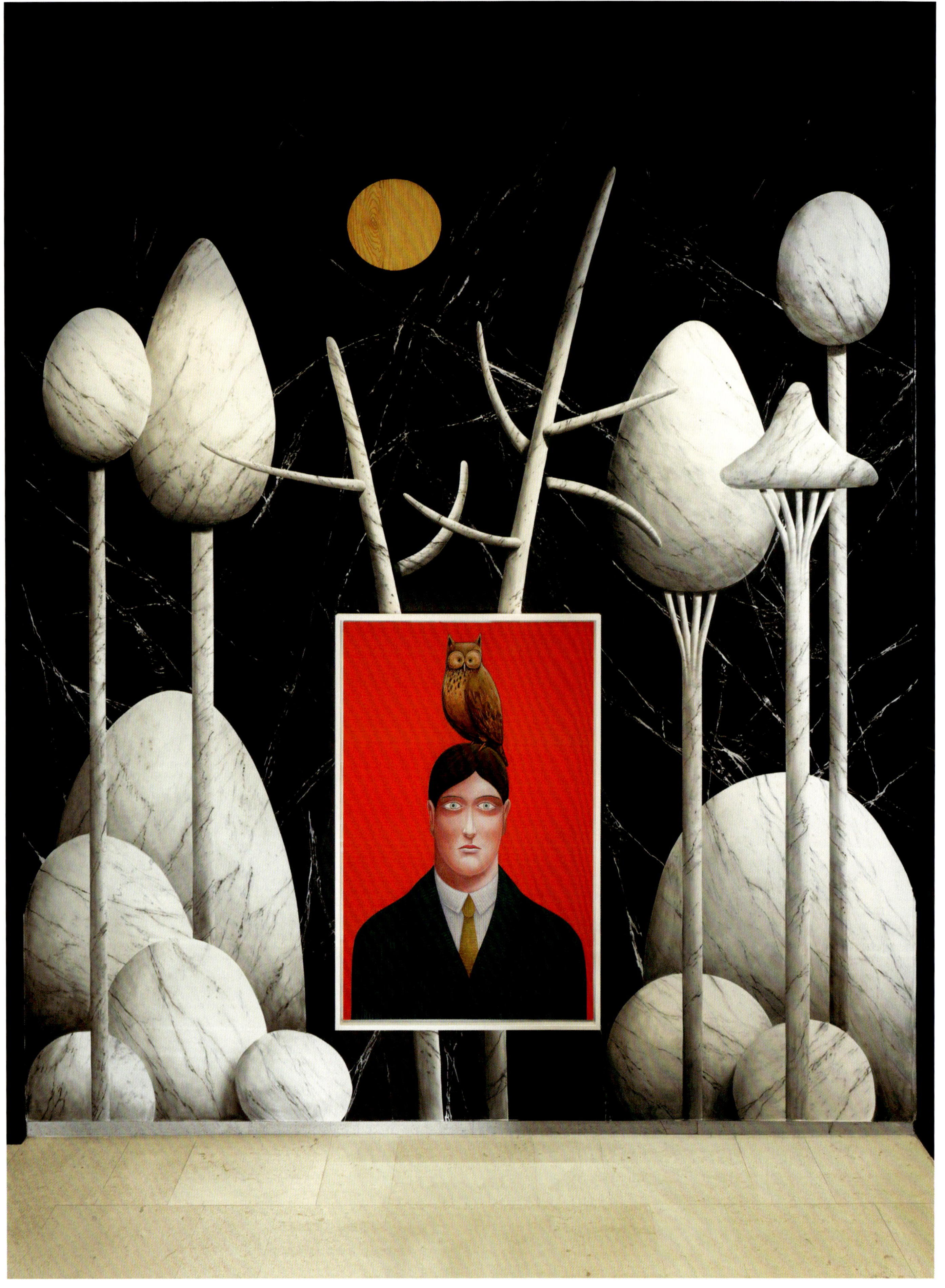

PORTRAIT WITH AN OWL, 2018
SOFT PASTEL ON LINEN
110 X 180 CM

MURAL: OIL ON WALL

INSTALLATION VIEW AT
MAGRITTE MUSEUM,
BRUSSELS, 2018

STONE FRUITS, 2018
SOFT PASTEL ON PASTEL CARD
100 X 68 CM

wood grain or the fur of big cats, while the apparently trained cats in Party's paintings seem to unconditionally obey the distinguished lady sitting behind them. This painting is also framed with an imitation marble mount. This time, however, it is the much less familiar and more exotic black marble. And so we automatically think of the well-known German saying 'Zweimal dasselbe ist nicht dasselbe' (Twice the same is not the same), a credo that played a significant role in the exhibition 'Pastel' at The FLAG Art Foundation in New York a year later.

Pastel

'Pastel' ran from 10 October 2019 to 15 February 2020, occupying two floors of The FLAG Art Foundation in New York. Here, the artist merged the two exhibitionary approaches he had utilized at Kunsthall Stavanger and the Musée Magritte Museum, while at the same time extending them conceptually. He transformed the spaces into a colourful, multi-part environment with four pastel pictures, which managed to be both delicate and monumental. Their subjects were drawn from the Rococo period and they served as a backdrop for a selection of pastels by other artists, both historical and contemporary. At the same time, he paid homage to the heyday of pastel painting in the eighteenth century and its niche-like survival into the twenty-first century, until it became the primary art medium for Party himself. In addition to his four monumental murals and some additional pastel works by Party, works were also on show by Rosalba Carriera (1673–1757), Mary Cassatt (1844–1926), Edgar Degas (1834–1917), Louis Fratino (b. 1993), Marsden Hartley (1877–1943), Loie Hollowell (b. 1983), Julian Martin (b. 1969), Toyin Ojih Odutola (b. 1985), Chris Ofili (b. 1968), Jean-Baptiste Perronneau

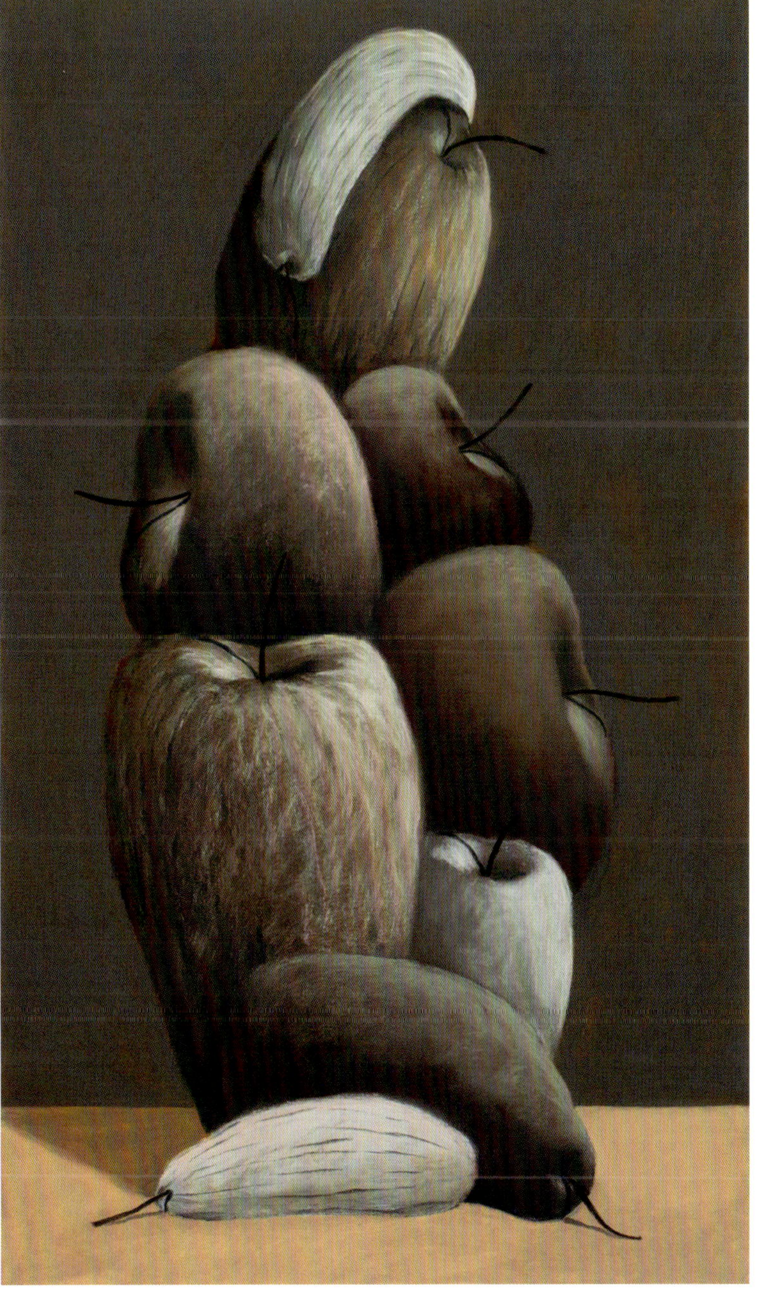

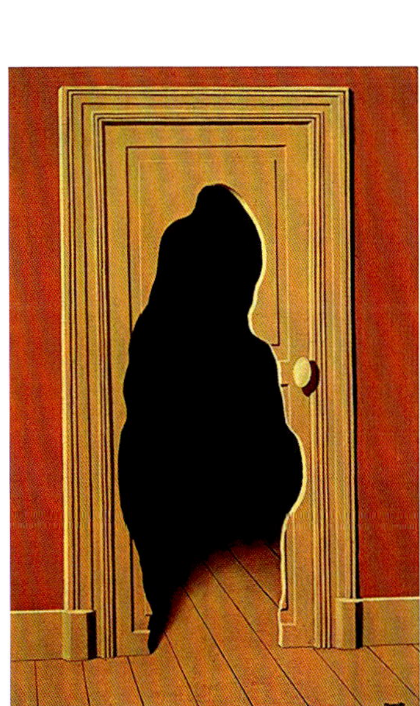

RENÉ MAGRITTE
LA RÉPONSE IMPRÉVUE, 1932
OIL ON CANVAS
82 X 55 CM

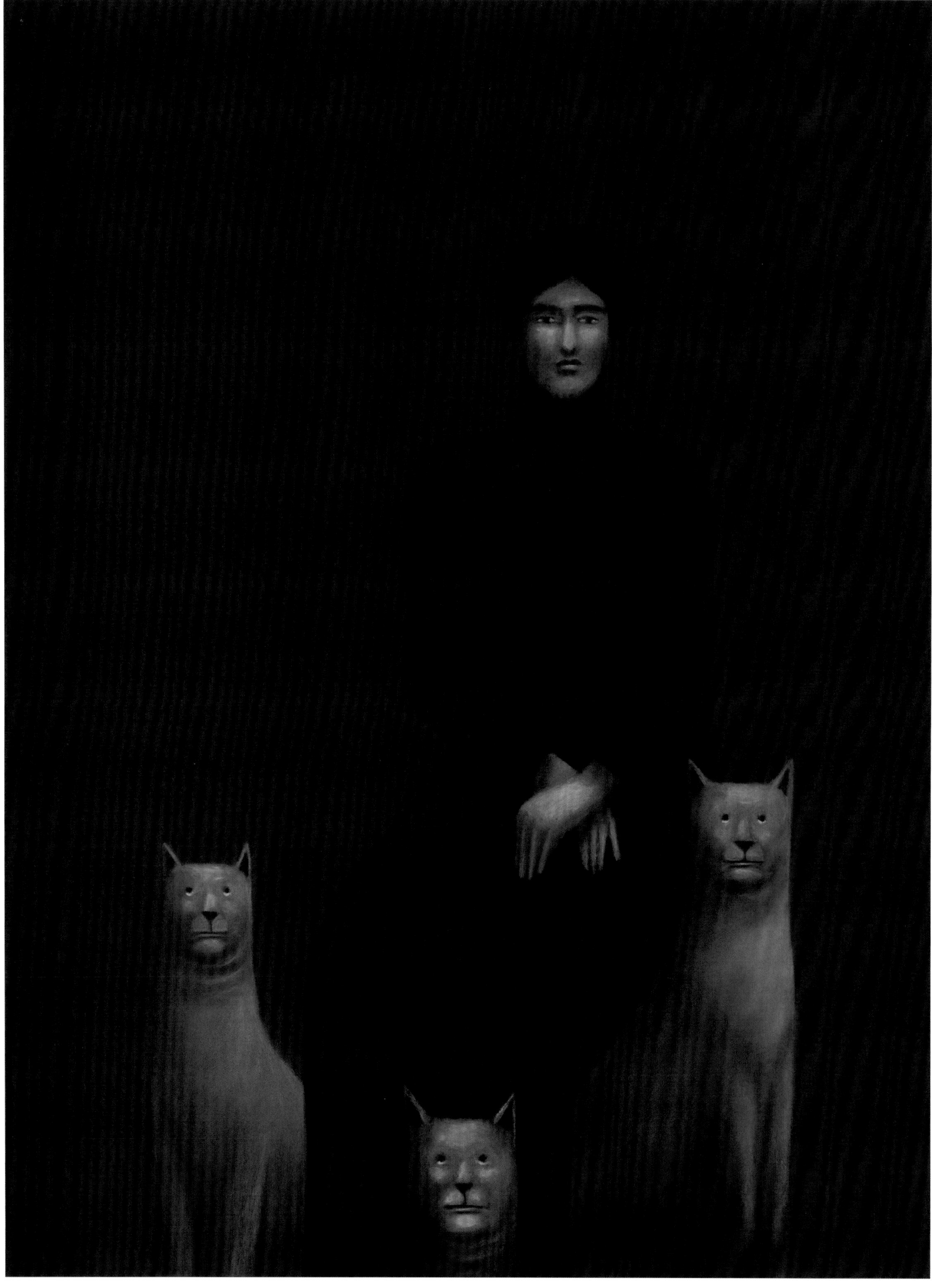

ROBIN F. WILLIAMS
ALIVE WITH PLEASURE
(STUDY), 2018
PASTEL ON PAPER
130 X 98 CM

background,
FROM JEAN-HONORÉ
FRAGONARD, BIRTH OF VENUS,
1753–55, 2019
SOFT PASTEL ON WALL
401 X 282 CM

INSTALLATION VIEW AT THE
FLAG ART FOUNDATION,
NEW YORK, 2019

opposite,
PORTRAIT WITH THREE CATS,
2018
SOFT PASTEL ON PASTEL CARD
80 X 60 CM

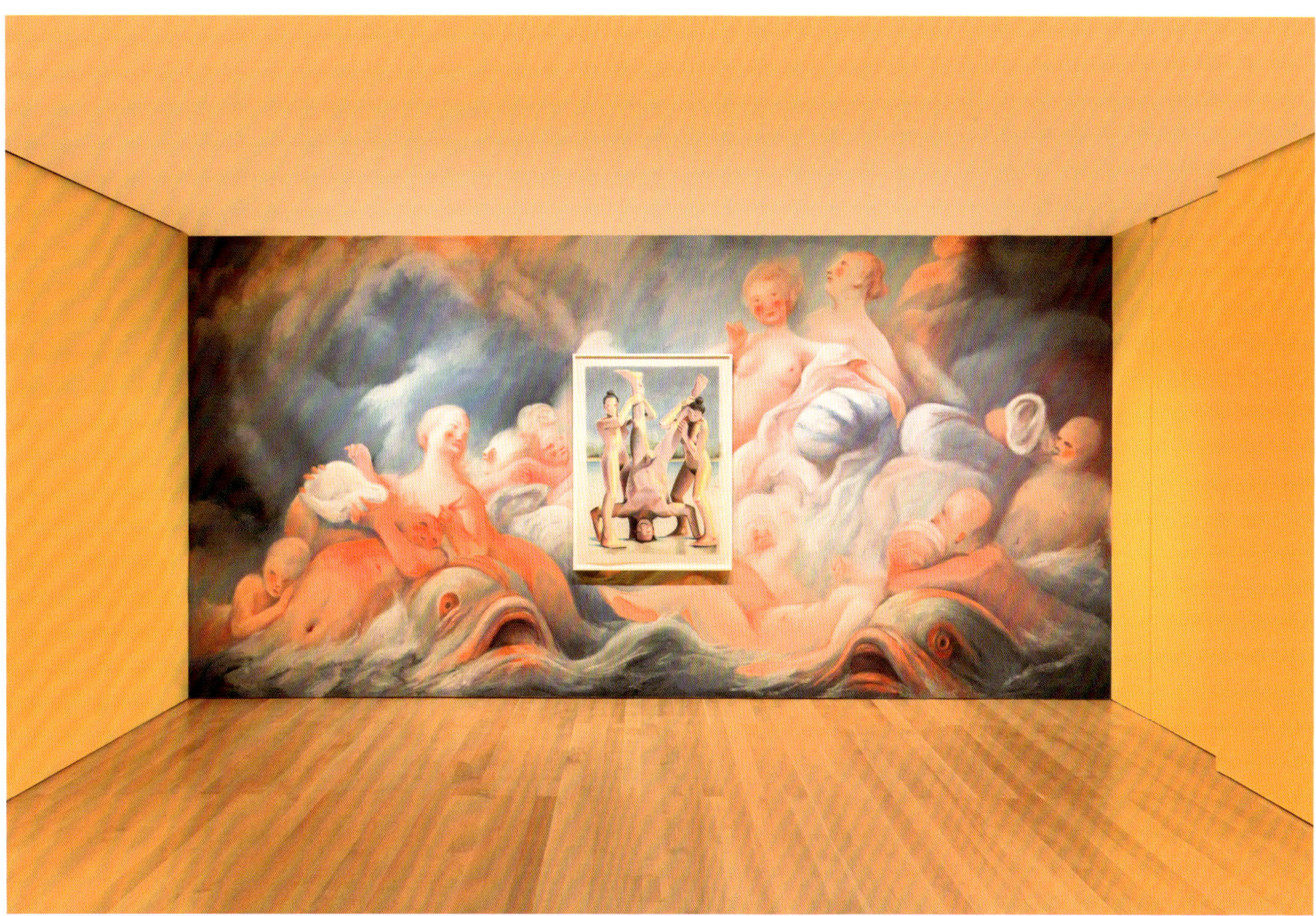

(1715–1783), Billy Sullivan (b. 1946), Wayne Thiebaud (b. 1920) and Robin F. Williams (b. 1984).

Pastel paintings by the Venice-born artist Rosalba Carriera were awarded special attention in this sweeping, typical Party-style mise-en-scène. Today, she is considered a pioneer of pastel painting, a delicate and ultimately ephemeral medium. Famous for her soft and graceful application of colour and the atmospheric shades of her portraits, she was one of the first female artists to achieve major international recognition before 1800. In this exhibition Carriera also represented the short-lived obsession with exaggeration during the Rococo.[10] Together with Jean-Baptiste Perronneau, she depicted the extravagant costumes and make-up of the aristocracy of the time: pale skin, rose-bud lips, artificial beauty marks,[11] powdered hair, elaborate wigs, masks, ostrich feathers, flowers, ribbons, jewels, decorated bodices cut to emphasise the breasts and décolleté of the sitter, and the colour pink, which Party used particularly lavishly in the exhibition to further emphasise the unique atmosphere of this historical excursion into the world of pastel.

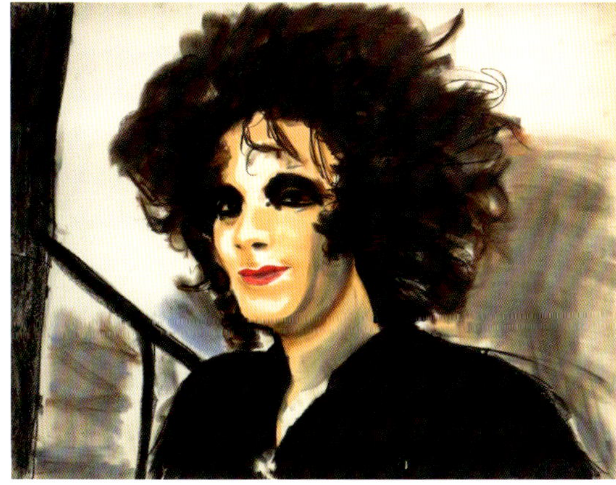

BILLY SULLIVAN
JACKIE CURTIS, 1971
PASTEL ON PAPER
89 X 117 CM

Executed and shaded by hand, fragile and easily smudged, pastel is an enormous challenge for an artist when applied onto large, unprotected walls. Party worked for a total of four weeks on the four murals, adapted from François Boucher's (1703–1770) and Jean-Honoré Fragonard's (1732–1806) paintings, whose frothy, theatrical and contrived allegories became the much maligned hallmark of the Rococo period. Although faithfully executing the works in the style of the two artists, Party nevertheless deviated from the originals. In one mural he cropped the source imager in order to concentrate on the contrasting fabrics of the elaborate dress in François Boucher's portrait of the *Marquise de Pompadour* (1758), in another on the artificial landscape in Fragonard's *The Progress of Love* (1771–73). And they also always formed the backdrop for the pastel pictures of the other artists selected by Party, which disturbed or unsettled the original thrust of the Rococo paintings.[12]

A particularly impressive example was Party's mural after Jean-Honoré Fragonard's *Birth of Venus* (1753–55), which he enlarged to 282 x 401 cm and on which he also hung the work of one of his contemporaries – American artist Robin F. Williams' pastel study *Alive with Pleasure* (p. 85). This combination established a richly metaphorical link between the naked protagonists at light-hearted play in the water in Fragonard's/Party's painting and the gymnastic exercises of the young nudists on display in Williams' picture.

Sunrises, Sunsets, Still Lifes, Trees, Coffee Pots and Caves

Along with another wall painting, a tondo of a fruit still life, on top of which he also hung a painting by Jean-Baptiste Perronneau, the exhibition included six additional works by Party. Especially noteworthy were the two paintings entitled *Sunrise and Sunset* (pp. 118–19), which had been shown for the first time in the exhibition 'Pastel' at Karma in New York. In their colouration and reduction, these two beguilingly beautiful compositions call to mind the famous seascapes of Milton Clark Avery (1885–1965). The difference from Avery's unsystematically painted pictures, however, lies in Party's markedly formalised depiction of the scenes, which nevertheless seem to be executed in a similarly unpremeditated way. The pronounced formalisation makes the depictions almost geometrical compositions, and yet they remain unmistakably figurative in their expression.

In many of his still lifes and tree depictions, however, Party drew his inspiration from the largely unknown Swiss painter Hans Emmenegger (1866–1940). Emmenegger was an outstanding artist, adept at capturing movement on canvas. But he also painted many unusual still lifes and lanscapes in which the subject is always reduced to the essential with impressionistic sensitivity: two cucumbers on a white cloth (p. 86), a fig tree in front of red earth or a forest interior illuminated by the sun (p. 94). Party formalizes the same subjects to a far greater extent (as for example with *Still Life*, 2014, or *Still Life*, 2014, p. 87) and then places them in new semantic contexts in his room settings. His world is the reinvention of the exhibition, of the Gesamtkunstwerk, while Emmenegger was interested in visualising the abstraction that he believed was already implicit in seeing.

Over the years, Party has stylized his tree depictions so rigorously in form and colour that they suddenly resemble his painted coffee pots (p. 90), which in turn, as strange as it may sound, are reminiscent of Marcel Duchamp's famous *Bottle Rack* (1915). On the other hand, the origins of the large-format paintings of grottos (pp. 92, 93), a recent arrival in his oeuvre, can be found in the Romantic period, for example, in Carl Gustav Carus' (1789–1869) idealized depictions of *Fingal's Cave* on the island of Staffa in Scotland and in Gustave Courbet's (1819–1877) realistic views of the *Source of the Loue*. Here, too, Party takes his subject to the brink of abstraction, so that we inevitably ask ourselves whether these pictures actually depict grottos or are perhaps more abstract compositions reminiscent of caves. Are they flattened, figurative paintings or perhaps spatial renditions of colours and forms? No matter how we ultimately read these works, the beguiling beauty of the compositions remains, lifting our spirits and encouraging us to see art and the world – life – with different eyes.

TRANSLATED FROM GERMAN BY TIM CHAFER

HANS EMMENEGGER
TWO CUCUMBERS, C. 1910–15
OIL ON CANVAS,
25 X 36 CM

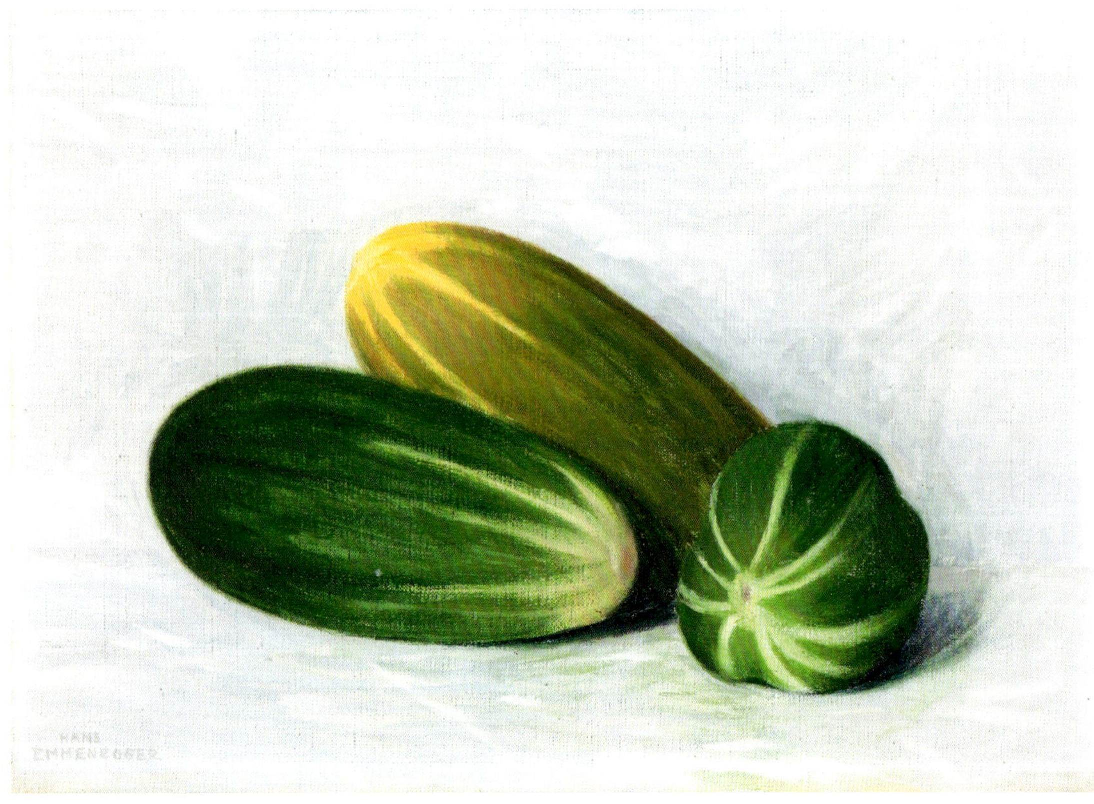

below,
STILL LIFE, 2014
SOFT PASTEL ON LINEN
100 X 150 CM

next pages, from left,
LANDSCAPE, 2020
SOFT PASTEL ON LINEN
114 X 97 CM

LANDSCAPE, 2018
SOFT PASTEL ON LINEN
180 X 150 CM

STILL LIFE, 2014
SOFT PASTEL ON LINEN
100 X 90 CM

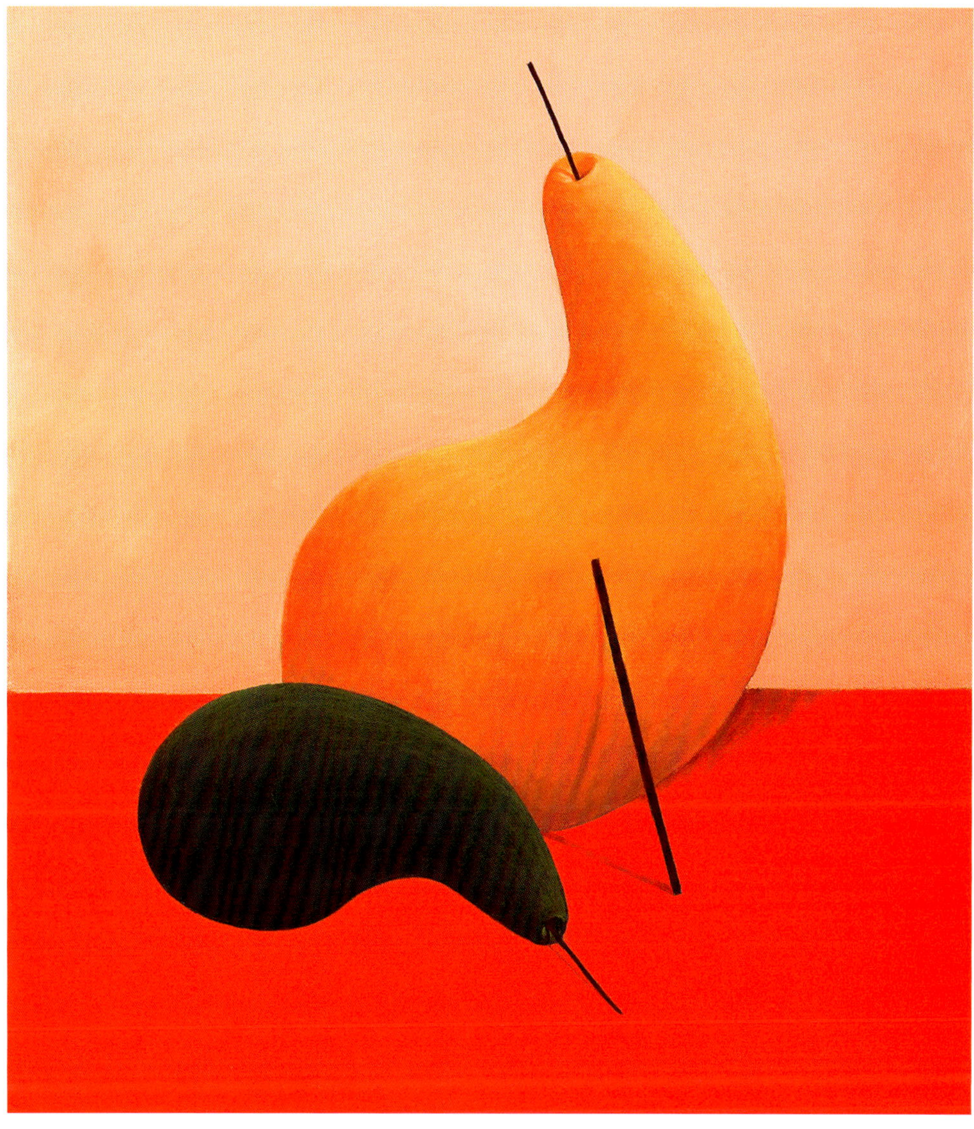

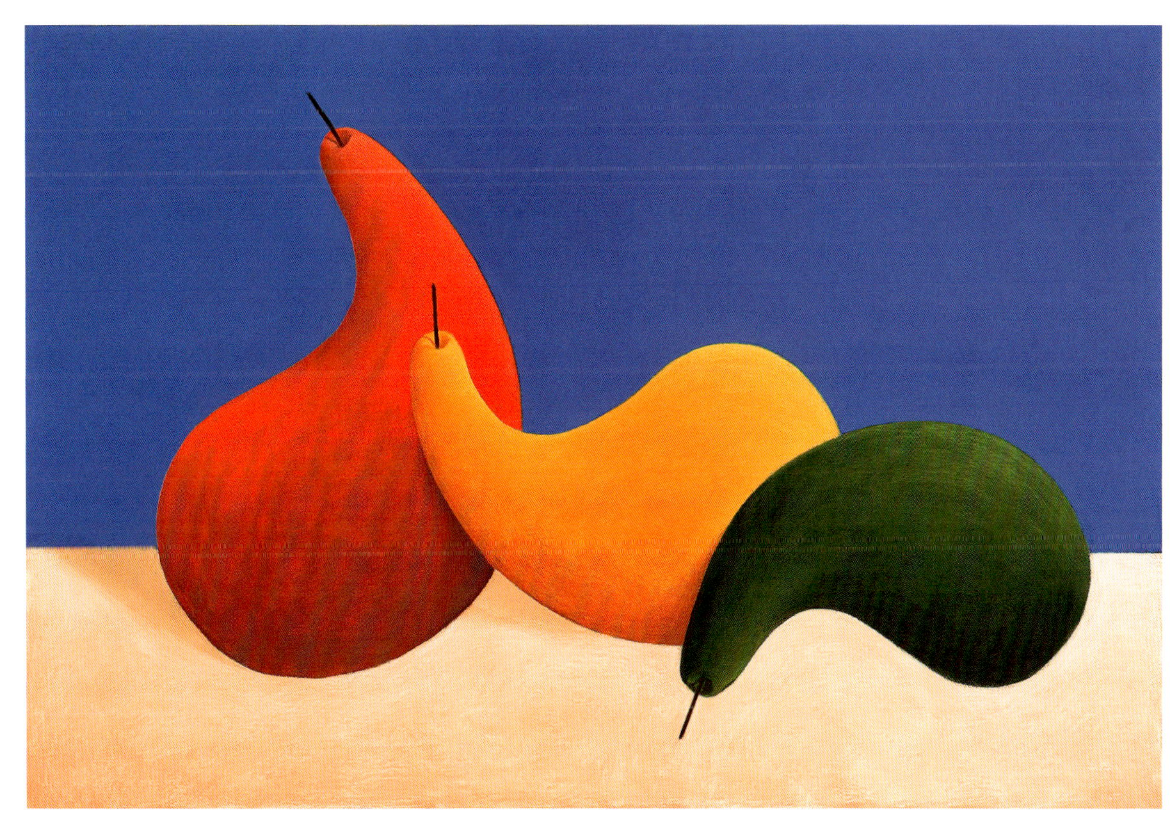

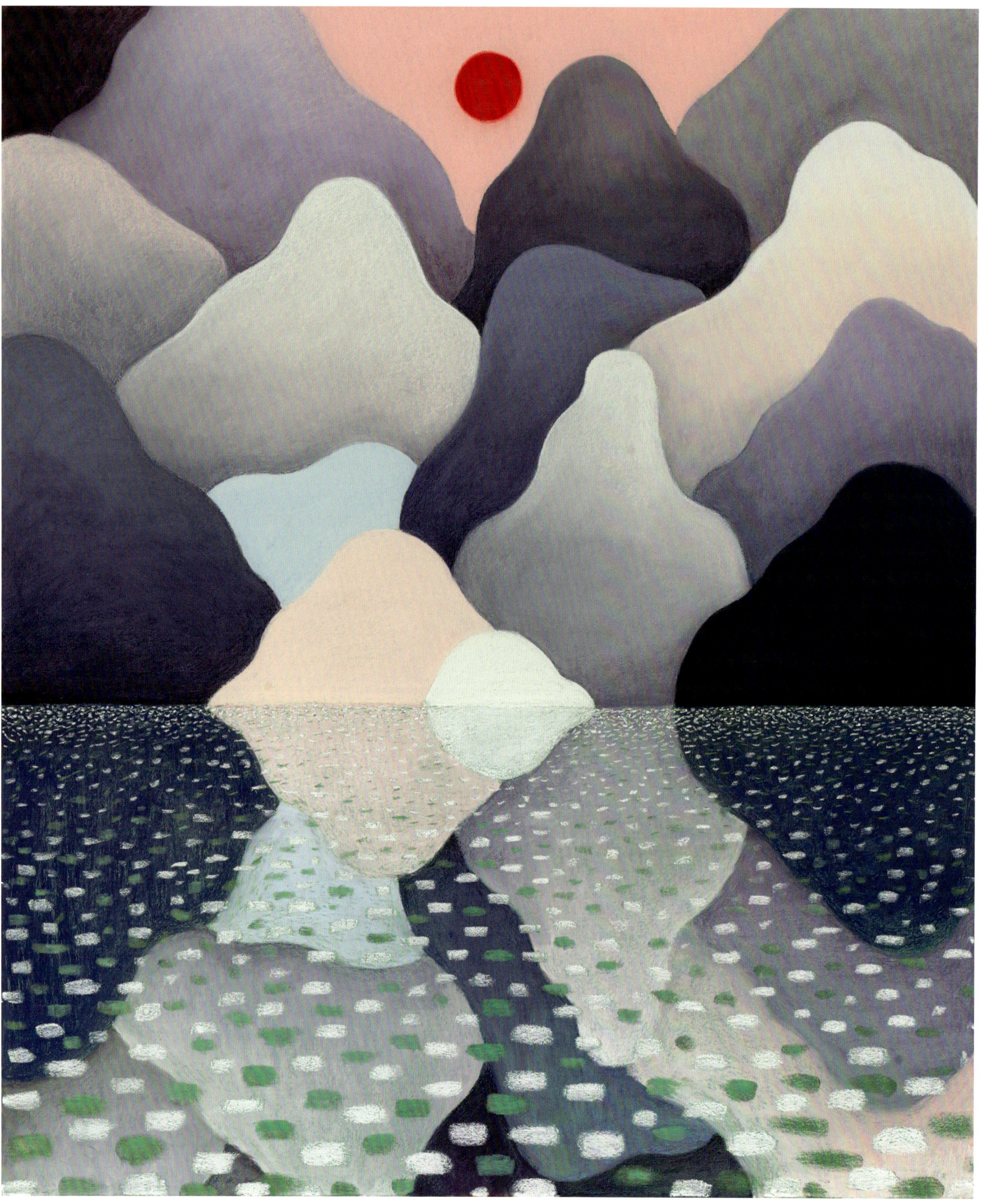

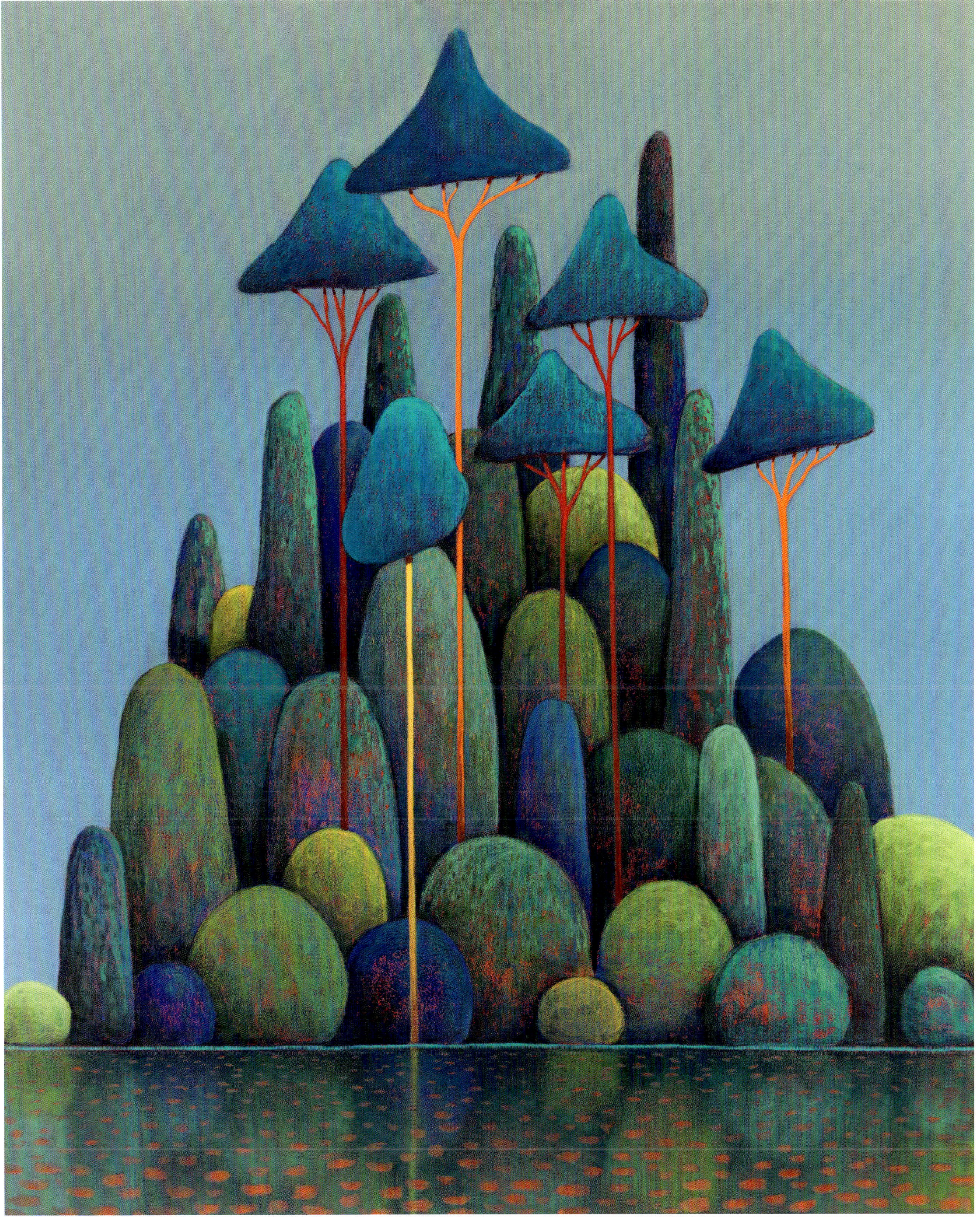

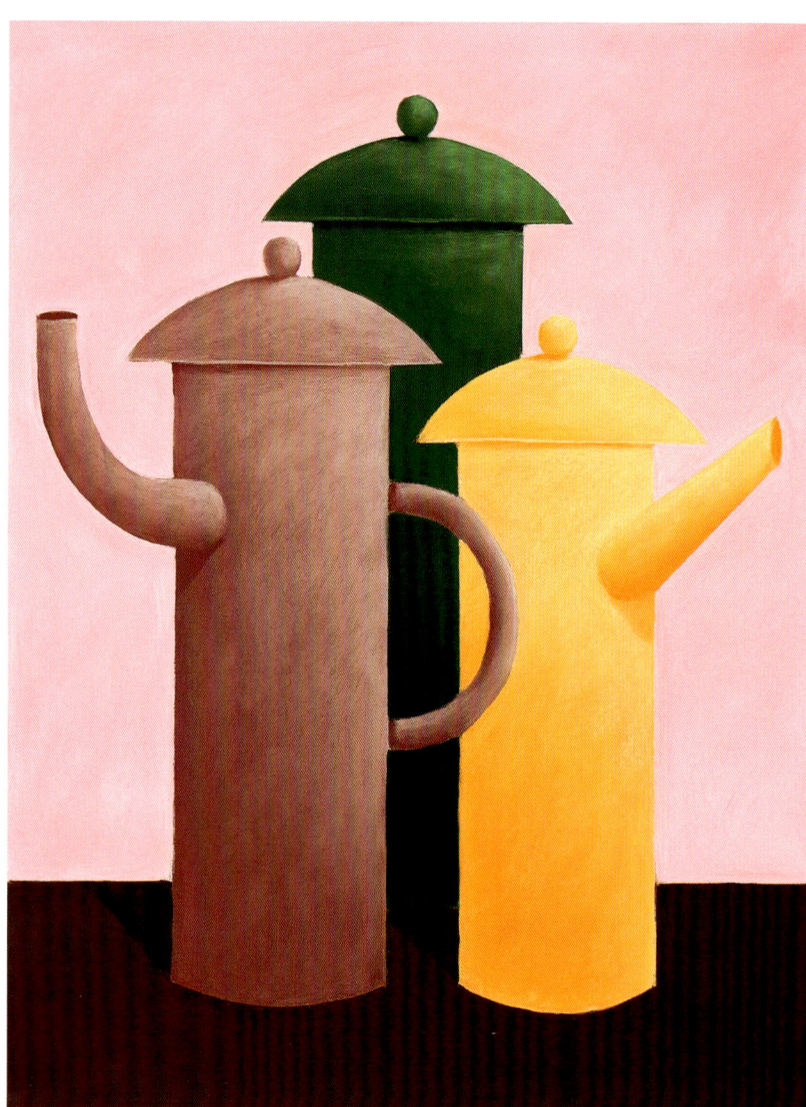

left,
STILL LIFE, 2014
SOFT PASTEL ON PASTEL CARD
65 X 50 CM

below,
STILL LIFE, 2015
SOFT PASTEL ON LINEN
150 X 90 CM

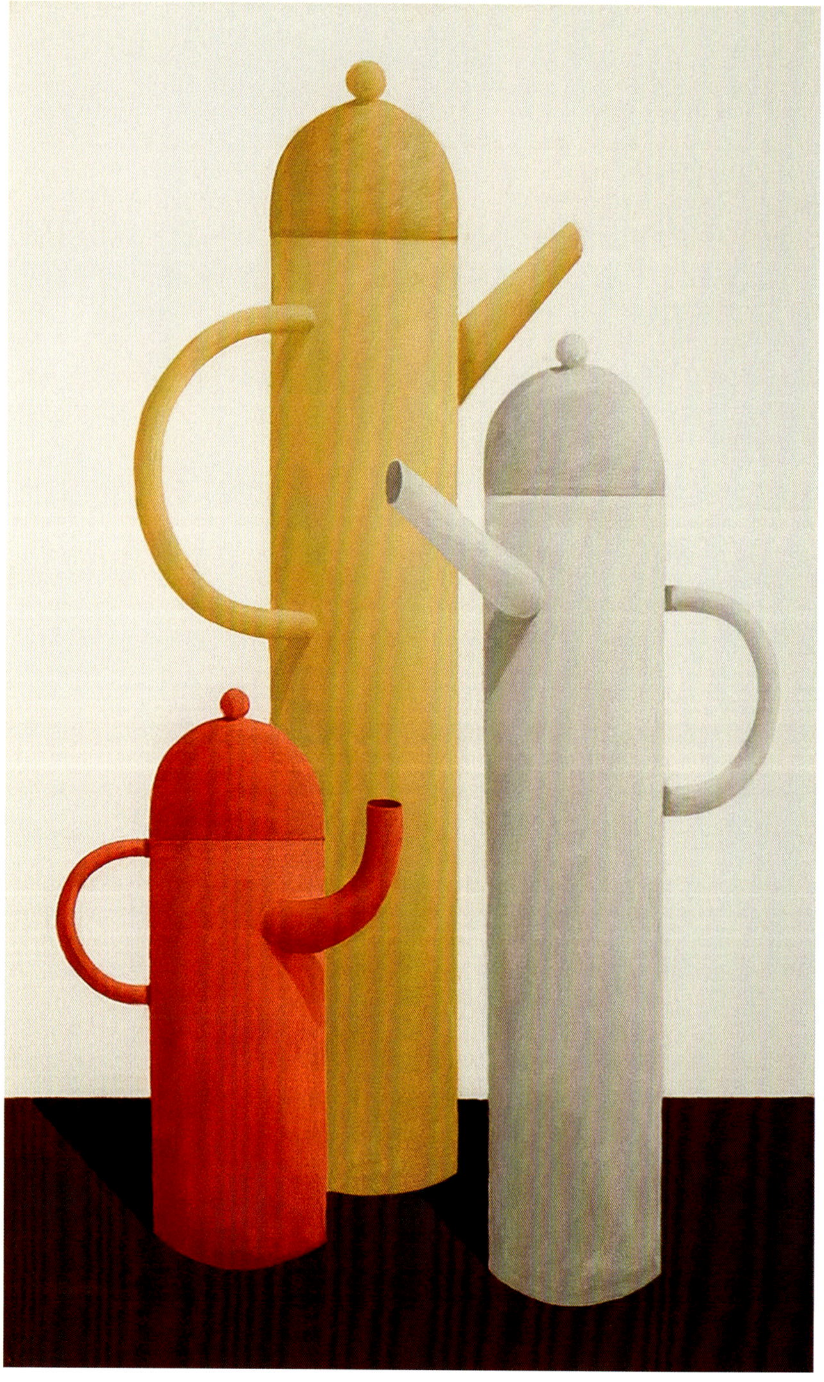

GROTTO, 2019
SOFT PASTEL ON LINEN
165 X 191 CM

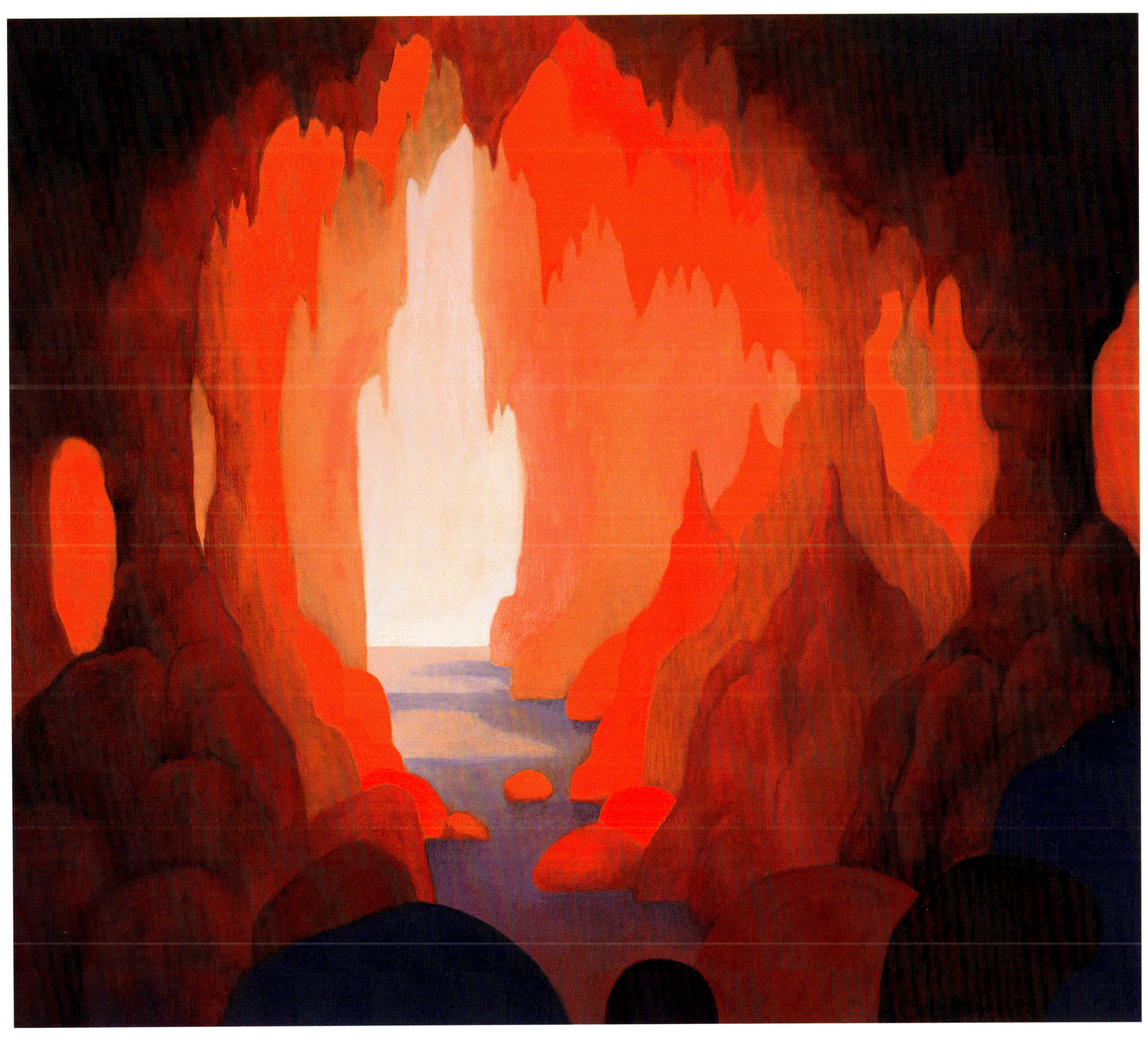

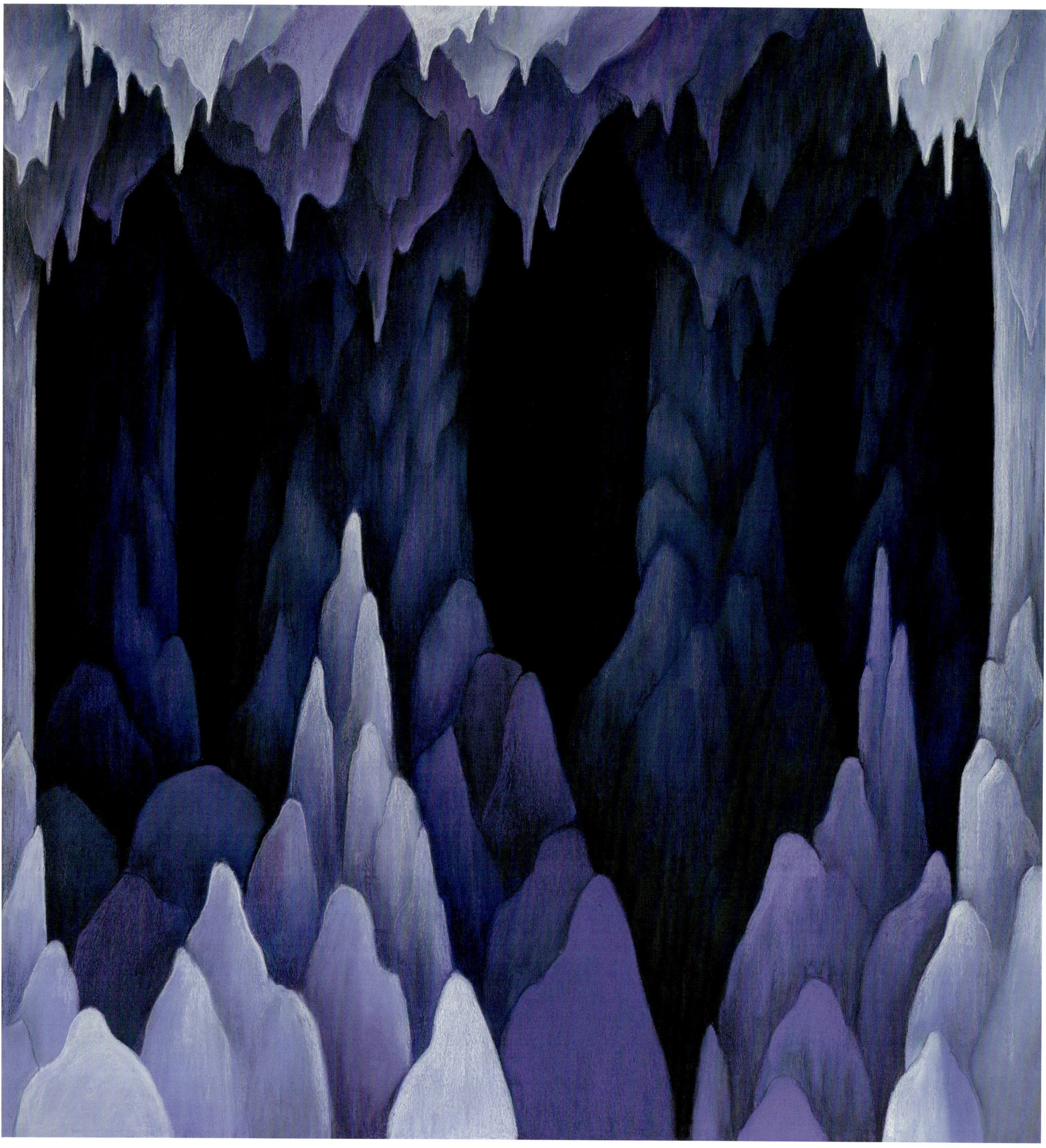

opposite,
CAVE, 2020
SOFT PASTEL ON LINEN
142 X 135 CM

CAVE, 2020
SOFT PASTEL ON LINEN
135 X 143 CM

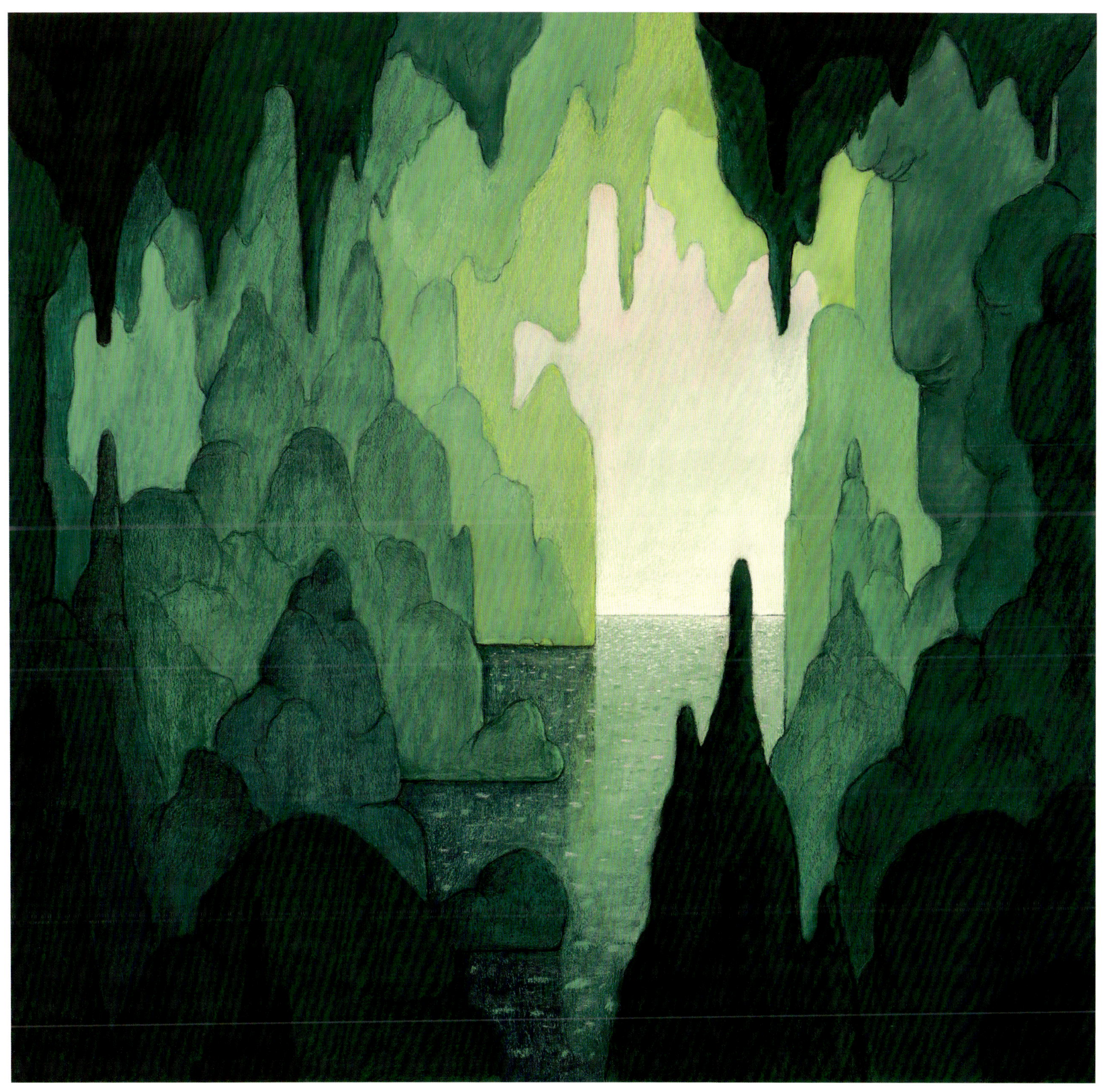

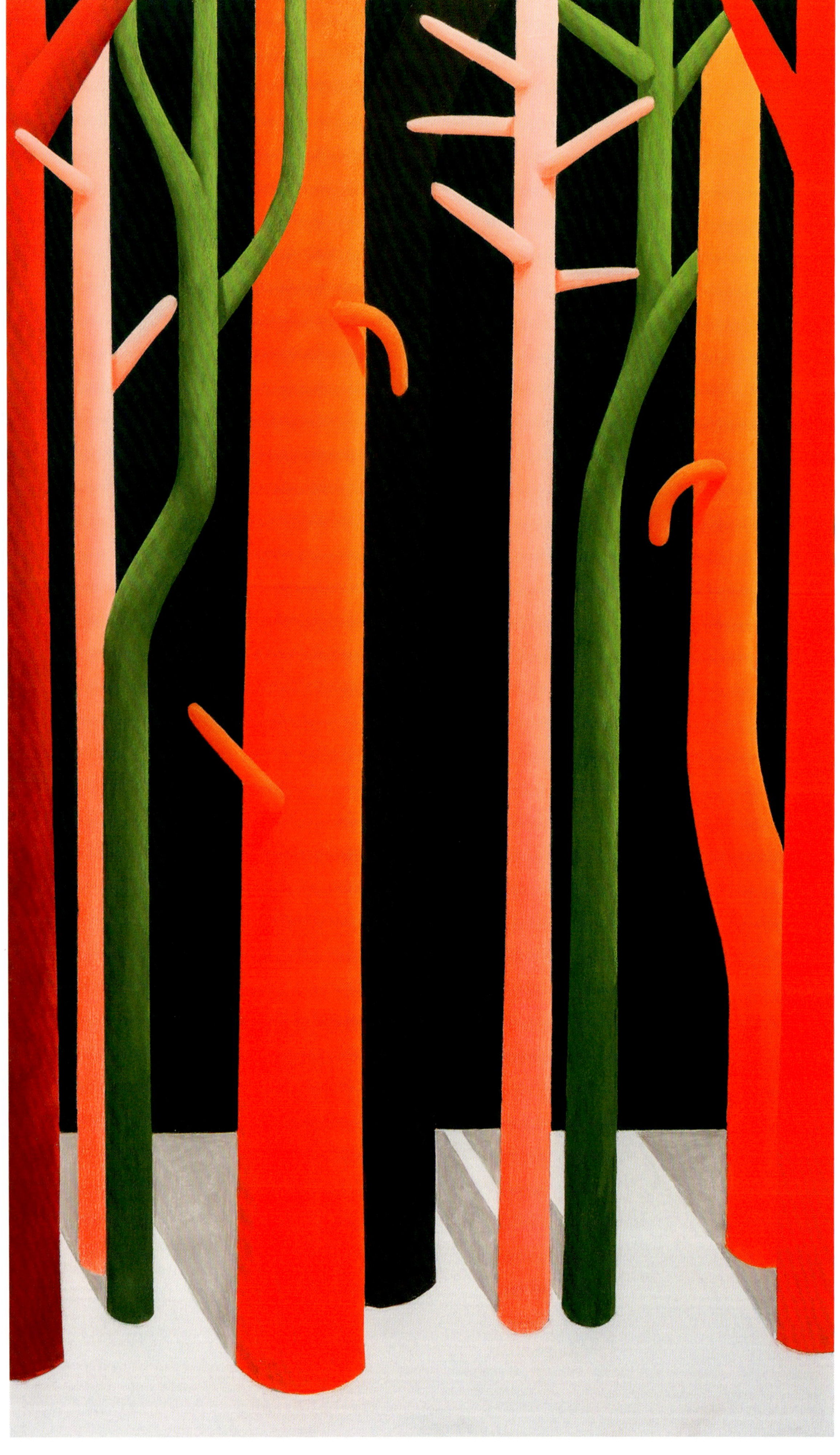

TREE TRUNKS, 2015
SOFT PASTEL ON LINEN
200 X 120 CM

TREES, 2020
SOFT PASTEL ON LINEN
89 X 64 CM

next pages,
LANDSCAPE, 2013
SPRAY PAINT ON WALL
600 X 3000 CM

INSTALLATION VIEW AT THE WALLED GARDEN, GLASGOW, 2013

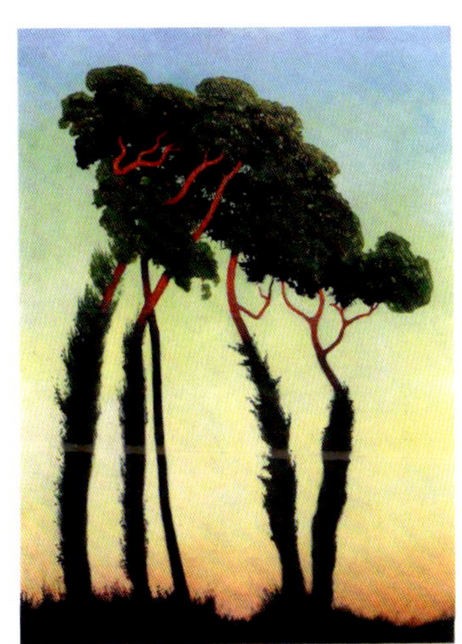

FÉLIX VALLOTTON
DERNIERS RAYONS OU PAYSAGE AVEC DES ARBRES, 1911
OIL ON CANVAS
100 X 73 CM

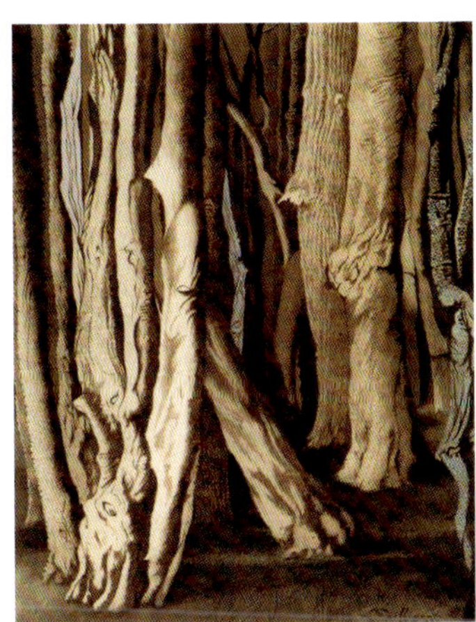

LÉON SPILLIAERT
TRONCS NOUEUX (GNARLED TREES), 1938
INDIA INK, BRUSH, PEN, BLACK CHALK AND GOUACHE ON PAPER
59 X 47 CM

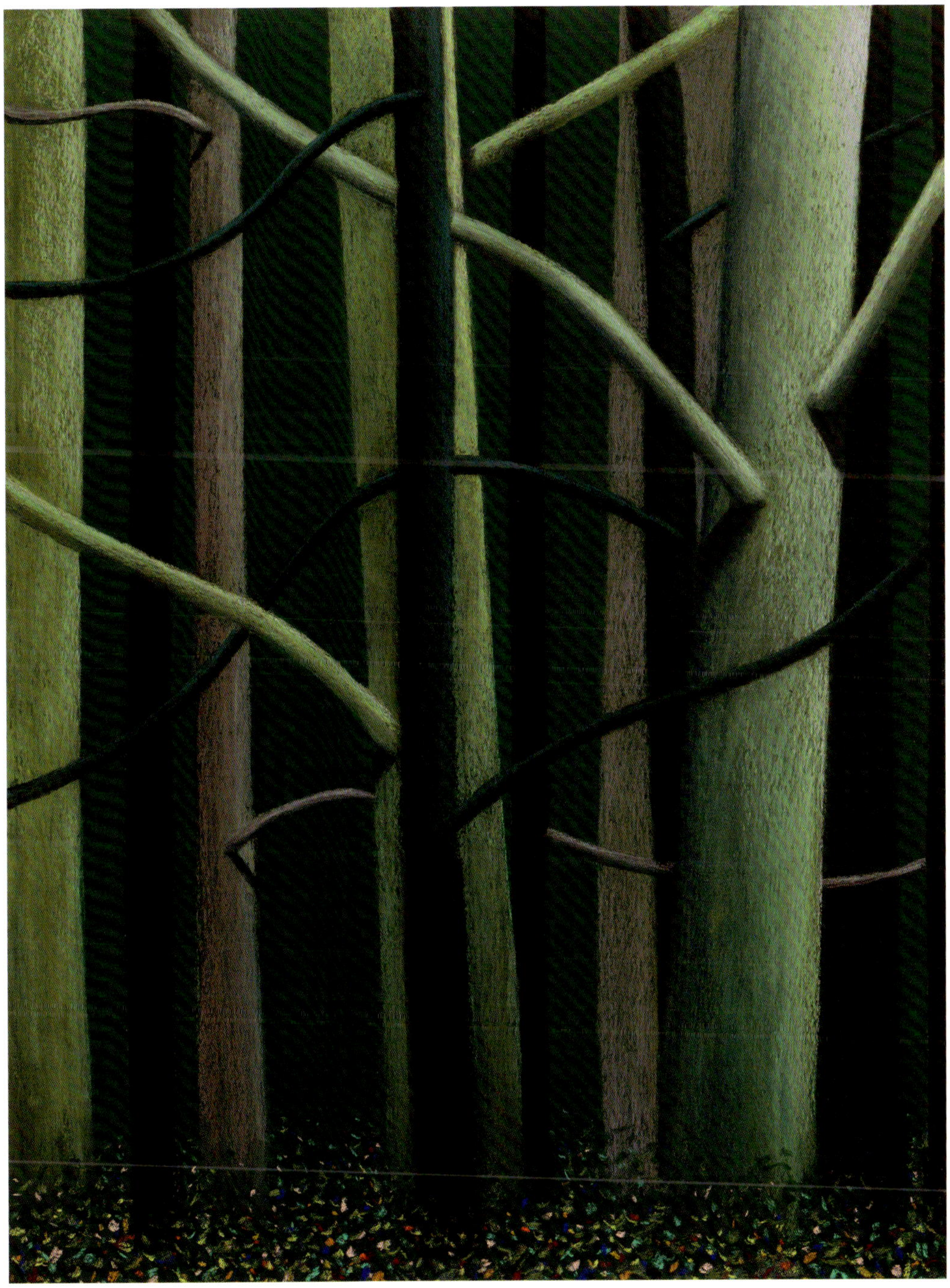

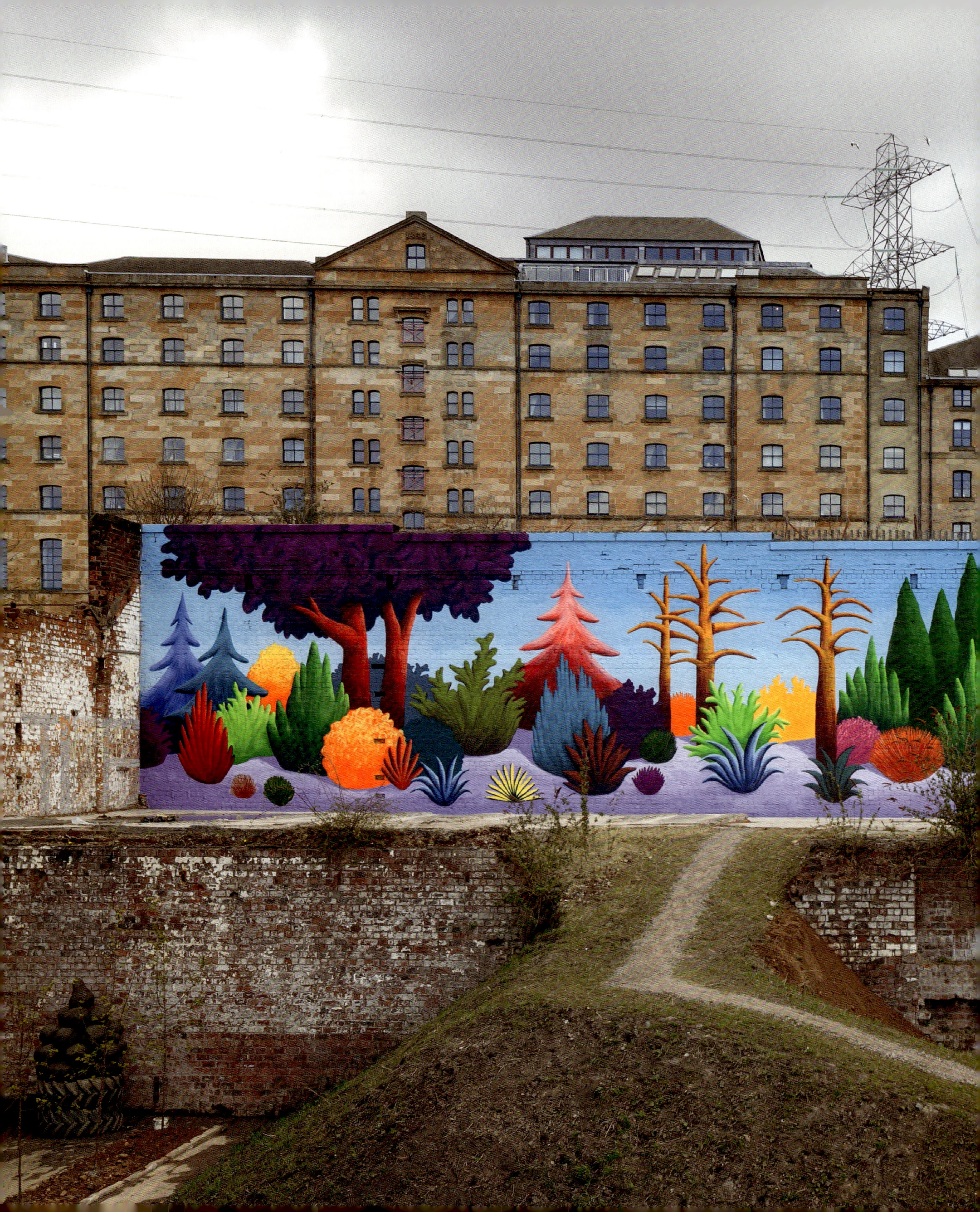

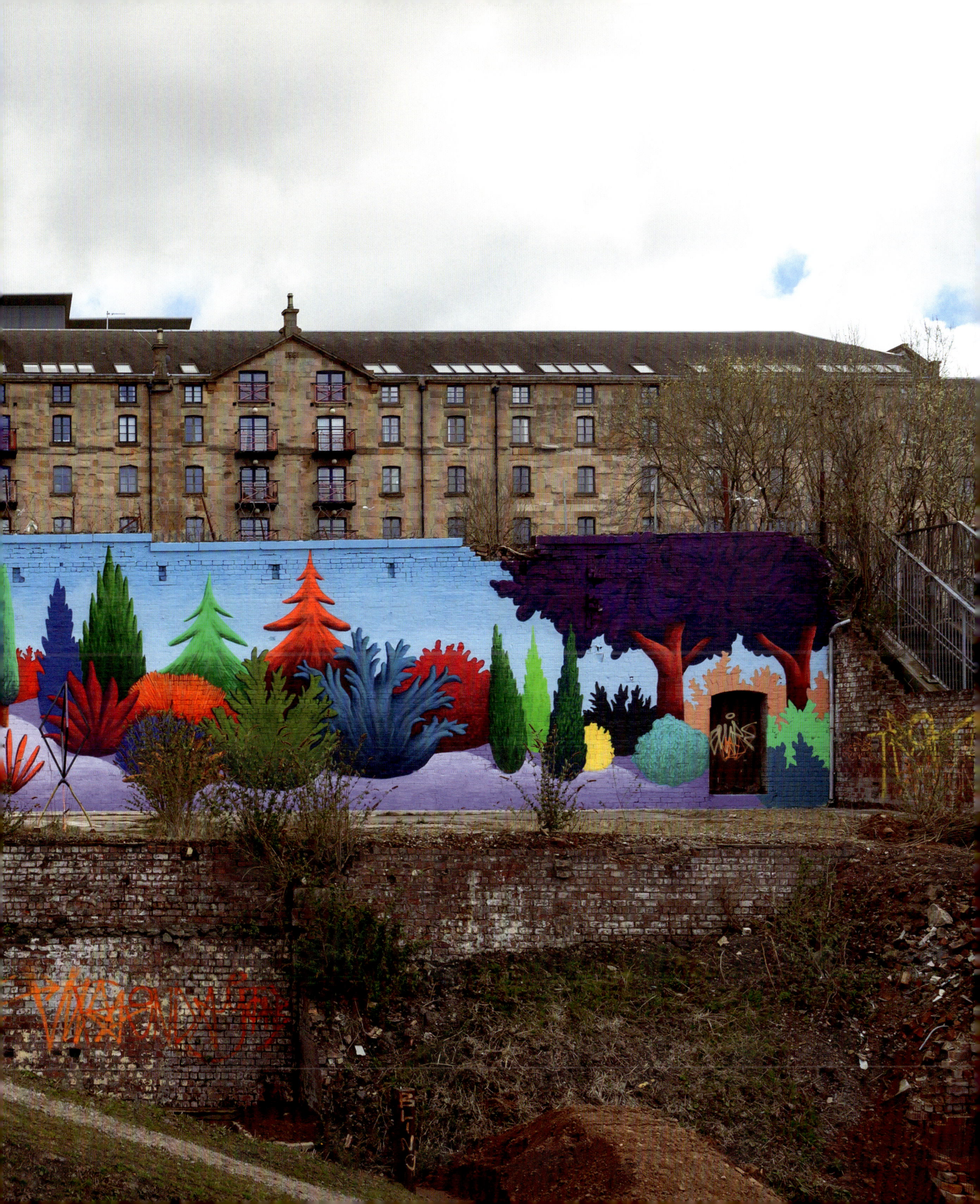

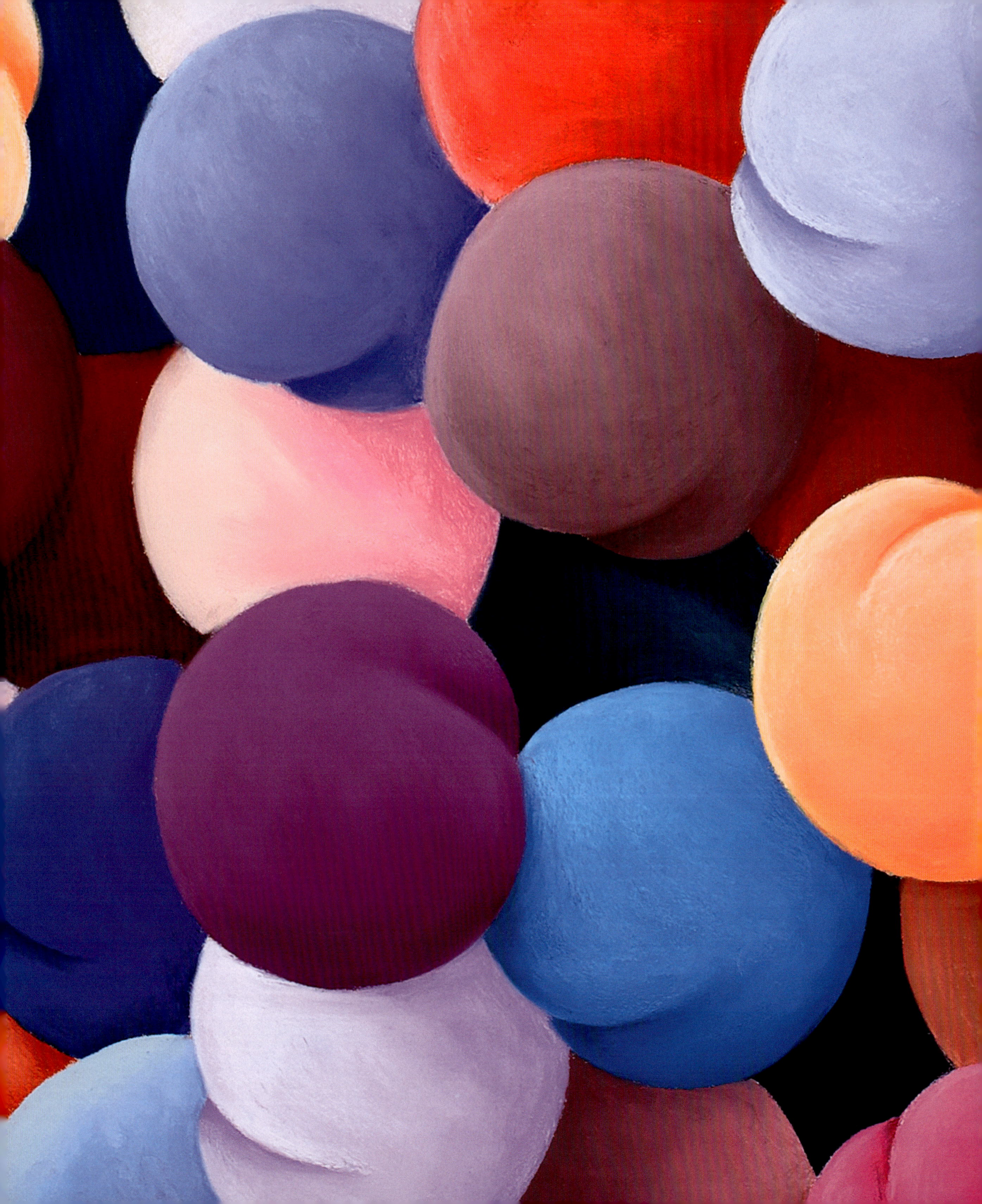

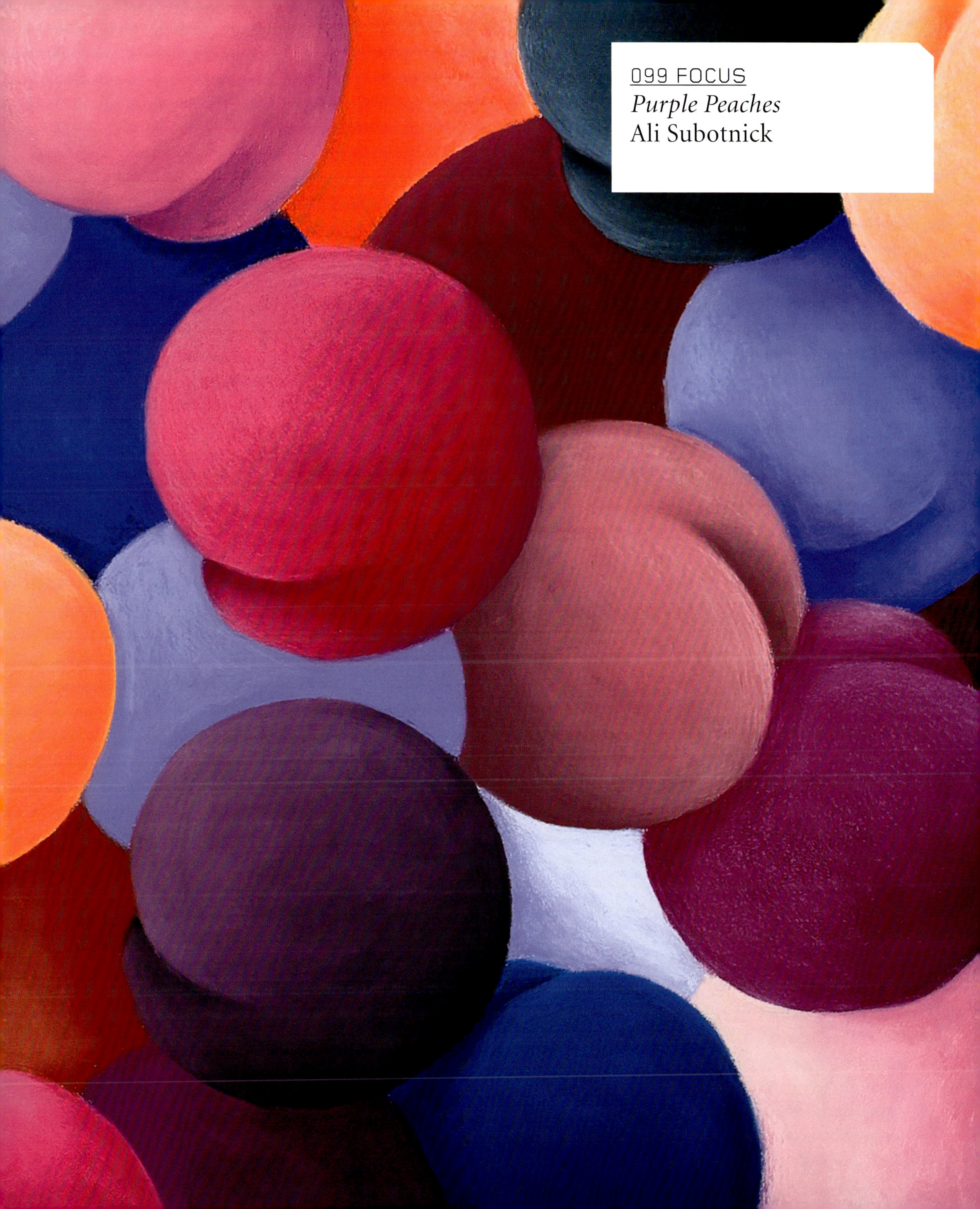

099 FOCUS

Purple Peaches

Ali Subotnick

HAMMER PROJECTS: NICOLAS PARTY, 2017
SOFT PASTEL, CHARCOAL AND OIL ON WALL

INSTALLATION VIEW AT THE HAMMER MUSEUM, LOS ANGELES, 2017

previous pages,
PURPLE PEACHES (DETAIL), 2017
SOFT PASTEL ON LINEN
240 X 60 CM

An enormous polished white marble bowl overflows with velvety peaches in purple, red, lavender, turquoise, pale pink, royal blue and indigo hues, each orb perfectly scaled for a giant. The bowl sits at the base of the wall, almost merging with the white marble trim at the wall's base and on the landing below. An immense index finger swipes left, leaving a polished white marble smear in its wake. On the walls flanking the marble staircase several more carefully rendered pointer fingers swipe up, down, left and right, each leaving a trail of white or green marble as if the finger had just been dipped in liquid marble. At the top of the staircase another larger-than-life marble bowl – this one composed of alternating white and green marble bands – holds a jumble of banana-like fruits. Absent the typical creases and stems of normal bananas, these fruits are all uninterrupted elegant curves, and painted in the same incongruous shades of blues, purples and pinks, the yin to the peaches' yang. This is Purple Peaches, Nicolas Party's 2016 Hammer Projects exhibition at the Hammer Museum in Los Angeles.[1]

Party's perfectly pristine purple peaches (perhaps the start of a new tongue twister… Party's perfectly pristine provocative peaches perch precariously past probing peepers pondering partaking pleasantly perfumed prized peach pies) couldn't be more tantalizing. In Purple Peaches fourteen peaches pile up, one atop the other perfectly precarious. The oversize fruits incised with a delicate curving cleft, sensual and seductive in shape, scale and colour, are rendered with chalk pastel, a medium so fragile, so fleeting and sensitive that one minor tap could disrupt and distort the image severely. There's an inherent softness and richness to pastel that no other medium can attain, and like satin or velveteen it's irresistible, daring you to caress it. For this project, Party took advantage of the space with its high ceilings and enormous walls – which were out of reach for most humans, and thus safe from curious fingers or an accidental graze – and employed pastel on a wall mural for only the second time, a seemingly natural progression for the artist.[2]

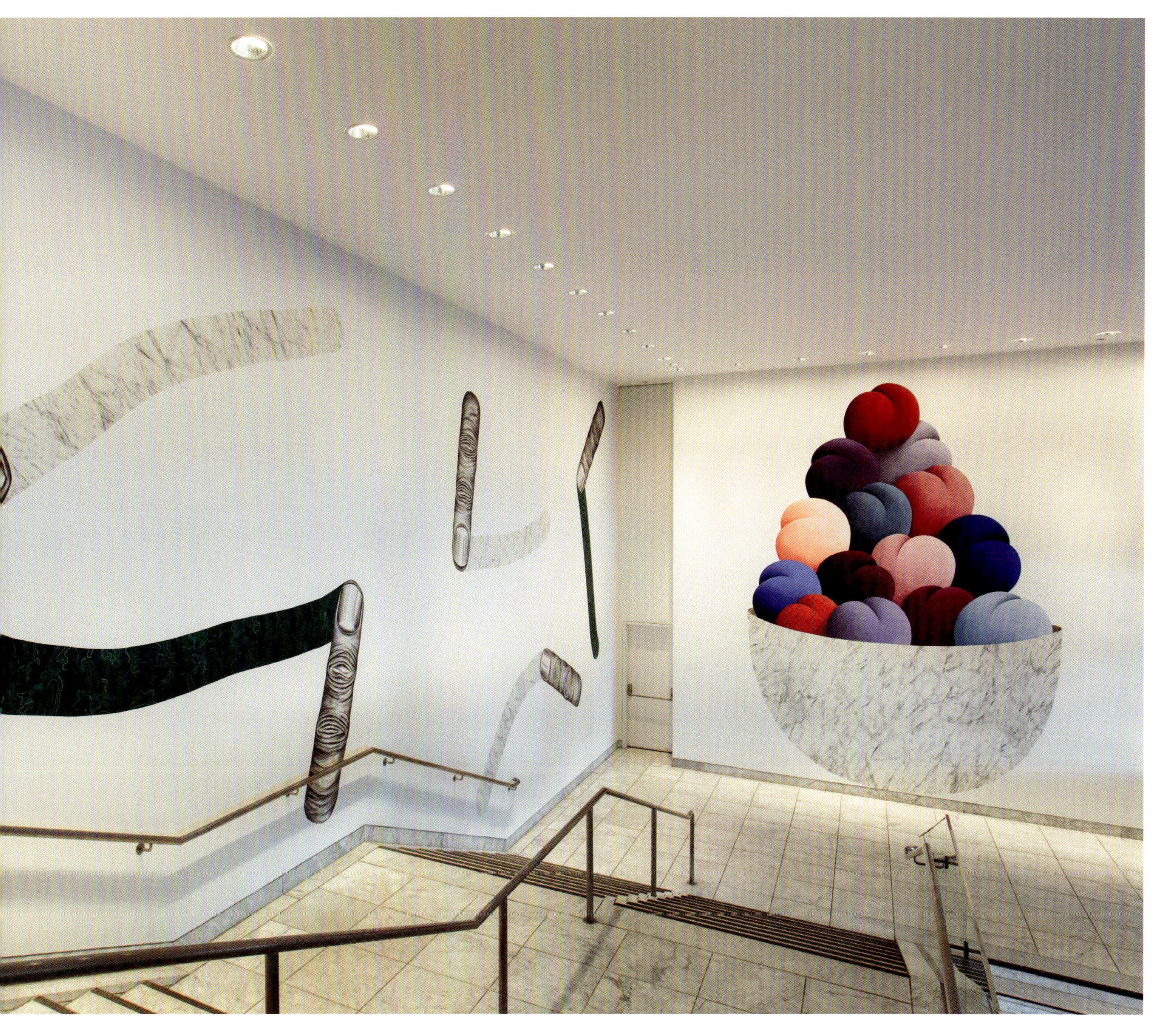

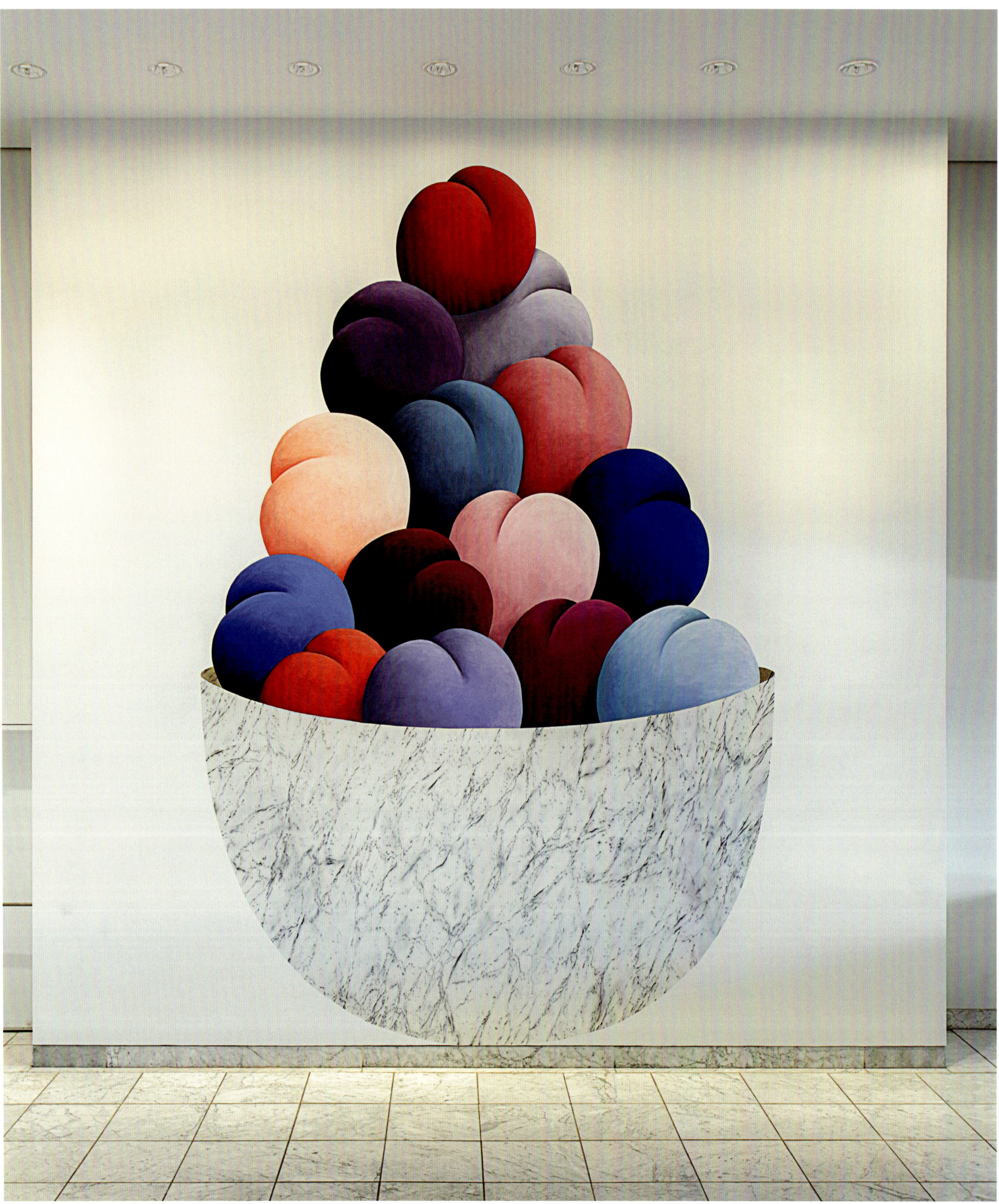

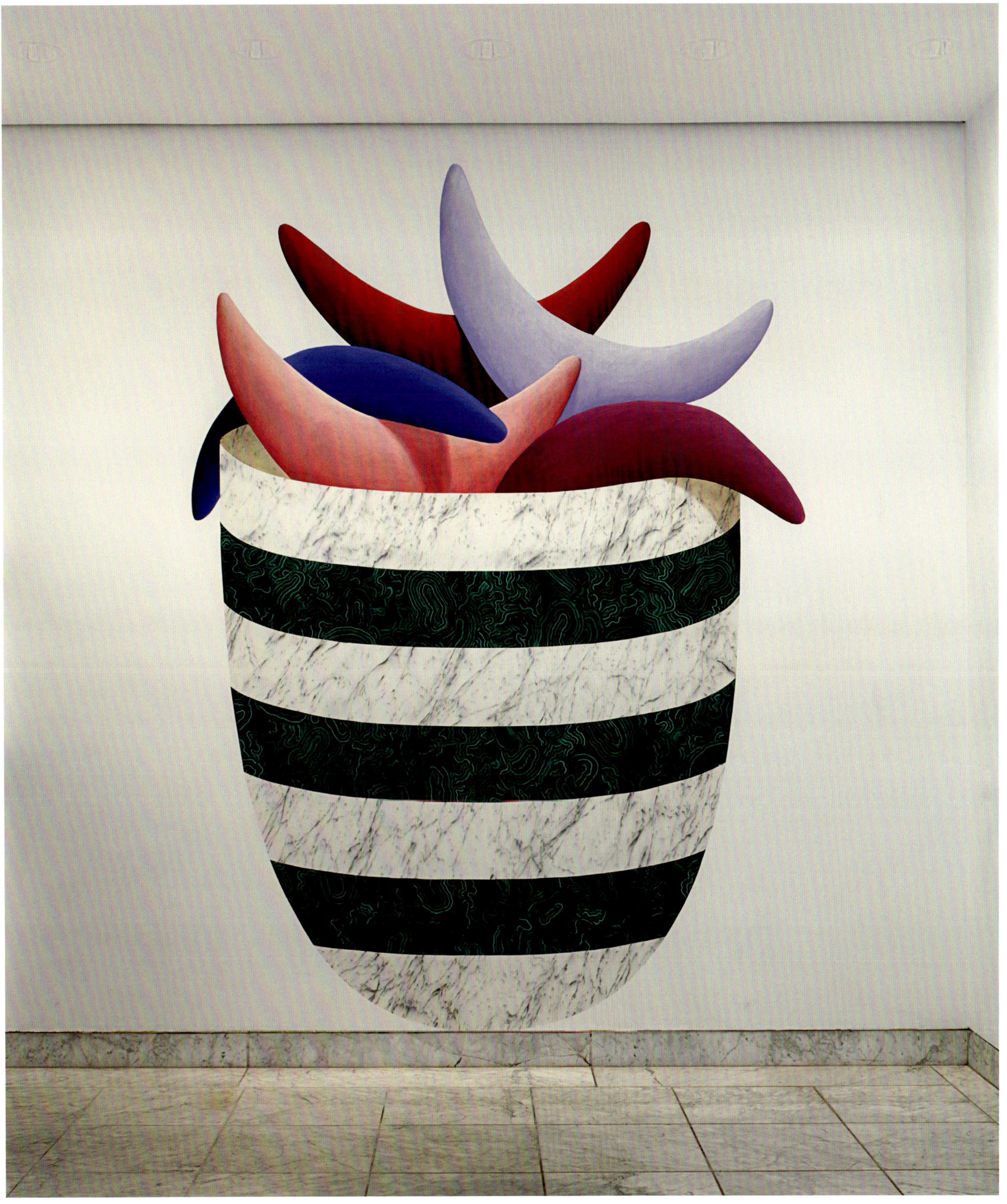

HAMMER PROJECTS: NICOLAS PARTY, 2017
SOFT PASTEL, CHARCOAL AND OIL ON WALL

INSTALLATION VIEW AT THE HAMMER MUSEUM, LOS ANGELES, 2017

opposite,
HAMMER PROJECTS: NICOLAS PARTY, 2017
SOFT PASTEL ON WALL

WORK-IN-PROGRESS IMAGE WITH SARAH MARGNETTI PAINTING OIL ON WALL, HAMMER MUSEUM, LOS ANGELES, 2017

previous pages,
HAMMER PROJECTS: NICOLAS PARTY (DETAIL), 2017
SOFT PASTEL, CHARCOAL AND OIL ON WALL

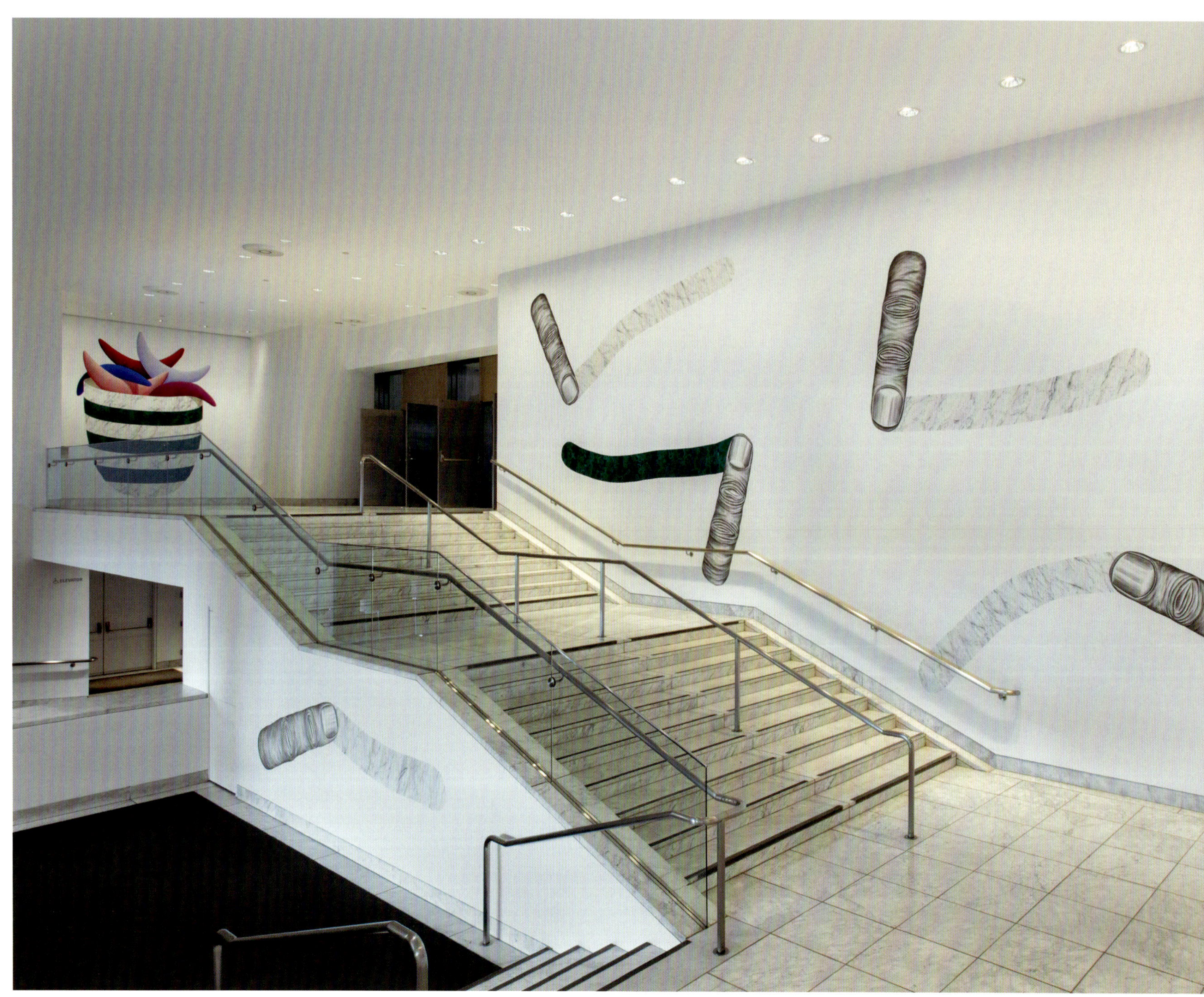

Prior to this, Party reserved the delicate medium with its soft matte finish for works that could remain protected behind glass, or otherwise secured from curious viewers unable to resist temptation. In this instance, Party exploits the powdery medium to create the illusion of the texture of the fuzzy fruit, luring us into a magical world where even those afflicted with a peach allergy (a common sensitivity, especially in the Mediterranean) are immune and able to appreciate, eat and touch these seductive and irresistible fruits. The colours chosen to depict the fruit enhance the whimsy and fantastical elements of the image. We're immediately transported to an alternate world where blue, lavender, and ruby red and pink peaches grow from trees. Like a Seussian landscape one imagines otherworldly characters plucking the tantalizing fruits to reveal a juicy succulent interior – perhaps its purple inside.

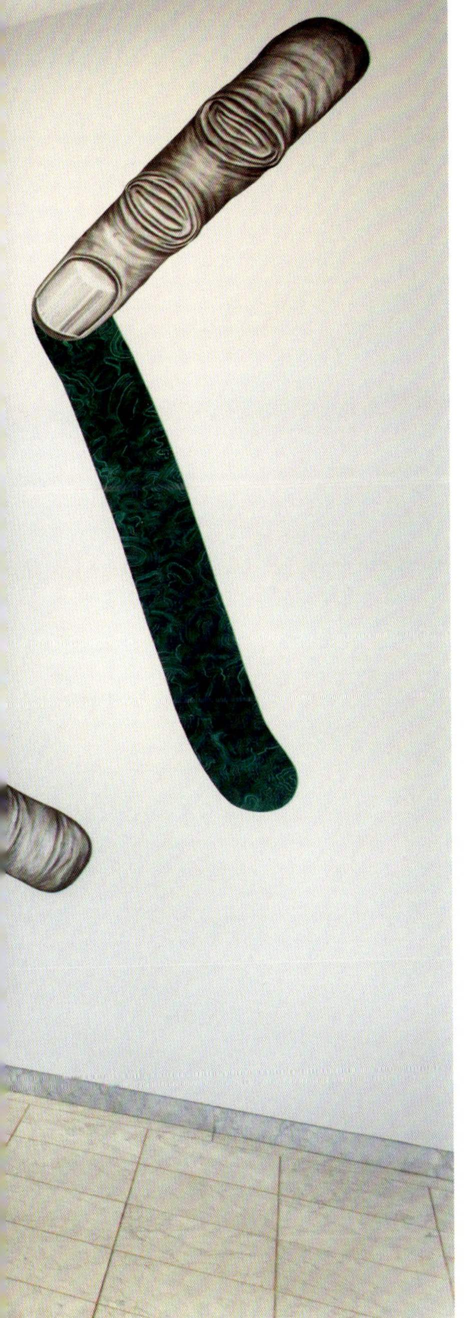

In 2013, inspired by Picasso's Tête De Femme (1921), Party began working with chalk pastel to create portraits in his now signature style of androgynous faces that recall classical Greek sculpture. Party remarked of the experience, 'I felt I was applying make-up onto those pristine marble faces. Using my fingers to paint colourful shadows around the eyes and bright red lipstick. What a great feeling to paint with your fingers.'[3] It's likely no coincidence that the bowls of fruit are accompanied by painting fingers.

In Party's earlier pastel still lifes and portraits, the objects occasionally take on anthropomorphized attributes. A tea pot might resemble a person, just as his portraits with their sharp angles and sculptural rendering resemble inanimate objects. In his 2016 pastel on linen, Two Pots, for instance, two (purple) teapots appear as if they're about to start a tango. Pastel lends itself to abstraction and curvilinear marks that make up the

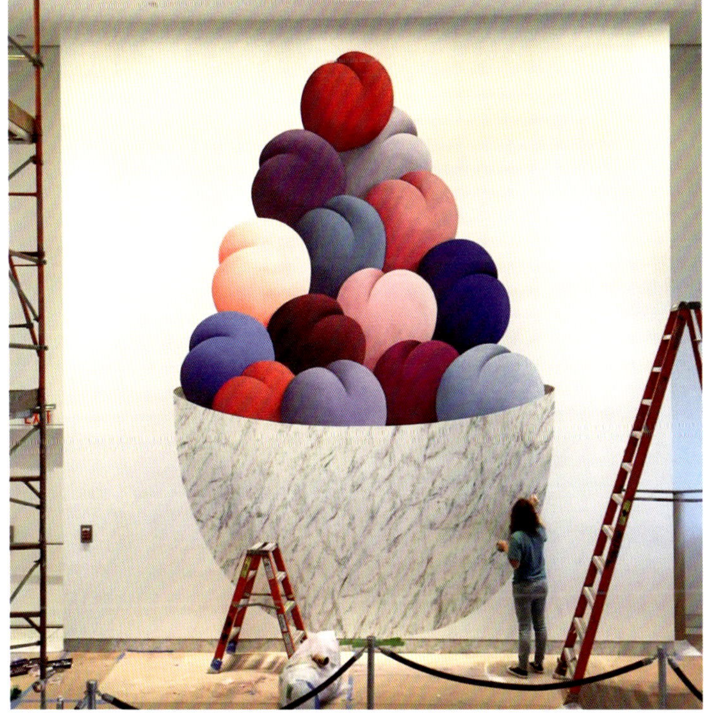

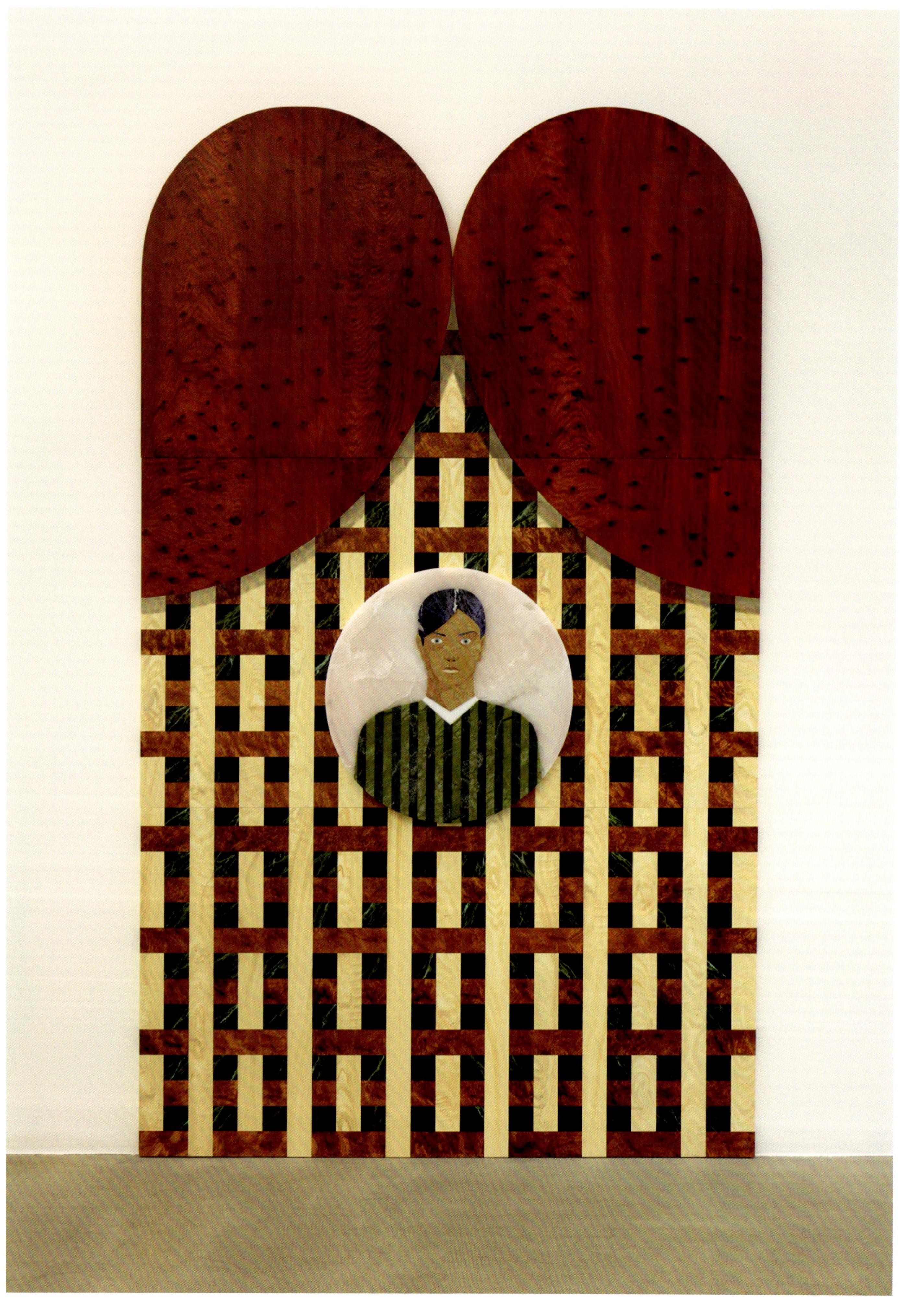

foreground,
PORTRAIT, 2018
MARBLE INLAY
80 X 80 X 3 CM

background,
OIL ON WOOD

INSTALLATION VIEW AT
KAUFMANN REPETTO,
MILAN, 2018

peaches and bananas in the Hammer exhibition, and the decision to depict the peaches in pastel was a pivotal move for this project, which along with the marbelizing, marked a new development in Party's arsenal of materials and techniques.

For his wall murals, Party carefully considers the context – in this case, a somewhat cold and corporate lobby that could just as easily be a bank entrance (that's actually next door). Party's project both embraces and contradicts the space. In addition to taking advantage of the space's high ceilings to employ pastel, Party deliberately acknowledges the marble, rather than attempting to conceal or disguise it. At the time of the project, Party had only recently begun working with the tromp l'eoil technique of marbelizing in his paintings, but he had not yet incorporated it into his murals. He looked at Italian frescoes and Giotto as references, as well as contemporary artists Richard Artschwager and Lucy McKenzie, for their precise renderings of the delicate, vein-like ribbons that are the main characteristic of polished marble.[4] Marbelizing or faux marbling was in wide use even before the Renaissance (when the technique was perfected) and requires expert attention and skill. Party collaborated with the Swiss artist Sarah Margnetti, a trained marbelizing painter, to create the convincing illusion.

The giant swiping fingers modelled after Party's own digits were rendered in charcoal, another ancient organic material. These fingers liberally spread seemingly weightless smears of the marble, in stark contrast to the heaviness implied by the marble bowls. With his painting fingers, Party adds a bit of magic to a gesture that has taken on a new relevance in today's digital world full of touch screens. Swiping left and right symbolizes acceptance or rejection, thanks to dating apps such as Tinder, and in this instance, Party plants a personal Easter egg of sorts – he met his long-time partner through the app. Additionally, the gesticulation reminds us of the childhood activity of finger painting, which Party recalled fondly in his comments about painting with pastel.

Party often revisits subjects in various scales, colours and materials. Peaches, and more specifically purple peaches, are no exception, and the fruit appears in several pastel on linen paintings from 2016 and 2017. In Tea Pot and Purple Fruits (2016), the purple peaches nestle around a large white tea pot, like a litter of puppies looking up to mom to nurse them. And Purple Peaches with a Stick (2017) features a pile of colourful peaches resting inside a generous white bowl inexplicably held up with a thin, delicate stick. Purple Fruits (2017) reveals an early version of the large striped marble bowl with bananas, this one featuring multicoloured banana-like fruits that appear to be making a slow escape from the bowl as if they were banana slugs. The delightful painting, Purple Peaches (2017), a narrow, vertical work, consists of a crowd of peaches (in all these same shades) bumping up against one another as if placed inside a rectangular vitrine.

With his vibrant palette and singular style, Party puts a refreshing spin on the traditional genres of portraiture, still life and landscape. His depictions of fruits and marble bowls are timeless and cannot be situated in any era or location. They also convey an impression of weight and volume (likely informed by Party's experience working in 3D animation in the early 2000s), which deepens with the soft curves afforded by the pastel and the hyperreal marbelizing. It is evident that Party carefully considers how to

STILL LIFE, 2015
SOFT PASTEL ON LINEN
150 X 140 CM

MURAL: CHARCOAL
AND ACRYLIC ON WALL

INSTALLATION VIEW
AT INVERLEITH HOUSE,
EDINBURGH, 2015

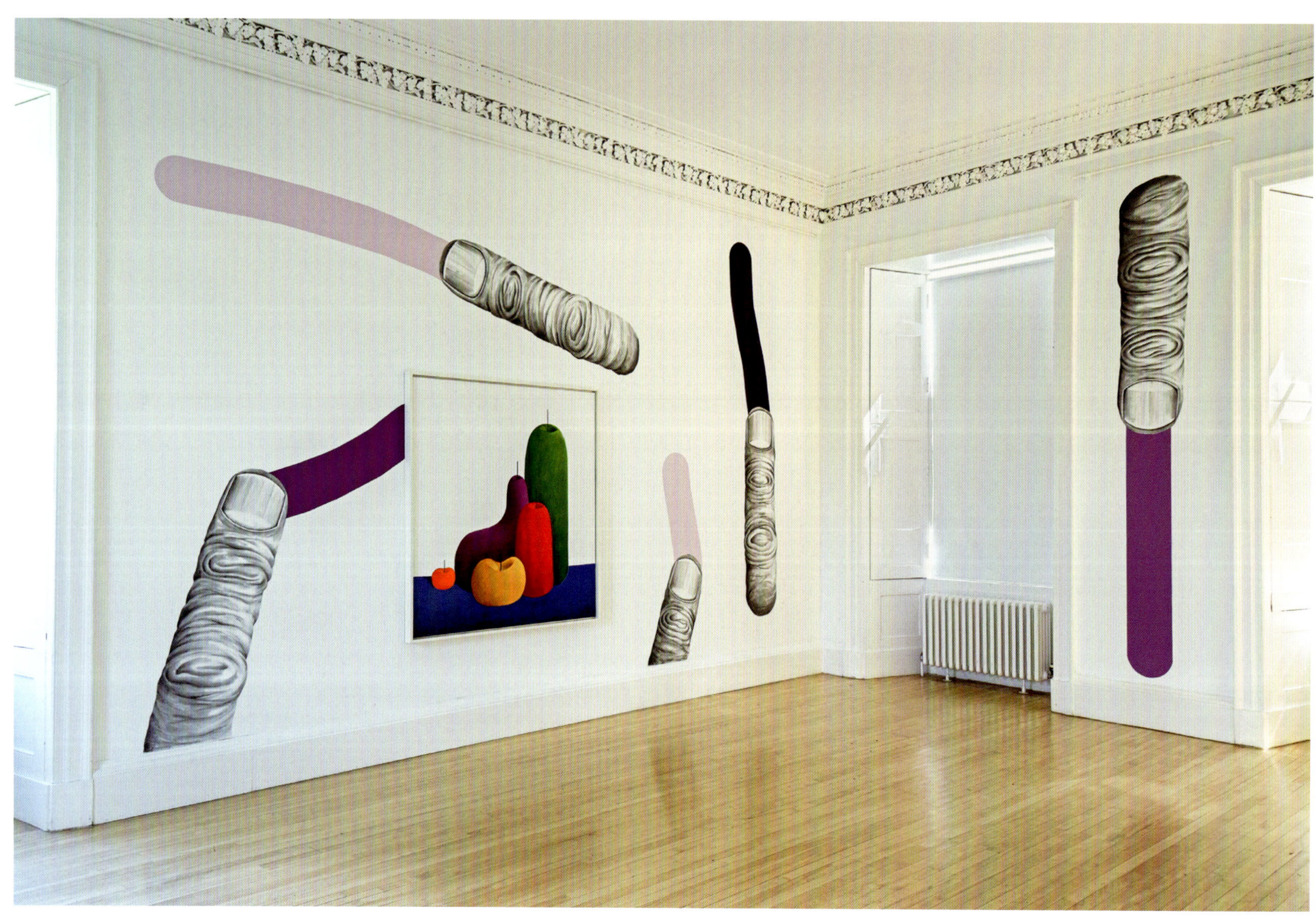

TEAPOT AND PURPLE FRUITS,
2016
SOFT PASTEL ON LINEN
105 X 85 CM

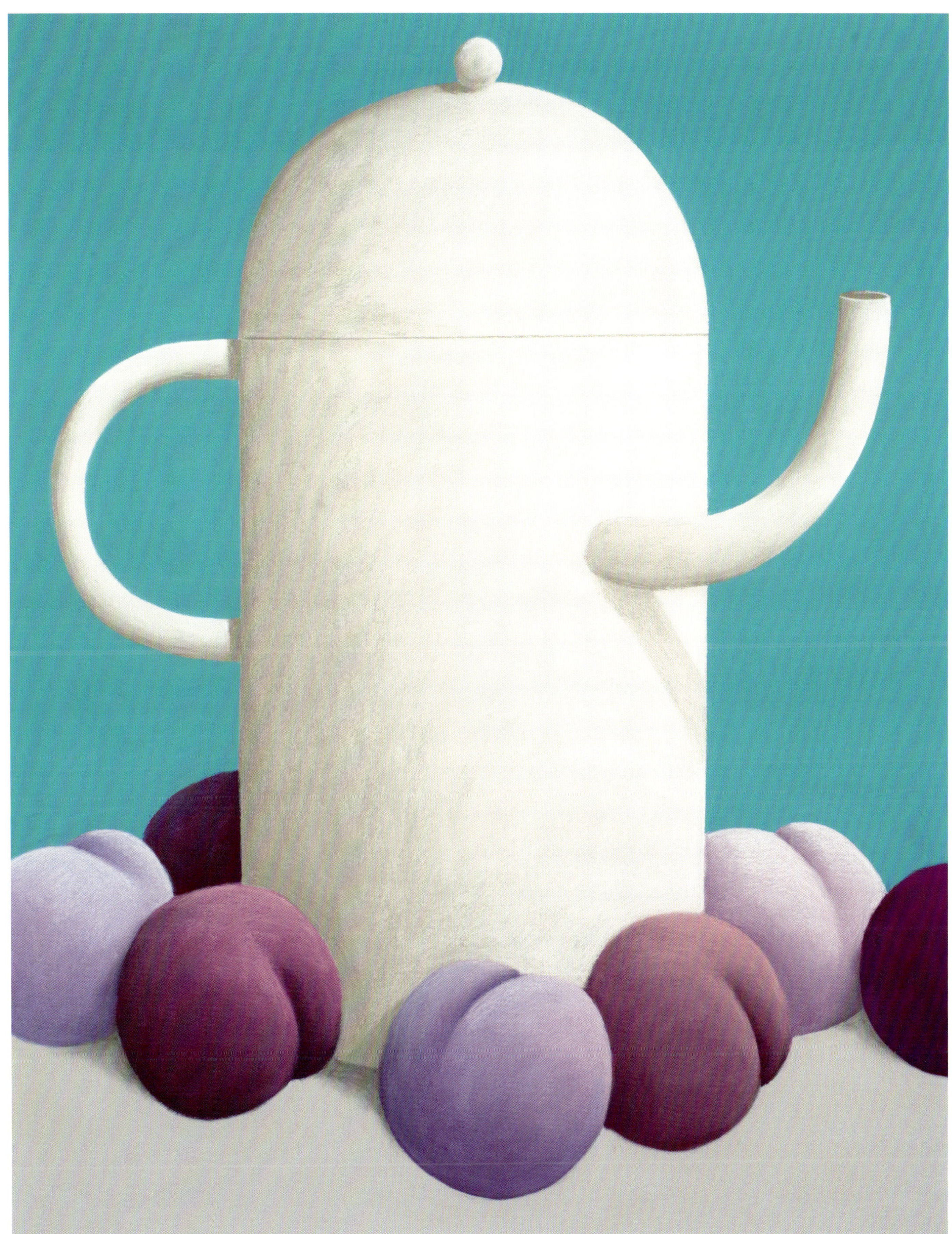

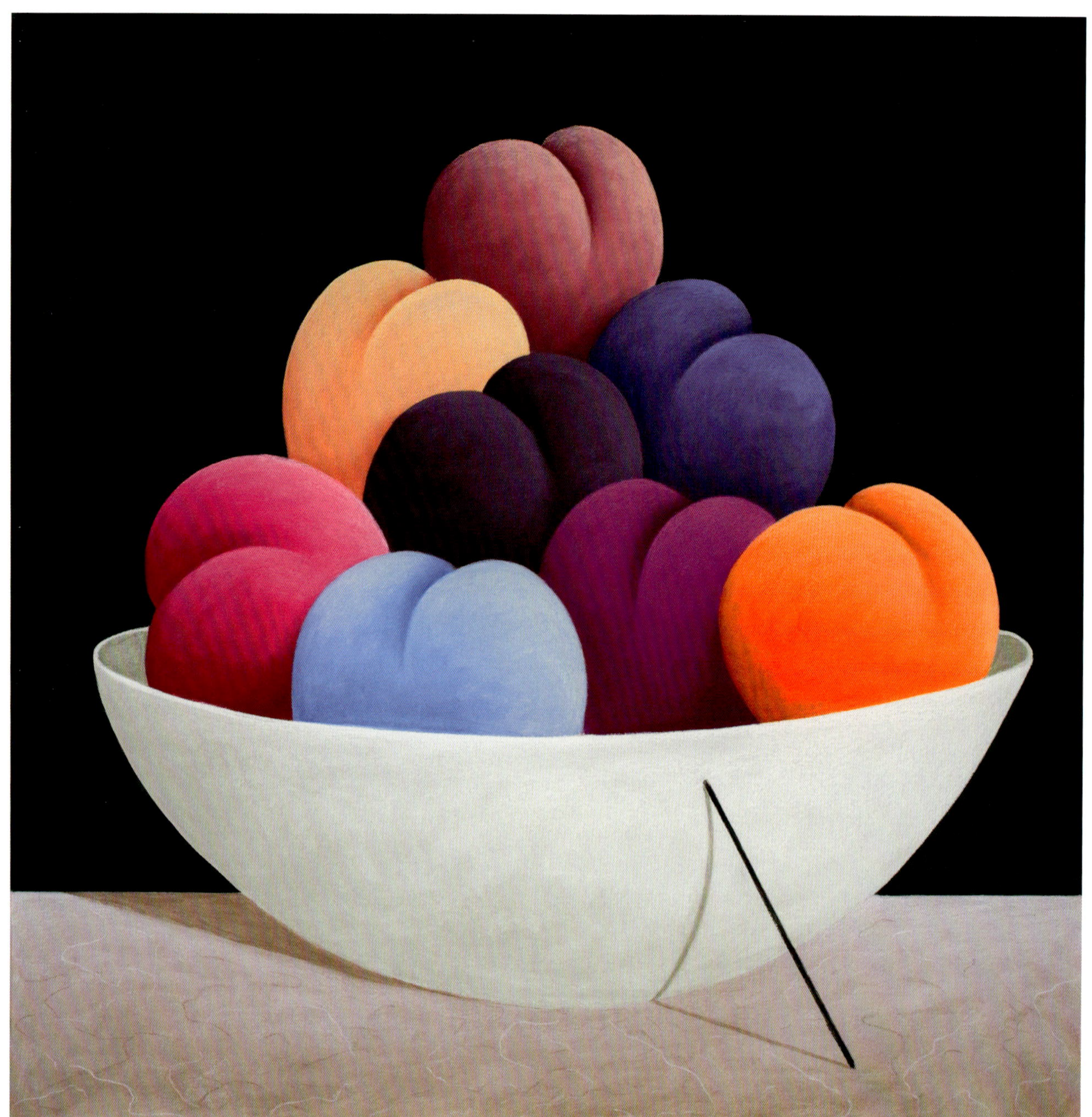

Purple Peaches with a Stick, 2017
Soft pastel on linen
120 x 120 cm

render these familiar objects and things, as he has developed his signature style. For example, the surreal soft pastel-on-canvas painting Still life (2016) depicts distorted apples and pears, and maybe a cherry, elongated in some cases, flattened out in others, wider in some areas, narrow in others, so they become not just anthropomorphized but almost alien.

A still life commonly includes fruit, but why did Party opt for the peach? The stone fruit originated in Northwest China and was cultivated in Persia (thus the scientific name Prunus persica) and from there was introduced to Europe. One account credits Alexander the Great for bringing the peach to Europe after conquering Persia; however, this has not been validated, peaches were well known to the Romans in the 1st century AD.[5] In the 16th century, Spanish explorers brought the peach to the Americas, and in the 17th century the peach made its way to England and France, where it was a delicacy. Archeobotanists have identified 'the oldest artistic representations of peaches in Italy' to two fragments of fresco from the 1st cent. AD, in Herculaneum, Casa di corvi, now preserved in the National Archaeological Museum in Naples.[6]

The still life, which became a popular genre during the Renaissance, was a frequent subject for Northern Renaissance painting in the 16th and 17th centuries.[7] Party's inspirations and references for Purple Peaches include French painters Jean-Baptiste-Siméon Chardin (for example, Basket of Peaches, with Walnuts, Knife and Glass of Wine of 1768) and Jean-Étienne Liotard's pastel Still-life: A Basket of Apples (c. 1786). These vanitas paintings, with eternally ripe fruits, reflected the fleeting nature of life and often symbolized bounty, abundance and wealth. Interestingly, the aforementioned allergy to peaches is rare in present-day Northern Europe. However, perhaps three centuries ago, before the advent of excessive washing and treating of produce, even Northern Europeans were allergic to peaches. This would have made the exotic fruits even more decadent.

Party also looked at ceramic Chinese fruit pyramids, that are composed with tall piles of fruit, like the composition of his pastel peaches.[8] For instance, the pastel on linen painting 20 Purple Peaches (2017), depicts 20 peaches in various shades of purple, violet, peach, pink and blue, arranged in a pyramidal shape.

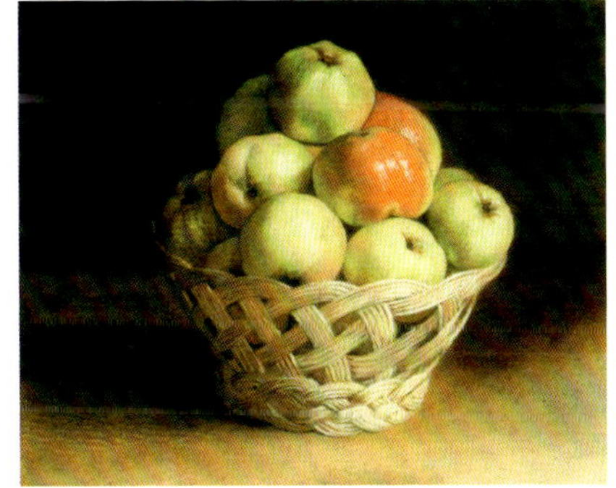

JEAN-ÉTIENNE LIOTARD
STILL-LIFE: A BASKET OF APPLES, C. 1786
OIL ON CANVAS
36 X 46 CM

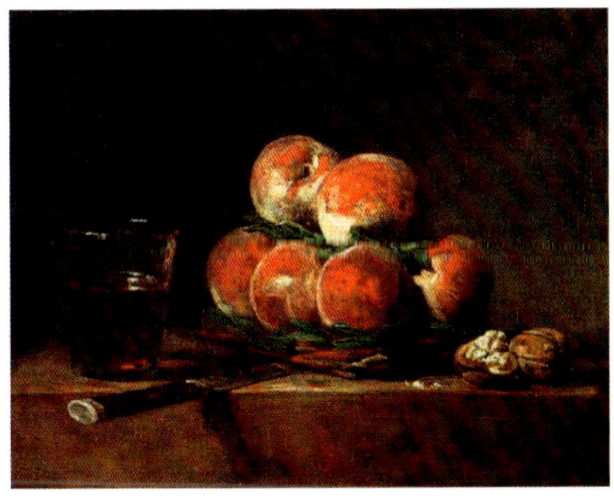

JEAN-BAPTISTE-SIMÉON CHARDIN
BASKET OF PEACHES, WITH WALNUTS, KNIFE AND GLASS OF WINE, 1768
OIL ON CANVAS
39 X 32 CM

The peach has a centuries-long history of eroticization and was a frequent subject for Caravaggio, as well as burlesque Italian poets such as Francesco Berni and Francesco Molza. The Italian word for peach, 'pesca' has a second meaning: 'a young man's bum', and the fruit has been adopted as a queer symbol. In contemporary culture, the peach emoji has been adopted as a stand-in for a derriere. Then there's that scene in the 2017 film Call Me By Your Name (if you haven't seen it, go watch it, words can't do it justice). After an intimate engagement with the peach, the character Elio (played by Timothée Chalamet) sets a spent peach on a desk, and the exquisitely lit scene looks straight from a Northern Renaissance still life with a peach. Peach references also abound in music. The late, great Prince wrote and recorded a song called 'Peach' in 1993, the moaning on the song reportedly contributed by American actress Kim Basinger (known for, among other things, her role in the soft-core film 9 ½ Weeks (1986), which coincidentally features a titillating scene in which she's being finger fed by her lover, although in this case there are no peaches, only strawberries and cherries, amongst other edibles). There's also a horribly annoying song 'Peaches' by The Presidents of the United States, which is allegedly about a crush on a girl that the songwriter wrote while sitting under a peach tree. Peaches can be a euphemism for breasts but also used as an idiom to express gratitude and declare someone as prized, desirable and/or delicious, as in 'You're a peach, doll.' Party's peaches bear a striking resemblance to a perfectly round and supple, perky even, rear end, crease and all. Of course, the

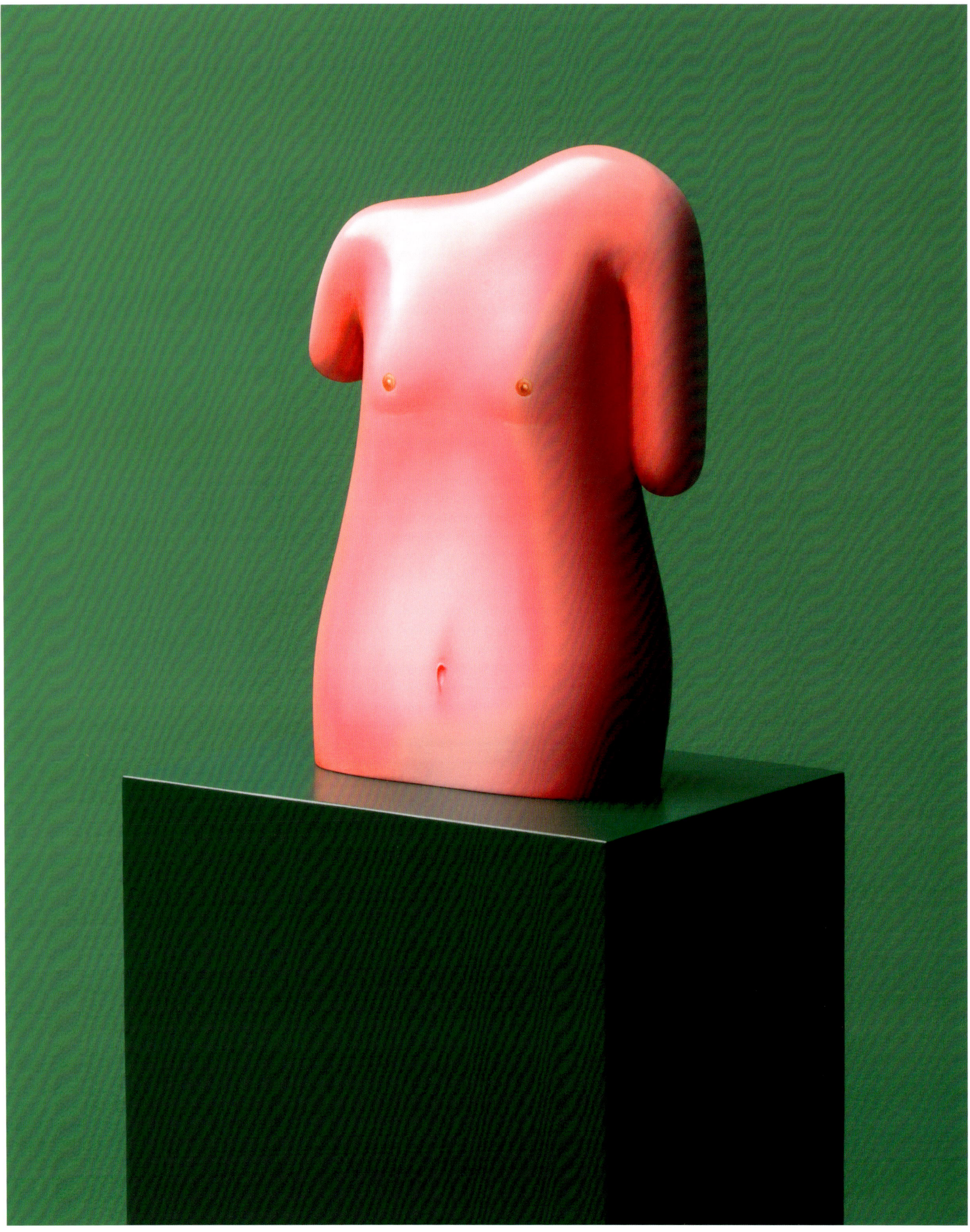

opposite,
TORSO, 2019
ACRYLIC AND OIL
ON BASS WOOD
30 X 20 X 11 CM

INSTALLATION VIEW AT XAVIER HUFKENS, BRUSSELS, 2019

below,
FINGER, 2019
ACRYLIC AND OIL
ON BASS WOOD
120 X 18 X 25 CM

INSTALLATION VIEW AT MARBLE HOUSE, NEWPORT, 2019

next pages, from left,
STILL LIFE, 2017
SOFT PASTEL ON LINEN
140 X 110 CM

STILL LIFE, 2020
SOFT PASTEL ON LINEN
140 X 110 CM

peach, as with most fruits, also often refers to female genitalia, and the act of eating a peach is a common metaphor for cunnilingus. Making Party's purple peaches the perfect partner to his purple bananas.

Starting with these rather unremarkable objects – peaches, fingers and marble, each rendered in a different material – initiates an endless dive into the numerous references and connotations in art, literature, science and technology, for all three subjects. This exemplifies one of Party's special gifts: his ability to deepen our understanding and appreciation of essential human and earthly things. The project also demonstrates Party's technical acuity and skill. Fluent in all aspects of painting, he can nimbly move from pastel to charcoal to gold leaf, marbelizing, oil, or spray paints. He seduces us with the technique, scale, colour and texture of these compelling representations and transforms our understanding of and relationship to each element. After experiencing Party's Purple Peaches, how can one ever look at a peach in the same way again?

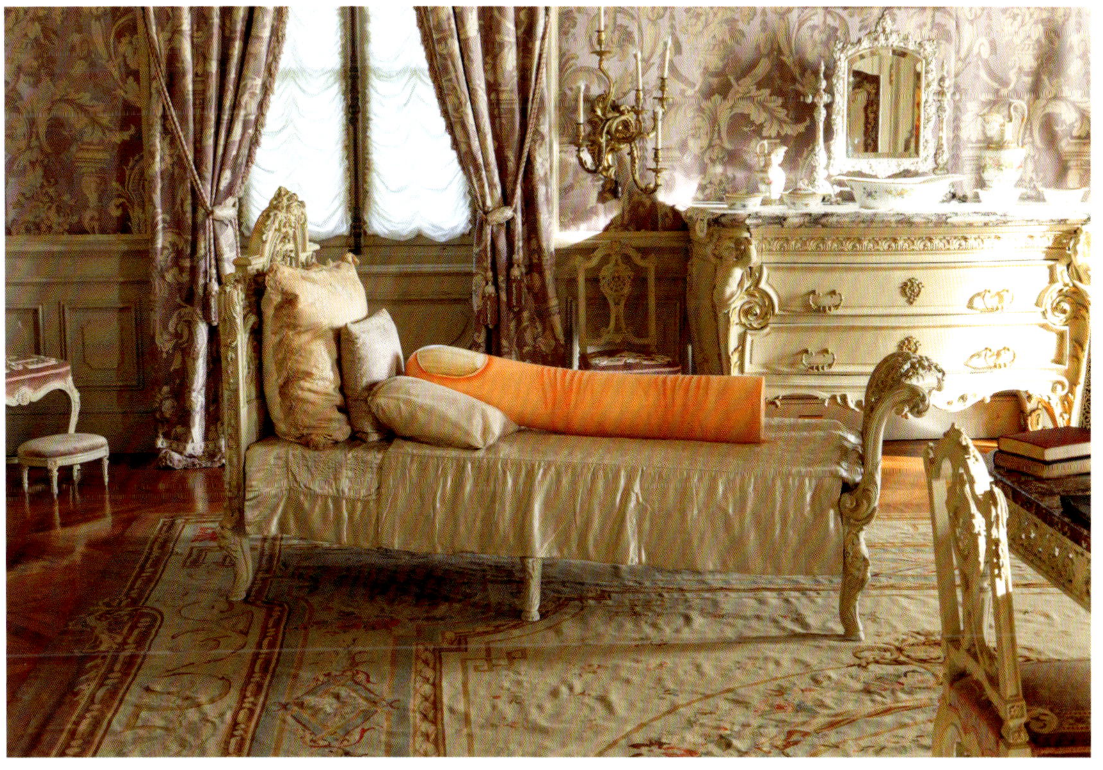

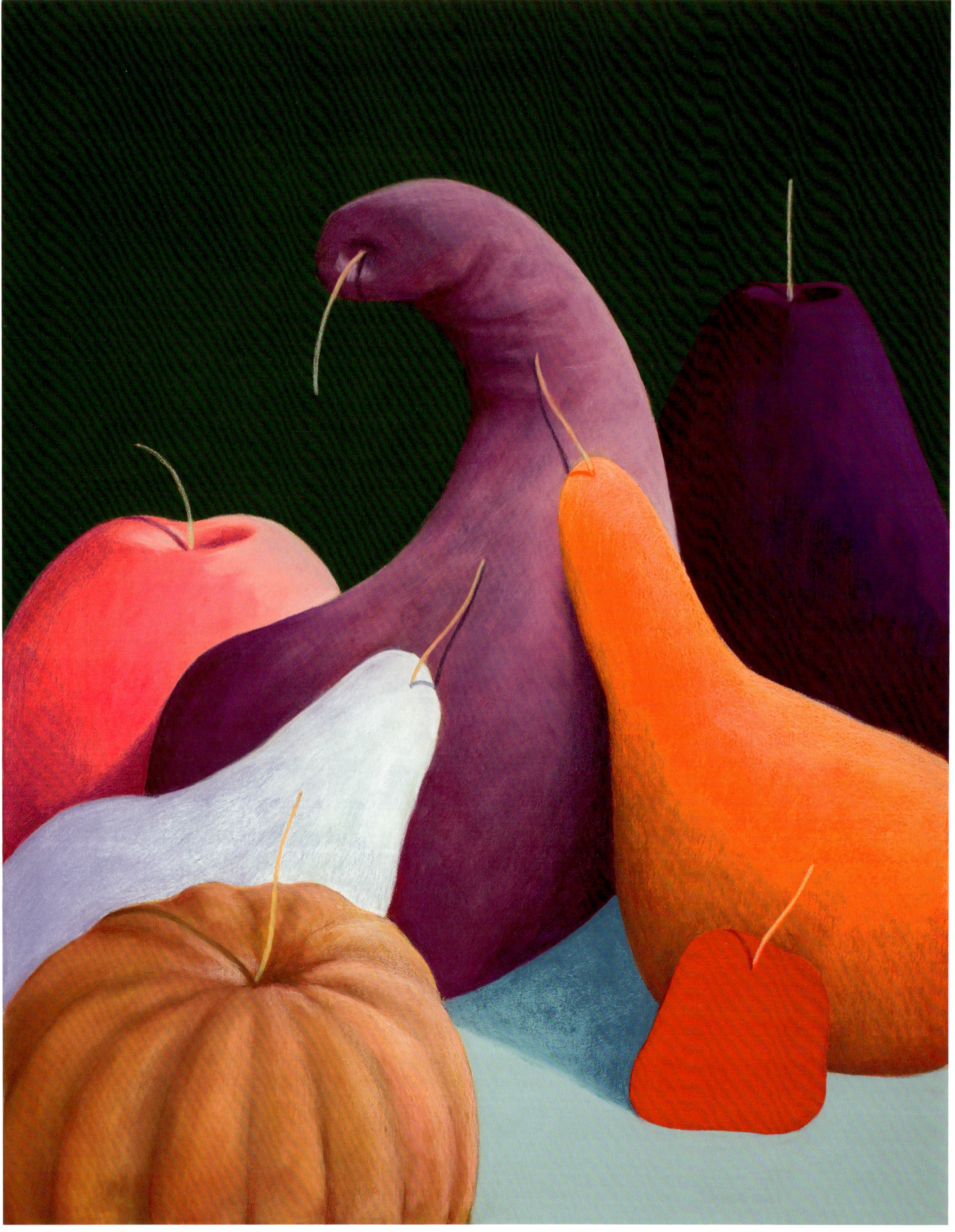

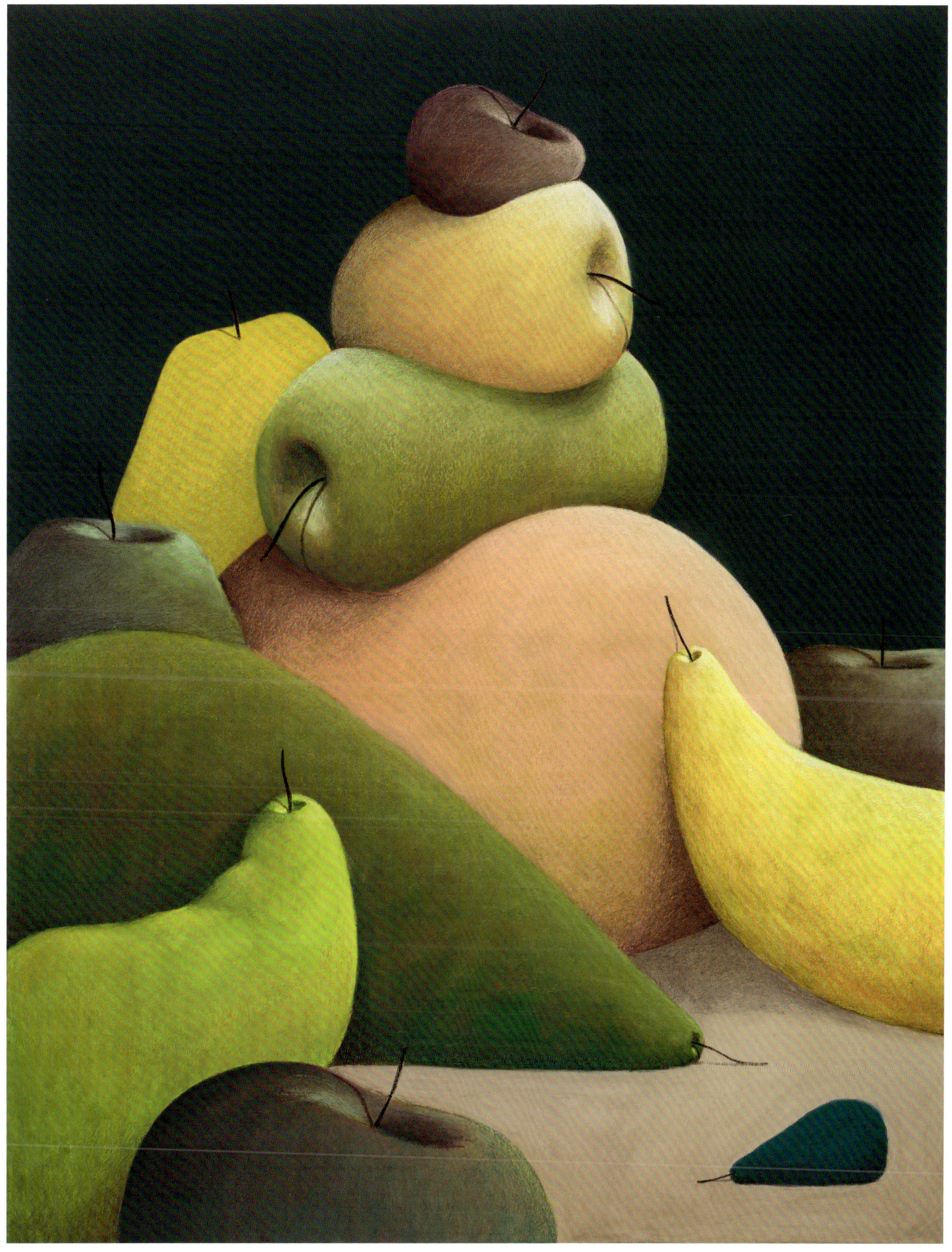

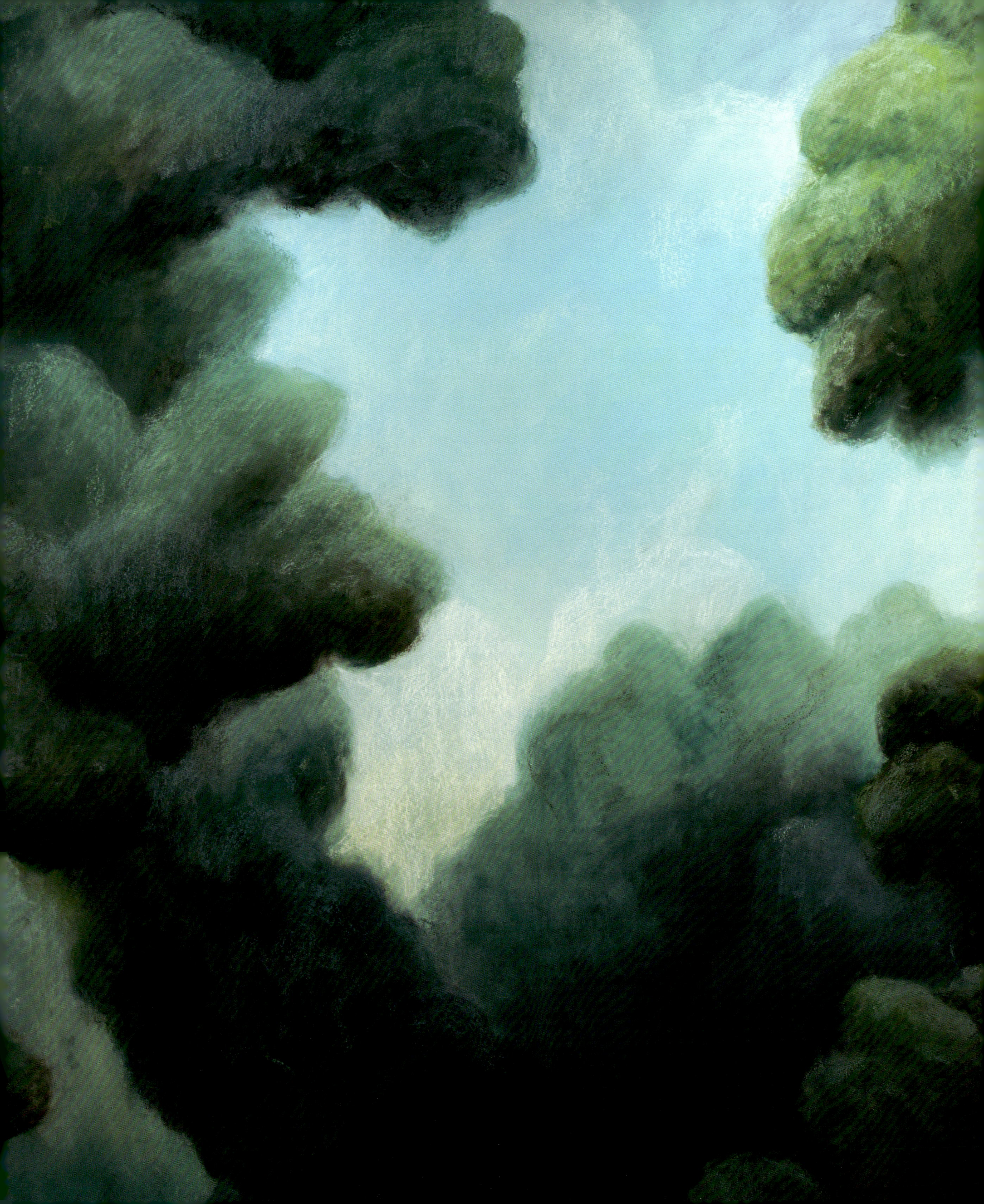

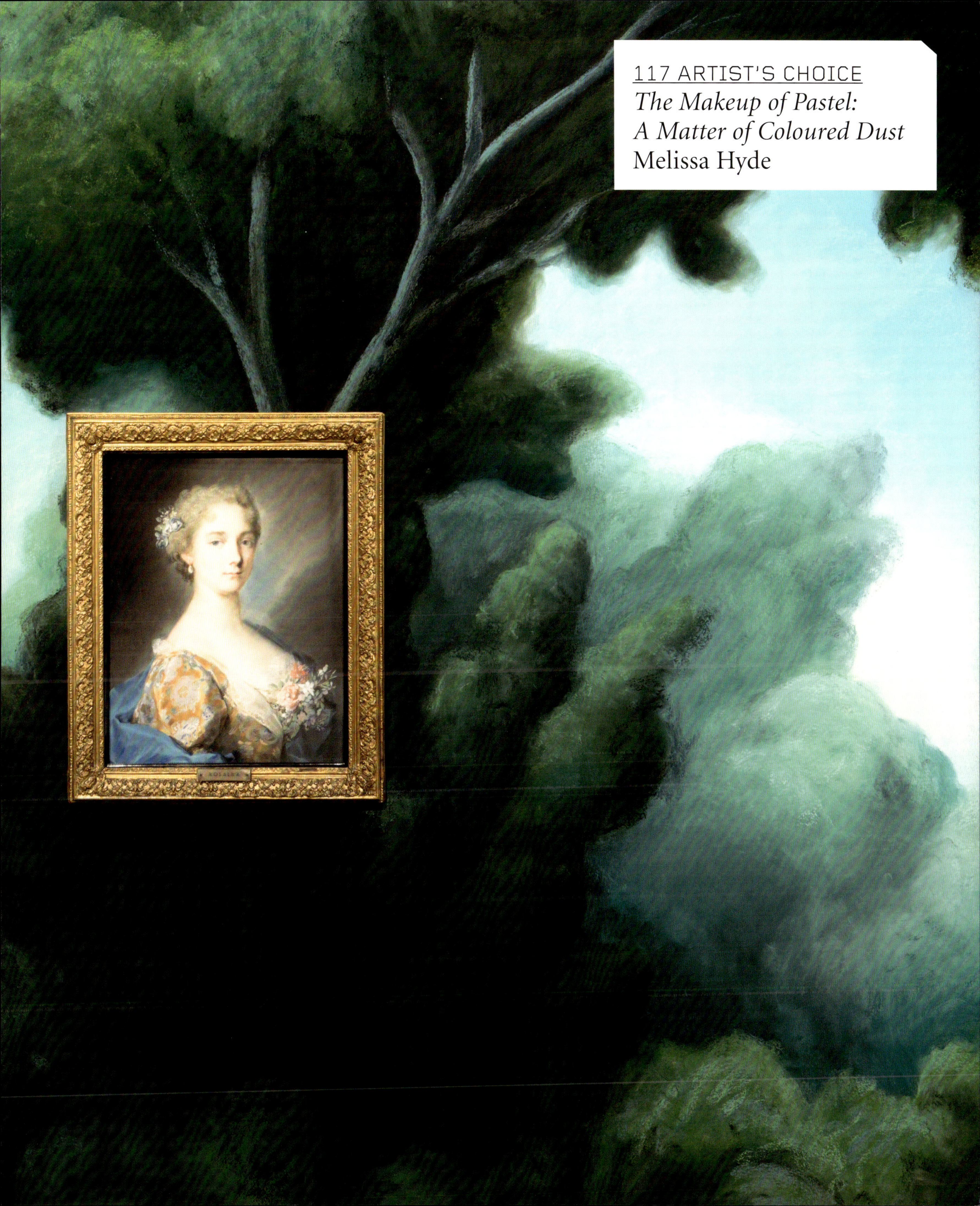

117 ARTIST'S CHOICE

The Makeup of Pastel: A Matter of Coloured Dust

Melissa Hyde

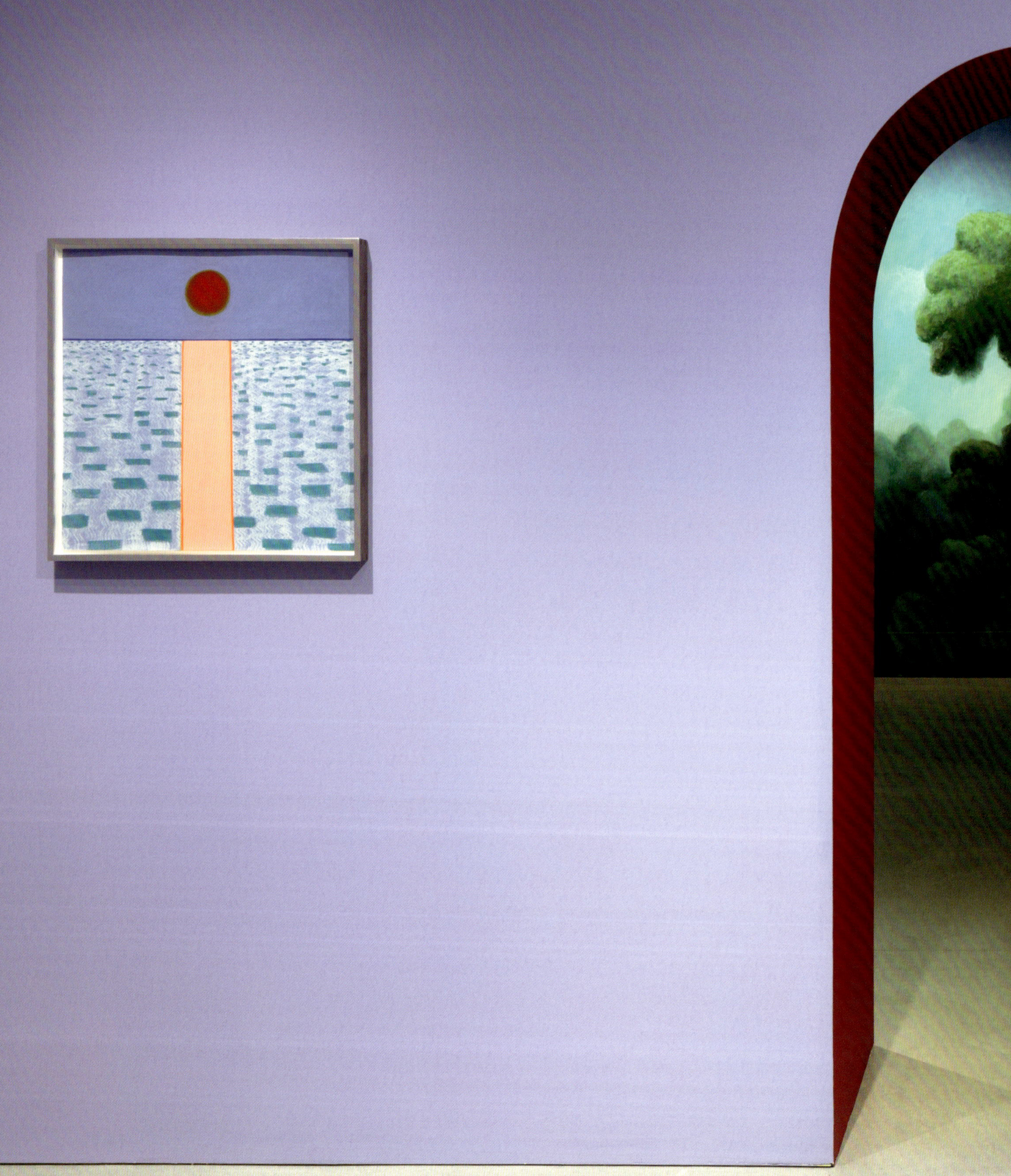

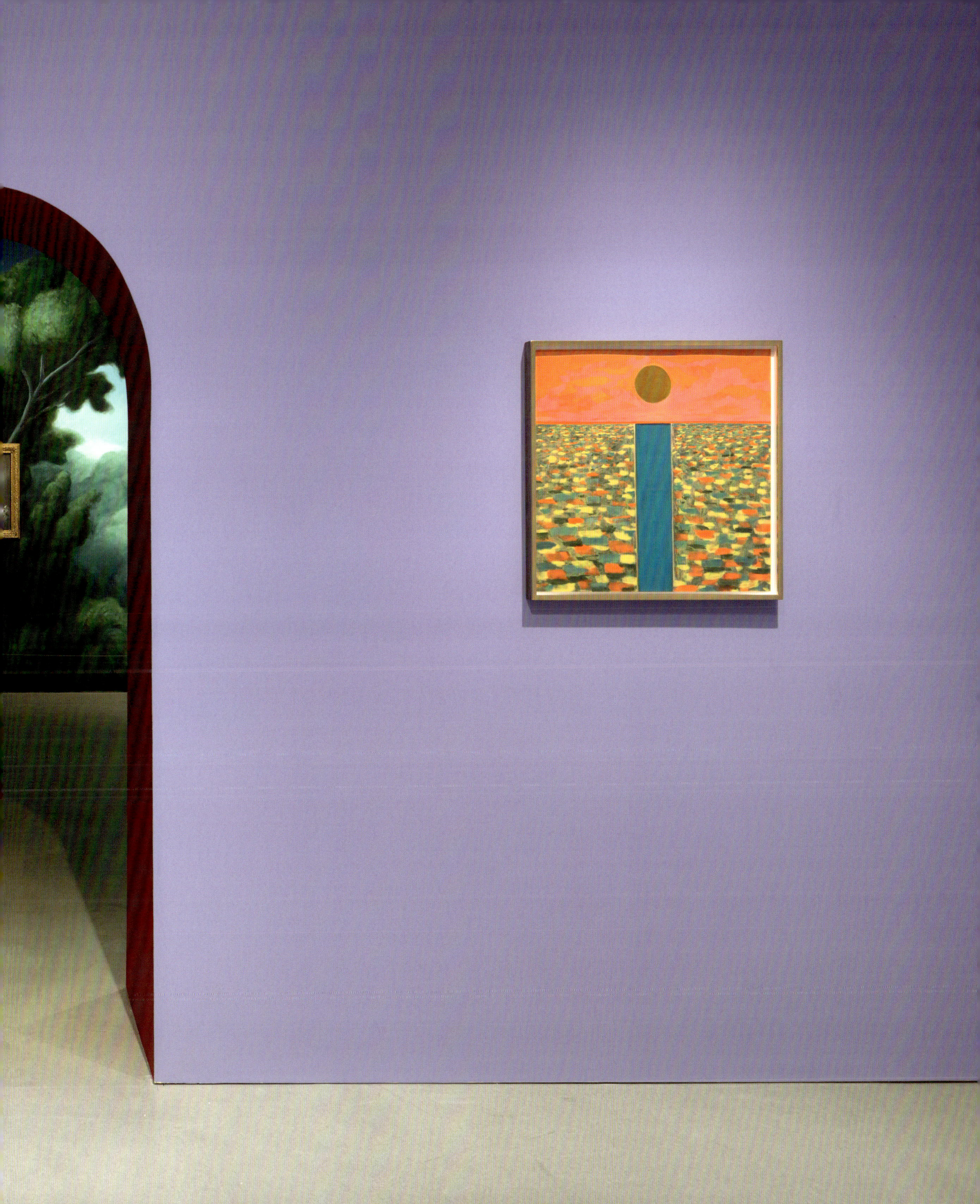

'Pastel: the face of all made-up women, so that in loving their beauty, one loves only a painting of crayon.'
– Louis-Antoine Caraccioli, *Dictionnaire critique*, 1768

'Pastel is a matter of dust. It is powdery and dry, and settles on the surface of what it figures like a cloud of makeup.'
– Jean-François Lyotard, *Pierre Skira: Pastels*, 1990

'Soft pastel is very different. It's very gentle. It's just dust.'
– Nicolas Party, *Arches*, 2018

Rosalba Carriera (1673–1757), an eighteenth-century Venetian 'paintress' (1731, p. 40) seems an improbable point of reference for the practice of a twenty-first century, Swiss-born, New York-based male artist – unless that artist is Nicolas Party. Like Carriera, who was known in her lifetime as 'The Queen of Pastel', Party found his calling as an artist when he began working with these friable sticks of pigment, a process by which he 'basically paints with dust', as Party has put it.[1] He has taken the trouble to learn that this delicate, fugitive medium has a surprisingly involved history, in which Carriera was a pivotal figure.

Though too often forgotten or dismissed by art history, Carriera was the first artist to be internationally renowned as a pastel painter and she was phenomenally successful.[2] Her handling of pastel, her distinctive, vaporous style and refined palette, had a marked influence on the art of her time. It helped to define the aesthetics of the stylistic mode to which we now refer as Rococo, a mode that has historically been placed squarely under the sign of the feminine. Carriera's importance in the formation of a Rococo aesthetic of portraiture contributed to a 'feminization' of the medium as well. Her unprecedented success as pastel painter and as a woman artist meant that her medium of choice was closely identified with her. Pastel in turn, came to be associated with women more generally, not least of all because so many of Carriera's subjects were women and because so many of them followed her example and became pastel painters themselves.[3] The particularities of pastel's materiality further contributed to its association with the feminine: its powdery, coloured pigments were physically similar to the cosmetics used (mainly) by women, an affinity that was accentuated by eighteenth- and nineteenth-century critics, who also frequently regarded pink – the colour of rouge for the cheeks, the quintessential Rococo hue – as the blushing handmaiden of pastel.

The origins of this constellation of pastel's associations can be traced to aesthetic, cultural (and ultimately political) debates in eighteenth-century France about what and who art was for, what should be its aesthetic priorities, and who should be making it. These were questions that, in turn, intersected with contested matters of class identity and ideals of masculinity and femininity, and were at the heart of a critical reaction against the Rococo that began in the middle of the eighteenth century shortly before Carriera's death in 1757.[4]

The medium of pastel has been in and out of favour over the past 300 years (mostly out, since the French Revolution). Party is bringing it back. He has made it part of his brief as an artist to rehabilitate, or at least to reclaim, pastel, which has been described aptly as a 'dethroned medium'.[5] There is a certain missionary zeal to Party's affection for pastel. He has observed that the traditional bias against it is alive and well: 'Masterpieces aren't made in pastel.'[6] 'If you use it, people will say, 'Well, that's not really *serious*. Why don't you [use] metal or oil paint on a big canvas? [Like] Richard Serra or Jackson Pollock.'[7] Happily, Party does not seem to take the requirement of 'seriousness' too seriously. He has made an agile (and perhaps post-postmodernist) swerve around the modernist emphasis on a self-critical, autonomous, 'deep' and serious-minded (oil) painting that operates in a realm far remote from that of decoration or even representation. His work, noted for its intensity and sometimes uncanny effects, resists the persuasive power of the modernist aesthetics and art-historical narratives that have long made the Rococo unpalatable to so many; that could only regard the 'pretty-

previous pages, foreground, from left,
SUNRISE, 2017
SOFT PASTEL ON PASTEL CARD
60 X 60 CM

SUNSET, 2017
SOFT PASTEL ON PASTEL CARD
60 X 60 CM

foreground,
ROSALBA CARRIERA
PORTRAIT OF A LADY AT THREE-QUARTER LENGTH, EARLY 1700s
PASTEL ON PAPER
56 X 44 CM

background,
FROM JEAN-HONORÉ FRAGONARD, THE PROGRESS OF LOVE, 1773, 2019
SOFT PASTEL ON WALL
233 X 340 CM

INSTALLATION VIEW AT THE FLAG ART FOUNDATION, NEW YORK, 2019

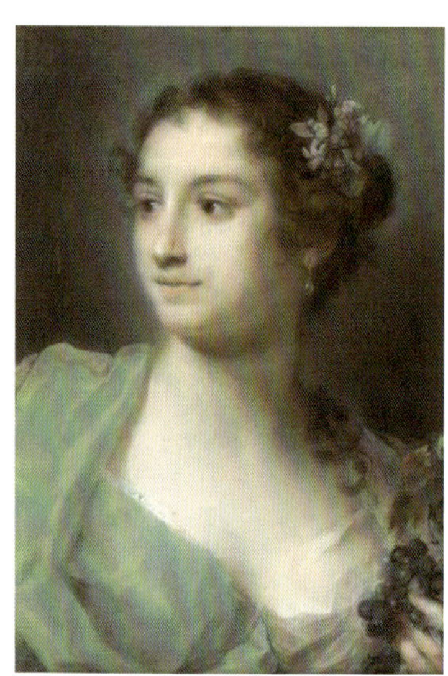

ROSALBA CARRIERA
PORTRAIT OF A LADY, BUST-LENGTH, LOOKING TOTHE RIGHT, HOLDING GRAPES (AN ALLEGORY OF AUTUMN), EARLY 1700s
PASTEL ON PAPER
46 X 33 CM

JEAN-BAPTISTE PERRONNEAU
PORTRAIT OF A WOMAN WITH PINK RIBBONS, C. 1770
PASTEL ON PAPER
55 X 45 CM

STILL LIFE, 2019
SOFT PASTEL ON WALL
84 INCHES

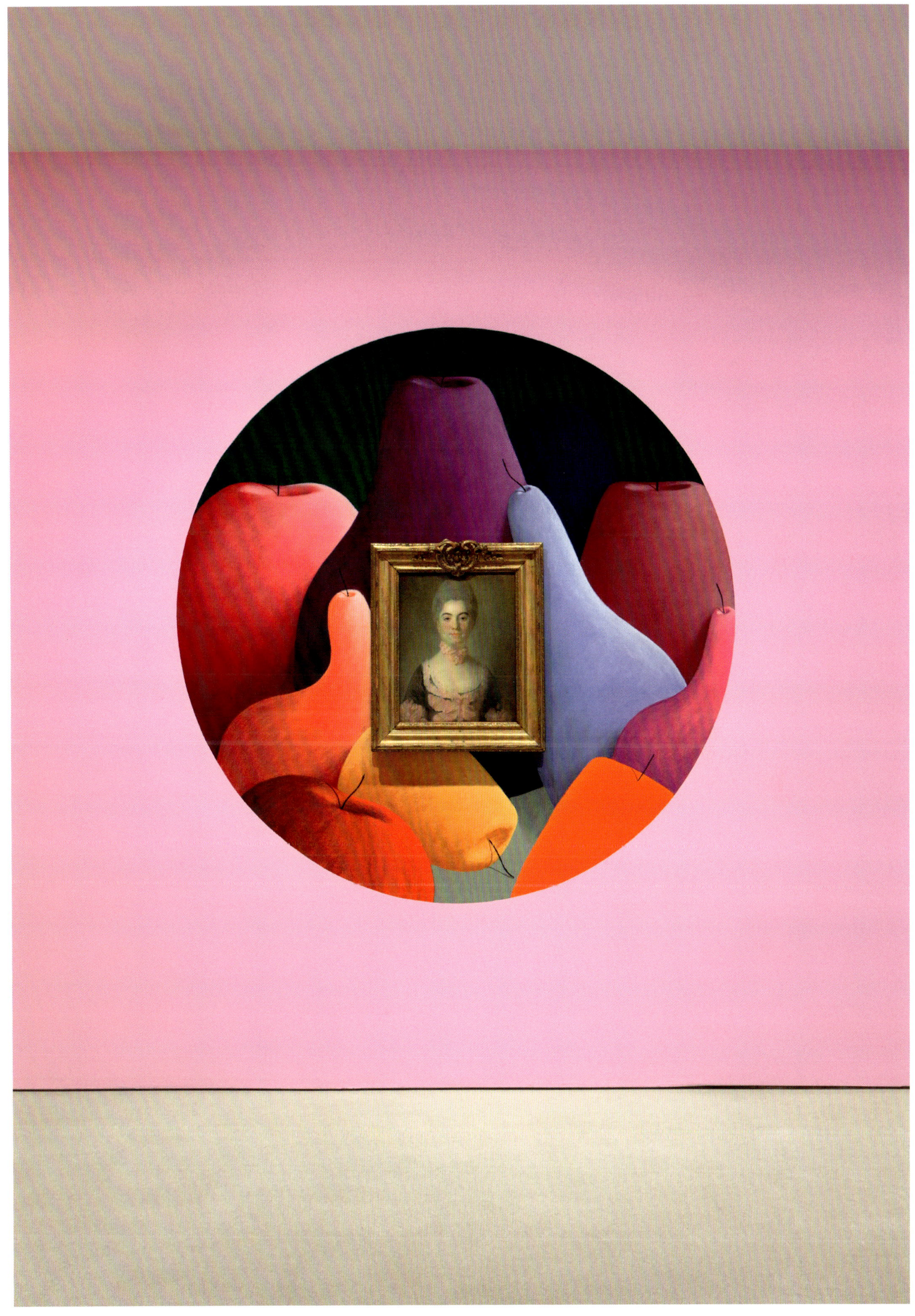

pretty school' of Boucher or Fragonard as examples of what was once denigrated as a 'hysterical and effulgent' Rococo.[8]

Party unabashedly rejoices in pastel's association with the Rococo and its collateral resonances. This accounts for the prominence given to Rococo painters, François Boucher and Jean-Honoré Fragonard in his exhibition 'Nicolas Party: Pastel', held at The FLAG Art Foundation in 2019. Party's 'walk-in celebration of pastel' included a series of installations of epically scaled murals rendered in pastel, each appropriated from an existing Rococo painting. The most immersive and perhaps alluring of these was the *Progress of Love* mural (2019), which unfolded contiguously around three sides of the room. It honed in on a detail from Fragonard's *The Pursuit* (c. 1771–73), one of a series of four fanciful scenes of aristocratic courtship painted for the last mistress of Louis XV, and now in the Frick Museum. It is perhaps misleading to speak in terms of a 'detail', since Party greatly expanded the scope and scale of the upper register of lush greenery in Fragonard's scene. In keeping with the Rococo aesthetics, which held that a painting should arrest and seduce the viewer, this work drew one in irresistibly, inviting one to luxuriate in the enveloping coolness of soft greens and lyrical blues, to delight in Party's rollicking version of the exuberance and fecundity of the picturesque garden in Fragonard's original. In this work, Party transformed the gallery space into an evanescent space of encounter with the actual Rococo itself in the form of Carriera's fetching *Portrait of a Lady at Three-Quarter Length*. This diminutive picture was the focal point of the room (and a centrepiece of the overall project). The juxtaposition of Carriera's pastel, its bloom still radiant after three centuries, and Party's ambitious excursion into pastel, a work of extremely recent vintage that was deliberately and pointedly impermanent, created a conjunction of past and present that highlighted the paradoxical nature of pastel itself: its extreme fragility and its remarkable power to retain its colour and freshness over centuries.

It is little wonder that Party, an artist whose practice is so deeply engaged with pastel, has turned his sights on the eighteenth century. In the spirit of that period, he playfully pays homage to it, and puts his work in witty dialogue with its art, even as he energetically extends the possibilities of the medium and intervenes in the received wisdom about it. The importance of Carriera's example for Party thus makes perfect sense. He not only delights in the connotations, both past and present, of his idiosyncratic choice of medium, but also those of the colour pink, one of the central chromatic themes in 'Nicolas Party: Pastel'. At the same time, the plush reds, fuchsias and shocking pinks of works like the outsized *Still Life* (2019) that opened the exhibition at The FLAG Art Foundation, so provocatively paired with Jean-Baptiste Perronneau's rouged and powdered *Portrait of a Woman with Pink Ribbons* (c. 1770, p. 121), give new meaning to 'pastel pink'. In Party's hands, it is as if the art of pastel itself is getting a complete makeover.

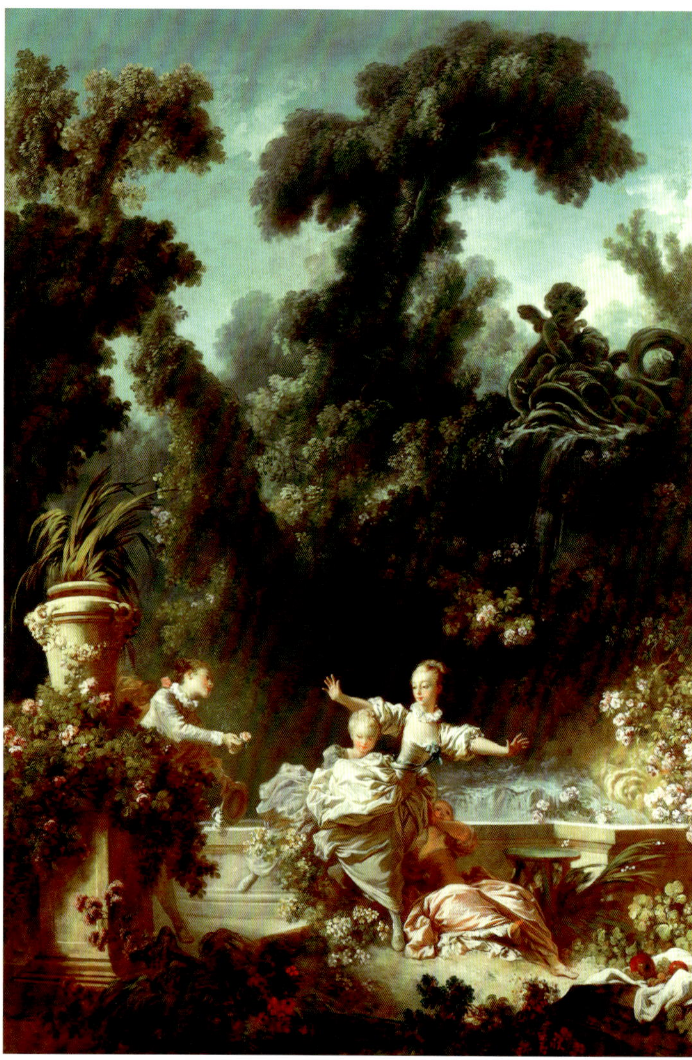

JEAN-HONORÉ FRAGONARD
THE PROGRESS OF LOVE: THE PURSUIT, 1771–72
OIL ON CANVAS
318 X 216 CM

Making Up with Carriera

... it was just a 'small step' to go from powders and painting makeup on the face to drawing pastel portraits ... [thanks to] Rosalba Carriera, who pioneered new techniques in pastel portraiture in the Rococo.
– Julie M. Johnson, *The Memory Factory: The Forgotten Women Artists of Vienna 1900*, 2012

foreground,
ROSALBA CARRIERA
PORTRAIT OF A LADY AT THREE-QUARTER LENGTH,
EARLY 1700s
PASTEL ON PAPER
56 X 44 CM

background,
FROM JEAN-HONORÉ FRAGONARD, THE PROGRESS OF LOVE, 1773, 2019
SOFT PASTEL ON WALL
233 X 340 CM

INSTALLATION VIEW AT THE FLAG ART FOUNDATION, NEW YORK, 2019

Pastel's meteoric rise in popularity in Europe was sparked by Carriera's stellar success during her sojourn in Paris from 1720–22. She went to Paris already an established artist with an international reputation. But once there, she became a phenomenon. Fashionable Parisians fell in love with the sophistication and refinement of her evanescent style, as did many artists who would emulate her. She was besieged by commissions, receiving far more requests for works than she could deliver. The ten-year-old Louis XV was one of Carriera's sitters. Her portrait of him won her the exceptional honour of being unanimously elected to the famed Académie Royale de Peinture et de Sculpture, abrogating its mandate of 1706 to accept no more women into its ranks.[9]

Carriera was largely a painter of small-scale portraits and female allegorical figures. Her work was especially prized by patrons and collectors of both sexes for its radiant palette, lustrous velvety tones and lush surfaces (mid-1720s). Part of the value of her pictures resided in their power to surprise, enchant and please. For connoisseurs like Pierre Crozat, the wealthy financier who sponsored her trip to Paris, Carriera's art had the power to seduce in just the way described by Crozat's protégé, the art theorist Roger de Piles: through a refined play of art and illusion. Considered from a de Pilesian perspective, one of the things that was and is most fascinating about Carriera's work is the way in which it invites awareness of the image as both illusion and artifice.[10] As such, it meets perfectly de Piles's ideals about pleasure and illusion – that the aim of art is to please and deceive the eye. It is in this context that he made his famous statement: 'We already know that all painting is only makeup [*la peinture n'est qu'un fard*], that it is part of its essence to deceive, and that the greatest deceiver in this art is the greatest

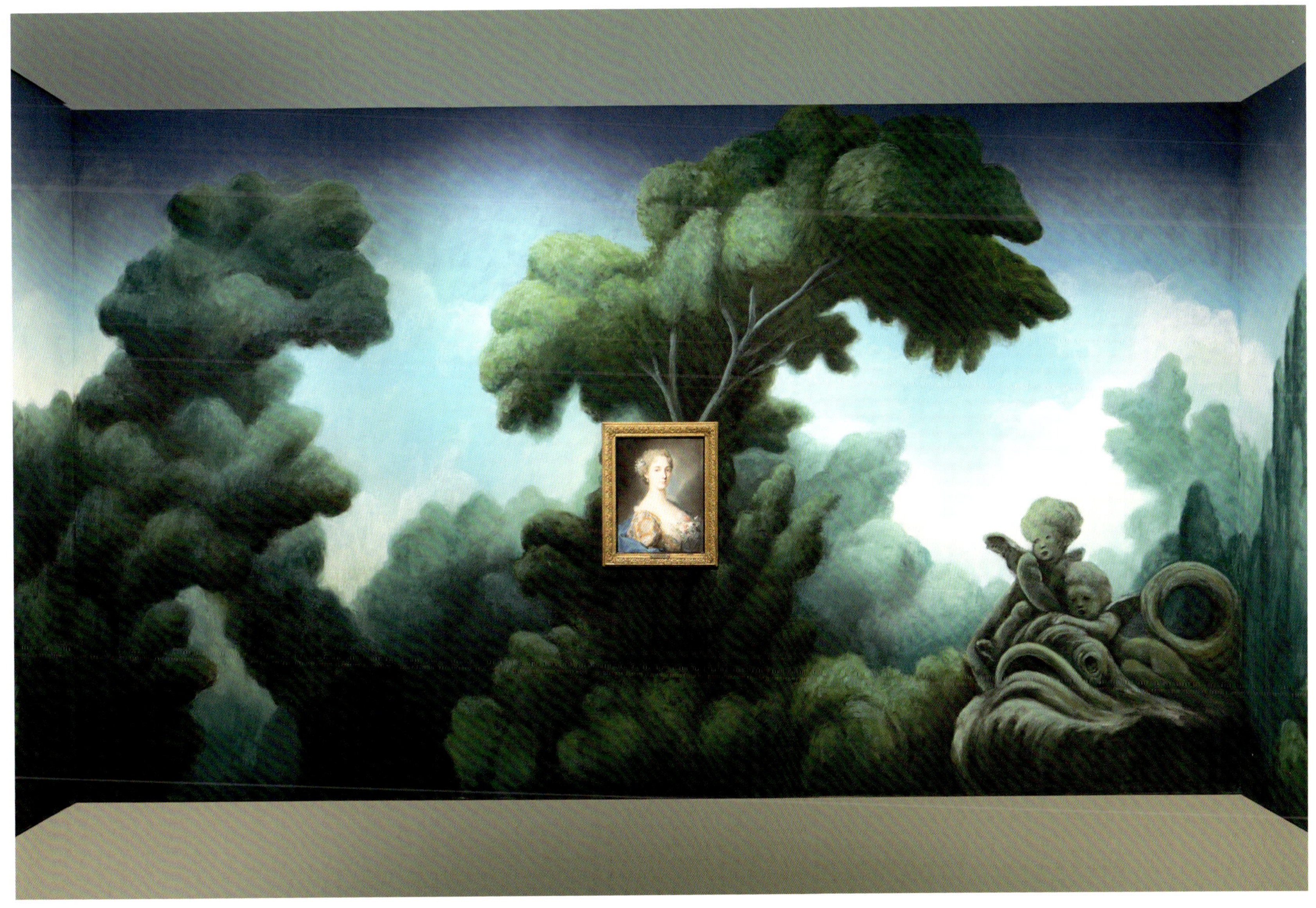

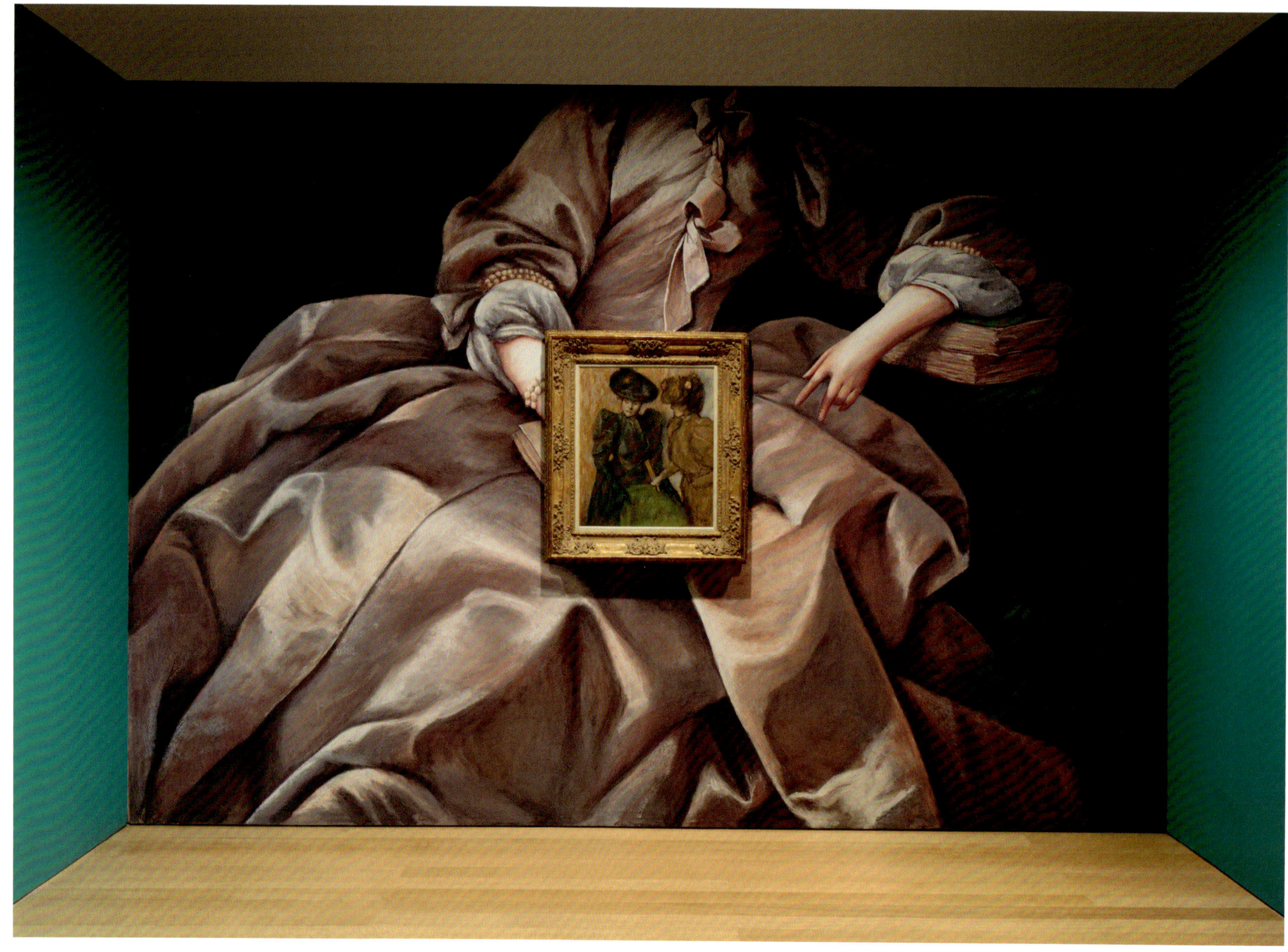

painter.'[11] Thanks to Carriera's handling of her pastel crayons, which variously calls attention to and effaces the means of representation, the spectator is invited to marvel at both the illusion Carriera creates and the materiality of pastel itself. The constant interruption of illusion in Carriera's pastels privileges the material aspects of the painting and prevents complete absorption into the image by never letting you forget that it is a representation, a made object (c. 1730, p. 127).

In many of Carriera's works, seductive illusionism is heightened by the intersections between her practice of pastel portraiture and the homologous cultural practice of 'making up' with cosmetics. To provide some context, let me say a few words about *le fard* (makeup) in its broader cultural and theoretical frameworks. Traditionally associated with forms of rhetoric and with painting, as well as actual cosmetics, *le fard*, in all its forms, had always had critics. Since antiquity, it had been associated with deception, illicit pleasure and seduction.[12] But with the Enlightenment's emphasis on transparency and truth, and its celebration of nature and sensibilité, criticism of *le fard* reached a new pitch during the second half of the eighteenth century. Social critics censured French women for their heavy-handed application of red and white that masked their faces and made them all look alike.[13] These writers celebrated a new aesthetic of natural female beauty that privileged the truthful unmade-up face as the expression of personal authenticity.[14]

opposite, background
EDGAR DEGAS
LA CONVERSATION, 1895
PASTEL ON PAPER
65 X 50 CM

foreground,
FROM FRANÇOISE BOUCHER, PORTRAIT OF MADAME DE POMPADOUR, 1758, 2019
SOFT PASTEL ON WALL
127 X 282 CM

below,
PORTRAIT WITH PINK BOW
2019
SOFT PASTEL ON LINEN
127 X 102 CM

The taste for naturalism extended to the painting of pictures, as well. After 1750, painters of *les grâces factices*, like Boucher and Jean-Marc Nattier, were increasingly taken to task for their made-up (*fardé*) painting – usually, but not always, in reference to their representations of women. The two streams of social and art criticism *contre le fard* were often intermingled, as when Louis-Antoine Caraccioli mockingly compared women's boudoirs to painter's studios, and important art-world figures like Charles-Nicolas Cochin satirized fashionable painters as makeup artists.[15]

The quite literal connections between pastels and *le fard* are confirmed by a 1788 treatise on pastel, which includes recipes for making cosmetics as well as pastels: both used carmine or cinnabar to make reds for the cheeks, for example, and they came in the same powdered and paste forms.[16] Like Boucher after her, Carriera capitalized on the similarities between *le fard*, art and artifice. In works like the *Allegory of Painting* (c. 1730s), which is an exquisite example of Carriera's artful depiction of a made-up face, she not only offers an allegorical image of the art of painting but also explores the self-referential qualities of pastel in terms of the de Pilesian metaphor of paint-as-*fard*. She was painting painting itself.[17] However, even in her portraits of sitters who didn't wear makeup, she paints the seductive surface, the mask, the social persona.

A Talent for Women?

'Pastel can rescue so many young women from the tedium of solitude and is one of the resources against idleness, the source of so many indiscretions.'
– [Chaperon] *Traité de la peinture au pastel*, 1788

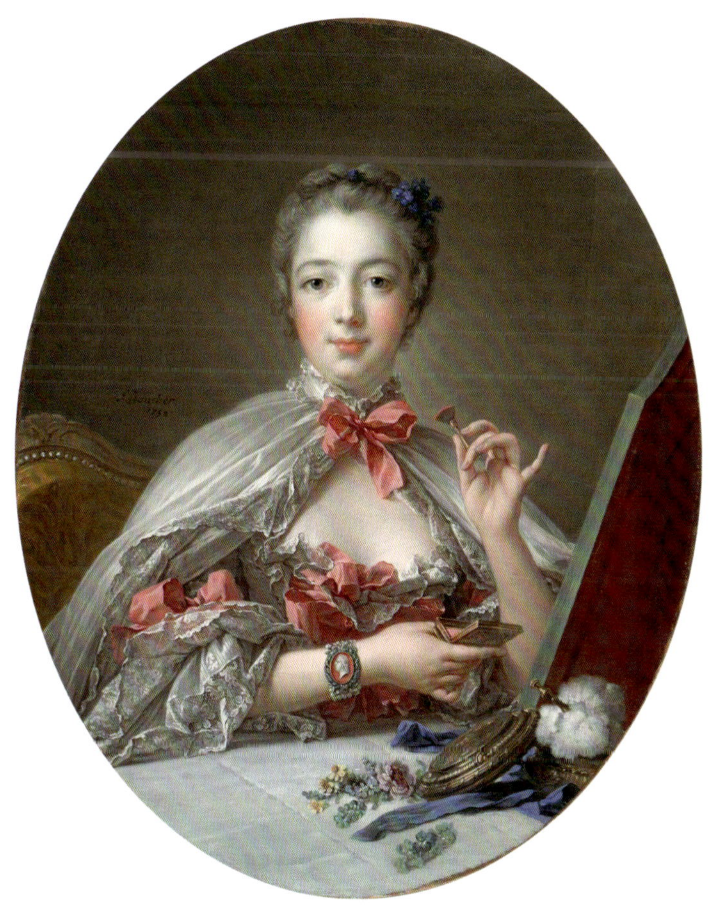

FRANÇOIS BOUCHER
JEANNE-ANTOINETTE POISSON, MARQUISE DE POMPADOUR, C. 1750
OIL ON CANVAS
81 X 65 CM

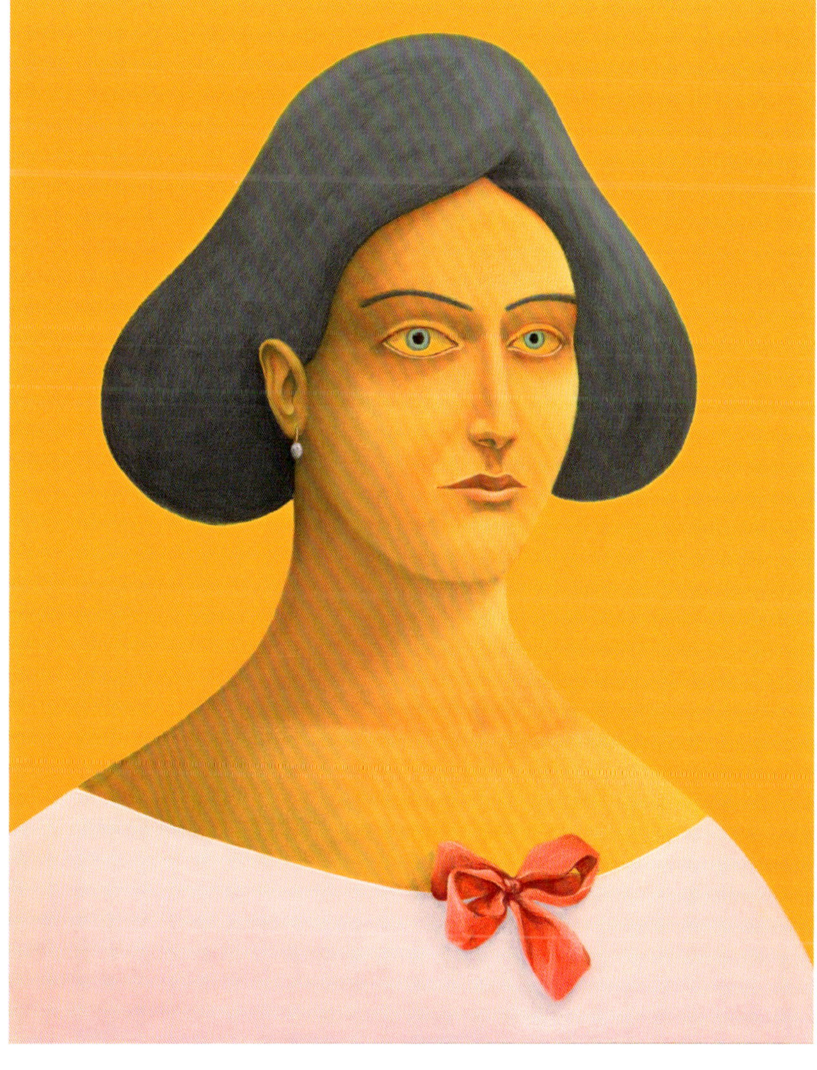

Despite the fact that pastel was practised by canonical artists who came after Carriera, such as Quentin de la Tour and Jean-Baptiste-Siméon Chardin, the medium never attained official legitimacy, at least in part because of its fragility and consequent ephemerality. Instead, pastel was increasingly identified during the eighteenth century as an art form executed by women. It was often taken up by young ladies as an elevating, tasteful pastime intended to enhance their matrimonial prospects. The treatise of 1788, mentioned above, recommended pastel specifically for them. Pastels were also marketed to women. One prominent pastel manufacturer, for instance, offered a selection for ladies containing a range of colours ideal for 'flowers, figures, and landscapes' – subjects considered suitable for the female artist.[18]

By the nineteenth century, women had long been regarded as the primary practitioners of pastel painting. Already by 1755, the association between pastel and amateur women artists was an established trope, as evidenced by Sir Joshua Reynolds' comment that the art of prominent Swiss pastellist Jean-Étienne Liotard was 'just what ladies do when they paint for their own amusement'.[19] The remark bespeaks Reynolds's low regard for Liotard, but also comports with a general antipathy toward pastel that emerged at mid-century in France, in official quarters, anyway.[20] The feminine 'domestication' of pastel also contributed to a sense that the medium belonged to the realm of the private, whereas oil painting was the medium for the public domain and the proper vehicle for serious, advanced painting.

In a publication of 1823, the writer and educator Madame de Genlis noted that pastel painting 'had been completely abandoned'.[21] She lamented that any form of art should be thus forsaken, especially when it was 'agreeable and easy', thereby alluding to the widely accepted idea that pastel was easy to master, but also referring to its convenience.[22] 'Many people who were put off by all the equipment, the difficulties and inconveniences of oil painting, painted in pastel', she observed.[23] A similar point had been made by De Piles, who described pastel as 'the most commodious type of painting', for, as recently noted, it 'required relatively little preparation, no assistants, and few tools: a box of crayons, paper, a drawing board, and stumps for blending'.[24] These are some of the reasons why pastel could so readily be practised by amateur artists. Additionally, one did not need a studio to accommodate the mess and smells of oil paint, pastel did not require drying time, one could pick it up and put it down at a moment's notice. All of these factors made pastel a particularly congenial medium for women.

According to Genlis, the essential reason why pastel had been abandoned was that 'in the end, this was a talent for women'.[25] She mentioned the renowned Elisabeth Louise Vigée Le Brun (1755–1842) as an example of a woman who had exercised this talent professionally. The evidence suggests, however, that what really doomed pastel as a feminized, second-class medium was not its identification with professional women artists, but rather its ever-increasing association in the nineteenth century with genteel ladies who practised it 'for their own amusement', as Reynolds had put it.

In the Pink: the Unbearable Lightness of Being Rococo

'For all too long we have seen artificial, illuminated style of colouring obscure the colours of nature, and a feeble pink emasculate all our artists' pictures. When Boucher imagined that he was conforming to the taste of his times, he ruined it.'
– Étienne Falconet, *Letter to Diderot,* 1770

In the eyes of reformist art critics of the eighteenth century, pastel, like the Rococo with which it was intimately allied, was redolent of twee aristocratic frivolity and the *ancien régime* – a regime that was itself said to be under the sway of women. (Jean-Jacques Rousseau was the most prominent purveyor of this line of thought.) During the second half of the century, anti-Rococo sentiment increasingly attacked the supposed feminization of society and, by association, pastel and its inherent artifice. Pastel, with its Rococo tinge, would eventually fall from grace.

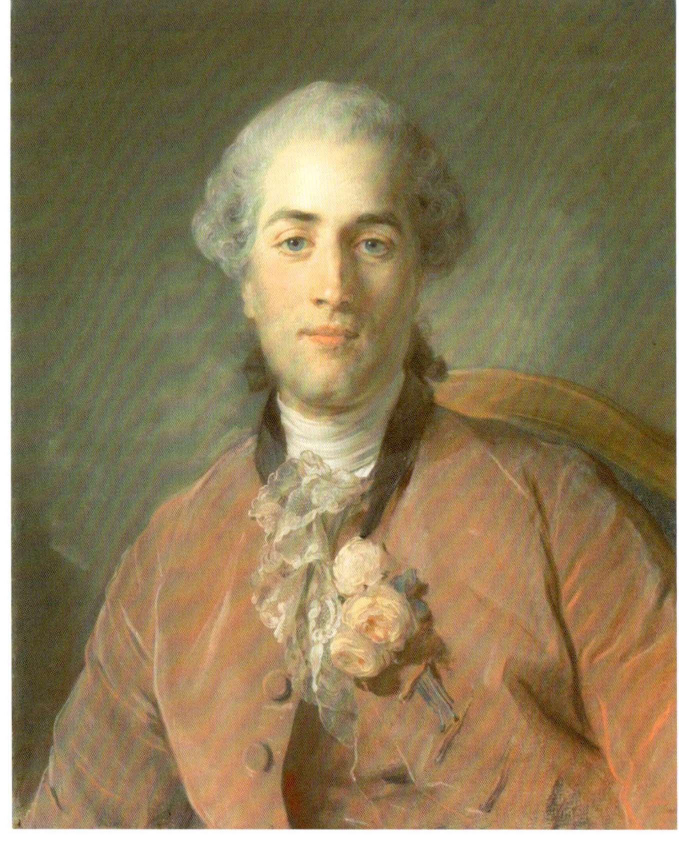

JEAN-BAPTISTE PERRONNEAU
PORTRAIT OF OLIVIER JOURNU, 1756
PASTEL ON BLUE-GRAY LAID PAPER
58 X 47 CM

If one is to speak literally of 'tinge' in relation to the Rococo, the feminine, and the aristocratic, the tinge in question would most certainly have to be pink. In anti-Rococo criticism, pink is emblematic, and not in a good way, of fashionable society, of artifice and dissimulation, of softness and weakness, and of the ascendancy of women – symbolized by Madame de Pompadour, the mistress of Louis XV, whose favourite colour was pink. Her best-loved painter, Boucher, allegedly the author of the demise of the French School, was singled out time and again for his 'abuse' of pink. Paintings such as *The Setting of the Sun* (1752) and *The Rising of the Sun* (1753) were criticized for their false, made-up (*fardé*) appearance.[26] Pink, along with white, also comprised the tonalities – racially inflected – of the cosmeticized faces of elite French women, and sometimes also men. That pastel could so seductively mimic the appearance of made-up (Caucasian) flesh, deepened its association with Rococo artifice and *le fard*, making pink a pastel colour (pastel in the sense of both hue and medium) par excellence.

One picture that thematizes all of these aspects of the Rococo is Boucher's *Jeanne-Antoinette Poisson, Marquise de Pompadour* (1758, p. 125). It depicts her seated before a mirror, applying rouge to her cheeks. Shades of pink and white dominate the composition: the delicate pallor of her artificially alabaster skin and the rosiness of her cheeks and lips are variously echoed in the ribbons adorning her gown, the tablecloth, the cameo on her wrist, the little rouge brush in her hand, loaded with pink powder and matched by the bow at the throat of her creamy white pelisse. That bow, by the way, makes a knowing appearance in Party's *Portrait with Pink Bows* (2019, p. 125) – an eye-catching, connotative detail that, with the wry esprit of the eighteenth century, gives a polite nod to an era that celebrated le fard and the 'feminine' medium of pastel, an era that loved pink and knew how to use it.

Boucher was not the first eighteenth-century artist to revel in pink, and if he set the tone for his time, as it were, he was certainly in good company, as so many eighteenth-century pictures can attest. A happy example is to be found in Perronneau's *Portrait of a Woman* (1773), which I mentioned at the outset. Pink is not a defining colour of Perronneau's oeuvre, but as this image shows, he did not shy from it and used the colour masterfully when he did take it up. In *Portrait of a Woman,* he delighted in the visual effect of the sinuous pink ruching that trims the bodice of the woman's gown, and contrasts vividly with its dark grey silk; and he subtly played off the pink ribbon trimmings against the slightly different shade of pink in the artificially rosy blush of his sitter's cheeks and lips. Even more 'in the pink' is Perronneau's splendid *Portrait of Olivier Journu* (1756), which portrays the handsome sitter in a suit of deliciously peachy-pink velvet, jauntily sporting a *boutonnière* of tea roses. This elegant portrait makes plain that seductive beauty and a taste for fashions in pink were hardly the province of women alone. Pink only became a 'feminine' colour when anti-Rococo critics defined it as such in order to disparage it as part of the Enlightenment project to challenge the social and political structures of the *ancien régime.*

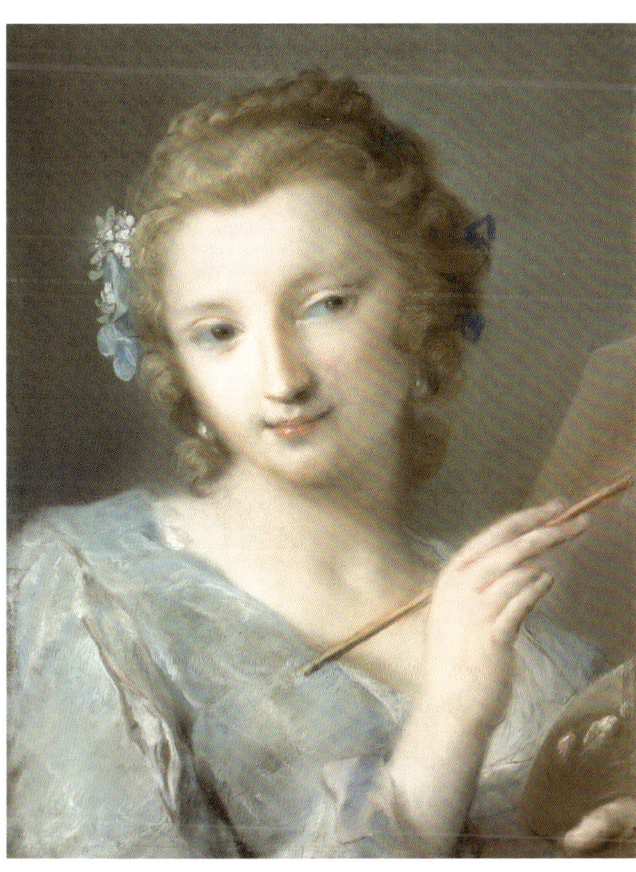

ROSALBA CARRIERA
ALLEGORY OF PAINTING, C. 1730
PASTEL AND RED CHALK ON BLUE LAID PAPER MOUNTED ON CANVAS
44 X 34 CM

Fêted or Ill-Fated?

'This coloured dust, for some people, seems eternally condemned to a smile.'
– Louis Soullié, *Peintures, aquarelles, pastels, dessins de Jean-François Millet* (L. Soullié, Paris, 1900)

During the French Revolution, oil portraiture would play an important role in defining citizens and new subjectivities for republican France.[27] Pastel portraiture, however, all but disappeared from public view after its final eighteenth-century efflorescence during the Salon of 1793, when the number of pastels exhibited reached a historic peak. By that time, the Salon had been democratized by the revolutionary regime and was open to all artists, so that a record number of women exhibited that year, as well. In the decades that followed, a few artists continued to practise pastel, and a market for this work remained, but it was no longer a fashionable medium and all but disappeared as an art form.[28]

Pastel painting languished in obscurity for the first thirty years of the nineteenth century. During that time, pastel chalk was still used, as it had been originally (going back to the Renaissance), for preparatory drawings. However, Romanticism's rejection of academic orthodoxy opened the way for pastel's return to favour, above all during the latter part of the century, when it was taken up by Impressionists who embraced the radiance of pastel colour and the bold effects of immediacy that could be achieved with it. But even before that, pastel inspired inventiveness and exploration by artists working in various modes and genres: from history painting to landscape and Realist subjects – the latter best represented by Jean-François Millet, who produced numerous pastels depicting the world of rustic peasants. With Millet's forays into pastels, 'the medium's entire tradition of aristocratic femininity was uprooted'.[29]

Despite these moments of revival and renewed interest, pastel was generally regarded as a medium for second-class talents and was disparaged as a serious material – as it still is. It was only with the coming of the Indépendants and their supporters that pastel enjoyed a rebirth, as Édouard Manet, Berthe Morisot, Eva Gonzalès, Mary Cassatt and many others associated with Impressionism began experimenting with avant-garde techniques. This light, ephemeral medium proved eminently well suited for the depiction of the transient pleasures of fashionable life that so fascinated the Impressionists.

Pastel à la Party

'Pastel scatters with the lightest breath, like dust from a butterfly's wing.'
– Théophile Gautier, *Histoire de l'art dramatique en France*, 1859

Pastel was primarily associated with portraiture (which the English aptly called 'face painting') because it could so beguilingly mimic the appearance of flesh, made-up or otherwise. In works like *Portrait with Pink Bows* (2019) Party evokes this traditional genre of 'face painting' and refers slyly to other portraits that are explicitly about 'putting on a good face', as it were (namely, it cites the pink bow in Boucher's portrait of *Madame de Pompadour at her Toilette*, but also the pearl earring in Carriera's *Portrait of a Lady at Three-Quarter Length*). But he takes up the formal language of the portrait genre, rather than seeking to make a likeness of a specific individual. In *Pink Bows*, Party's subject is a dreamily mythic figure, which is a recurring archetype in his work, rendered in his own idiom and formal vocabulary. Here, rather than the powdery, transitory qualities of pastel, Party emphasizes its velutinous opacity and, smoothing away the visual flourishes of his painterly touch (a technique dubbed 'sweetening' in the eighteenth century), he magnifies the matte intensity of colours, which makes the image look deceptively durable. Pastel's simultaneity as at once line and colour is highlighted in the arching, linear contours that define the figure's unnaturally colourful head, neck, and shoulders, which are rendered in expanses of unmodulated, glowing shades of goldenrod, sunflower, ochre, charcoal-grey, and pale-rose pink. The simultaneity of pastel (what we would nowadays call its nonbinary quality) is ideally suited to the neither/nor androgyny of this figural type. What is more, in works like these, where traces of process have been all but effaced, Party plays a sense of timeless presence against the impermanence and fragility of crumbly crayons made of coloured dust.

The ephemerality and fragility of the medium (the very things that were problematic in the past for Diderot and so many others) are essential to Party's interest in it.[30] They were thematized in the three large-scale installation works of The FLAG Art Foundation exhibition: *From Jean-Honoré Fragonard, The Progress of Love*, 1733 (2019), *From Jean-Honoré Fragonard, Birth of Venus*, 1753–55 (2019), and *From François Boucher, Portrait of Madame de Pompadour* (1758). All three site-specific works engaged directly with the Rococo and representative works by Boucher and Fragonard. Energetically improvisational, playful, and full of visual flourishes attesting to the facility of the artist, they no longer exist (like 'dust from a butterfly's wing' scattered by a breath) and must now be referred to in the past tense. They poignantly emblematized

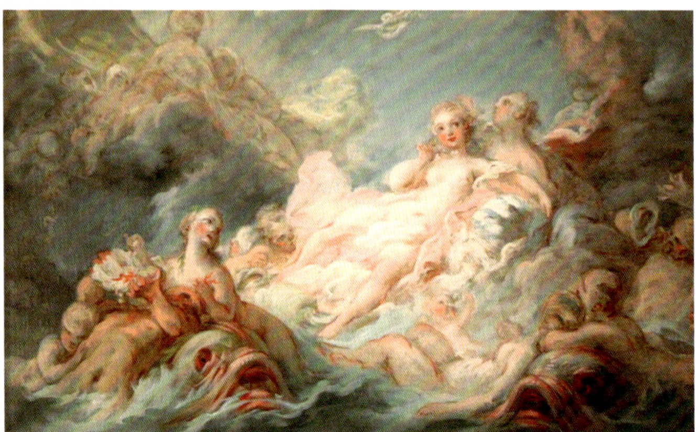

JEAN-HONORÉ FRAGONARD
THE BIRTH OF VENUS, 1753–55
OIL ON CANVAS
49 X 80 CM

foreground,
ROBIN F. WILLIAMS
ALIVE WITH PLEASURE
(STUDY), 2018
PASTEL ON PAPER
130 X 98 CM

background,
FROM JEAN-HONORÉ
FRAGONARD, BIRTH OF VENUS,
1753–55 (DETAIL), 2019
SOFT PASTEL ON WALL
401 X 282 CM

INSTALLATION VIEW AT THE
FLAG ART FOUNDATION,
NEW YORK, 2019

the fleeting, the transitory, the ineffable, the unbearable lightness of the Rococo – all qualities of pastel that Party embraces and celebrates.[31] As a recent interviewer noted:

When Party has completed site-specific murals in the past, he has grown used to visitors lamenting how those works will eventually just be destroyed. 'That's actually what I like,' he counters. 'There's something very reassuring, relaxing and soothing to do things that go back to dust.' 'I fell in love with the fact that pastel is super fragile,' Party says. 'There's a poetic edge to an artwork that can so easily become nothing more than "dust in the air"'.[32]

The history of the 'feminine' medium of pastel, which might be called oil painting's 'other', still inflects how it is perceived and how it signifies. This history animates and enriches Party's own engagement with pastel. If at times, in his murals, for example, he makes pastel perform in a way that is almost without precedent, he conceptualizes the medium itself in a way that would have been familiar to an eighteenth-century viewer: 'The nature of the pastels is really like makeup', he has said – a comment that resonates with the ironic definition of pastel by the eighteenth-century social critic, Louis-Antoine Caraccioli: 'Pastel: the face of all made-up women, so that in loving their beauty, one loves only a painting of crayon.'[33] Working on the poetic edge of an art that can so easily become 'dust in the air' or a 'cloud of makeup' (as Jean-François Lyotard would have it), Party seriously delights in the irony.

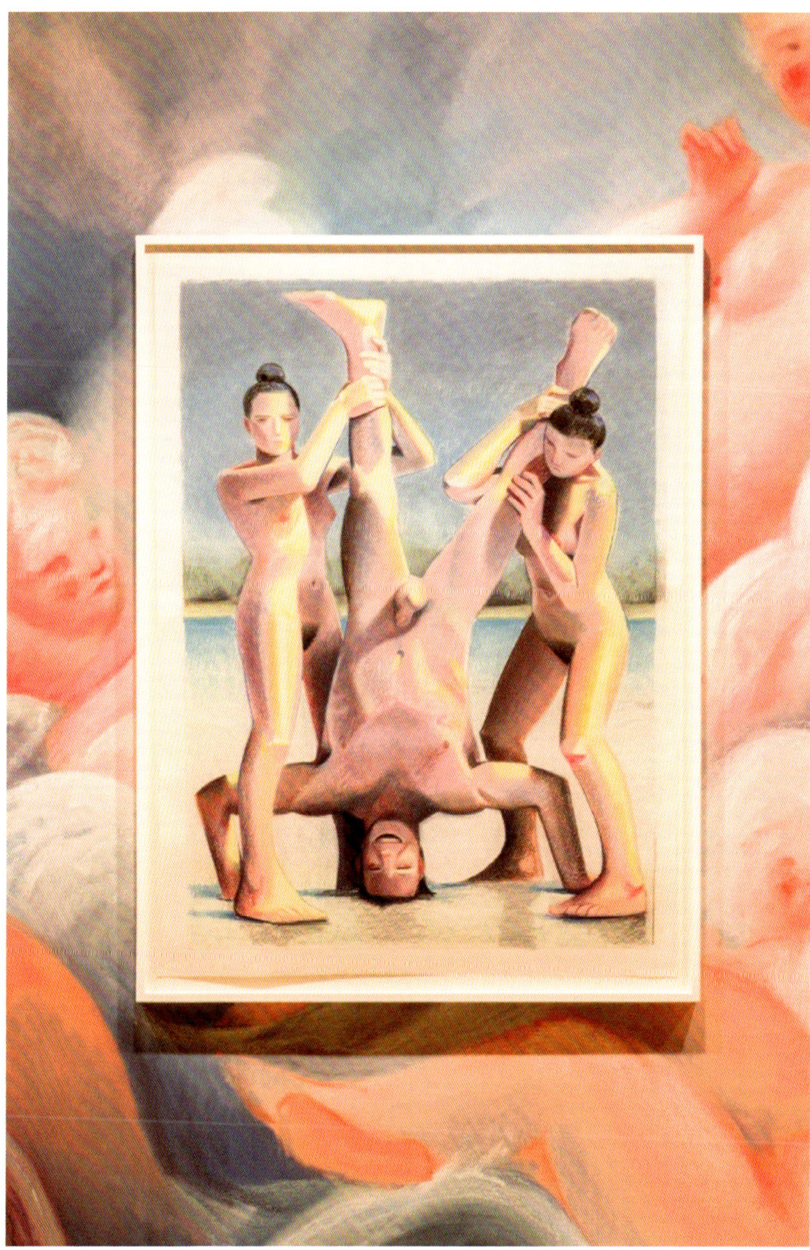

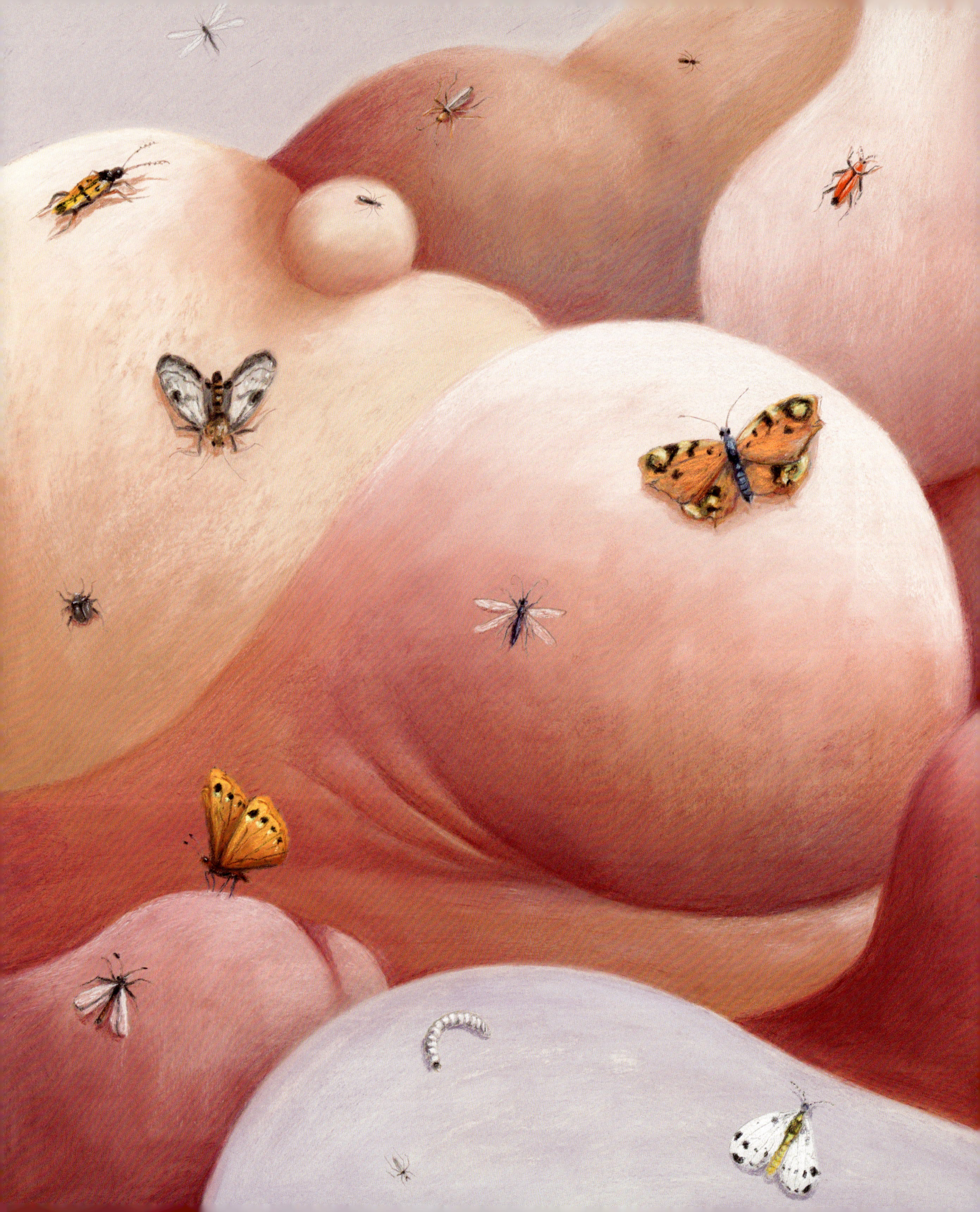

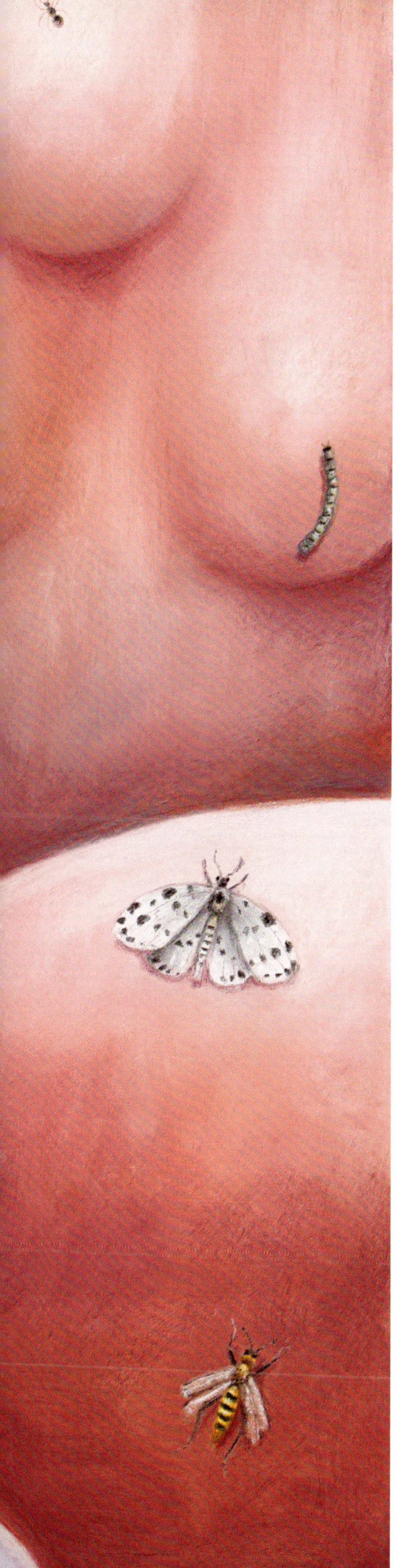

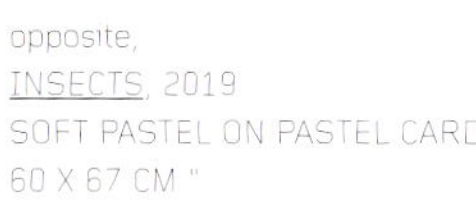

opposite,
INSECTS, 2019
SOFT PASTEL ON PASTEL CARD
60 X 67 CM

CREASES, 2019
SOFT PASTEL ON PASTEL CARD
76 X 56 CM

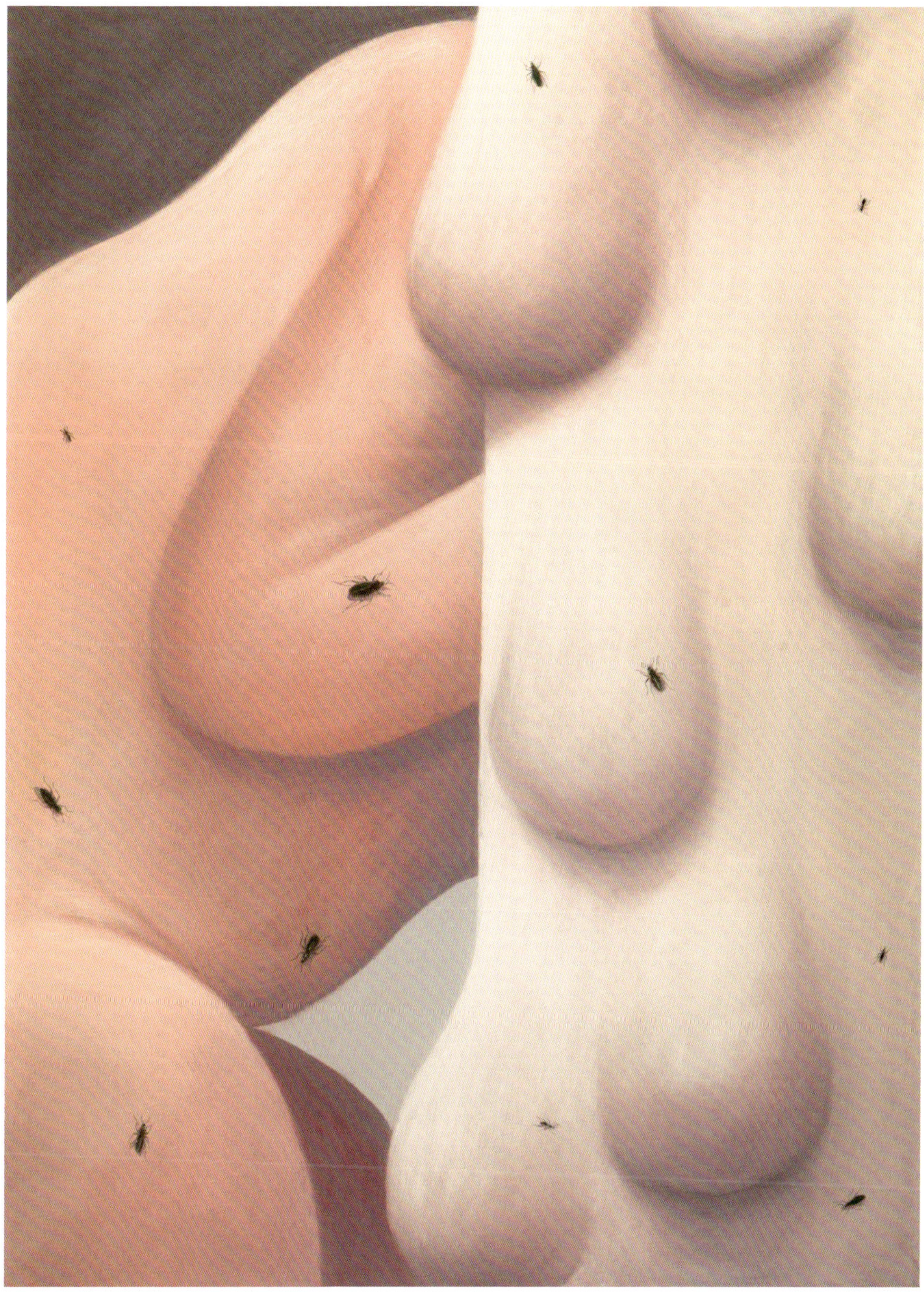

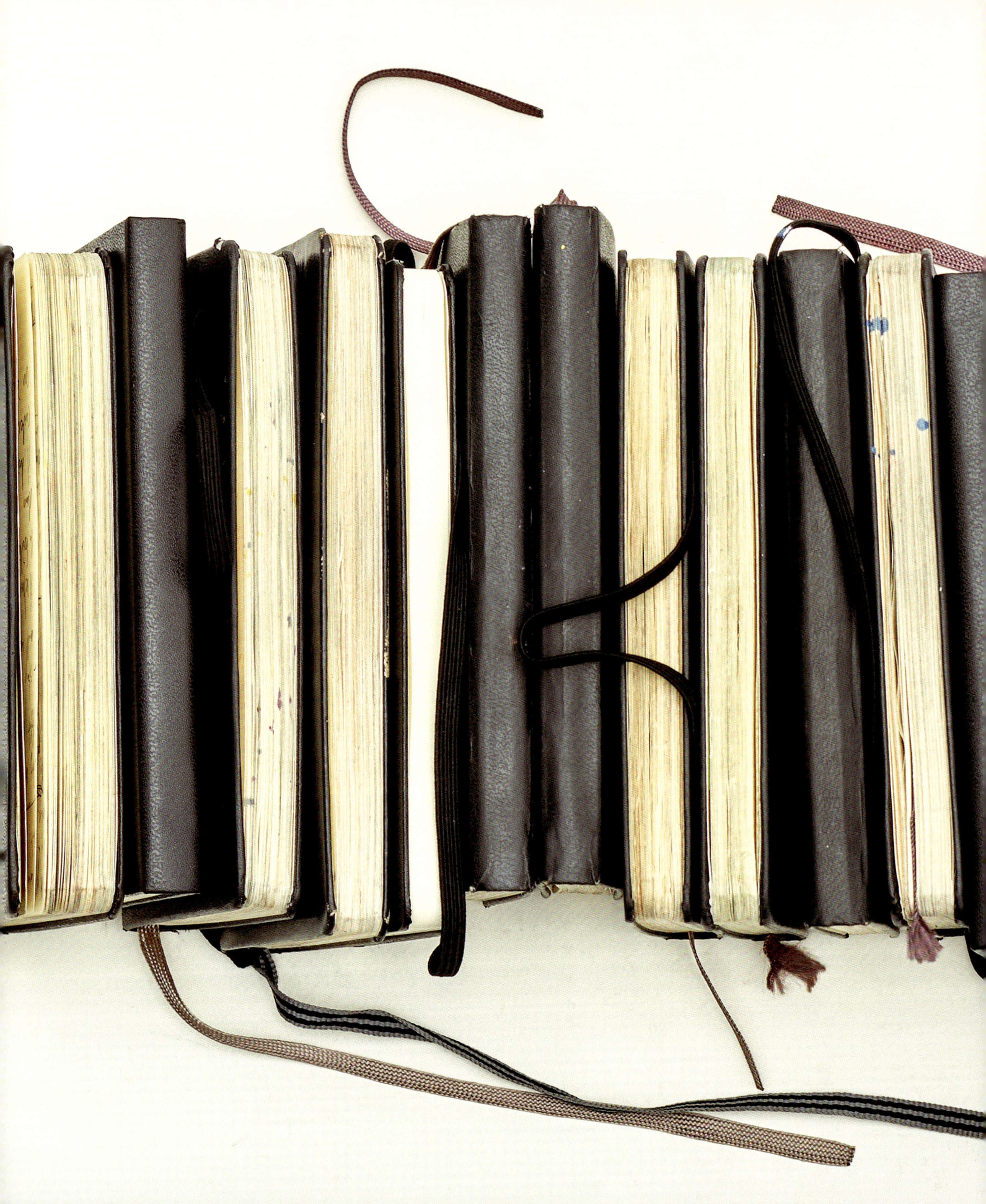

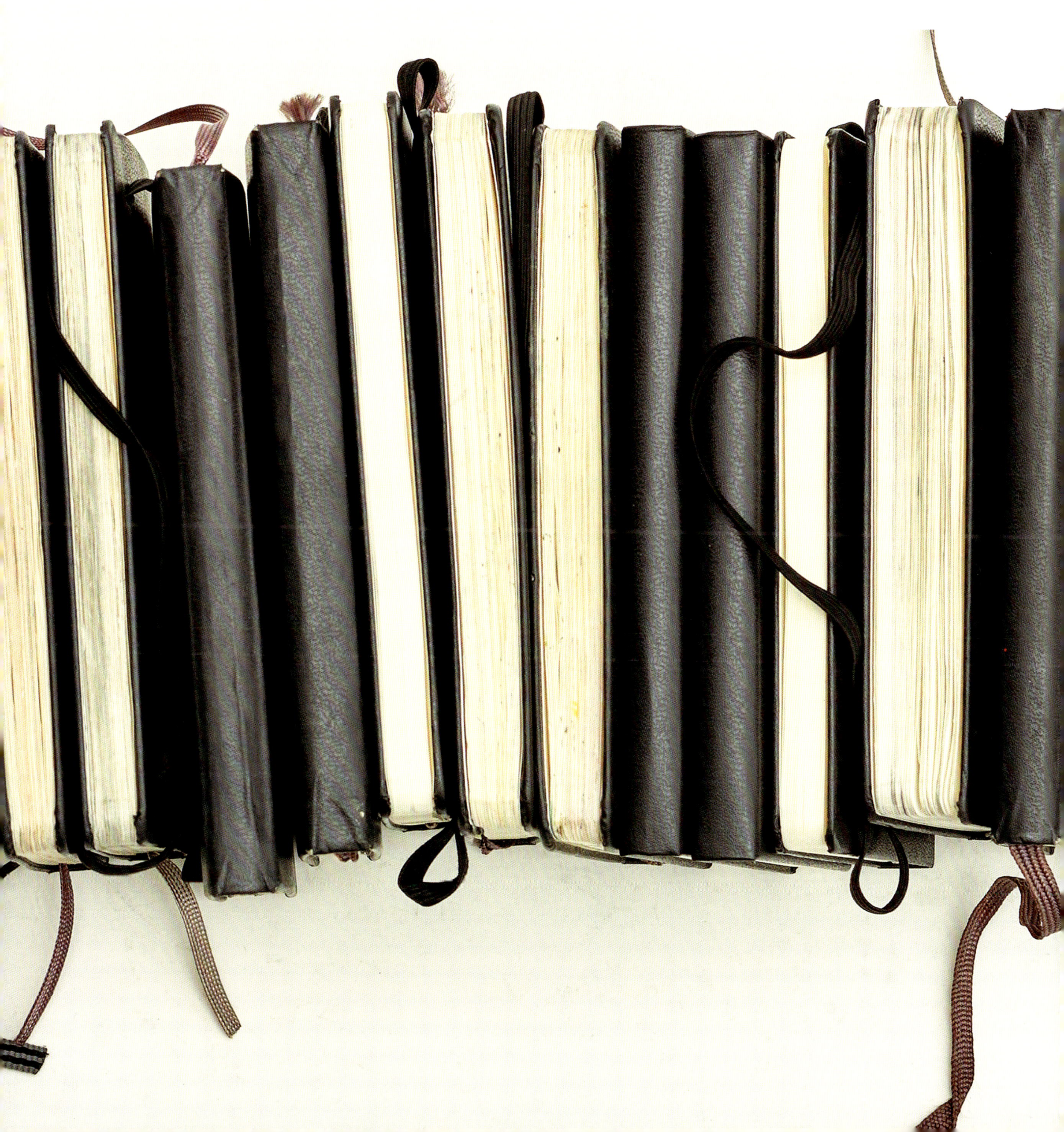

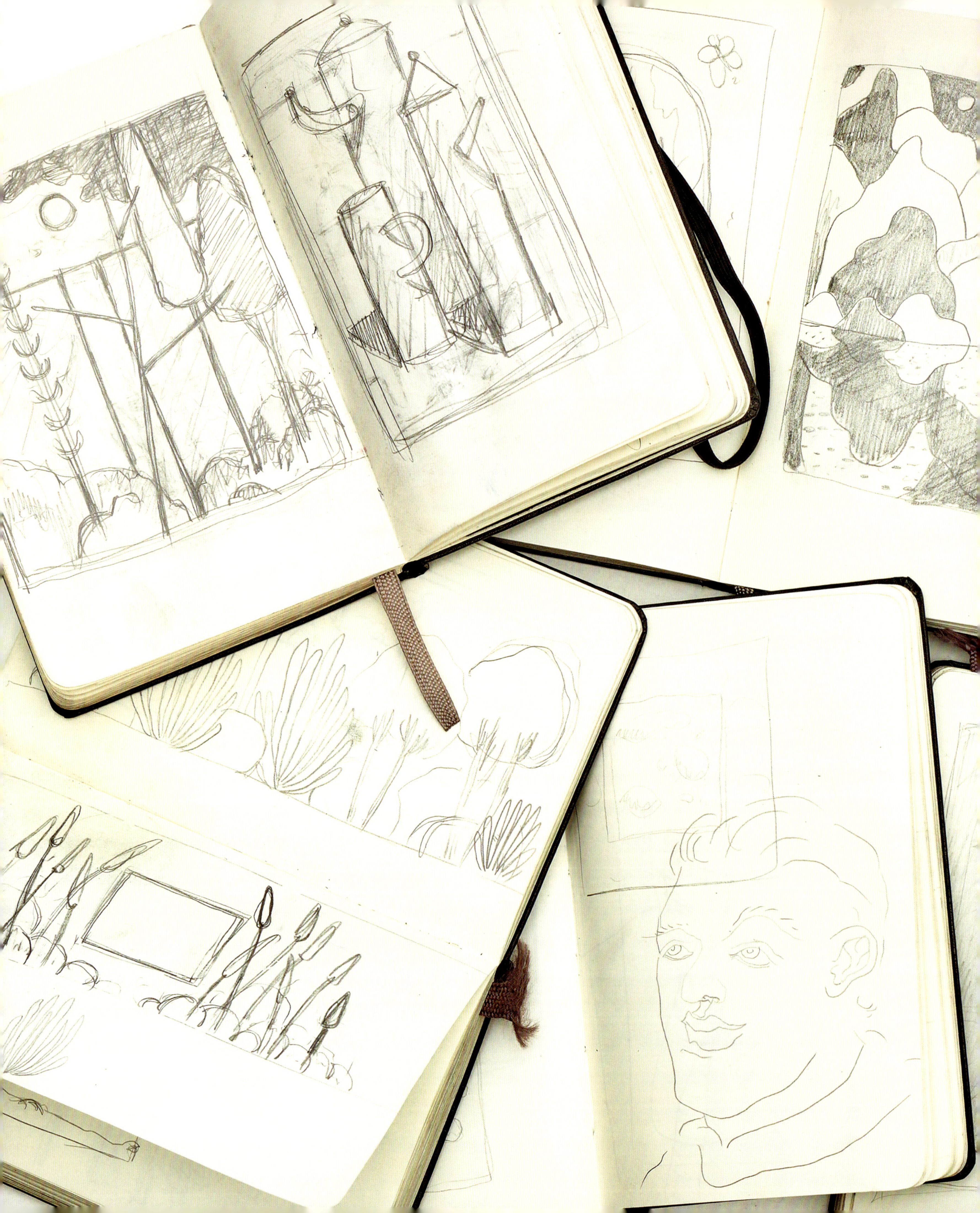

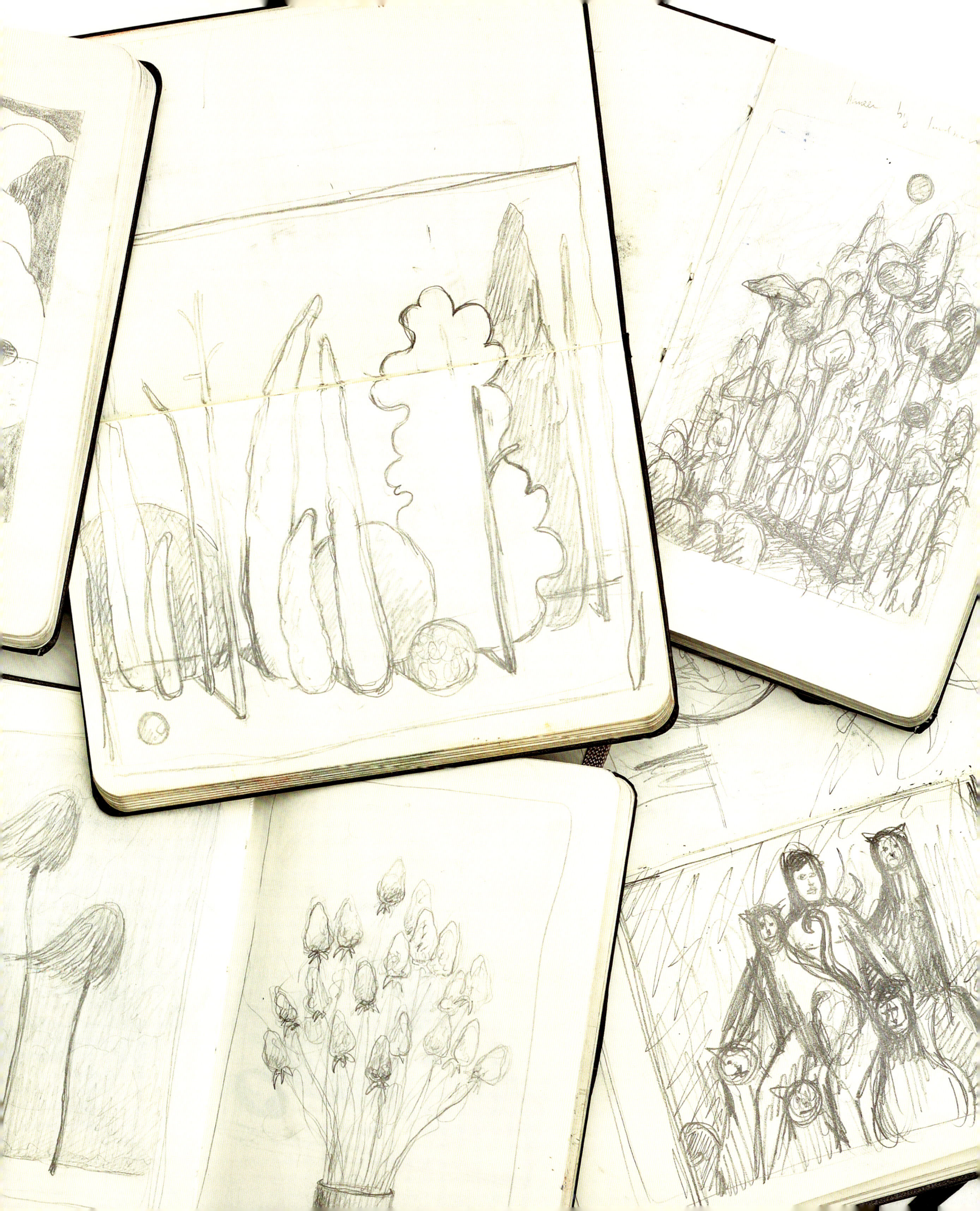

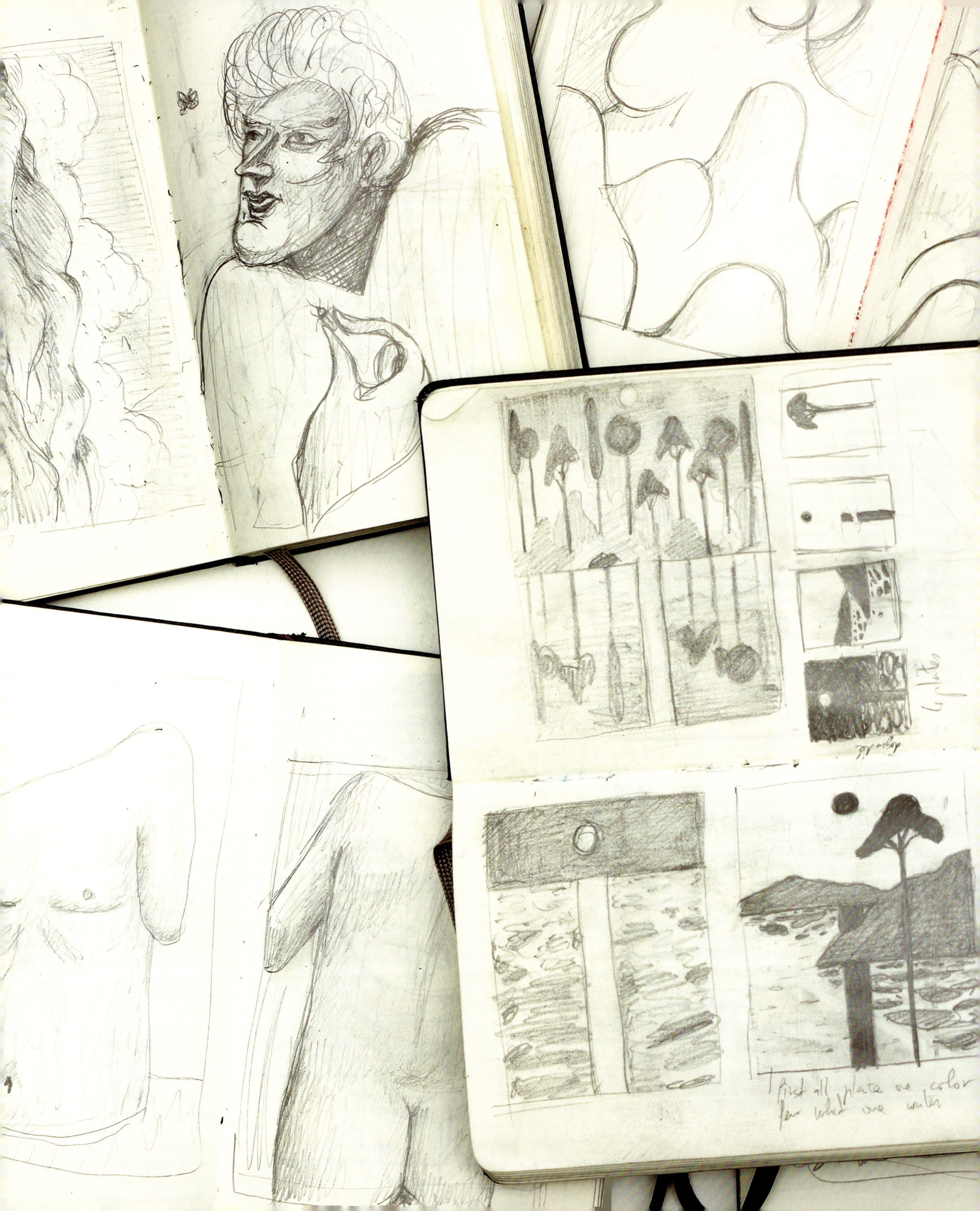
4 plates
first all plate one color

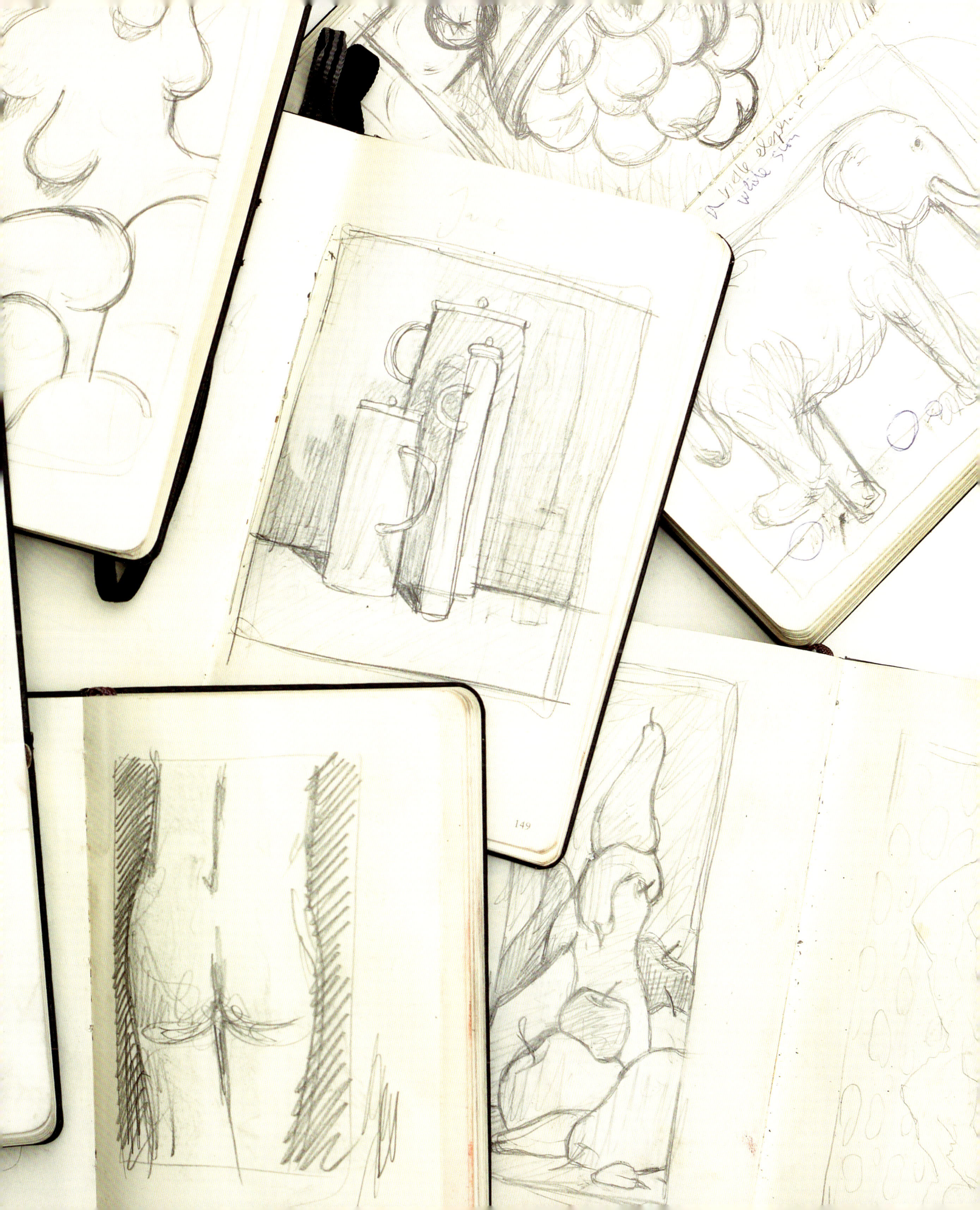
149

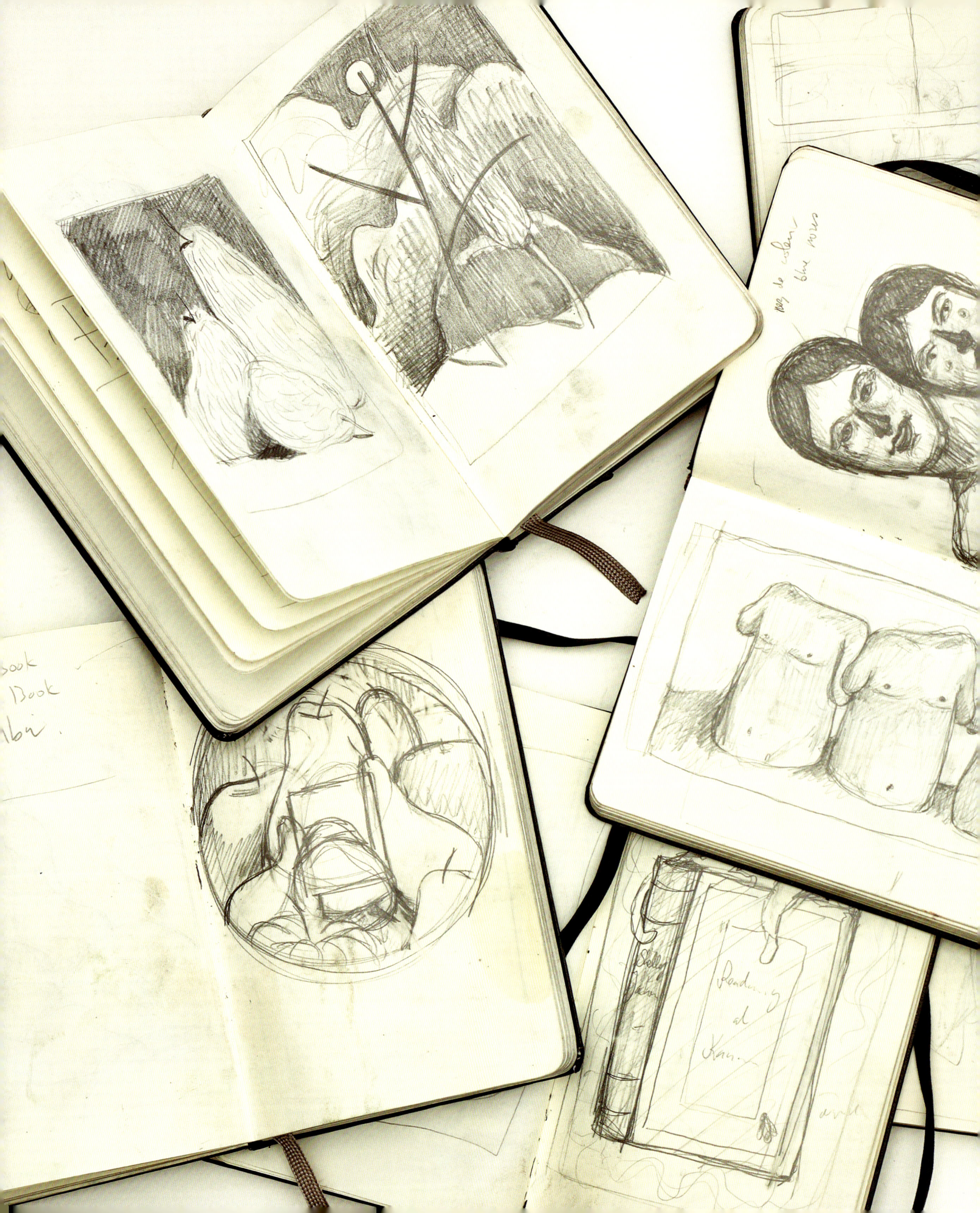

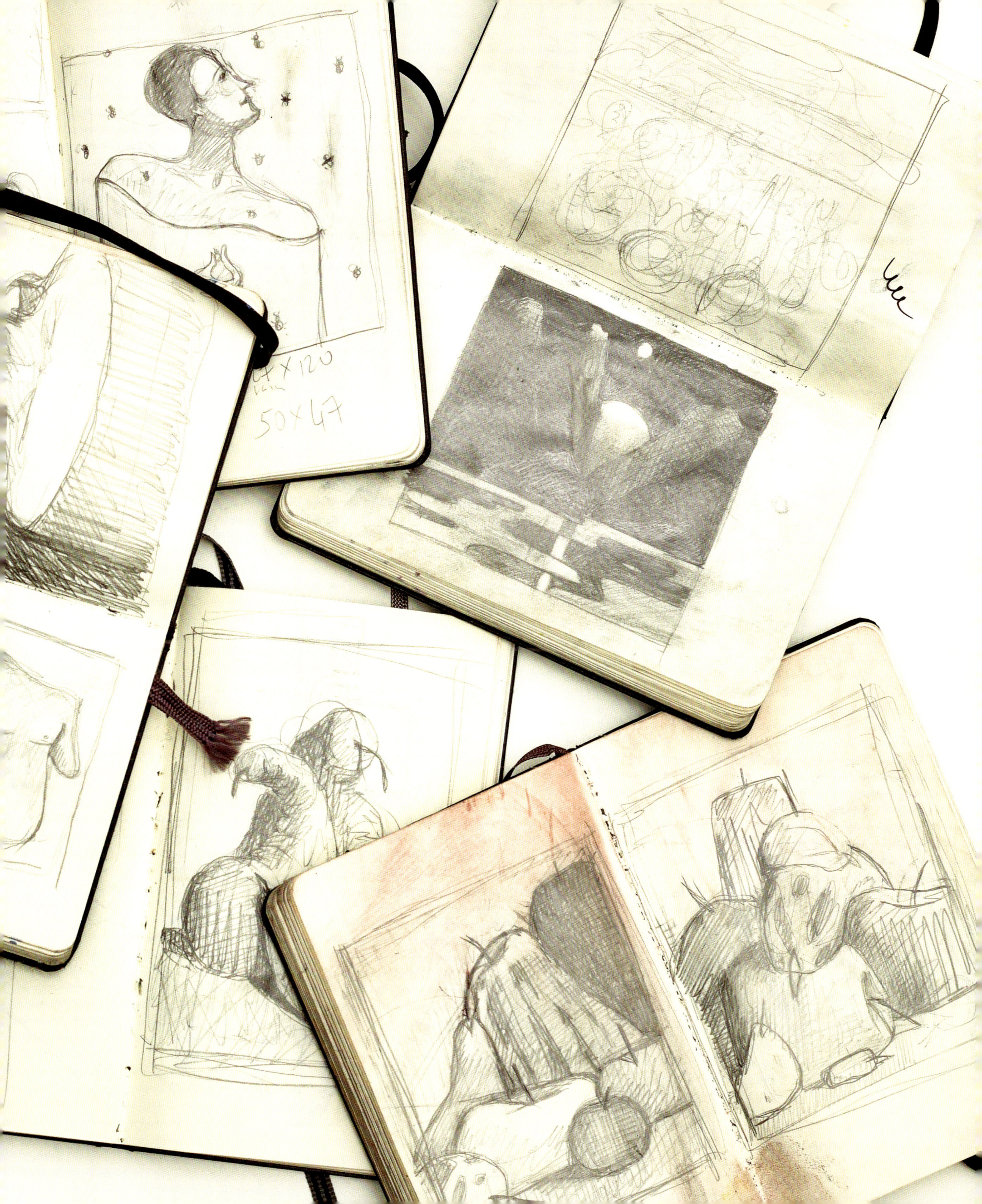
X 120
50 X 47

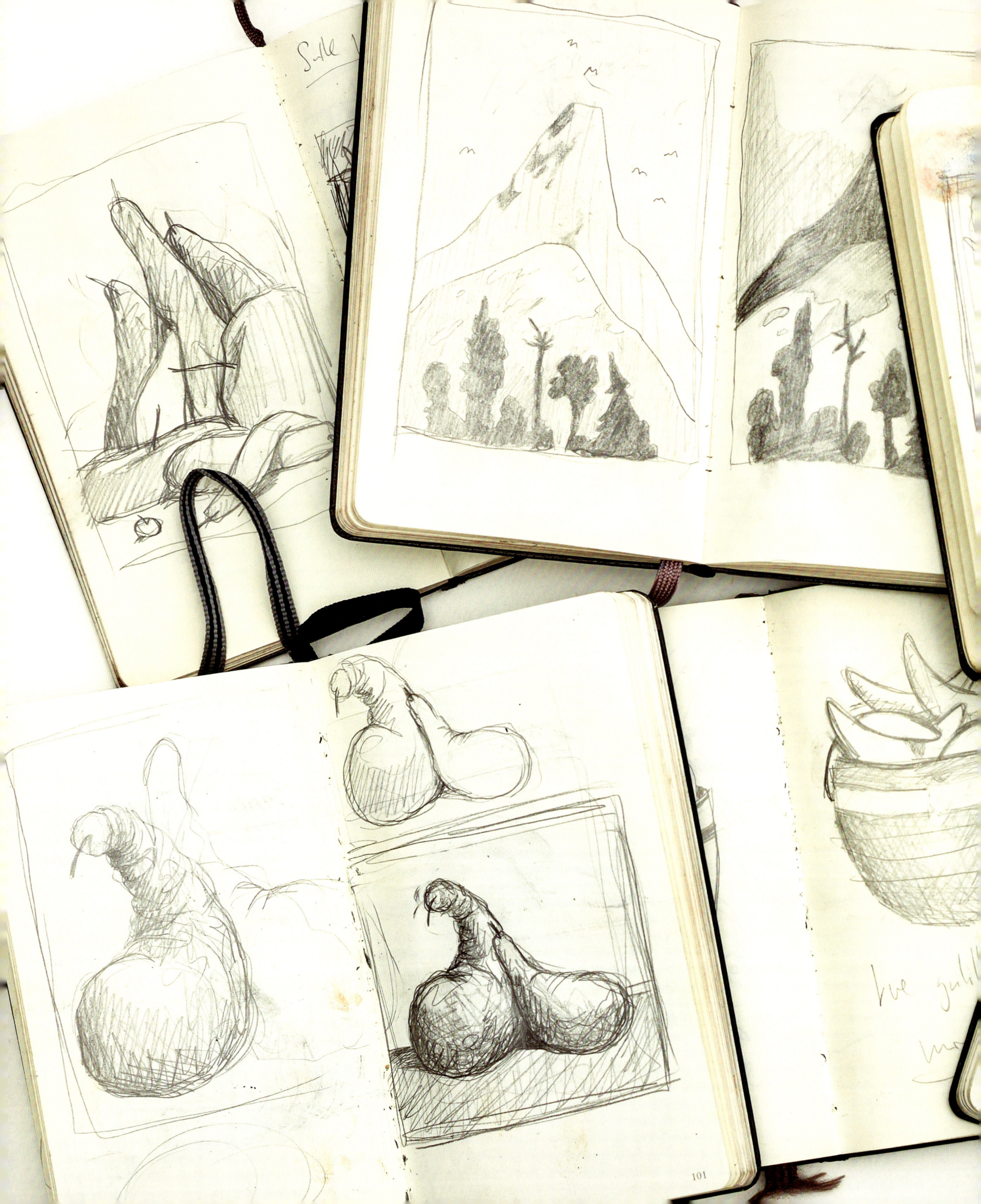
101

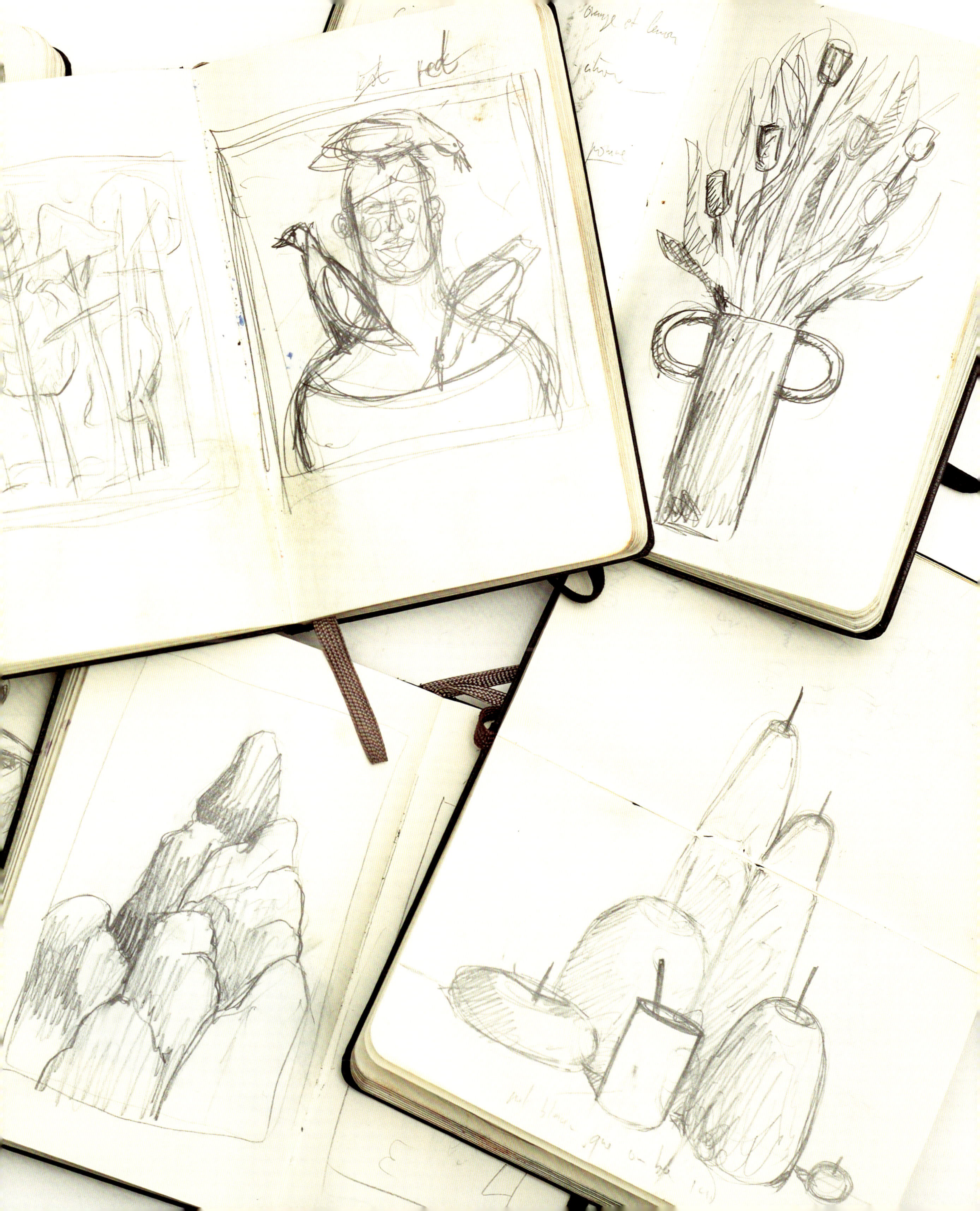

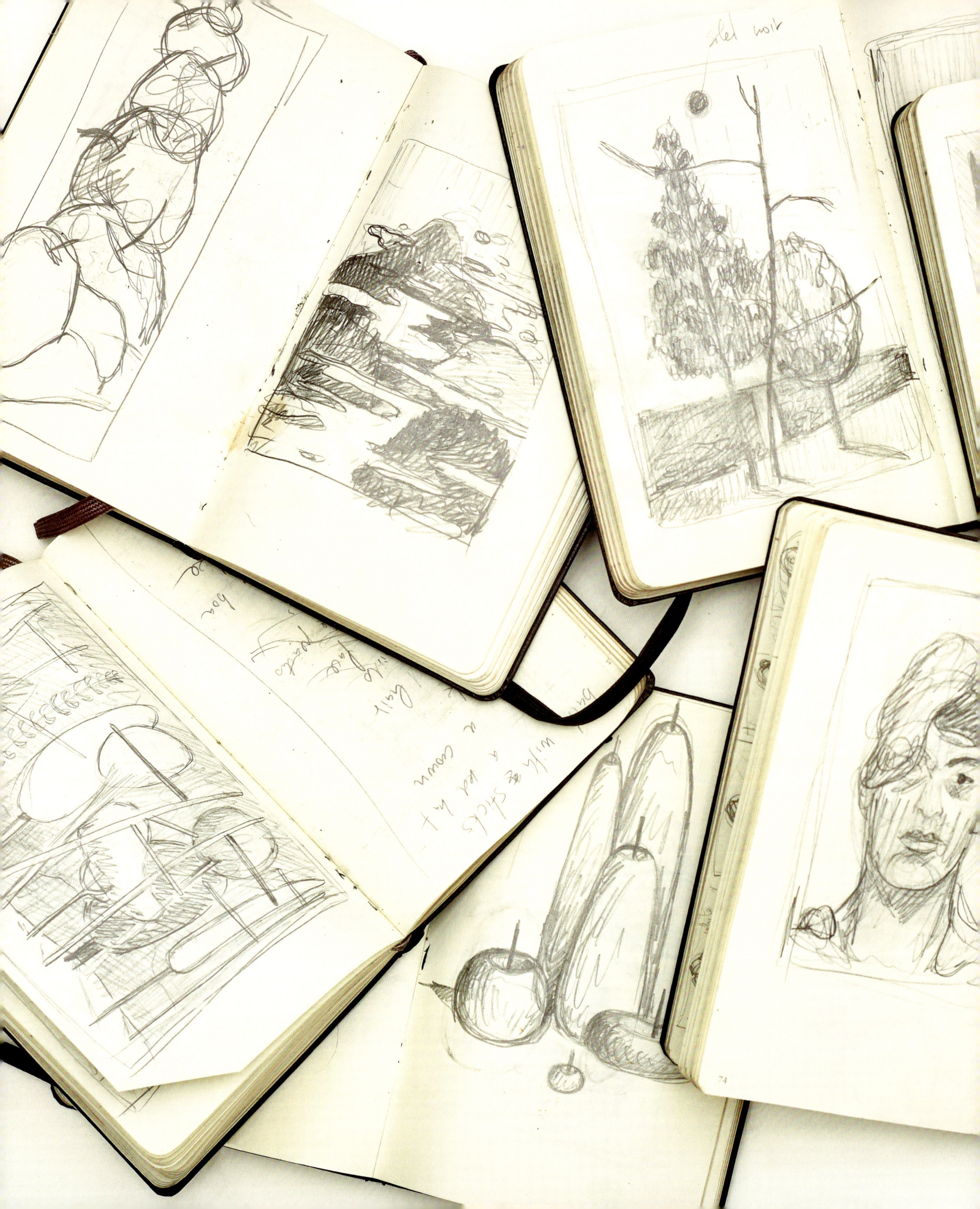

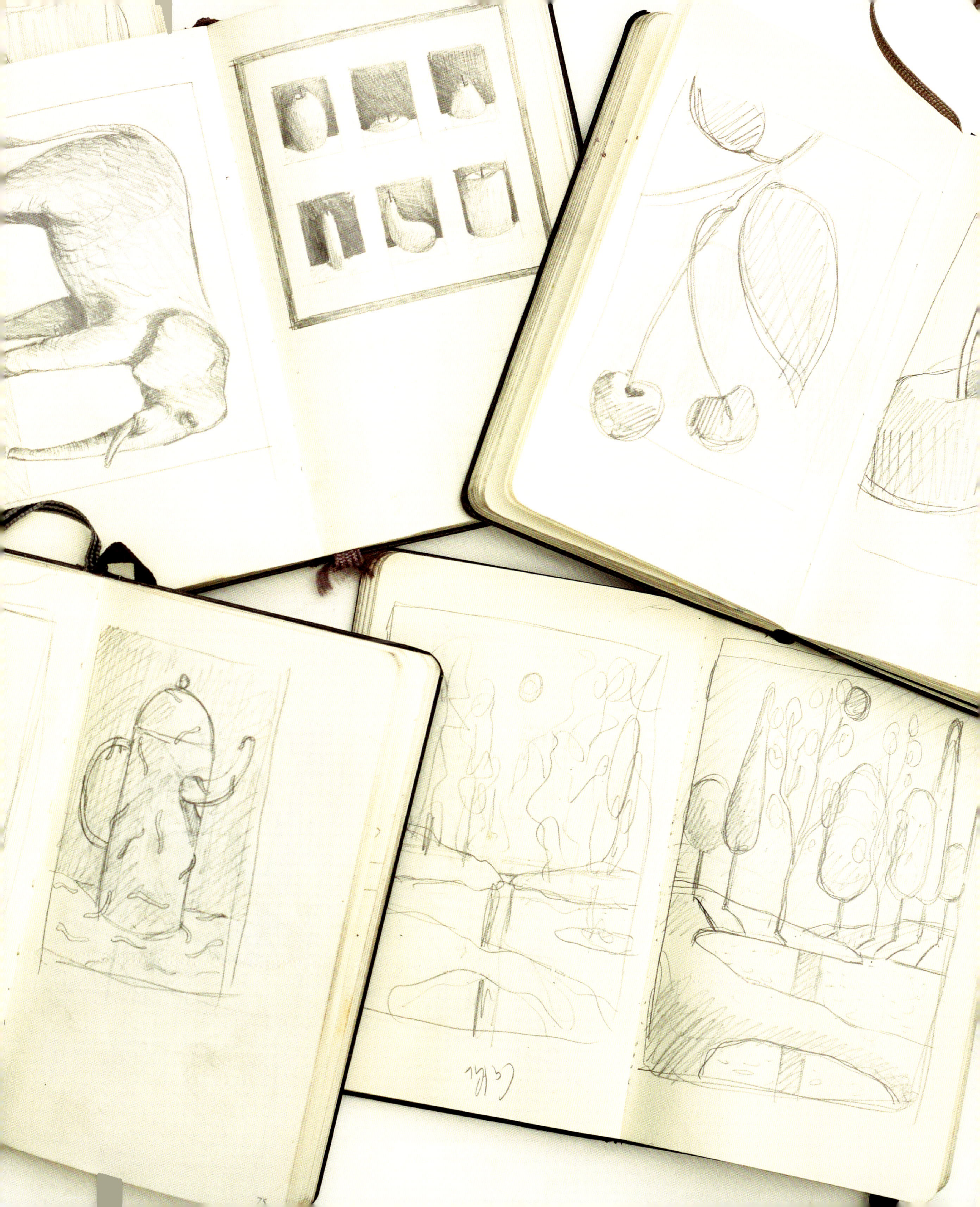

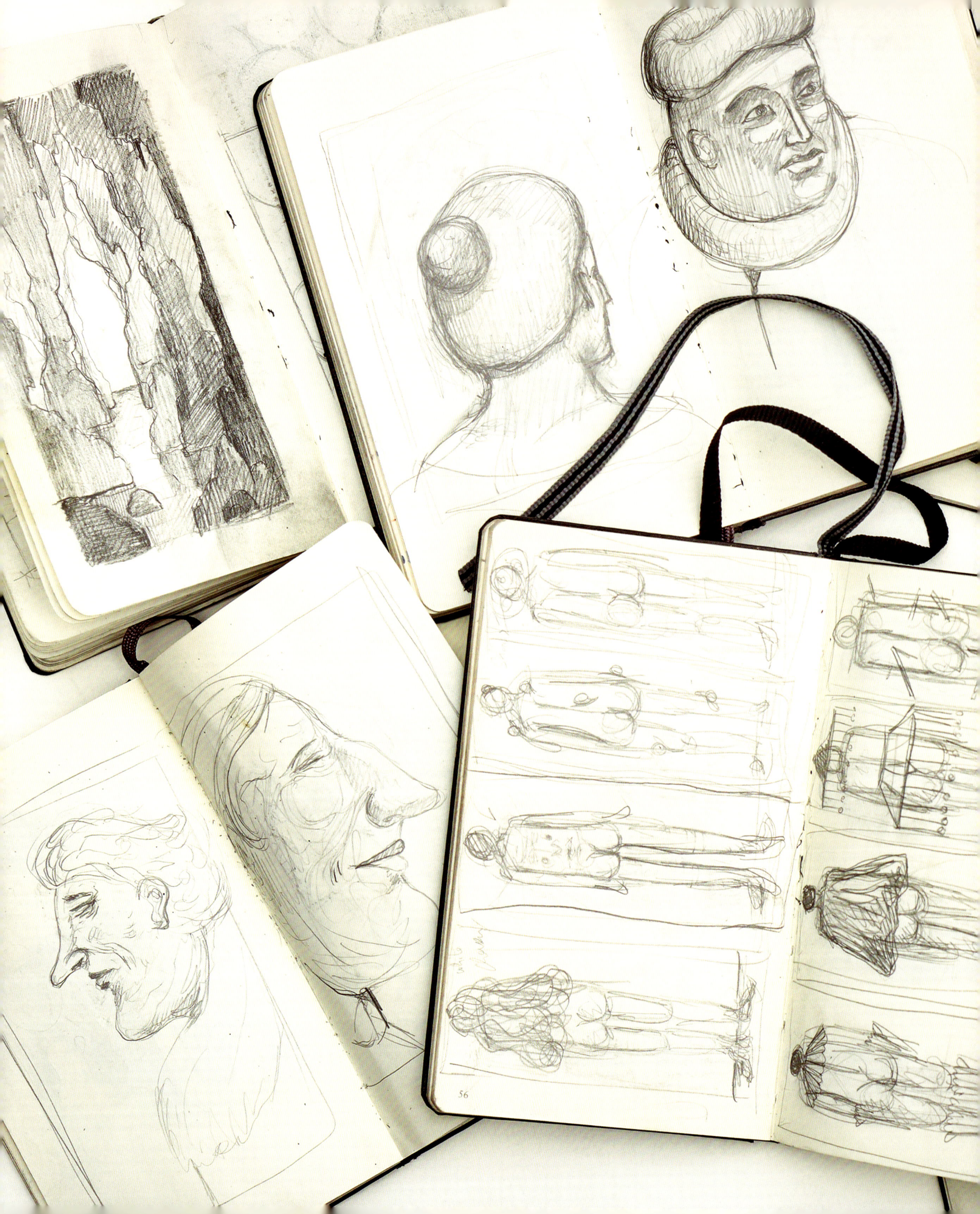

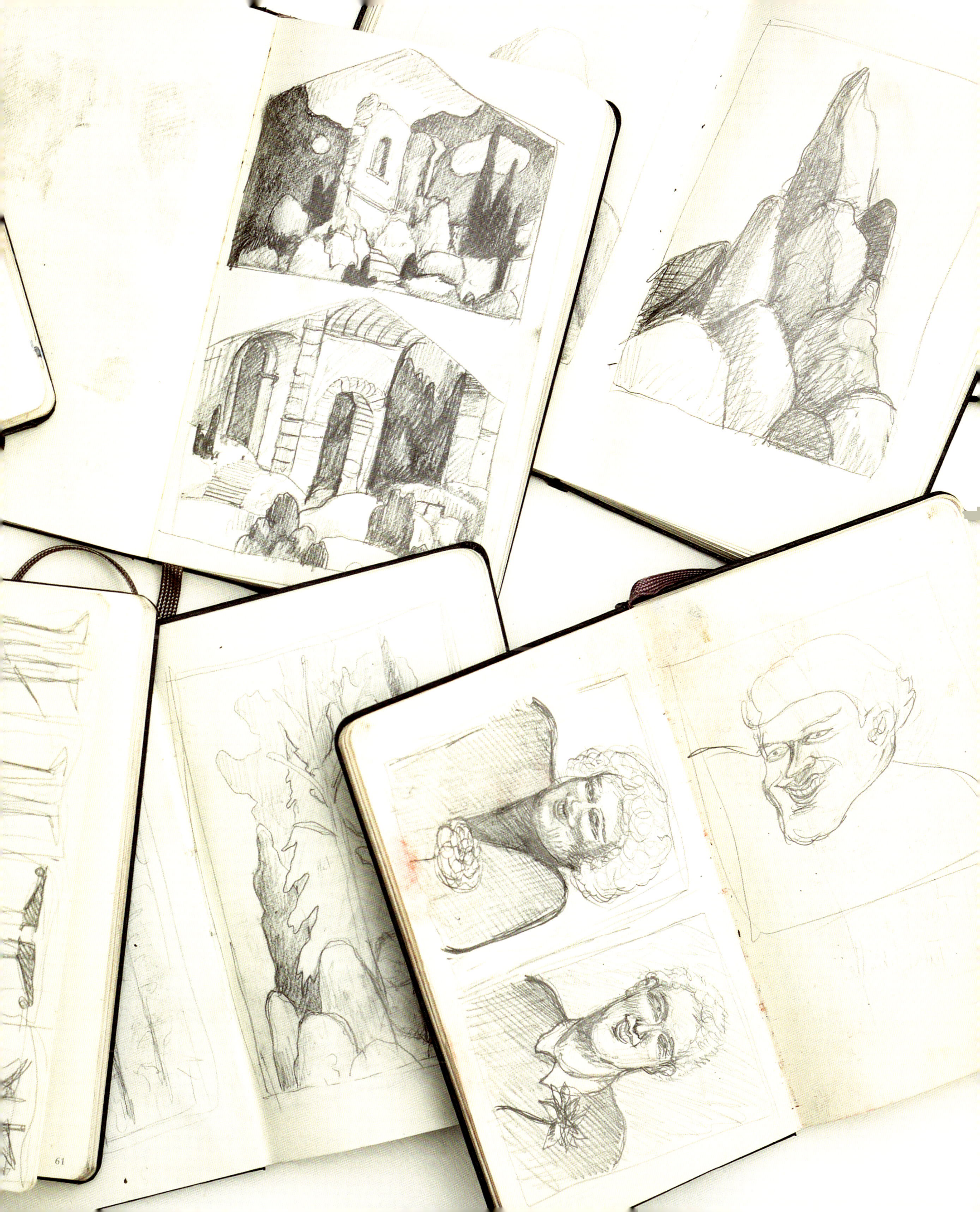
61

NOTES

next pages, from left,
LANDSCAPE, 2014
SOFT PASTEL ON LINEN
150 X 100 CM

PORTRAIT, 2014
SOFT PASTEL ON LINEN
120 X 120 CM

MURAL: CHARCOAL ON WALL

INSTALLATION VIEW AT
GALERIE GREGOR STEIGER,
ZURICH, 2014

opposite,
PANORAMA, 2016
ACRYLIC ON WOOD
585 X 618 X 500 CM

INSTALLATION VIEW AT SALTS,
BASEL, 2016

SURVEY PAGES 057–097

1 See Annette Kuptz-Klimpel, *Elefant*, https://www.symbolonline.de/index.php?title=Elefant (accessed 16 September 2020).
2 See Morton L. Schamberg's readymade *God* from 1917, consisting of a drainpipe: Stefan Banz, Morton L. Schamberg: *God*, Les Éditions KMD, Cully, Switzerland, 2020, and distributed as a digital document on the website of Les Presses du Réel, Dijon: https://www.lespressesdureel.com/EN/ouvrage.php?id=8228 (accessed 20 September 2020).
3 In Barcelona on 23 April 1916 Cravan fought a boxing match against the former heavyweight world champion Jack Johnson and – as agreed in advance – was knocked out in the sixth round so that he could finance his passage to New York with his performance fee.
4 'Emerging: Nicolas Party. John Calcutt examines this painter's dynamic visual lexicon,' *MAP Magazine*, no. 25, Summer 2011, see https://mapmagazine.co.uk/nicolas-party (accessed 18 September 2020)
5 Party had become acquainted with Eilshemius' work through my comprehensive monograph *Eilshemius: Peer of Poet-Painters. Collected Documents, a Novel of Facts by and about Louis M. Eilshemius; and a Study of his Influence on Marcel Duchamp* (JRP|Ringier, Zurich, 2015) and had studied his paintings in detail. He is also a collector of the works of Caroline Bachmann (b. 1963, Lausanne), a Swiss painter.
6 Stefan Banz (ed.), *Louis Michel Eilshemius: Six Musical Moods*, Verlag f ür Moderne Kunst, Vienna, and Les Presses du Réel, Dijon, 2018, p. 60.
7 Ibid.
8 Ibid, p. 61.
9 From 19 May to 28 October 2018.
10 The Rococo era began in France in 1730 (continuing to around 1770) before it eventually spread to the United Kingdom, Austria, Germany, Bavaria, and Russia. See also: http://flagartfoundation.org/exhibitions/nicolas-party-pastel/ (accessed 20 September 2020).
11 See Maggie Angeloglou, *A History of Make-Up*, Studio Vista, London, 1970, p 73. See also: http://flagartfoundation.org/exhibitions/nicolas-party-pastel/.
12 See: http://flagartfoundation.org/exhibitions/nicolas-party-pastel.

FOCUS PAGES 099–115

1 Full disclosure, I was the curator of the exhibition.
2 Party first used pastel for a wall mural at Neuchâtel, Switzerland in 2016.
3 Quoted on the back cover of Nicolas Party, *Pastel*, Karma, New York, and The Modern Institute, Glasgow, 2017.
4 From an email conversation with the artist on 15 October 2020.
5 Catherine Geissler, *The New Oxford Book of Food Plants*, Oxford University Press, 2009, Oxford, p. 82.
6 Laura Sadori, Emilia Allevato, Giovanna Bosi and Giulia Caneva, *The Introduction and Diffusion of Peach in Ancient Italy* (PDF), Edipuglia, 2009, Archived (PDF) from the original on 14 January 2013.
7 One explanation for the regional variance might be due to an allergy to lipid transfer protein (LTP) that is quite common in the Mediterranean countries but virtually absent in Northern Europe. It's been hypothesized that handling, brushing washing and packaging peaches before they're shipped to Northern Europe may desensitize the allergens on the surface of the peach fuzz, the likely agent for LTP. http://research.bmh.manchester.ac.uk/informall/allergenic-food/index.aspx?FoodId=37.
8 From an email conversation with the artist on 15 October 2020.

ARTIST'S CHOICE PAGES 117–131

1 Christy Kuesel, 'Beloved for his Popping Pastels, Nicolas Party Take a Darker Turn', *Artsy*, 12 February 2020. https://www.artsy.net/article/artsy-editorial-beloved-popping-pastels-nicolas-party-takes-darker-turn darker-turn. Here, Party echoes the poetic evocations of many writers of the past who likened pastel to 'the dust from a butterfly's wing'. For further discussion, from which the present essay is drawn, Melissa Hyde, '"Dust from a Butterfly's Wing": The Gentle Art of Pastel. A Short History', in Glenn Fuhrman, Melissa Hyde, Louis Fratino, Loie Hollowell, Billy Sullivan, Robin F. Williams and Dodie Kazanjian, *Nicolas Party: Pastel*, The FLAG Art Foundation, New York, 2021.
2 For the first monograph on Carriera in English, see Angela Oberer, *The Life and Work of Rosalba Carriera (1673–1757). The Queen of Pastel*, Amsterdam University Press, 2020.
3 Following her example, something in the order of 500 of the 2,500 pastellists working before 1800 were women. See Neil Jeffares, 'Prolegomena to Pastels and Pastellists', *Dictionary of Pastellists before 1800*, Unicorn Press, London, p. 102. (Pastellists, hereafter.) http://www.pastellists.com/misc/prolegomena.pdf.
4 Melissa Hyde, *Making Up the Rococo. François Boucher and his Critics*, Getty Research Institute, Los Angeles, 2006.
5 Karen Chernick, 'The Remarkable Success Story of Rosalba Carriera, the Original "Queen of Pastel",' *Hyperallergic*, 14 October 2020. https://hyperallergic.com/594151/the-life-and-work-of-rosalba-carriera/. See Jeffares' 'Florilegium' in *Pastellists*, op. cit., for a compendium of commentary on pastel from the seventeenth century to the present.
6 In conversation with the artist, February 2019.
7 Quoted in Scott Indrisek, 'Explore Nicolas Party's Unbelievable Pastel Wonderland', *All Arts*, 7 November 2019. https://allarts.org/2019/11/nicolas-party-pastel-flag-art-foundation-scott-indrisek/
8 Christopher Lazare, Review of 'Old Masters at the World's Fair. From Giotto to David', *The North American Review*, Autumn, 1939, p. 181. For the impact of modernist aesthetics on attitudes toward the Rococo see Melissa Hyde and Mark Ledbury, *Rethinking Boucher*, 'Introduction', Getty Research Institute, Los Angeles, 2006.
9 For an overview of académiciennes, see Mary D. Sheriff, 'Academies of Art. France', in Delia Gaze (ed.), *Dictionary of Women Artists*, Fitzroy Dearborn Publishers, London and Chicago, 1997, pp. 1, 45–48.
10 For further discussion of these aspects of Carriera's work, see Thea Burns, *The Invention of Pastel*, Archetype, London, 2007.
11 Roger de Piles, *Cours de Peinture par principes*, Arkstée & Merkus, Amsterdam, 1766, p. 274. For the racial dimensions of de Piles' conceptualization of colour, see Anne Lafont, 'How Skin Color Became a Racial Marker: Art Historical Perspectives on Race', *Eighteenth-Century Studies*, Fall 2017, pp. 89–113.
12 See Jacqueline Lichtenstein, 'Making Up Representation: The Risks of Femininity', *Representations*, Fall 1987, pp. 77–97.
13 Lapeyre, *Les Moeurs de Paris*, Amsterdam, 1748; Louis Antoine de Caraccioli, *La critique des dames et des messieurs à leur toilette*, Paris, 1770.
14 Morag Martin, 'Casanova and Mlle. Clairon: Painting the Face in a World of Natural Fashion', *Fashion Theory*, no. 1, 2003, pp. 57–78.
15 Louis Antoine de Caraccioli, *Dictionnaire critique, pittoresque et sentencieux, propre à faire connoitre les usages du Siecle, ainsi que ses bisarreries*, Duplain, Lyon, 1768, pp. 2, 205. On cosmetics in eighteenth-century art criticism see Melissa Hyde, *Making Up the Rococo. François Boucher and his Critics*, op. cit.
16 M. P. R. de C... C. à P. de L [Paul Romain de Chaperon], *Traité de la peinture au pastel*, Defer de Maisonneuve, Paris, 1788. Discussed at length in Thea Burns, *The Invention of Pastel Painting*, op. cit.
17 Hyde, *Making Up the Rococo*, op. cit., pp. 133–35.
18 Stacey Sell, 'The Touch Color: Pastels at the National Gallery. Sept. 29, 2019-Jan. 26, 2020', p. 7. https://www.nga.gov/content/dam/ngaweb/exhibitions/pdfs/2019/touch-of-color-pastels.pdf
21 Cited in Jeffares, 'Jean-Étienne Liotard', *Pastellists*, op. cit., p. 5.
22 Hyde, 'The Gentle Art of Pastel', in *Nicolas Party: Pastel*, op. cit.
23 Cited in Jeffares, 'Treatises and other historical texts related to Pastels and pastellists', *Pastellists*, op. cit., p. 95.
24 Ibid.
25 Ibid.
26 Marjorie Shelley, *Pastel Portraits. Images of 18th-Century Europe*, Metropolitan Museum of Art, New York, 2011, p. 11.
27 Cited in Jeffares, 'Treatises', *Pastellists*, op. cit., p. 95.
28 See Hyde, *Making Up the Rococo*, op. cit., pp. 86–90.
29 Amy Freund, *Portraiture and Politics in Revolutionary France*, College Penn State University Press, State College, Pennsylvania, 2014.
30 As Thea Burns and Philippe Saunier have noted in their indispensable, *The Art of Pastel*, Abbeville Press, New York, 2015, pp. 162–72.
31 Ibid, 224.
32 See 'Conversation avec Nicolas Party', op. cit., pp. 201–02.
33 Gautier, *Histoire de l'art dramatique*, 1859, op. cit., p. 331.
34 Indrisek, 'Explore…', *All Arts*.
35 *Nicolas Party: In the Studio*, 26 June 2019, https://www.youtube.com/watch?v=ZozkE6dyBx0. Louis-Antoine Caraccioli, *Dictionnaire critique*, 1768, op. cit.

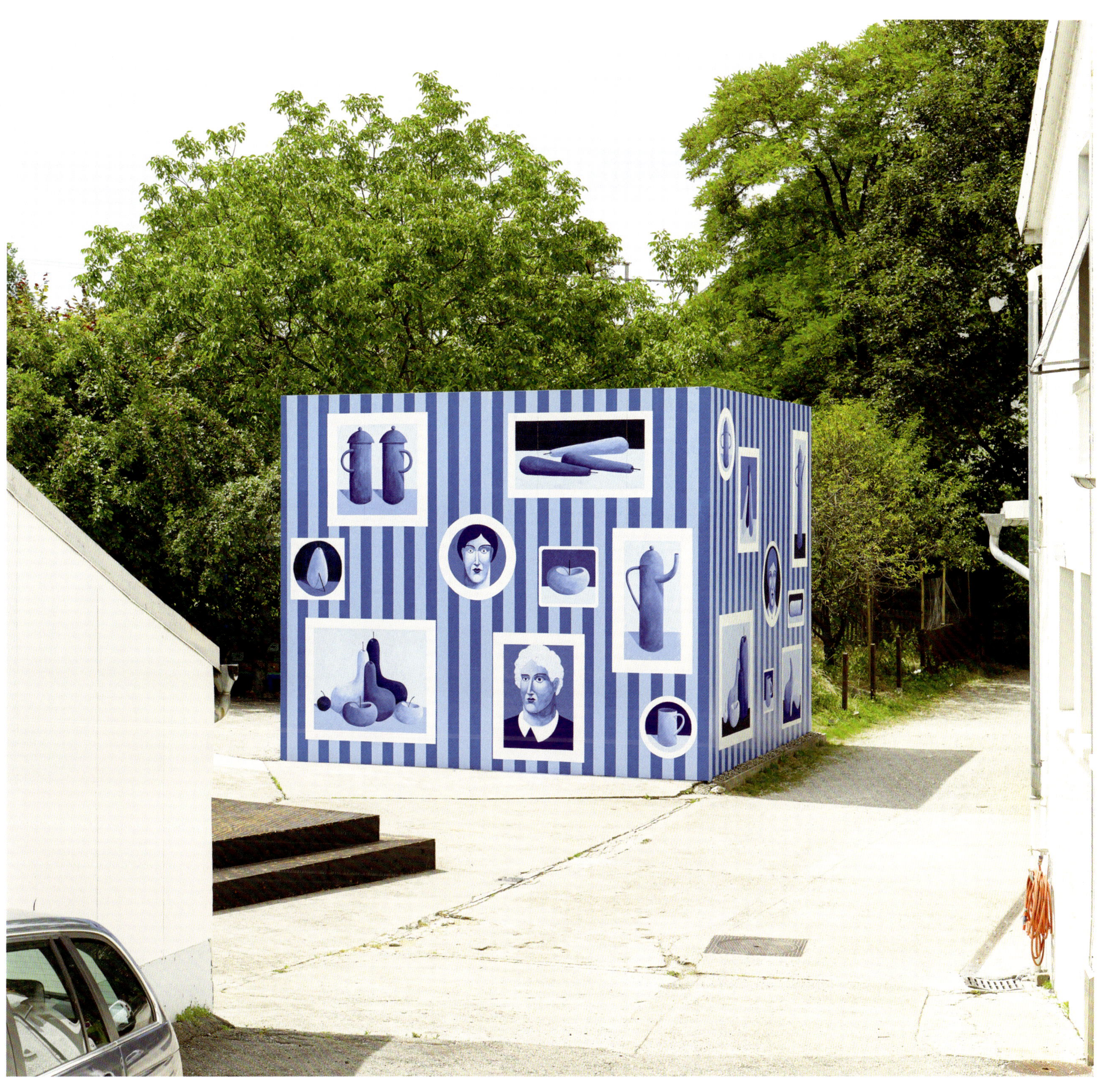

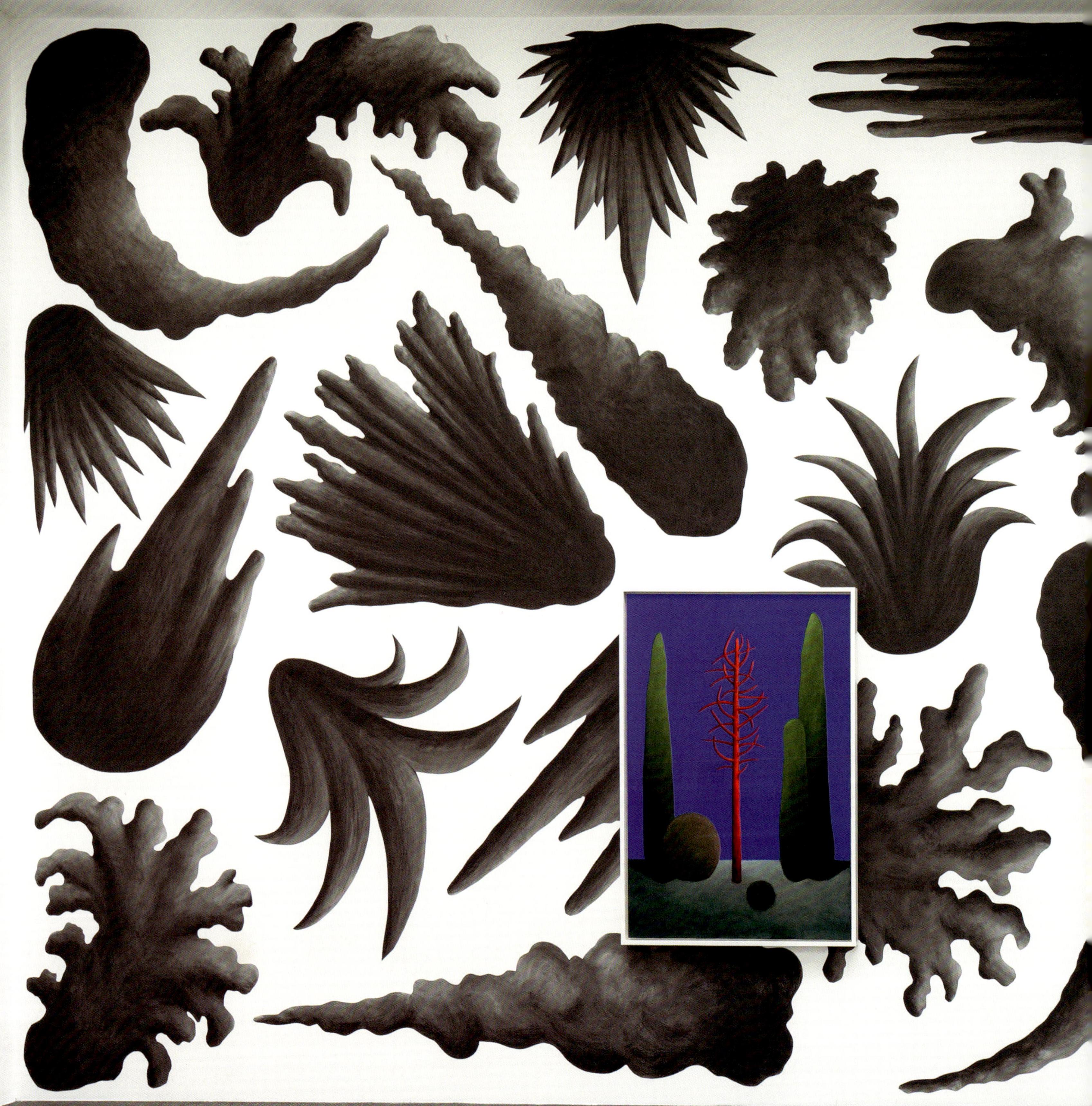

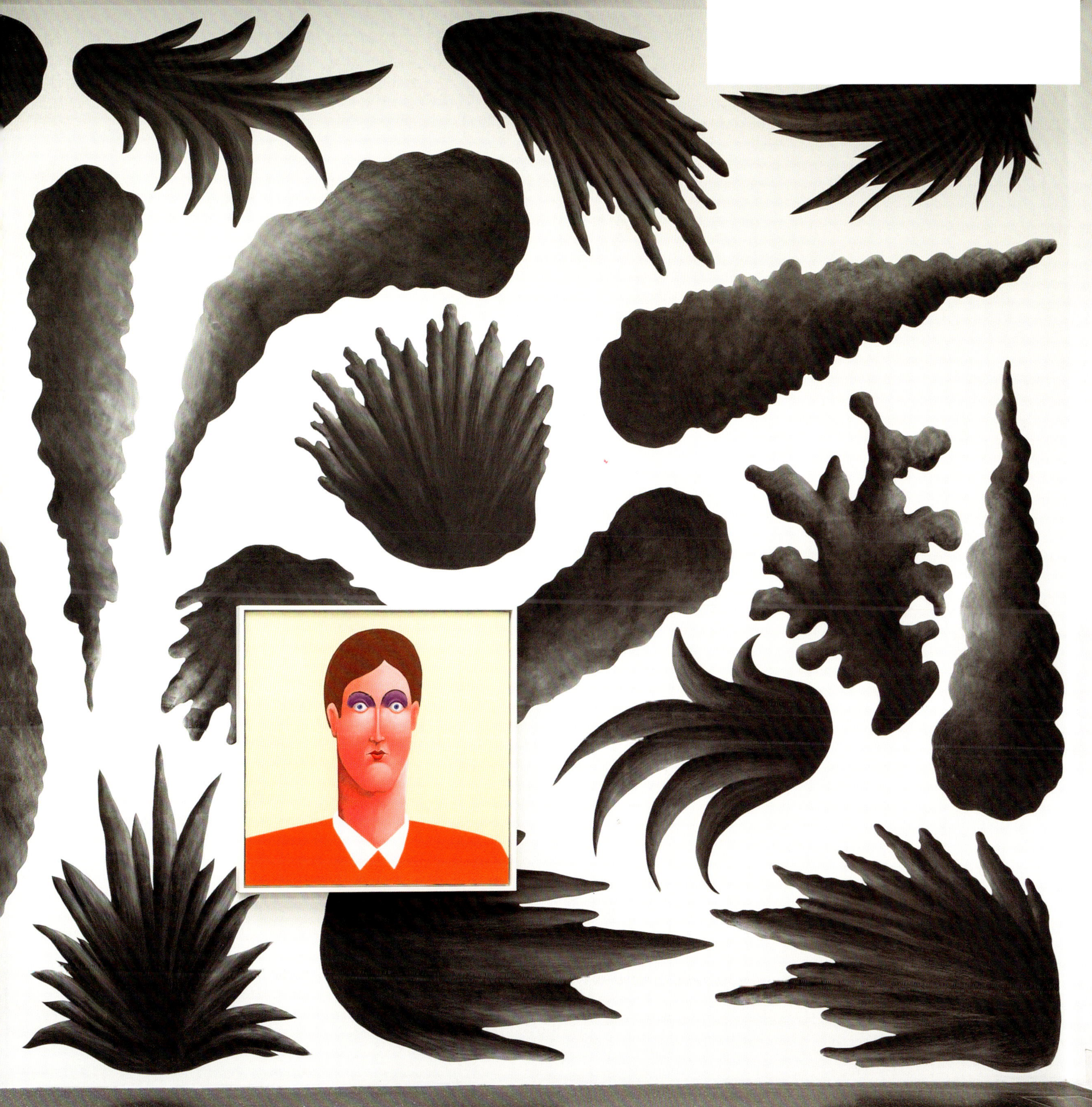

CHRONOLOGY: Nicolas Party, born 1980 in Lausanne. Lives and works in New York.

SELECTED EXHIBITIONS AND PROJECTS
2002–08

SELECTED ARTICLES AND INTERVIEWS
2002–08

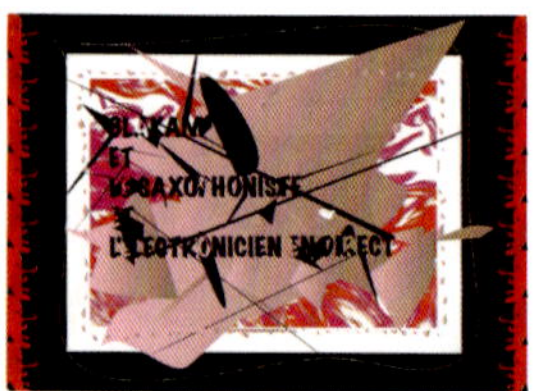

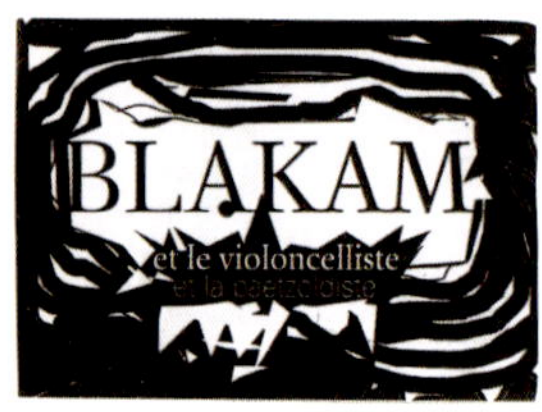

2002
'Viper 22 Replay 2',
PLUG.IN, Basel (group)

2003
'Désire Design',
MUSÉE DE DESIGN ET D'ARTS APPLIQUÉS CONTEMPORAINS (MUDAC), Lausanne (group)

'MediaSpace Suiza',
CENTRO CULTURAL CONDE DUQUE, Madrid (group)

'Viper Basel 03',
KUNSTHALLE BASEL (group)

2004
'Cinquième partie',
L'ARSENIC, Lausanne (group)

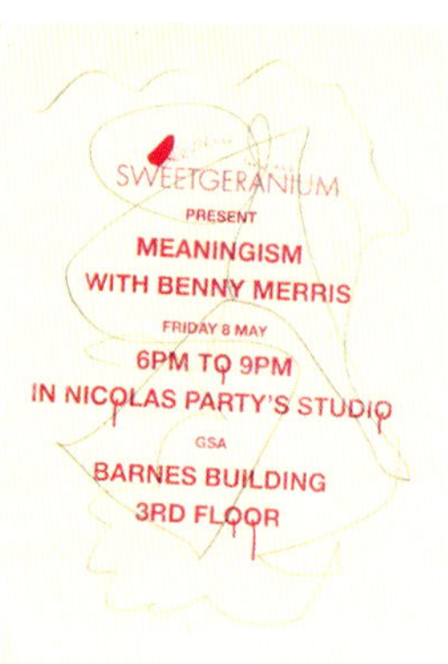

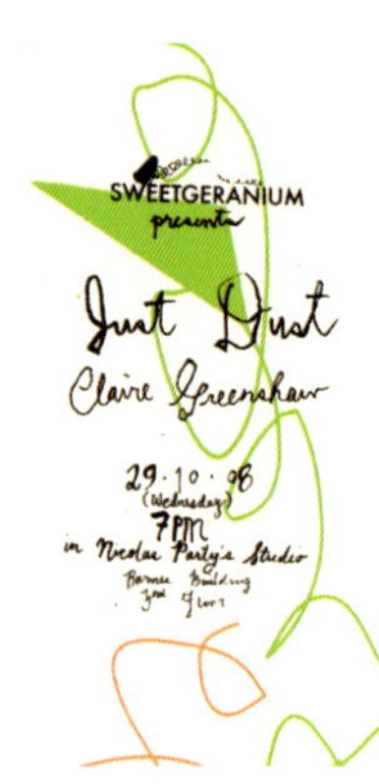

2005
'Elle procure des plaisirs qui n'ont rien à voir avec le plaisir de se gratter',
LA RUSILLE, Vallorbe, Switzerland (group)

'Swiss Videolandscape Today/Lopped Sensations',
PARK TOWER HALL, Tokyo, toured to GOETHE INSTITUTE, Kyoto (group)

BA in Fine Arts at the École Cantonale d'Art de Lausanne

2006
ESPACE BELLEVAUX (with Blakam), Lausanne (solo)

'Blakam Madame 2' (with Blakam),
ESPACE BELLEVAUX, Lausanne (solo)

'Mini Golf' (with Blakam),
CIRCUIT, Lausanne (group)

'Viper Basel 06' (with Blakam),
KUNSTHALLE BASEL (group)

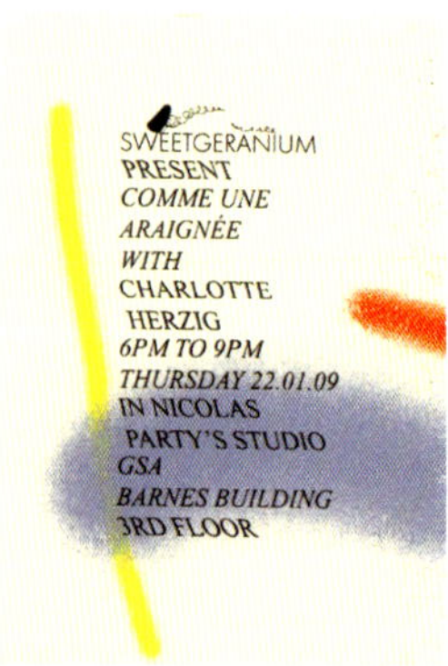

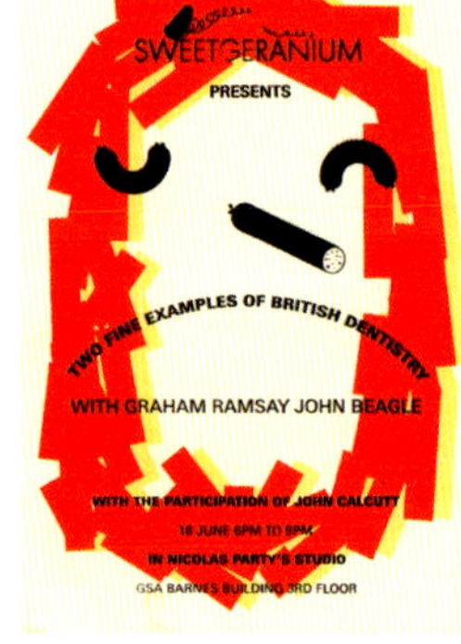

2007
'Blakadama' (with Blakam),
FORD, Geneva (group)

'Les Urbaines' (with Blakam),
DOCKS, Lausanne (group)

'OB zine' (with Blakam),
FORD, Geneva (group)

'Swiss Art Award' (with Blakam),
MESSE, Basel (group)

'Unter < 30' (with Blakam),
CENTRE PASQUART, Biel, toured to KUNSTHALLE LANGENTHAL, Switzerland (group)

'Wunder Stanza' (with Blakam),
FORD, Geneva (group)

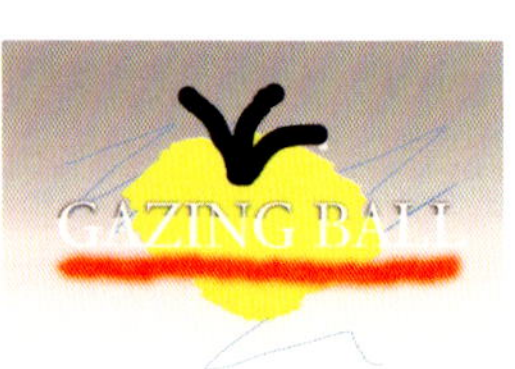

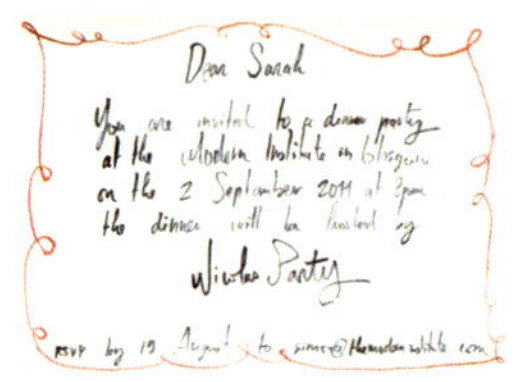

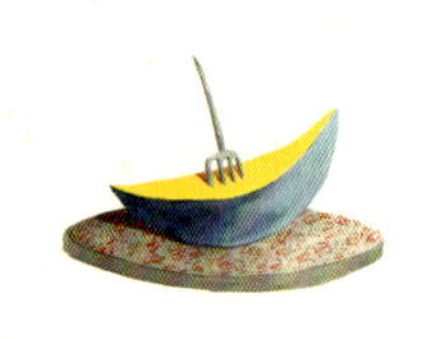

GAZING BALL
A collection of works by Christian Newby with interruptions by Nicolas Party
Preview
Thursday November 5th
7pm–9pm
Tuesday November 10th to Saturday November 14th
Opening hours 11am to 5pm
Project Room
Trongate 103
Glasgow

Glasgow Independent Studios
Project Room
First floor
Trongate 103
Glasgow G1 5HD
www.gis.uk.com
0141 552 1472

www.christiannewby.org

2008
'Swiss Art Award',
MESSE, Basel (group)

SELECTED EXHIBITIONS AND PROJECTS
2008–11

SELECTED ARTICLES AND INTERVIEWS
2008–11

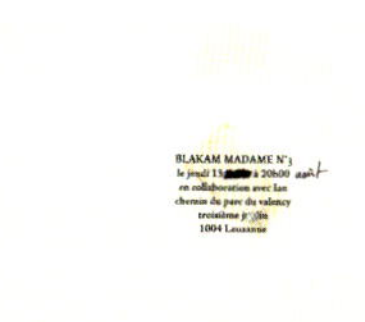

2008 (cont.)
'Fertiles Differences',
GALERIE ANALIX FOREVER, Geneva (group)

'Royal Scottish Academy Exhibition',
ROYAL SCOTTISH ACADEMY, Edinburgh (group)

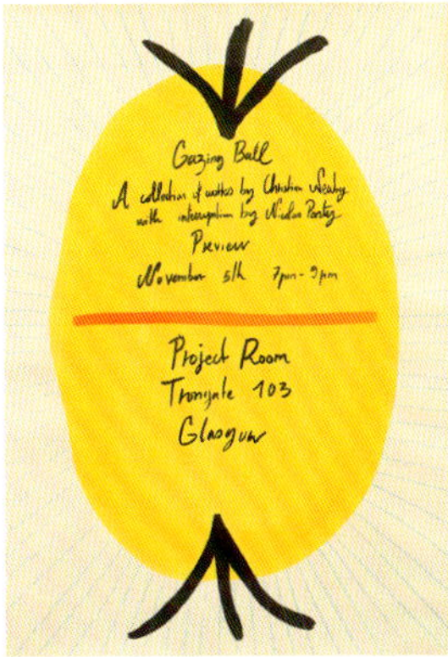

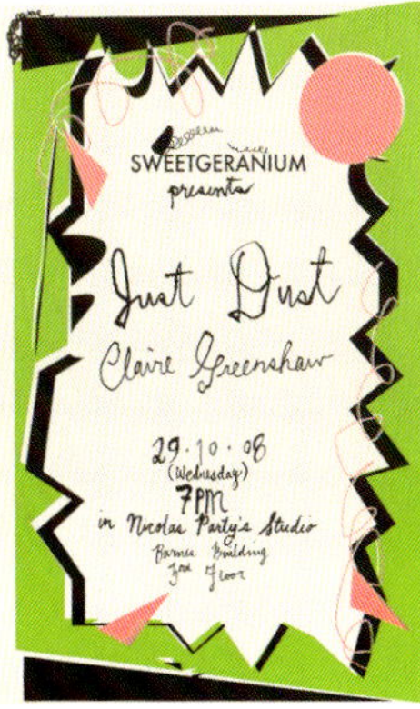

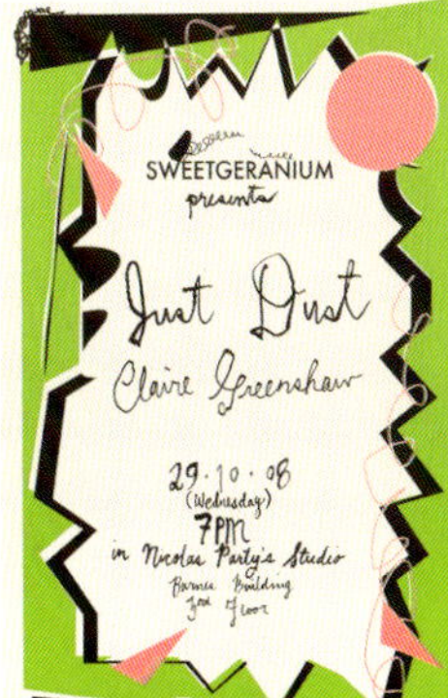

2009
'Gazing Ball',
PROJECT ROOM, Glasgow (group)

'MFA Show',
TRAMWAY, Glasgow (group)

'Set Up and Go',
APS ARTNEWS PROJECT+TWINSPACE, Berlin (group)

'The Complete World History of Terrorism as it is Known Today + Solution',
PLATEAUX FESTIVAL MOUSONTURM, Frankfurt, toured to L'ARSENIC, Lausanne (group)

MA in Fine Arts at the Glasgow School of Art

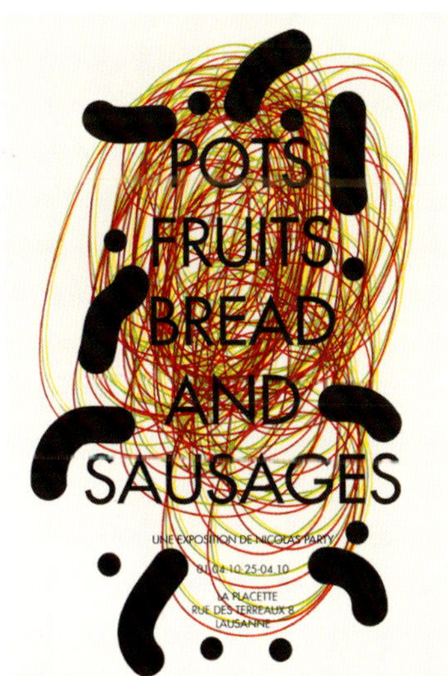

2010
'Elephants, spoons and sausage rolls',
LE REZ DE CHAUSSEE, Glasgow (solo)

'New Work Scotland',
COLLECTIVE GALLERY, Edinburgh (solo)

'Teapots and Sausages',
INTERMEDIA, Glasgow (solo)

'Teapots, Bread and Sausages',
LA PLACETTE, Lausanne (solo)

'Air de jeux',
LE QUARTIER CENTRE D'ART CONTEMPORAIN, Quimper, France (group)

'Interference with Twigs',
MARY MARY, Glasgow (group)

'Kiss of Death',
THE GLUE FACTORY, Glasgow (group)

'The Show in the Shoe' (organized by Nicolas Party and Jim Lambie),
TEMPORARY SPACE, Glasgow (group)

2010
Edbrook, Laura, 'A Space on Stage, The Dinner Party', New Work Scotland Programme, no. 7

'New Work Scotland', Map, no. 23, September

Cattanach, Andrew, 'NWS 2010: Nicolas Party and Catherine Payton', The Skinny, no. 61, October

Lammer, Elise, 'Sweet Geranium', Novembre, no. 2, Fall–Winter

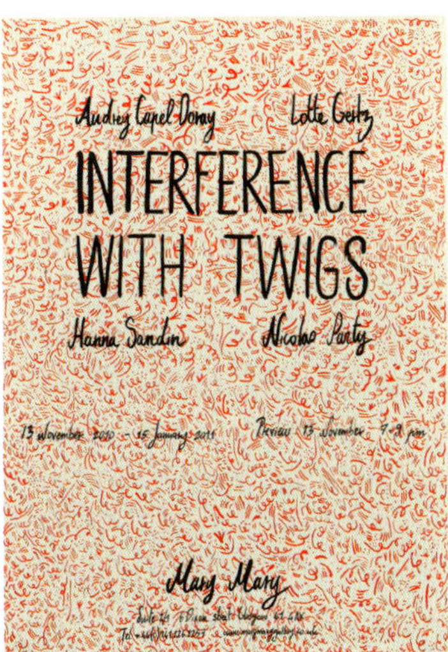

2011
'Charlotte' (with Stéphane Devidal),
DOLL ESPACE D'ART CONTEMPORAIN, Lausanne (solo)

'Still Life, Gold and Peeling Paint',
REMAP 3, Athens (solo)

'Dinner for 24 Elephants',
THE MODERN INSTITUTE, Glasgow (solo)

'Elephants at the Woodmill',
THE WOODMILL, London (solo)

'Painting Show',
EASTSIDE PROJECTS, Birmingham (group)

'Poster Club',
EASTSIDE PROJECTS, Birmingham (group)

2011
Calcutt, John, 'Emerging: Nicolas Party', MAP Magazine, no. 25, Summer

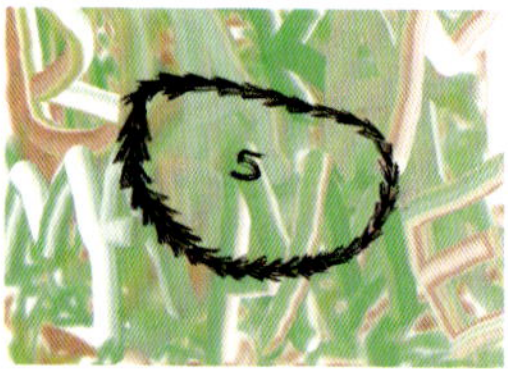

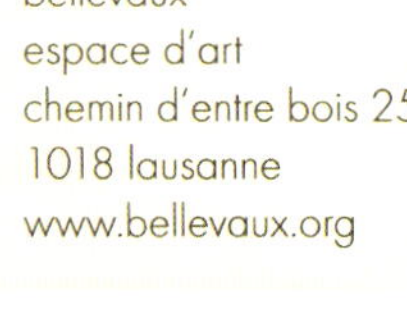

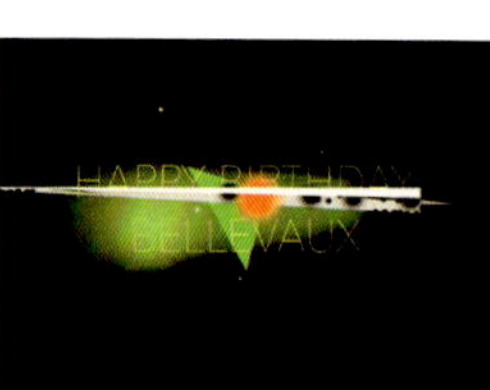

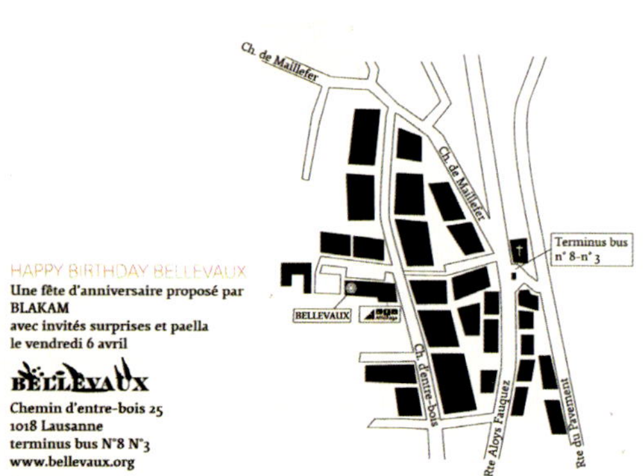

SELECTED EXHIBITIONS AND PROJECTS
2011–14

2011 (cont.)
'Poster Chaud',
GLASGOW PRINT STUDIO (group)

'Blueprint for a Bogey',
GALLERY OF MODERN ART, Glasgow (group)

'Draw In',
TRAVELLING GALLERY, Edinburgh (group)

'Elephants at The Royal Standard',
THE ROYAL STANDARD, Liverpool (group)

2012
'Dinner for 24 Dogs'
SALON 94, New York (solo)

'Still Lifes and Big Naked Women',
GALERIE GREGOR STAIGER, Zurich (solo)

'Still Life, Stones and Elephants',
SWISS INSTITUTE, New York (solo)

'Carpets of Distinction',
DOVECOT STUDIOS, Edinburgh (group)

'Allez-y',
R4, Ile Seguin, Paris (group)

'Arrives In Starting',
THE DUCHY GALLERY, Glasgow (group)

2013
'Still Life Oil Paintings and Landscape Watercolours',
THE MODERN INSTITUTE, Glasgow (solo)

'Cully Jazz',
DAVEL 14, Cully (solo)

'Funktion/Disfunktion: Kunstzentrum Glasgow/Function Dysfunction: Contemporary Art from Glasgow',
NEUES MUSEUM, Nürnberg (group)

'Ihre Geschichte(n)',
BONNER KUNSTVEREIN, Bonn (group)

'Just What is Not is Possible: Painting in Space',
MUSEUM FOLKWANG, Essen (group)

'157 Days of Sunshine',
THE BOTHY PROJECT AT THE WALLED GARDEN, Glasgow (group)

'40/40',
GLASGOW PRINT STUDIO (group)

2014
'Trunks and Faces',
WESTFÄLISCHER KUNSTVEREIN, Münster (solo)

'Landscape',
KUNSTHALL STAVANGER, Norway (solo)

'Pastel',
GALERIE GREGOR STAIGER, Zurich (solo)

'Carrot Stairs',
DAVID DALE GALLERY, Glasgow (solo)

'Three Elephant's Day' (with Serge Vuille),
BONNER KUNSTVEREIN, Bonn (solo)

SELECTED ARTICLES AND INTERVIEWS
2011–14

2012
Hoberman, Mara, 'Five Questions for Nicolas Party', Swiss Institute Contemporary Art, no. 1, March

Katsof, Alhena, 'Meet Nicolas Party', Kaleidoscope, no. 17, Winter

Morgan, Elinor, 'Painting Show', Modern Painters, December

2013
Benmakhlouf, Adam, 'Art Review', The Skinny, no. 91, April

Herbert, Martin, 'Now See This', Art Review, April

Patience, Jan, 'An Arty Party', The Daily Record, 12 April

Patience, Jan, 'Gallery Round-Up', The Herald, 13 April

Mansfield, Susan, 'Art Reviews: Nicolas Party at The Modern Institute', The Scotsman, 25 April

Sharratt, Chris, 'Nicolas Party at The Modern Institute', Frieze, no. 156, June–August

Halpern, Clara, 'Daily Servings: The Art World's Food Pyramid', Modern Painters, October

Lack, Jessica, 'Party Coloured', The World of Interiors, December

Sharratt, Chris, 'Strange Fruits', Frieze d/e, no. 12, December–February

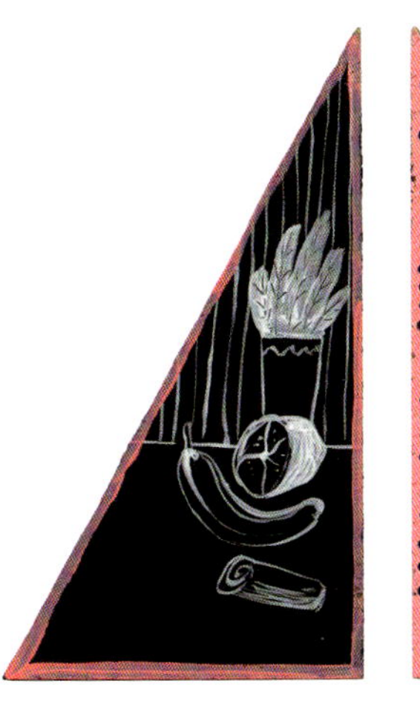

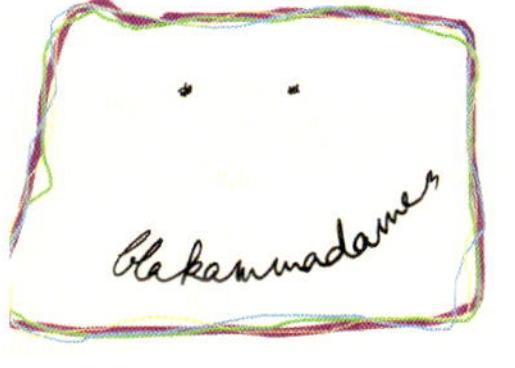

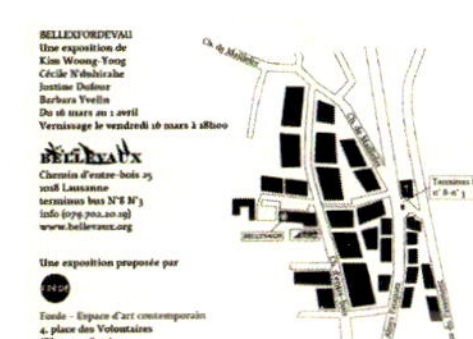

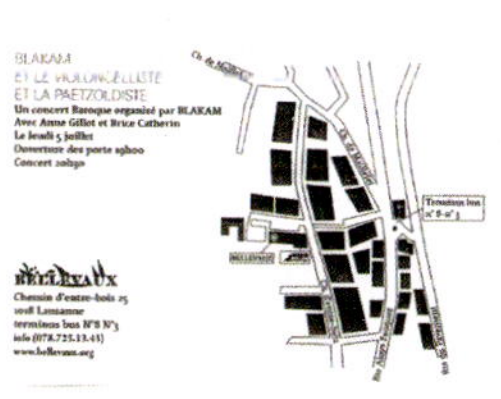

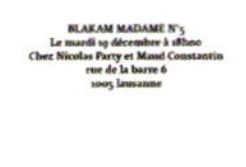

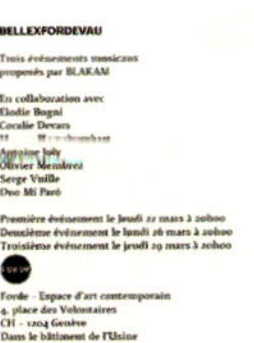

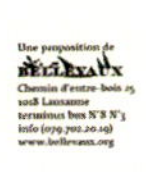

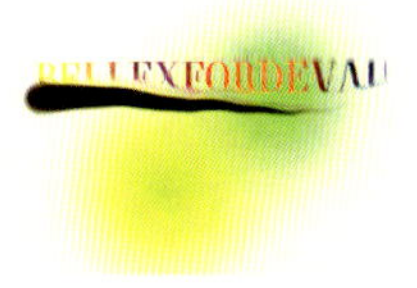

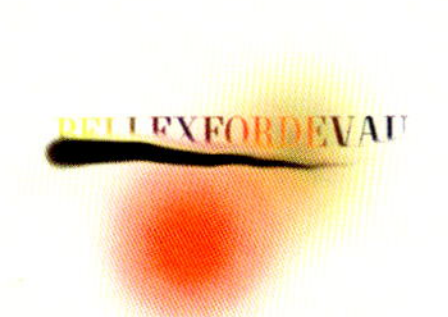

SELECTED EXHIBITIONS AND PROJECTS
2014–16

2014 (cont.)
'I'm So Green',
NATALIA HUG GALLERY, Cologne (group)

'I'm a Painting',
KUMU ART MUSEUM, Tallinn (group)

2015
'Snails in Notting Hill' (with Jesse Wine),
RISE PROJECTS, London (solo)

'Two Naked Women',
KAUFMANN REPETTO, Milan (solo)

'Boys and Pastel',
INVERLEITH HOUSE, Edinburgh (solo)

'Pastel et Nu',
CENTRE CULTUREL SUISSE, Paris (solo)

'Snail's Chapel',
KAUFMANN REPETTO, Milan (solo)

'Panorama',
SALTS, Basel (group)

'Full House',
SHANAYNAY, Paris (group)

'Tiger Tiger',
SALON 94, New York (group)

'Still-Life Remix',
CANTINA DEL BARGINO, Antinori nel Chianti Classico, Italy (group)

2016
'Hammer Projects: Nicolas Party',
THE HAMMER MUSEUM, Los Angeles (solo)

'Nicolas Party in the Garden Room',
PALAZZO ANTINORI, Florence (solo)

'Three Cats',
THE MODERN INSTITUTE, Glasgow (solo)

'Cimaise' and 'Sorcières et Escargots' (with Jesse Wine),
CENTRE D'ART NEUCHÂTEL (CAN), Switzerland (solo)

'Snails in Notting Hill' (with Jesse Wine),
RISE PROJECTS, London (solo)

'Nicolas Party: Pathway',
DALLAS MUSEUM OF ART (solo)

'Mezzotint',
GLASGOW PRINT STUDIO, Glasgow (solo)

'Surreal',
KÖNIG GALERIE, Berlin (group)

'Olympia',
GALERIE PATRICK SEGUIN, Paris (group)

'I Still Believe in Miracles',
INVERLEITH HOUSE, Edinburgh (group)

'These Strangers... Painting and People',
STEDELIJK MUSEUM VOOR ACTUELE KUNST (SMAK), Ghent, Belgium (group)

SELECTED ARTICLES AND INTERVIEWS
2014–16

2015
Krell, Cynthia, 'Konzept-Bilder und Interventionen', Kunst Bulletin, February

Cotter, Holland, 'Independent Art Fair Combines Less Is More and Growth', The New York Times, 6 March

Campanini, Cristiana, 'La pittura che dialoga coi graffiti', La Repubblica, 28 March

Clark, Robert, 'Nicolas Party', The Guardian, 9 May

'Nicolas Party: Boys And Pastel, Inverleith Gallery, Edinburgh', The Herald, 9 May

Vitorelli, Rita, 'Portrait Nicolas Party', Spike Art Magazine, no. 44, Summer

Wine, Jesse, 'Apples and Pairs', Frieze, no. 175, November–December

McCrory, Sarah, 'Best of 2015', Artforum, December

2016
'News of the Print World', Art in Print, no. 6, March–April

Holderegger Rossier, Katharina, 'Nicolas Party', Kunst Bulletin, July–August

Spence, Rachel, 'I Still Believe in Miracles, Inverleith House, Edinburgh: Improbable loveliness', Financial Times, 21 August

'Art Review: Nicolas Party/Jennifer West', The Scotsman, 19 September

Hatfull, Nicholas, 'Nicolas Party "Three Cats" at The Modern Institute, Glasgow', Mousse Magazine, no. 55, October–November

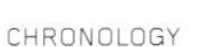
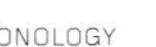

SWEETGERANIUM
PRESENT
COMME UNE
ARAIGNÉE
WITH
CHARLOTTE
HERZIG
6PM TO 9PM
THURSDAY 22.01.09
IN NICOLAS
PARTY'S STUDIO
GSA
BARNES BUILDING
3RD FLOOR

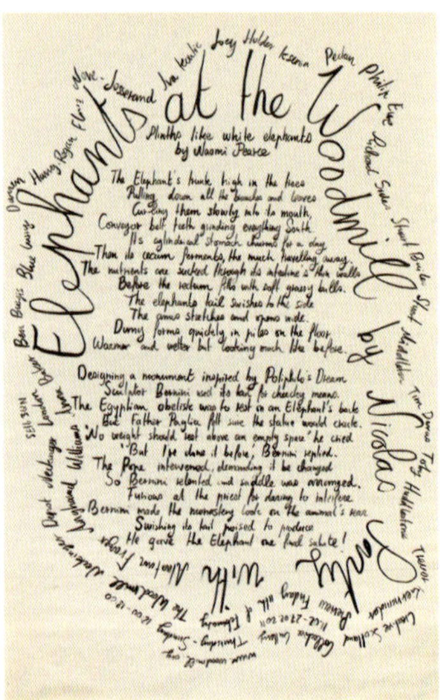

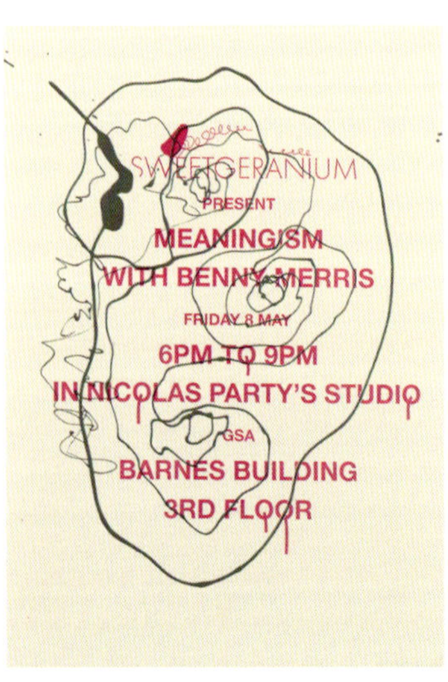

SELECTED EXHIBITIONS AND PROJECTS
2017–19

2017

'Speakers',
MODERN ART OXFORD (solo)

'Pastel',
KARMA, New York (solo)

'Sunrise, Sunset',
HIRSHHORN MUSEUM AND SCULPTURE GARDEN, Washington DC (solo)

'Three Seasons',
XAVIER HUFKENS, Brussels (solo)

'La vie simple/Simplement la vie',
FONDATION VINCENT VAN GOGH, Arles (group)

'Wie werden wir uns wiedererkennen',
KÜNSTLERHAUS BREMEN (group)

2018

'Arches',
M WOODS MUSEUM, Beijing (solo)

'Magritte Parti',
MUSÉE MAGRITTE MUSEUM, Brussels (solo)

'Heads',
GALERIE GREGOR STAIGER, Zurich (solo)

'Head',
THE MODERN INSTITUTE, Glasgow (solo)

'Pietra Dura',
KAUFMANN REPETTO, Milan (solo)

6th BIENNIAL OF PAINTING, Deurle, Belgium (group)

'Pastels du 16e au 21e siècle',
FONDATION DE L'HERMITAGE, Lausanne (group)

'Open House',
JESSICA SILVERMAN GALLERY, San Francisco (group)

'Vous me rappelez quelqu'un/You Remind Me of Someone',
FONDS RÉGIONAL D'ART CONTEMPORAIN (FRAC) LORRAINE, France (group)

2019

'Grotto',
XAVIER HUFKENS, Brussels (solo)

'Marble Ghosts',
MARBLE HOUSE, Newport, Rhode Island (solo)

'Trees',
MARCIANO ART FOUNDATION, Los Angeles (solo)

'Polychrome',
THE MODERN INSTITUTE, Glasgow (solo)

'Pastel',
THE FLAG ART FOUNDATION, New York (solo)

'Away in the Hill',
GRIMM, New York (group)

'Drawn World: Zeichnungen von Menzel Bis Warhol',
GALERIE LUDORFF, Düsseldorf (group)

Receives the RxArt Inspiration Award, New York

SELECTED ARTICLES AND INTERVIEWS
2017–19

2017

Koller, Denise, 'Gegen die Wand. Interview mit Künstler Nicolas Party', Interview Magazin, January

Subotnick, Ali, 'The First Form of Art', Parkett, No. 100/101

Ostroff, Hannah S., 'Vibrant Nicolas Party landscapes embellish Hirshhorn's third-floor circle gallery, Smithsonian Magazine, June

McGrath, Charles, 'The Met's Dinner That Never Ends', The New Yorker, 9 October

Godfrey Lamon, Annie, 'Nicolas Party at Karma, New York', Artforum, December

Provenzi, Romina, 'Nicolas Party: Oxford, Revisited', Elephant Magazine, December

2018

Owen Rowlands, Lili, 'Nicolas Party: Speakers/Hannah Ryggen: Woven Histories', The White Review, no. 20, February

Casavecchia, Barbara, 'As far as the eye can see', L'Officiel Art, no. 26, April

Mackovic, Sinisa, 'Nicolas Party', Apartamento, no. 21, April

Kazanjian, Dodie, 'Party Time', Vogue, June

Shaw, Anny, 'London's contemporary art summer season in flux as middle market comes out on top', The Art Newspaper, June

Grandjean, Emmanuel, 'Grand Classique', T: Le Magazine du Temps, June

Behrens, Katja, 'Nicolas Party', Kunst Bulletin, December

2019

Tudor, Elisabetta, 'A Tinte Accese', Vogue Italia, February

Truax, Stephen, 'Pastel Then, Pastel Now', Hyperallergic, 12/2019
Loos, Ted, 'Artist Nicolas Party Revives the Language of Pastel', Cultured, March

Troncy, Éric, 'Nicolas Party, King of Oneiric Flamboyance', Numéro, August

Guadagnino, Kate, 'At a "Dinner with Ghosts," Everything Is Art', The New York Times, 28 August

Yerebakan, Osman Can, 'Nicolas Party Is Painting Pastels on Everything From Museum Walls to Hospital Halls', The Observer, 6 November

Hong, Catherine, 'Nicolas Party's Audacious Sense of Color', Surface, no. 154, December

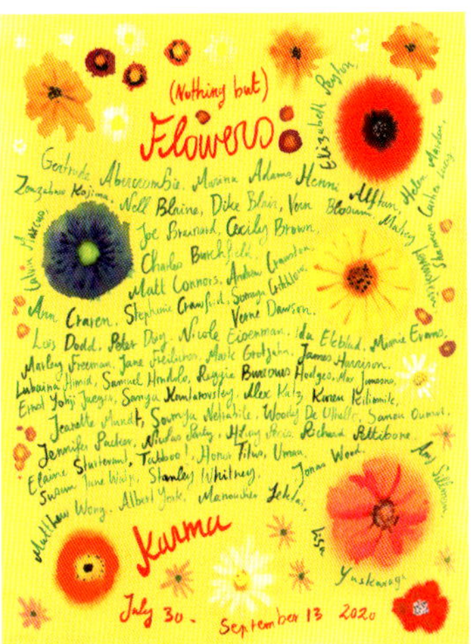

SELECTED EXHIBITIONS AND PROJECTS
2020–22

2020
'Sottobosco',
HAUSER & WIRTH, Los Angeles (solo)

'Al filo de la navaja/On the Razor's Edge',
MUSEO JUMEX, Mexico City (group)

7th BIENNALE GHERDËINA, Urtijëi, Italy (group)

'Nothing but Flowers',
KARMA, New York (group)

'Shall und Rauch',
KUNSTHAUS ZÜRICH (group)

'Figures and Faces',
McCABE FINE ART, New York (group)

'Vent'anni/Twenty Years',
KAUFMANN REPETTO, Milan (group)

2021
'Nicolas Party: Rovine',
MUSEO D'ARTE DELLA SVIZZERA ITALIANA (MASI), Lugano (solo)

'Heads and Cave',
KUNSTHALLE MARCEL DUCHAMP, Cully, Switzerland (solo)

'Nicolas Party: Boilly',
LE CONSORTIUM, Dijon, France (solo)

'Stage Fright',
KESTNER GESELLSCHAFT, Hannover (solo)

AÏSHTI FOUNDATION, Beirut (solo)

KARMA, New York (solo)

'Draw the Curtain',
HIRSHHORN MUSEUM AND SCULPTURE GARDEN, Washington, DC (solo)

'Hans Emmenegger',
FONDATION DE L'HERMITAGE, Lausanne (group)

'Yes. this is how we pierce the vault of heaven',
GALERIE GREGOR STAIGER, Zurich (group)

'And I will wear you in my heart of heart',
THE FLAG ART FOUNDATION, New York (group)

2022
'L'heure mauve'
MONTREAL MUSEUM OF FINE ARTS, Montreal (solo)

MUSEO POLDI PEZZOLI, Milan (solo)

SELECTED ARTICLES AND INTERVIEWS
2020–22

2020
Abrams, Amah-Rose, 'Painting the Town', Esquire, Winter

Leydier, Richard, 'Nicolas Party Game Over', Art Press, no. 474, February

Martorelli, Manuela, 'Nicolas Party. Interview', Odda, March

Belcove, Julie, 'Art Therapy', Robb Report, May

Klingelfuss, Jessica, 'West Side Story', Wallpaper*, May

Edugyan, Esi, 'How Silk-Making Represents a More Hidden Side of Georgia's Past', T: The New York Times Magazine, 11 May

Bogojev, Sasha, 'A Hug From On Top of You', Juxtapoz, no. 215, September

Loos, Ted, 'Auction Price that take your breath away', The New York Times, 15 September

Lee, Jonathan, 'Nicolas Party', Bomb Magazine, no. 152

Zham, Oliver, 'Nicolas Party', Purple, no. 34

Bennett, Alex, 'The Sweet Potato and the Jar: Alex Bennett in Conversation with Nicolas Party', Novembre, Fall

2021
Reyburn, Scott, 'Blue-chip artists move over, here come the red chips', The Art Newspaper, January

'Nicolas Party: Cover', Public Art, no. 174, March

Lee, Gajin, 'Nicolas Party: Landscape and Portrait', Public Art, no. 175, April

Delisi, Alessia, 'Party surreale: Tra ritratti onirici e panorami fiabeschi, il MASI di Lugano svela il talento immaginifico del pittore svizzero', Marie Claire, June

Capps, Kriston, 'Hide and Seek: Hirshhorn Museum to cover entire building in a giant painting by Nicolas Party', The Art Newspaper, July–August

BIBLIOGRAPHY

MONOGRAPHS AND ARTIST'S BOOKS

Party, Nicolas, Joanne Tatham and Tom O'Sullivan, Staub: A Journal of Entropy, Sweet Geranium, Glasgow, 2010

Party, Nicolas, and Corin Sworn, Teapots and Sausages, Intermedia, Glasgow, 2010

Party, Nicolas, and Naomi Pearce, Nicolas Party, The Modern Institute, Glasgow, 2011

Party, Nicolas, Pastel, Galerie Gregor Staiger, Zurich, 2014

Party, Nicolas, Nicolas Party: Pastel, Karma, New York, and The Modern Institute, Glasgow, 2017

Party, Nicolas, Nicolas Party: Still Life. Paintings by William Nicholson, Giorgio Morandi, Euan Uglow, Félix Vallotton, Karma, New York, 2019

Party, Nicolas, Nicolas Party: Arches, M WOODS, Beijing, 2019

Party, Nicolas, and Michel Draguet, Magritte Parti: A conversation between René Magritte & Nicolas Party, Musées Royaux des Beaux-Arts de Belgique/Koninklijke Musea voor Schone Kunsten van België and Musée Magritte Museum, Brussels, 2020

Party, Nicolas, Glenn Fuhrman, Melissa Hyde, Louis Fratino, Loie Hollowell, Billy Sullivan, Robin F. Williams and Dodie Kazanjian, Nicolas Party: Pastel, The FLAG Art Foundation, New York, 2021

Party, Nicolas, Tobia Bezzola, Francesca Bernasconi and Michele Robecchi, Nicolas Party: Rovine, Museo della Svizzera Italiana, Lugano, and Scheidegger & Spiess, Zurich, 2021

Party, Nicolas, Stéphane Aquin, Stefan Banz, Ali Subotnick and Melissa Hyde, Nicolas Party, Phaidon, London, 2021

EXHIBITION CATALOGUES AND SURVEYS

Als, Hilton, and Helen Molesworth, Nothing but Flowers, Karma, New York, 2021

Bezzola, Tobia, Denis Bury, Simon Dybbroe Møller, Samuel Gross and Marcel Schumacher, Just What is Not is Possible: Painting in Space, Museum Folkwang, Essen, and Steidl, Göttingen, Germany, 2013

Bottura, Massimo, The Kitchen Studio: Culinary Creations by Artists, Phaidon, London, 2021

Budack, Adam (ed.), A Breath? A Name? The Ways of Worldmaking, Istitut Ladin Micurá de Rü, San Martin de Tor, and Biennale Gherdëina, Urtijëi, Italy, 2020

Curiger, Bice (ed.), La vie simple/Simplement la vie, Fondation Vincent Van Gogh Arles, France, 2017

Deitch, Jeffrey, Alison Gingeras, Johanna Fateman and Aria Dean, Unrealism: New Figurative Painting, Rizzoli Electa, New York, 2019

Emin, Tracy, Wayne Koestenbaum and Andrea K. Scott (eds), Feelings: Soft Art, Skira Rizzoli, New York, 2015

Hammons, Kit, and Patricia Marshall, Al filo de la navaja/On the Razor's Edge, Museo Jumex, Mexico City, 2020

Hoste, Ann (ed.), These Strangers... Painting and People, Stedelijk Museum voor Actuele Kunst, Ghent, Belgium, and Roma Publications, Amsterdam, 2016

Hug, Cathérine, Petra Joos, Gioia Mori, Alexis Schwarzenbach and Jakob Tanner, Schall und Rauch: Die wilden 20er/Smoke and Mirrors: The Roaring Twenties, Kunsthaus Zürich, 2020

Kliege, Melitta (ed.), Funktion/Dysfunktion: Kunstzentrum Glasgow/Function Dysfunction: Contemporary Art from Glasgow, Verlag für Moderne Kunst, Nuremberg, and Neues Museum, Nürnberg, Germany, 2013

Schwabsky, Barry, Vitamin P3: New Perspectives in Painting, Phaidon, London, 2016

Stein, Jordan, Gertrude Abercrombie, Ann Craven, Nicolas Party, Matthew Wong, Karma, New York, 2019

Stout, Katharine, and Gunda Luyken, Drawn World: Zeichnungen von Menzel Bis Warhol, Galerie Ludorff, Düsseldorf, 2019

Wuhrmann, Sylvie, and Aurélie Couvreur (eds.), Pastels, du 16e au 21e siècle, La Bibliothèque des Arts and Fondation de l'Hermitage, Lausanne, 2018

SELECTED PUBLIC COLLECTIONS

READING AT KARMA, HERMIONE HOBY, 2018
POSTER
SOFT PASTEL ON PASTEL CARD
65 X 50 CM

ALBRIGHT-KNOX GALLERY, Buffalo

FONDAZIONE FIERA, Milan

HAMMER MUSEUM, Los Angeles

HIRSHHORN MUSEUM AND SCULPTURE GARDEN, Washington, DC

JUPITER ARTLAND, Edinburgh

K11 ART FOUNDATION, Hong Kong

KUNSTHALL STAVANGER, Norway

KUNSTHAUS ZURICH

LONG MUSEUM, Shanghai

LOS ANGELES COUNTY MUSEUM OF ART

M WOODS, Beijing

THE MENIL COLLECTION, Houston

MIGROS MUSEUM FÜR GEGENWARTSKUNST, Zurich

MUSÉES ROYAUX DES BEAUX-ARTS DE BELGIQUE/KONINKLIJKE MUSEA VOOR SCHONE KUNSTEN VAN BELGIË, Brussels

MUSEO D'ARTE SVIZZERA ITALIANA, Lugano, Switzerland

MUSEUM FOLKWANG, Essen, Germany

MUSEUM OF FINE ARTS, Houston

PHOENIX ART MUSEUM

SIFANG ART MUSEUM, NANJING, China

WESTFÄLISCHER KUNSTVEREIN, Münster, Germany

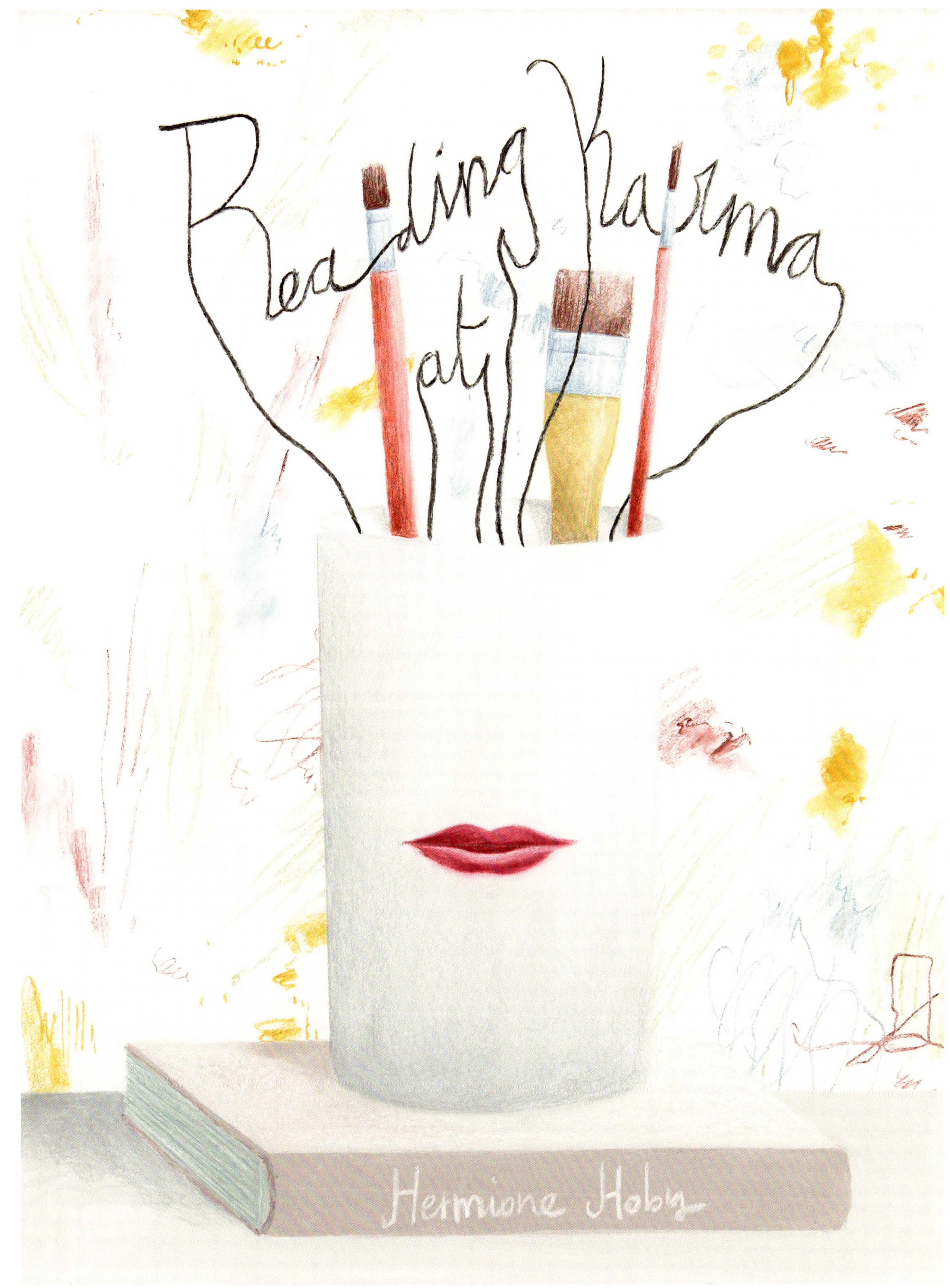
Reading Karma
at
Hermione Hoby

ILLUSTRATED WORKS

COMPARATIVE IMAGES

PHAIDON PRESS LTD.
2 COOPERAGE YARD
LONDON E15 2QR

PHAIDON PRESS INC.
65 BLEECKER STREET
NEW YORK, NY 10012

PHAIDON.COM

First published 2021
Reprinted 2022

ISBN:
978-1-83866-166-3
Limited Edition:
978-1-83866-380-3
Signed Edition:
978-1-83866-379-7

A CIP catalogue record of this book is available from the British Library and the Library of Congress.

Commissioning Editor
Michele Robecchi

Production Controller
Nerissa Dominguez Vales

Design
Melanie Mues, Mues Design, London

Layout
Rita Peres Pereira

Printed in China

PUBLISHER'S ACKNOWLEDGEMENTS

Special thanks to Kathryn Sawabini and August Krogan-Roley at Nicolas Party Studio, New York; Toby Webster and Andrew Hamilton at The Modern Institute, Glasgow; Catherine Serrano and Barbara Corti at Hauser & Wirth, New York; Xavier Hufkens, Barthélémy Schöller and Joris Dockx at Xavier Hufkens, Brussels; Caroline Bachmann, Sarah Blakley-Cartwright, Stéphane Devidal, Katharina Fritsch, Charlotte Herzig, Melissa Hyde, Francesca Kaufmann, Melissa Larner, Marie Lusa, Sarah Margnetti, João Mota, Marta Perovic, Tracey Smith, Daniel Spoerri, Gregor Staiger, John Stezaker, Hans Stofregen, Billy Sullivan, Robin F. Williams.

We would also like to thank the following institutions: Karma, New York; Kaufmann Repetto, Milan and New York; Galerie Gregor Staiger, Zurich; Fondation Beyeler, Riehen/Basel, Switzerland; The Frick Collection, New York; Gemäldegalerie Alte Meister, Dresden; Hammer Museum at the University of California, Los Angeles; Harvard Art Museums/Fogg Museum, Bequest of Charles E. Dunlap, Boston; The Metropolitan Museum of Art/Rogers Fund/Wrightsman Fund, New York; Musées Royaux des Beaux-Arts de Belgique, Brussels; Musée des Beaux-Arts de Quimper, France; Musée Grobet-Labadié, Marseille; Musée du Louvre, Paris; Museo Nazionale di San Marco, Florence; Museum für Moderne Kunst, Frankfurt; Mu.ZEE, Ostend, Belgium; Nasjonalmuseet for Kunst, Arkitektur og Design, Oslo; Samuel H. Kress Collection/National Gallery of Washington, DC; Société d'Auteurs Belge – Belgische Auteurs Maatschappij (SABAM), Brussels; Acquavella Galleries, New York; The Approach, London; Matthew Marks, New York; P.P.O.W Gallery, New York.

ARTIST'S ACKNOWLEDGEMENTS

In loving memory of Stefan Banz.

I would like to thank Keith Fox, Michele Robecchi, Nerissa Vales and everyone at Phaidon; the writers who contributed to this book – Stéphane Aquin, Stefan Banz, Ali Subotnick and Melissa Hyde; my galleries – Galerie Gregor Staiger, Zurich; Hauser & Wirth, Hong Kong, London, Los Angeles, New York and Zurich; KARMA, New York; Kaufmann Repetto, Milan and New York; The Modern Institute, Glasgow; Xavier Hufkens, Brussels; and my studio – August Krogan-Roley, Kathryn Sawabini and Robert Zehnder.

Thanks to Gregor Staiger and Marie Lusa at Galerie Gregor Staiger; Ursula Hauser, Iwan and Manuela Wirth, Marc Payot, Barbara Corti and Catherine Serrano at Hauser & Wirth; Brendan Dugan and Siniša Mačković at KARMA; Chiara Repetto, Francesca Kaufmann, Astrid Welter and Amanda Schmitt at Kaufmann Repetto; Toby Webster, Andrew Hamilton and Bobby Sinclair at The Modern Institute; Xavier Hufkens and Barthélémy Schöller at Xavier Hufkens.

Thanks to all the institutions who welcomed me over the years – Bonner Kunstverein, Bonn; Bothy Project, Scotland; Centre Culturel Suisse, Paris; Centre d'Art Neuchâtel, Switzerland; Collective Gallery, Edinburgh; Le Consortium, Dijon; Dallas Museum of Art; David Dale Gallery & Studio, Glasgow; Dovecot Studio, Edinburgh; East Side Project, Birmingham, United Kingdom; The FLAG Art Foundation, New York; Fondation Vincent van Gogh, Arles; Gallery Met, New York; Glasgow Print Studio; The Glue Factory, Glasgow; Hermitage Foundation, Lausanne; Hirshhorn Museum and Sculpture Garden, Washington, DC; Intermedia Gallery, Glasgow; Inverleith House, Edinburgh; Kestner Gesellschaft, Hannover; Kumu Art Museum, Tallinn; Kunsthalle Marcel Duchamp, Cully, Switzerland; Kunsthall Stavanger, Norway; Kunsthaus Zürich; Mary Mary, Glasgow; Neues Museum, Nüremberg; Musée Magritte Museum, Brussels; Museo d'Arte della Svizzera Italiana (MASI), Lugano, Switzerland; Museum Folkwang, Essen, Germany; Modern Art Oxford; La Placette, Lausanne; RISE Projects, London; The Royal Standard, Liverpool; Westfälischer Kunstverein, Münster, Germany; The Woodmill, London; M WOODS, Beijing; Salon 94, New York; Stedelijk Museum voor Actuele Kunst (SMAK), Gent, Belgium; Swiss Institute, New York; SALTS, Basel.

Specifically from those institutions – Lea Altner, Stéphane Aquin, Tobias Bezzola, Adam Budak, Caroline Cassidy, Simon Castets, Melissa Chiu, Bice Curiger, Gavin Delahunty, Michel Draguet, Merike Estna, Jean-Paul Felley, Claire Forsyth, Glenn Fuhrman, Fanny Gonella, Jeanne Greenberg, Sandy Guttman, Lin Han, Paul Hobson, Michael Xufu Huang, Cathérine Hug, Gianni Jetzer, Olivier Kaeser, Elise Lammer, Wanwan Lei, Samuel Leuenberger, John Mackechnie, Hanne Mugaas, Paul Nesbitt, Bobby Niven, Jon Rider, Silka Rittson-Thomas, Stephanie Roach, Ellie Royle, Kristina Scepanski, Max Slaven, Fabienne Stephan, Stephanie Straine, Éric Troncy, Christina Végh, Gavin Wade, Sylvie Wuhrmann, Marie Lea Zwahlen.

Dodie Kazanjian, Calvin Tomkins, Caroline Bachmann, Carroll Cartwright, Sarah Margnetti, Valérianne Poidevin, Jesse Wine, Cassie Griffin, Sanya Kantarovsky, Marta Perovic, Robin F. Williams, Billy Sullivan, Claire Greenshaw, Serge Vuille, Hermione Hoby, Adam Reich, Isabelle Arthuis, Christophe Coënon.

My friends and family; Sarah, thank you for your eternal support.

And Pepoli.

PHOTOGRAPHERS
Thorsten Arendt, Isabelle Arthuis, Thomas Barratt, Dawn Blackman, Cathy Carver, Ruth Clark, Christophe Coënon, Brian Forrest, Keith Hunter, HV Studio, Paul Knight, Nikos Kokkas, Stephan Jaeggi, Patrick Jameson, Max C Lee-Russell, Jeff McClane, Thomas Mueller, Robert Niven, George Oliver, Daniel Perez, Chad Redmon, Adam Reich, Andrea Rossetti, Marc Slaven, Gregor Staiger, Ben Westoby, Annik Wetter, Michael Wolchover.

CONTEMPORARY ARTISTS:

Contemporary Artists is a series of authoritative and extensively illustrated studies of today's most important artists. Each title offers a comprehensive survey of an individual artist's work and a range of art writing contributed by an international spectrum of authors, all leading figures in their fields, from art history and criticism to philosophy, cultural theory and fiction. Each study provides incisive analysis and multiple perspectives on contemporary art and its inspiration. These are essential source books for everyone concerned with art today.

MARINA ABRAMOVIĆ KLAUS BIESENBACH, KRISTINE STILES, CHRISSIE ILES / VITO ACCONCI FRAZER WARD, MARK C. TAYLOR, JENNIFER BLOOMER / AI WEIWEI HANS ULRICH OBRIST, KAREN SMITH, BERNARD FIBICHER / DOUG AITKEN DANIEL BIRNBAUM, AMANDA SHARP, JÖRG HEISER / PAWEŁ ALTHAMER ADAM SZYMCZYK, ROMAN KURZMEYER, SUZANNE COTTER / FRANCIS ALŸS CUAUHTÉMOC MEDINA, RUSSELL FERGUSON, JEAN FISHER, MICHAEL TAUSSIG / UTA BARTH PAMELA M. LEE, MATTHEW HIGGS, JEREMY GILBERT-ROLFE / CHRISTIAN BOLTANSKI DIDIER SEMIN, TAMAR GARB, DONALD KUSPIT / MONICA BONVICINI ALEXANDER ALBERRO, JANET KRAYNAK, JULIANE REBENTISCH / LOUISE BOURGEOIS PAULO HERKENHOFF (WITH THYRZA GOODEVE), ROBERT STORR, ALLAN SCHWARTZMAN / MARK BRADFORD ANITA HILL, SEBASTIAN SMEE, CONNIE BUTLER / CECILY BROWN COURTNEY J. MARTIN, JASON ROSENFELD, FRANCINE PROSE / CAI GUO-QIANG DANA FRIIS-HANSEN, OCTAVIO ZAYA, TAKASHI SERIZAWA / MAURIZIO CATTELAN NANCY SPECTOR, FRANCESCO BONAMI, BARBARA VANDERLINDEN, MASSIMILIANO GIONI / VIJA CELMINS ROBERT GOBER, LANE RELYEA, BRIONY FER / NIGEL COOKE DARIAN LEADER, TONY GODFREY, MARIE DARRIEUSSECQ / RICHARD DEACON PIER LUIGI TAZZI, JON THOMPSON, PETER SCHJELDAHL, PENELOPE CURTIS / TACITA DEAN JEAN-CHRISTOPHE ROYOUX, MARINA WARNER, GERMAINE GREER / MARK DION LISA GRAZIOSE CORRIN, MIWON KWON, NORMAN BRYSON / PETER DOIG ADRIAN SEARLE, KITTY SCOTT, CATHERINE GRENIER / STAN DOUGLAS SCOTT WATSON, DIANA THATER, CAROL J. CLOVER / MARLENE DUMAS DOMINIC VAN DEN BOOGERD, BARBARA BLOOM, MARIUCCIA CASADIO, ILARIA BONACOSSA / JIMMIE DURHAM LAURA MULVEY, DIRK SNAUWAERT, MARK ALICE DURANT, KATE NESISN / OLAFUR ELIASSON MADELEINE GRYNSZTEJN, DANIEL BIRNBAUM, MICHAEL SPEAKS / ELMGREEN & DRAGSET LINDA YABLONSKY, MARTIN HERBERT, CONNIE BUTLER / PETER FISCHLI AND DAVID WEISS ROBERT FLECK, BEATE SONTGEN, ARTHUR C. DANTO / TOM FRIEDMAN DENNIS COOPER, BRUCE HAINLEY, ADRIAN SEARLE / THEASTER GATES CAROL BECKER, LISA YUN LEE, ACHIM BORCHARDT-HUME / ISA GENZKEN ALEX FARQUHARSON, DIEDRICH DIEDERICHSEN, SABINE BREITWIESER / ANTONY GORMLEY ERNST GOMBRICH, JOHN HUTCHINSON, LELA B. NJATIN, W. J. T. MITCHELL / DAN GRAHAM BIRGIT PELZER, MARK FRANCIS, BEATRIZ COLOMINA / PAUL GRAHAM ANDREW WILSON, GILLIAN WEARING, CAROL SQUIERS / HANS HAACKE WALTER GRASSKAMP, MOLLY NESBIT, JON BIRD / MONA HATOUM GUY BRETT, MICHAEL ARCHER, CATHERINE DE ZEGHER, NANCY SPECTOR / SHARON HAYES JULIA BRYAN-WILSON, JEANNINE TANG, LANKA TATTERSALL / THOMAS HIRSCHHORN BENJAMIN H. D. BUCHLOH, ALISON M. GINGERAS, CARLOS BASUALDO / JIM HODGES JANE M SAKS, ROBERT HOBBS, JULIE AULT, TIM HAILAND /JENNY HOLZER DAVID JOSELIT, JOAN SIMON, RENATA SALECL / RONI HORN LOUISE NERI, LYNNE COOKE, THIERRY DE DUVE / CHRIS JOHANSON CORRINA PEIPON, BOB NICKAS, JULIE DEAMER / ILYA KABAKOV BORIS GROYS, DAVID A. ROSS, IWONA BLAZWICK / ALEX KATZ ROBERT STORR, CARTER RATCLIFF, IWONA BLAZWICK, BARRY SCHWABSKY / ON KAWARA 'TRIBUTE', JONATHAN WATKINS, RENÉ DENIZOT / MIKE KELLEY ISABELLE GRAW, JOHN C. WELCHMAN, ANTHONY VIDLER / MARY KELLY MARGARET IVERSEN, DOUGLAS CRIMP, HOMI K. BHABHA / WILLIAM KENTRIDGE CAROLYN CHRISTOV-BAKARGIEV, DAN CAMERON, J. M. COETZEE / JANNIS KOUNELLIS 'TRIBUTE', PHILIP LARRATT-SMITH, RUDI FUCHS / YAYOI KUSAMA AKIRA TATEHATA, LAURA HOPTMAN, UDO KULTERMANN, CHATERINE TAFT / CHRISTIAN MARCLAY JENNIFER GONZALEZ, KIM GORDON, MATTHEW HIGGS / KERRY JAMES MARSHALL CHARLES GAINES, GREG TATE, LAURENCE RASSEL / PAUL McCARTHY KRISTINE STILES, RALPH RUGOFF, MASSIMILIANO GIONI, ROBERT STORR / CILDO MEIRELES PAULO HERKENHOFF, GERARDO MOSQUERA, DAN CAMERON / LUCY ORTA ROBERTO PINTO, NICOLAS BOURRIAUD, MAIA DAMIANOVIC / JEAN-MICHEL OTHONIEL GAY GASSMANN, CATHERINE GRENIER, ROBERT STORR / TREVOR PAGLEN LAUREN CORNELL, JULIA BRYAN-WILSON, OMAR KHOLEIF / JORGE PARDO CHRISTINE VÉGH, LANE RELYEA, CHRIS KRAUS / NICOLAS PARTY STÉPHANE AQUIN, STEFAN BANZ, ALI SUBOTNICK, MELISSA HYDE / ADAM PENDLETON ALEC MAPES-FRANCES, ADRIENNE EDWARDS, ANDRÉA PICARD / RAYMOND PETTIBON DENNIS COOPER, ROBERT STORR, ULRICH LOOCK / RICHARD PRINCE ROSETTA BROOKS, JEFF RIAN, LUC SANTE / LILI REYNAUD-DEWAR ÉLISABETH LEBOVICI, DIEDRICH DIEDERICHSEN, MONIKA SZEWCZYK / PIPILOTTI RIST HANS ULRICH OBRIST, PEGGY PHELAN, ELIZABETH BRONFEN / DAAN ROOSEGAARDE NICO DASWANI, FUMIO NANJO, CAROL BECKER / STERLING RUBY KATE FOWLE, FRANKLIN SIRMANS, JESSICA MORGAN / ANRI SALA HANS ULRICH OBRIST, MARK GODFREY, LIAM GILLICK / DORIS SALCEDO NANCY PRINCENTHAL, CARLOS BASUALDO, ANDREAS HUYSSEN / WILHELM SASNAL ANDRZEJ PRZYWARA, DOMINIC EICHLER, JÖRG HEISER / THOMAS SCHÜTTE JULIAN HEYNEN, JAMES LINGWOOD, ANGELA VETTESE / STEPHEN SHORE MICHAEL FRIED, CHRISTY LANGE, JOEL STERNFELD / ROMAN SIGNER PAULA VAN DEN BOSCH, GERHARD MACK, JEREMY MILLAR / LORNA SIMPSON KELLIE JONES, THELMA GOLDEN, CHRISSIE ILES, NAOMI BECKWITH / NANCY SPERO JON BIRD, JO ANNA ISAAK, SYLVÈRE LOTRINGER / SIMON STARLING FRANCESCO MANACORDA, DIETER ROELSTRAETE, JANET HARBORD / FRANK STELLA ANDRIANNA CAMPBELL, KATE NESIN, LUCAS BLALOCK, TERRY RICHARDSON / JESSICA STOCKHOLDER BARRY SCHWABSKY, LYNNE TILLMAN, LYNNE COOKE, GERMANO CELANT / SARAH SZE OKWUI ENWEZOR, BENJAMIN H. D. BUCHLOH, LAURA HOPTMAN / WOLFGANG TILLMANS PETER HALLEY, JAN VERWOERT, MIDORI MATSUI, JOHANNA BURTON / LUC TUYMANS ULRICH LOOCK, JUAN VICENTE ALIAGA, NANCY SPECTOR, HANS RUDOLF REUST / BERNAR VENET FLORENCE DERIEUX, BARRY SCHWABSKY, CLAIRE LILLEY / ADRIÁN VILLAR-ROJAS HANS ULRICH OBRIST, CAROLYN CHRISTOV-BAKARGIEV, EUNGIE JOO / JEFF WALL THIERRY DE DUVE, ARIELLE PÉLENC, BORIS GROYS, JEAN-FRANÇOIS CHEVRIER, MARK LEWIS / GILLIAN WEARING RUSSELL FERGUSON, DONNA DE SALVO, JOHN SLYCE / LAWRENCE WEINER BENJAMIN H. D. BUCHLOH, ALEXANDER ALBERRO AND ALICE ZIMMERMAN, DAVID BATCHELOR / FRANZ WEST ROBERT FLECK, BICE CURIGER, NEAL BENEZRA / JONAS WOOD MARK GROTJAHN, HELEN MOLESWORTH, IAN ALTEVEER / YIN XIUZHEN HOU HANRU, WU HUNG, STEPHANIE ROSENTHAL / ZHANG HUAN ROSELEE GOLDBERG, YILMAZ DZIEWOR, ROBERT STORR